For Love of the Prophet

For Love of the Prophet

An Ethnography of Sudan's Islamic State

Noah Salomon

PRINCETON UNIVERSITY PRESS
PRINCETON AND OXFORD

Published by Princeton University Press,
41 William Street, Princeton, New Jersey 08540
In the United Kingdom:
Princeton University Press, 6 Oxford Street, Woodstock, Oxfordshire OX20 1TR

press.princeton.edu

Cover art: Detail from the painting, *Min mufakkirat al-shaykh Tāj al-Dīn al-Bahārī* (from the Diary of Shaykh Taj al-Din al-Bahari) by Dr. Ahmed Abdel Aal (d. 2008). Photograph by Rik Sferra.

Library of Congress Cataloging-in-Publication Data
Names: Salomon, Noah, author.
Title: For love of the Prophet : an ethnography of Sudan's Islamic state / Noah Salomon.
Description: Princeton : Princeton University Press, 2016. | Includes bibliographical references and index.
Identifiers: LCCN 2016010110| ISBN 9780691165141 (hardcover : alk. paper) | ISBN 9780691165158 (pbk. : alk. paper)
Subjects: LCSH: Islam and state—Sudan. | Islam—Sudan. | Islam and politics—Sudan. | Sudan—Politics and government—1985- | Islamic law—Sudan.
Classification: LCC BP64.S8 S27 2016 | DDC 320.55709624—dc23
LC record available at https://lccn.loc.gov/2016010110

British Library Cataloging-in-Publication Data is available

This book has been composed in Linux Libertine O

Printed on acid-free paper. ∞

Printed in the United States of America

10 9 8 7 6 5 4 3 2 1

For Amel, Aya, and Ayman.

Contents

Figures

Acknowledgments

This section of my book is both the final one I am writing and the most difficult one to formulate. The volume you have in your hands represents a small portion of the fieldwork I conducted over more than three years in Khartoum, North Kordofan, Jazira, and Sinnar states. I completed the bulk of this work between February 2005 and August 2007, though the groundwork for my research was laid during the summers of 2003 and 2004. Five short visits since that time—in 2009, 2010, 2012, 2013, and 2015—as well as extended fieldwork for a newer project in South Sudan (undertaken in 2011 and 2012) have kept me connected to developments in Sudan, but very little of the research I did during these later trips made it into this book. So many friends and colleagues helped me during these stays as I worked on multiple projects simultaneously, never exactly sure what I would publish first: from annotated translations of popular Sufi verse (some of which can be found in Salomon 2010) and an ethnography of the work and lives of Sudanese *mudāḥ* (itinerant singers of Islamic praise poetry), to the grammar of *daʿwa* training among Salafi Muslims, to the present project on the intricacies of the Islamic state. It is difficult to untangle exactly who helped me with which project, as each of them informed the others in countless ways.

The first person who opened the door to Sudan for me was Professor Steve Howard of Ohio University. Shortly after I contacted him at the suggestion of AbdouMaliq Simone (to whom I'd written moments after completing his spellbinding book *In Whose Image,* which I cite heavily in this book) he generously invited me to a conference he had organized at which several Sudanese academics were speaking. Steve Howard and his colleague Asma Abdel Halim put me in touch with a wonderful community of people in Khartoum who welcomed me at the airport in 2003 and took care of me day-in and day-out as I made the often clumsy transition to Sudanese life. In those early years, no one helped me more than ʿIzz al-Din Siddiq, whose car reliably showed up at my doorstep each and every day *baʿd al-maghrib,* and took me to multiple *munāsabāt* (weddings, condolence calls, arrivals, and departures) around the capital. These visits were my first and best school in both the Sudanese dialect and culture and customs. Ahmad ʿAbd al-Majid, ʿAbd al-Halim Hasan, Dr. al-Fatih Mahjub, Limya Siddiq, Maha Zaki, the staff and directors of Mutaʿawwinat Legal Aid Society (where I spent the summer of 2003 interning), my neighbors in *nimra ithnayn,* the members of the Kwato theater troupe (who bravely employed me as an actor in their play *al-Ḥarba* in 2007), especially Derek Alfred and Al-Fatih Atem, the Gorani and Arbab families, and my friends in Wad Madani and al-ʿUbayd offered me much friendship and kindness during my time in Sudan and shared their knowledge of the joys and challenges of Sudanese life. It was they who made Sudan not only a research site for me, but a true home.

In academic circles in Sudan, Dr. ʿAli Muhammad ʿAbd al-Majid was extremely helpful, welcoming me into the community at *al-Markaz al-Qawmī li-l-Buḥūth*, as was Dr. Tariq Ahmad ʿUthman of African University, who served as a frank and insightful sounding board during the first stages of my research. In later years Agnès de Geoffroy and Einas Ahmed of the Centre d'études et de documentation économique, juridique et sociales (CEDEJ), Khartoum, were extremely helpful interlocutors, as were many others I met at the University of Khartoum, chief among them Mohamed Abdelsalam Babiker and Akram ʿAbbas. On a day-to-day basis, two extremely committed research assistants, Dalil Muhammad Dalil and Tariq Ahmad Husayn, pored over hours and hours of recordings of sermons and *madīḥ*, books, pamphlets, and poetry in my often electricity-less apartment, explaining to me in plain Arabic the complicated theological and historical references that populated the material with which I was working. The process of what Brinkley Messick has called in his lectures "ethnographic reading," that is, reading texts with a person who is intimately familiar with the milieu in which they were written, was an essential, almost daily part of my fieldwork in Khartoum.

The leaders and regular folks at all the field sites where I worked were extremely selfless with their time and energy in their willingness to help me. One of the things I loved most about Sudan was that it seemed everywhere I went people were as excited about my research topics as I was. In fact, on arriving at field sites, I was often delighted to find that the conversation I wanted to have was already unfolding, without any prompting on my part. Few restrictions were imposed on my access to Muslim organizations in Sudan across the doctrinal and political spectrum. I thank their members and leaders for welcoming me so warmly and for trusting me to record what they told me with accuracy and seriousness. I hope they find this book is worthy of their trust.

Countless people from the Salafi organization Ansar al-Sunna, the various Sufi orders with which I worked, and the worlds of academia and politics helped me on my research path and I trust they are aware of my gratitude even if I do not have the space to mention them all here by name. The Ashraf of Karkoj, the members of the Republican Brotherhood and the people of the *masīd* of al-Zariba were particularly generous conversation partners. Among the many interlocutors I met in Sudan, three deserve special mention. Al-Sharif Munaf al-Sharif al-Nur provided an amazing introduction to the world of *madīḥ*, and to the landscape of contemporary Sufism more broadly, and I am only sorry that so little of what he taught me made it into the pages of the present volume. I hope to have the opportunity in the not-so-distant future to reanimate those notes and write more on the topics we discussed. My travels with Munaf across central Sudan (many times accompanied by the brilliant *mādiḥ* Muhammad Shukr Allah) are some of the most memorable moments of my time there, if not of my life. Taj al-Din Amin Sabun showed me warmth, hospitality, and friendship during my time in al-Zariba and on pilgrimage to al-Kirayda and served as a steady *qudwa* (exemplar) of the moral life. Muhammad Khalifa Siddiq, journalist, intellectual, and political analyst, has been an extremely generous interlocutor throughout my time in Sudan and remains so through the present day, providing thorough introductions to many areas of shared interest and helping me with countless contacts. I have benefited tremendously from both our conversations and his written work.

Those who helped me in my time in Sudan had little sense of what the finished product you hold in your hands would look like, and in this sense they were quite a bit like me. This book grew out of questions that pulled on me as much during the years subsequent to my field research in Sudan as in my time there. It was written during an eighteen-month sabbatical at the Institute for Advanced Study (IAS) in Princeton, where I was a member in the School of Social Science during the 2013–14 academic year and then a visitor in the fall of 2014. It was edited and revised over the summer of 2015, again at IAS. There is no person who deserves more credit for this book seeing the light of day than Joan Scott, who read each and every chapter as I wrote them (often in multiple drafts), and served unwittingly as my deadline minder, helping me to give structure to this lengthy period of "free time." Joan's comments shaped this book in countless ways and her encouragement gave me the courage to move on when it was time to do so. Without her support, I suspect this book would have remained a draft in perpetuity.

IAS was an extremely fecund space for unbridled thinking, and many colleagues helped facilitate the ideas I formed there. I benefited from so many, among them Danielle Allen, Nikhil Anand, Beth Berman, Patricia Crone, Elizabeth Davis, Omar Dewachi, Jeffrey Flynn, Marion Katz, Joseph Hankins, Joseph Masco, Ramah McKay, Vanessa Ogle, Manuela Picq, Sabine Schmidtke, and Judith Surkis. Didier Fassin deserves special mention among this group both for his insight and encouragement and for welcoming me into the various IAS cohorts he so generously formed.

Several other colleagues read the manuscript in full or in great part. Talal Asad, Elizabeth Shakman Hurd, Saba Mahmood, Benjamin Schonthal, Kabir Tambar, and Jeremy Walton helped shape this book in countless ways, and I am extremely grateful to them for the time they took to comment on the manuscript with such insight and in such careful detail. My office neighbor during my last months at IAS, Anver Emon, was a daily conversation partner, and those conversations as well as his comments on the full manuscript were indispensable as I put the finishing touches on my book. Several presentations of this material to academic audiences at a variety of institutions also helped shape my ideas. None was more valuable than the two-day workshopping of the manuscript I undertook in 2015 at the University of California, Santa Cruz, and I thank Mayanthi Fernando both for her comments there and for setting up such an engaging visit. The two anonymous reviewers from Princeton University Press, as well as my editor, Fred Appel, each contributed to the book in vital ways, and I thank them for the thoroughness and seriousness of their readings. The editorial work of Nathan Carr, Basit Iqbal, and Eva Jaunzems helped immensely with the clarity and cleanliness of my prose. It is most certainly to my readers' detriment that I have not been able to incorporate all of the many excellent suggestions I received in the final draft of this book.

The foundation for this book was laid in my PhD dissertation (Salomon 2010), though it has strayed far from that early effort. I was inspired then, as I am now, by the work of my graduate advisor, Saba Mahmood. The ethical and political underpinnings of her research agenda motivated my own, and learning with her opened up infinite intellectual vistas. She has been both a loyal supporter and an unfailing critic throughout my academic career and I feel extremely lucky to have her as an interlocutor. Malika Zeghal, who coadvised my dissertation with Saba Mahmood, read countless drafts and helped shape many of the ideas that took full form in this book. My interest in state politics emerged in part from the conversations I had with her in graduate school and in the years since, and I am so grateful for her time and support. Michael Sells and Amy Hollywood, who also sat on my dissertation committee, helped put the Sufism I was working on into historical, theological, and theoretical context and always pushed my work in unexpected directions. Winnifred Fallers Sullivan has been a great support and strength throughout all stages of this project. Indeed many portions of this book were written at her prompting, and the various initiatives that she has spearheaded have inspired a great deal of my thinking here. The dissertation was physically written in the libraries of Columbia University, where I was an exchange scholar, and at Yale University, where I was a postgraduate associate in the Council on Middle East Studies. Narges Erami, Frank Griffel, Marsha Inhorn, Brinkley Messick, Mahmood Mamdani, Andrew March, and Nadia Marzouki all provided lively intellectual exchange while I was in New York and New Haven. Kambiz GhaneaBassiri of Reed College has been a mentor since that time and remains so now.

Several colleagues in the fields of Sudanese and African Studies have been ideal interlocutors throughout my time working on Sudan. None of them has more consistently provided inspiration than Rüdiger Seesemann. Rüdiger and I have often shared field sites and interlocutors, and he has always been an unflaggingly selfless senior colleague. Abdullahi An-Naʿim, Carolyn Fluehr-Lobban, Abdullahi Gallab, Albrecht Hofheinz, Susan Kenyon, Cherry Leonardi, Rebecca Lorins, Benjamin Soares, and many others in the Sudan Studies and African Studies communities have also been helpful conversation partners, in many cases opening up crucial doors for me in my early studies. I also thank Azza Mustafa Babikir, Mark Massoud, and Elena Vezzadini with whom I shared the joys and challenges of fieldwork in Sudan.

My colleagues at Carleton College, most prominent among them Stacy Beckwith, Kristin Bloomer, Pamela Feldman-Savelsberg, Zaki Haidar, Roger Jackson, Cherif Keita, Adeeb Khalid, Amna Khalid, Yaron Klein, Michael McNally, Louis Newman, Lori Pearson, Paul Petzschmann, Asuka Sango, Shana Sippy, Thabiti Willis, and Kevin Wolfe offered me wonderful engagement throughout the time I was writing this book. Philip Francis sparked me to think more critically about the relationship between art and religion. Additionally, the students in all of my classes have proved not only excellent sounding boards for many of the ideas I express in this volume, but helped me to think of them in new and more creative ways. President Steven Poskanzer and Dean Beverly Nagel offered me the confidence, support, and time on leave to get this project done, and I am extremely appreciative of the investment they put into faculty research.

Some sections of this book have been adapted (with permission) from previously published work. Revised paragraphs appear at various moments in the manuscript from Salomon 2004a, 2009, 2011, 2013, 2014, 2015b, and from Salomon and Walton 2012.

I am grateful to several academic institutions and foundations that supported my research at various stages. During my dissertation, I was supported by a Wenner Gren Foundation Dissertation Fieldwork Grant, a Fulbright Hays Grant, and a write-up grant from the American Council of Learned Societies/Andrew W. Mellon Foundation. An IAS membership grant, a grant from the Deutsche Forschungsgemeinschaft, and a Hewlett Mellon Fellowship and Smith Faculty Development Grant from Carleton College supported me during the writing of this book. A grant from the Islam Research Programme (Netherlands) via CEDEJ funded my research in South Sudan.

The people who deserve the most gratitude for this book are the members of my family: my birth family who raised me in a context of joy in learning, and my wife and children who afforded me the time to write. My wife, Amel Gorani, has been a loyal friend, companion, and conversation-partner, and it is her love and support that has kept me grounded throughout this process. She has challenged me to think in new ways about the material I researched and kept me smiling through its most difficult challenges. Both she and our two children, Aya and Ayman, showed amazing patience as I went through the seemingly endless steps in shepherding this volume to publication and dragged them back and forth across the US to the various places in which I wrote it. At age five, Aya, my daughter, avidly followed the progress of my IAS colleagues, interrogating them from the fence of her on-site daycare, and reminding me frequently that so-and-so just turned in his manuscript, and that she herself had written two in only the last three days. I apologize to her that mine took a bit longer to get to press. I hope the many nights away from home were worth this final product.

A Note on Transliteration and Translation

In this book, I use a version of the *International Journal of Middle East Studies* (IJMES) transliteration model for both spoken Sudanese and Modern Standard Arabic (MSA). However, I occasionally use vowels (e.g., o) and consonants (e.g., g) that are not found in MSA if the word in question was spoken as such in Sudanese Arabic and is not a common MSA term. In all other cases, I have leaned toward accuracy with orthography, rather than pronunciation, since this will help the scholar find the term in question in the relevant sources. I highly recommend Dr. ʿAwn al-Sharif Qasim's *Qāmūs al-lahja al-ʿāmmiyya fī-l-Sūdān* (Qasim 2002) to scholars who wish to explore the Sudanese terminology I use in this book further. For the sake of readability, I have omitted diacritical marks from names of places and people, Arabic terms found in English dictionaries, and certain repeated proper nouns (e.g., al-Inqadh, Ansar al-Sunna). These repeated proper nouns are fully transliterated in the index. The index also includes transliteration of the Arabic for some proper nouns that are only introduced in English translation in the body text.

All translations contained in the following pages are my own, unless otherwise noted. I use a very literal translation style, cleaving as closely to the Arabic as possible, so that at times clarifications are necessary if the passage is to make sense in English. Those clarifications are in brackets. When an Arabic term is not easily translatable into English, or when the technical term in question is useful for analysis, I place that term in parentheses following the English translation.

In my translated quotes I have used the abbreviation *swt* to refer to the formula recited/written after articulating the name of God (*subḥānahu wa taʿālā*, "glorified and exalted") and the abbreviation *ṣlʿm* to refer to the formula recited/written after speaking the name of the prophet Muhammad (*ṣallā allāhu ʿalayhi wa sallam*, "God bless him and grant him peace").

For Love of the Prophet

In Search of the Islamic State

Year after year, Sudan has placed among the top three countries on *Foreign Policy*'s annual Failed State Index.[1] Scoring a perfect ten for internally displaced persons, external intervention, group grievances, and factionalized elites, Sudan serves as a near archetype of the nonfunctioning state. Media portrayals of rampant interethnic violence, famine, and displacement reinforce this perception. Yet, even with the loss of territory following the secession of South Sudan in 2011, the persistent civil war in Darfur and the "new South" (those regions of Sudan that once were in the center of the country and now are in its southern reaches, following partition), and great economic uncertainty, the Sudanese state somehow continues to function, the National Congress (*née* National Islamic Front) party sitting firmly in power for over twenty-five years, despite persistent internal divisions. While the events of the Arab Spring and their reversal have made scholars of the region know better than to predict continuing stability, the itinerary of the longest-standing government in Sudan's postcolonial history and its experiment with establishing what its intellectuals called "the Islamic state" is in need of study, no matter what tomorrow may bring. This is particularly true now as a variety of regimes across the region are experimenting with their own Islamization projects or are seeking to unravel them. Indeed, while *Foreign Policy* looks at formal indicators such as "uneven development," "economic decline," and "external intervention" as evidence of a state's health (or, more precisely, the lack thereof), it overlooks a series of factors that make states like Sudan endure, despite their failure to meet the journal's indices of full-sovereignty and economic well-being. What would a study of Sudan look like that did not take its lacks and lacunas, its under-development and instability, as a starting point? What do we learn if we examine state power as productive and not solely repressive,[2] and if we explore the Sudanese public as made up of agents of its modernity and not merely victims of power struggles from on high? This book attempts to answer these questions.

1 http://www.foreignpolicy.com/articles/2013/06/24/2013_failed_states_interactive_map.

2 Whether the state is thereby *oppressive* is another question entirely. For many, certainly so; for those whose conditions have improved under it, perhaps not—but I leave the polemic against the state to others better positioned to wield it, given their more immediate stake in its success or failure.

My first foray into studying the Sudanese state was beset by a paradox not unrelated to that which confronts the Failed State Index. I initially went to Sudan in the summer of 2003 with the idea of studying how the state reproduced its Islamist ideology through an examination of the Sudanese national secondary school curriculum. At that point in time, Sudan was the only country in the Arabic-speaking world where an Islamist organization, so common as political opposition, had taken the reins of power.[3] While Islamist notions of government could be studied as a theoretical framework across the Arabic-speaking world, Sudan seemed to me then (and it still does now) the perfect place to find out what modern Islamic governance looks like in practice, when it is forced to confront the complexity of the modern nation-state and the diverse publics to which it must cater. Sudan was the first country in the Arabic-speaking world where a modern Islamist movement (in this case, an offshoot of the Muslim Brotherhood) had the chance to apply its elaborate theories, so often faulted for their vagueness on specifics.[4] The researcher had the added benefit in Sudan that its Islamic movement had been in power for a considerable time, enabling a diachronic view of policies as they responded to the complexities of governance, and as the governed responded to them.

Yet, when I arrived in Sudan, I made the rather unsettling discovery that I could not find the state in the places where I had expected it to be. I traveled to my field sites, to the Ministry of Education and to the curriculum-building

3 Outside of the Arab world, the reader with knowledge of Iran will likely be able to draw important parallels between its Islamic revolution of 1979 and Sudan's Islamist coup only ten years later. While the Sudanese Islamists were surely inspired by the Iranian model, Sudan's relationship to Iran (both ideological and political) has always been unstable due in great measure to popular antipathy towards Shiʿi modes of Islam (indeed, in recent years, as Sudan has moved closer to Saudi Arabia, the Iranian presence has been almost entirely erased with the formerly influential Iranian Cultural Center shuttered and diplomatic relations falling to an all-time low). There is not sufficient room here to explore what parallels we may draw between the two Islamist experiments, but I hope future researchers will examine this topic. For literature on Iran's Islamic state project, see Fischer 2003, Mottahedeh 1985, and Varzi 2006, as well as forthcoming work from a host of scholars currently doing interesting work in Iran including Alireza Doostdar, Narges Erami, Elham Mireshghi, Hosna Sheikholeslami, and Rose Wellman.

4 By "modern Islamist movement," I am referring to those groups that emerged out of the cauldron of European colonialism and saw their intervention as a response to the questions it posed, accepting, at least in part, the institutional and intellectual categories that colonialism provided, but filling them with Islamic content. The Muslim Brotherhood is the most famous representative of such a trend. So, for example, the eighteenth-century movement of Muhammad ibn ʿAbd al-Wahhab neither fits this category historically, emerging as it did out of internal theological dispute rather than colonial intervention, nor intellectually, addressing a series of doctrinal matters that have tended not to be of great concern to modern Islamist movements, preoccupied as the latter are with the challenge of secularism and Westernization. For a useful comparison of the difference between these two "Islamist" trends at their origins, see Haj 2009, particularly chapter 1.

center at Bakht al-Ridda on the White Nile, only to find that the curriculum that was now being discussed was one that had been developed by the United Nations.[5] This curriculum focused on peace-building and multicultural education, preparing for the "period of national unity" that the expected signing of the peace agreement with the restive South in 2005 would bring about. There was no discernible program of Islamic state-building. At first it seemed to me that the Islamic state was nowhere to be found, that the Sudanese state indeed was a failed project, existing in a position of international guardianship, in which, as in the case of the remnants of the colonial projects that had preceded it, some of the bureaucracy was nevertheless left intact. Frantically, I wrote my funders, asking if it would be acceptable if I spent my grants on another sort of project (intrareligious controversy? religious reform movements? Sufi revivalism?), since the Sudanese Islamic state project that I had come to study seemed to have vanished before I even arrived.

It was in this moment of crisis, however, ironically just when I began to contemplate abandoning the state as an object of inquiry, that I began to encounter the state in unexpected places. In my rather dejected travels on public transport from ministry to ministry, government office to government office—that is, in my quest to find the Islamic state in the places one would expect it to be—I began actually to listen to what was going on around me. So sure of the models of governance that I'd brought with me into the field, models that prepared me to find the state lodged in institutions that projected power downwards onto "society," I had deafened myself to the resonances of the state that emerged in other places. It was when I took out my virtual earplugs that the presence of the Islamic state, so elusive in those government offices, came blaring to the surface, and I began to find what I had come to study, though in very different places from where I had expected to find it.

The Sudanese soundscape was staffed with notes of this elusive state. It was on those bus rides across town that I began to hear them most clearly: bus radios constantly blasting popified *madīḥ* (Islamic praise poetry), which my fellow passengers informed me were enjoying a renaissance under the current regime that supported their resurgence through radio projects and state television; the cacophony of sounds emerging from new mosques built with state funds and broadcasting not only the call to prayer but myriad

5 The ability of NGOs to "see" and order the world like a state (Scott 1998) is a topic of increasing interest in anthropology, as several recent works have shown (e.g., Bernal and Grewal 2014; see also Trouillot 2001: 132). This parallel state was alive and well in Sudan during the entirety of my stay there, serving functions from education to security, though it is not the topic of my study here. Mark Massoud's recent book *Law's Fragile State: Colonial, Authoritarian and Humanitarian Legacies in Sudan* (2013) amply discusses the interaction of the humanitarian reason of international governance organizations and the legal apparatus of the formal state.

other pious activities going on under their roofs; debates over whose hands could touch whose as the young *kumsārī* (fare collector) returned riders' change, citing state-enforced norms on dress and public comportment, while reworking and reappraising them. While the integrity of the state seemed to be disintegrating in government offices, occupied as they were by international powers, on those bus rides the state seemed alive and vibrant all around me. Far from the ministries of central Khartoum, the state had become "a social subject in everyday life" (Aretxaga 2003: 395), reproduced in the discourses, the practices, and the very bodies of the subjects who lived in its midst.

The state may have failed according to the criteria of *Foreign Policy's* index, yet by producing and sustaining novel publics, it has in fact endured. The state seemed absent in my visits to the ministries, but on my bus rides across town I nevertheless seemed to find it everywhere. Clearly we are in need of not only new frameworks for understanding the state (a task I leave, for the most part, to political scientists), but also empirical research that can substantiate the life of the state from which such theorizing might proceed. Taking off from this challenge, this book is a study of the experiment with the Islamic state in Sudan. It looks primarily not at state institutions, but rather at the daily life that goes on in their shadows, examining the lasting effects of state Islamization on Sudanese society through a study of the individuals and organizations that function in its midst.[6] As such, it takes as its interlocutors Sudanese working within the conditions of possibility provided by the state and its Islamist project. For whether a critic or a champion of state Islamism, no one in Sudan could ignore its pull. This situation was partly a result of the power of the ruling Islamist elite and its dominance over political, legal, and economic realms, which shaped a bureaucracy in

6 Michel-Rolph Trouillot expresses this concept of the state unbounded from institutional life and describes the kind of ethnography necessary to study it. He writes, "Though linked to a number of apparatuses not all of which may be governmental, the state is not an apparatus, but a set of processes. It is not necessarily bound by an institution, nor can any institution fully encapsulate it. At that level, its materiality resides much less in its institutions than in the reworking of processes and relations of power, so as to create new spaces for the deployment of power. . . . Anthropology may not find the state ready-made, waiting for our ethnographic gaze in the known sites of national government. . . . We may have to insist on encounters that are not immediately transparent. We may indeed have to revert to the seemingly timeless banality of daily life" (Trioullot 2001: 127, 133). Political theorist Wendy Brown expresses a similar sentiment when she writes, "Despite the almost unavoidable tendency to speak of the state as an 'it,' the domain we call the state is not a thing, system or subject, but a significantly unbounded terrain of powers and techniques, an ensemble of discourses, rules and practices cohabiting in limiting, tension-ridden, and often contradictory relation to each other" (Brown 1995: 174; cited on p. 398 of Aretxaga 2003). Yael Navaro-Yashin's work (2002) takes up the kind of research Trioullot and Brown suggest and equally provides an inspiration for my observations in what follows.

which to be legible one had to be Islamic. Yet the magnetism of Islamism (here I mean the term simply to refer to the animation of the political sphere with Islamic principles) was also due to the fact that the Islam on which it relied was not merely a bureaucratic logic, but a normative framework that far exceeded the state, one that individuals inhabited regardless of their positions on the particular government in question.

While the authoritarian, and indeed despotic, features of Sudan's Islamic state project are well known and rightly decried, what is less understood is the kind of political culture the Islamic state enabled. Actors who previously had little political involvement were suddenly pulled into a political conversation they had not created but to which they came to contribute in increasingly creative ways by dint of their authority within the Islamic tradition. People who had understood themselves for generations as anti-Islamist began to express their political participation in Islamic terms, as the only recognized language of political discourse increasingly became that of Islam.

Yet, as the regime made Islam the primary source of political legitimacy, it paradoxically opened itself up to endless challenge. If Sunni Islam is known for not having a clergy, Sudanese Islam takes this in an even more robust direction. In Sudan, there is no single paradigmatic institution for the production of Islamic leadership, no al-Azhar as in Egypt, no Qayrawan as in Tunisia. While many have attempted to create such an institution (as we will see in Chapters 1 and 2), precisely to guard against the proliferation of claims to Islamic authority, none have been successful. This book will examine the political space that was opened by the Islamic state and the way that a surprising set of actors and classical Islamic genres (from hagiography to poetry to sermons on Muslim doctrine) came to fill that space. It will do so through framing contemporary Islamic politics not merely as a response to secularism or Western domination, as it is often positioned in the literature, but rather as situated in a much longer conversation in Islamic thought, here at the node of a more-than-two-decade-long experience with the Islamic state. In the process, this book will explore how the Islamic grammars produced by the state were fulfilled, augmented, and reappropriated as its projects of reform became objects of debate and controversy. Understanding this process is crucial today, in the first decades of the twenty-first century, when so many claimants to "the Islamic state" have arisen, but almost no research has taken place that has explored how such a political formation is sustained.

The chapters that follow are situated in conversation with a burgeoning literature on theories of the Islamic state that, while engaging political science and Islamic studies, has rarely been taken up in political anthropology or the anthropology of religion, the perspectives from which I approach this unique political model. In some of this literature, the idea of the "Islamic state" has served to fulfill aspirations for cultural sovereignty and new forms of ethical political practice (Abu Rabi 1996; Euben 1999). In others, of course, it is seen as a violator of the proper domains of both religion and politics (e.g., An-Naʿim 2008), evidence that the Muslim world is slipping backwards in what was once seen as a universal march toward history's end. Still others have argued for the incompatibility between Islam as a moral project and the mode of subjectivation forwarded by the modern state (Hallaq 2013). Yet, while much scholarship has focused on the idea and ideals of the Islamic state, its possibilities and impossibilities, surprisingly little work has analyzed how this novel political formation *is lived* in spite of, or in fact animated by, the tensions inherent in its achievement. Understanding the life of the Islamic state, as put into practice in Sudan, is the agenda of this book.

The State, Outside In

Within the anthropology of Islam, the state has not been a particularly popular topic of inquiry. While a few important exceptions exist (e.g., Agrama 2012; Fernando 2014; Messick 1993; Starrett 1998), the bulk of the anthropological literature on contemporary Islam has instead taken on the public sphere as the central locus in which to determine the nature of Muslim life. In this literature, the public sphere is imagined as a site of free deliberation, the place where one looks for an authentic expression of modern Islam outside of the constraints of the official sphere, identified primarily with the state.[7] At the heart of such an approach are some key assumptions about the nature of the state that this book seeks to disrupt. The state, in this literature, is deemed a realm of artifice and coercion, the expression of raw power, a category of life that is ontologically distinct from the public sphere, not an element or expression of the social but rather its prime adversary. Through an analysis of the way the state is established, experienced, and contested across a diverse spectrum of life in Sudan—from prayer circles to think tanks, from poetic performances to government religious councils—this book will challenge the apotheosis of state sovereignty on which such theories of the public sphere are based. Doing so will allow us to correct the misrecognition of the state as a creature that exists outside the political practice of everyday life.

The bulk of literature on the public sphere in the Muslim world has taken for granted a hard and fast divide between state and civil society, official

7 While what I critique here represents a pervasive trend in conceptualizing the public sphere, it is important to note that there exists a countercurrent of work on Islamic public spheres (e.g., Eisenlohr 2011; Hirschkind 2006; Mahmood 2005; Wedeen 2008) that has deeply challenged the Habermasian presuppositions about them that still pervade the majority of studies. I build on this countercurrent in more detail in the following.

domains and the public sphere. Studies of Sudan are no exception. The tendency there has been to see the state as a goliath, inhabited by a different species than the political actors of civil society, despite the recognition that its personnel come from the very same families as the opposition and despite the rapidity with which people fall into and out of state favor (Khalid 1990). In the case of Sudan (and Sudan is not unique, the same could be said about many places) this is of course, in part, a political strategy to deflect some of the embarrassment that surrounds the crimes of the state by insisting that the state is not *of us*. Here again the public sphere is celebrated, used as a proxy for a critique of the state.[8] It is everything the state isn't: free, deliberative, authentic, horizontal.

Despite its interest in elaborating the Muslim public sphere, the literature that has sought to include the Muslim world within the scholarly conversation on the topic has not only drawn on but also complicated some of Habermas's initial assumptions (Habermas 1991). Spearheaded by scholars such as Armando Salvatore (2007; Salvatore and LeVine 2005), Dale Eickelman, Jon Anderson (Eickelman and Anderson 2003), and Nilüfer Göle (Göle and Amman 2006), it has sought simultaneously to rethink the characteristics of the public sphere and to broaden our understanding of who participates in it and how, entering the conversation following the recalibration of Habermas's concept by his critics and interlocutors (Calhoun 1992). For these scholars, there is something unique about "*Islamic* public spheres," in that if we can conjure their existence we can destabilize not only what Nancy Fraser called Habermas's bourgeois presuppositions (Fraser 1992; Salvatore and LeVine 2005)—chief among them secularization—but also the narrative of the public sphere as an achievement of Western capitalist societies more broadly. Salvatore and LeVine explain in one of the edited volumes that serves as a key example of the burst in literature on Islamic public spheres that took place in the first decade of this century:

> In seeking to expand the definition of the public sphere, we are cautious not to adopt either a liberal or a republican-jacobian norm. For *shariʿa* notions such as *istislah* [which they define as seeking the public good] that are at the heart of Muslim understandings of the public sphere operate from a different orientation than the liberal or Jacobian European frameworks. . . . The resulting public sphere can potentially be seen as a positive-sum game, one that reflects a logic quite distinct from the scarcely plastic—if not zero-sum—notions of social justice based on standards of 'pure reason,' or, at least, from the zeroing

8 I thank Anver Emon of the University of Toronto for lending me this language, which I have borrowed from his article (in preparation) "Codification and Islamic Law: The Ideology behind a Tragic Narrative."

> formal culture—that is, the elision of specific cultural and even legal traditions—that often accompanies Western discourses of 'the public.' Such a singular kind of public reason silences other kinds of reason embodied by autonomous social actors, especially those grounded in a religious identity. (Salvatore and LeVine 2005: 2)

Moreover, the kinds of Islamic social movements that make up the new imaginary of the Islamic public sphere—a place for debate over the common good outside the boundaries of the state—are imagined as distinctly "unbounded" from the characteristics of liberal pubic spheres:

> [They are] unbounded by the strictures of liberal norms of publicness premised on atomistic views of the social agent and contractually-based notions of trust, by a strict interpretation of the dichotomy between private and public spheres, and by the ultimate basing of public reason on private interest. What socio-religious discourses and movements primarily base their public reason on is a practical reason sanctified by religious tradition, however variably interpreted. (Salvatore and LeVine 2005: 29)

Interestingly, despite the rather significant difference between the phenomena these scholars observe and that of the Habermasian public sphere, these scholars do not attempt to coin a new term for what they are seeing, but instead seem to think that the premises of the Habermasian concept are similar enough to what they are observing that their inclusion of the latter does not push the term "public sphere" to a breaking point. The reason for this seems to be that, for these scholars, both the bourgeois public sphere and the Islamic public sphere share a certain set of characteristics, ones essential for us to interrogate in any conversation about the state in the Muslim world, premised as they are on a clear notion of being outside of it.

The premises that these authors share coalesce around the type of communicative activity that goes on in the public sphere, which they term "deliberation" (e.g., Habermas 1996). Concepts of the public sphere, whether they emerge from Habermas or the proponents of the Islamic public sphere, seem to gather around this notion, which imbeds within it a certain thesis about the free circulation of such deliberative practices (not to mention a rather unspoken idea of the genre in which such deliberation takes place, what is loosely referred to as "talk"). While for Habermas the public sphere is a unique achievement of democracy, a place where citizens debate what laws best serve them, the literature on the Islamic public sphere does not assume this particular political order (or assumes that people can debate the common good in a whole host of political systems). Nonetheless, Habermas's foundational assumption about the public sphere, namely, that "[c]itizens behave as a public body when they confer in an *unrestricted* fashion—that is with the guarantee of freedom of assembly and association and the freedom to express and publish their opinions—about matters of general interest" (Habermas 1974: 49), remains central to these conceptions of the public sphere as well. Restrictions, discipline, authority: these are the conceptual enemies of the public sphere, whether Islamic or bourgeois. Too much of any of them and we risk losing the public sphere entirely, ending up in the realm of coercion, state totalitarianism, or worse. The public sphere for these thinkers has little place for the extension, the embodiment, or the production of authority; it is instead always an arena for the challenging of authority, which serves to increase individuals' capacity to gather and maintain voice. This is a voice that is understood to be the expression of their full and unfettered moral core, whether or not that core is idiomized or even limited by the discursive tradition of which these individuals are a part. The celebration of new media and new technologies of circulation in recent literatures has only highlighted the analytical importance of the deliberative character of the public sphere, as these tools are understood as the technical means that make possible this sort of deliberative space, leading to what these scholars maintain is an effervescence in the democratization of Islamic authority.[9]

In this regard, as a space of free deliberation and for challenging authority, the public sphere is always pictured as being outside of the state. Habermas writes:

> Although state authority is so to speak the executor of the political public sphere, it is not a part of it. . . . The expression of 'public opinion' refers to the tasks of criticism and control which a public body of citizens informally—and, in periodic elections, formally as well—practices *vis-à-vis* the ruling structure organized in the form of a state. . . . The public sphere as a sphere which *mediates between society and state*, in which the public organizes itself as the bearer or [*sic*] public opinion, accords with the principle of the public sphere—that principle of public information which once had to be fought for against arcane policies

9 One example of such a trend is found in the work of Jon Anderson, who observes:

> For well over a generation, the public sphere of Islam has been an arena of contest in which activists and militants brought forth *challenges to traditional interpretative practices* and authority to speak for Islam, especially to articulate its social interests and political agendas. . . . [T]heir claims draw on social and political experience as *alternatives* both to expertise in textual hermeneutics associated with the learned men of Islam (*ulema*) and to more illuminationist priorities exemplified in Sufi and generally mystical ways. Opening the social field to *new spokespeople* and *new discursive practices* not only *challenges authority* long since thought settled to interpret what religion requires, but also blurs boundaries between public and private discourse and fosters new habits of production and consumption tied to media and particularly to new media. (Anderson 2003: 887, my emphasis)

> of monarchies and which since that time has made possible the democratic control of state activities. (Habermas 1974: 49–50, my emphasis)

This deeply utopian democratic ideal of the public sphere as outside of the state permeates the literature on the Islamic public sphere as well, despite the fact that the empirical context in which such studies take place can often hardly be characterized as democratic, and thus the kind of mediation Habermas expects (or the democratic control of state activities) cannot be taken for granted. As anthropologist Jon Anderson has written: "As much as the public/private distinction introduced into the anthropology of the Middle East, South Asia, and Muslim world generally opened previously private realms of experience and expression, it is the public sphere, *separate from domestic and from formal structures of authority*, that needs thick description now" (Anderson 2003: 901, my emphasis).

For these authors, the public sphere is manifestly located outside the state and formal structures of authority in general. But where, one must ask, is the state's outside—not only in authoritarian contexts such as Sudan, where it is hard to escape the material context of the state no matter where one goes, but for all modern states given what we know about the workings of governmentality, from biopolitics (e.g., Foucault 2010) to the "state effect" (Mitchell 1991: 2006)? If we take the conclusions of this literature seriously, it becomes exceedingly difficult to imagine a conceptual (or actual) "outside of the state" where a distinct public sphere supposedly resides. For Mitchell, for example, what he calls "the state effect" is that "which arises from techniques that enable mundane material practices to take on the appearance of an abstract, nonmaterial form [here the state]," the ability to abstract power being itself "the distinctive technique of the modern political order" (Mitchell 2006: 170).[10] Like civil society, the state too is a conglomeration of human actors, whose distinct claims to sovereignty we have perhaps given more analytical credit than is due. Nevertheless, Mitchell reminds us that though the distinction between state and civil society may in some sense be a false one, "the elusiveness of the state-society boundary needs to be taken seriously, not as a problem of conceptual precision but as a clue to the nature of the phenomenon. Rather than searching for a definition that will fix

10 Begoña Aretxaga's extremely helpful review of the ethnographic literature of the state quotes two classic, but still relevant, articulations of this idea. For A.R. Radcliffe-Brown, the state "is usually represented as an entity over and above the human individuals that make up a society, having as one of its attributes something called 'sovereignty,' and sometimes spoken of as having a will . . . or as issuing commands. [Yet] the State in this sense does not exist in the phenomenal world; it is a fiction of the philosophers" (Aretxaga 2003: 400); or as reframed by sociologist Philip Abrams, "The state is not the reality which stands behind the mask of political practice. It is itself the mask which prevents our seeing political practice as it is" (Aretxaga 2003: 400; see also Aretxaga 2005).

the boundary, we need to examine the detailed process through which the uncertain yet powerful distinction between state and society [i.e., the state effect] is produced" (Mitchell 1991: 78). He argues then "that the task of a critique of the state is not just to reject such metaphysics, but to explain how it has been possible to produce this practical effect, so characteristic of the modern political order" (Mitchell 2006: 176). Understanding how this "structural effect"—that is, the ability of the state to appear "as an apparatus that stands apart from the rest of the social world" (2006: 180)—takes place (or, in other words, how the man behind the curtain becomes the Wizard of Oz, despite his mundanity)[11] is key to understanding how modern power works. For Mitchell, despite its constructedness, "[t]he state cannot be dismissed as an abstraction or ideological construct and passed over in favor of more real, material realities" (2006: 184).

I adopt such an approach to the state here, one that looks at it less as an institutional "site" and more as the effect of a series of processes that produce a novel form of modern power that is, however, no less real: a leviathan who is neither human nor entirely divorced from our collective will. It is the materiality of the state, which I observed through its effects in everyday life everywhere I went in Sudan, and this precisely at the moment of its displacement from the institutional bases in which it traditionally resides, that inspired me to write this book. The state, as a "social subject in everyday life" (Aretxaga 2003: 395), and the varying ways in which it has structured Sudanese life and in which Sudanese have come to terms with it, is the focus of the chapters that follow. Through the means of ethnography we are able not only to view this everyday life, to see the state from the bottom up, but to dissolve fantasies of its unity, to disaggregate the state into its constituent parts, which do not always act in concert (Sharma and Gupta 2006: 10–11). Aradhana Sharma and Akhil Gupta put it this way: "Once we see that the boundary between the state and civil society is itself an effect of power, then we can begin to conceptualize 'the state' *within* (and not automatically distinct from) other institutional forms through which social relations are lived, such as the family, civil society, and the economy [or, in my case, religious life]" (Sharma and Gupta 2006: 9).[12] In the example of Sudan, where the government came to power through a coup, the regime explicitly muddied the boundary between state and society in order to make itself seem less

11 As the Wizard famously exclaimed, "Pay no attention to the man behind the curtain!" http://www.youtube.com/watch?v=YWyCCJ6B2WE.

12 This sentiment is echoed in the work of Yael Navaro-Yashin: "There is an attempt to base this distinction [between state and civil society] empirically on historical and social grounds, as if the state and society were tangible things to be pinpointed and distinguished objectively from one another. The following questions, however, ought to be asked: where does the state end and society begin? Could one ever locate such division empirically?" (Navaro-Yashin 2002: 134).

foreign, a process that eventually led to its instability, as we will soon learn. Such a phenomenon has often been hard to detect, however, given that the essential otherness of the state has been upheld by many in civil society in order to maintain comfortable distance from the regime.

By rejecting the impenetrability of the boundary between state and civil society, official realms and the public sphere, this book also challenges presuppositions of the public sphere as necessarily a place where only free deliberation occurs, where traditional authority is challenged, where discourse takes place solely in the medium of talk. We will see that, in fact, public spheres are also very much the spaces of discipline (Hirschkind 2006: 105–8).[13] They are spaces that rely on (and reproduce) both traditional *and* state authority as much as they challenge them; and they not only make use of other sorts of communicative genres besides talk, but also do much more than merely communicate ideas to their participants, as Chapter 4 of this book on the affective training of Sudanese citizens shows. The social is not, then, an organic phenomenon that stands up to the artifice of the state, but is itself the place where the state is reproduced through a reiteration of the rules for membership in political society (Stevens 1999). Such a recognition of the circulation of power in public spheres should not be read gloomily, as a comment restricted to Africa or the Islamic world, nor as marking the end of the kind of deliberation we tend to see as central for the health of public spheres. Rather, it is an appreciation that the presence of the state, and of its disciplining techniques, can be located all across what we have come to call the public sphere. Recognizing this does not imply the end of agency, but rather appreciates the way in which the capacity for agency often comes within a roster of submissions, within a regime of discipline that makes meaningful action possible (Foucault 1990, 1997; Mahmood 2005: 27–29). Reading public spheres through this lens, rather than the one that sees them as outside of official bearers of authority, mobilized only in the challenging of that authority, helps us to understand how power circulates not only in Sudan, but in modern societies more generally.

13 Hirschkind takes works on the public sphere such as those I mention to task for assuming that the sphere of deliberation opened up by mass education and the modern public sphere is somehow free of the disciplinary constraints that characterized periods wherein knowledge was said to be monopolized by an entrenched scholarly elite. He writes that such approaches to the public "sustain this fiction of a purely self-organizing discourse . . . [by building] in a structural blindness to the material conditions of the discourses it produces and circulates, as well as to the pragmatics of its speech forms: the genres, stylistic elements, citational resources, gestural codes, and so on that make a discourse intelligible to specific people, inhabiting certain conditions of knowledge and learning" (Hirschkind 2006: 106). It is these material contexts and pragmatic codes that are the focus of this book. However, while Hirschkind's "counterpublics" exist in "disjunctive relationship to the public sphere of the nation and its media instruments" (2006: 117), the publics I am studying are deeply intertwined with state logics.

Chapters 1 and 2, which make up the section of this book I am calling "Interventions," look at the state from the inside out, tracing how the state-based political class, in both its colonial origins and in its postcolonial present, sought to shape Islam by means of official policies. Inspired by recent works in the ethnography of the state, such as those that I have cited above, Chapters 3, 4, and 5 (the section of the book I am calling "Itineraries") bring what scholars have understood as the state's outside (the public sphere, civil society, the individual) *into* a discussion of the state, explaining how the aspiration for an Islamic political order is lived in these domains. By examining the presence of the state in those spaces that scholars often situate as discursive outsides to it, I hope to question our fetishizing allegiance to state sovereignty, exploring the state as yet another function of our shared political life and not the distant goliath it is often misrecognized to be.

When the State Is Everywhere (or, Reconceiving the Islamic Public Sphere)

When the National Islamic Front came to power in a bloodless coup in Sudan in June of 1989, it promised not only to install new modes of governance but to reform Sudanese society at large. Proclaiming its movement the "Revolution of National Salvation" (*thawrat al-inqādh al-waṭanī*), what came to be called (sometimes pridefully, sometimes scornfully) the "Salvation (*inqādh*) regime" sought to reconstruct Sudanese civilization individual by individual, fusing personal piety and political commitment into an often-unstable whole. The title of my book is derived from a nationalist anthem released by a state-affiliated radio station that I will discuss in more detail in Chapter 4. The anthem, like the Salvation regime itself, sought to lay claim to the Islamic identity of the state and to conceive of the state as a political form for the development of an Islamic way of life that could meet the challenges of modernity. Yet, creating a community that not only submitted to the Islamic state but that desired it, that loved the Prophet so much that it would willingly seek to organize its political order on the model he bequeathed to humanity, was a difficult process. For love of the Prophet meant different things to different people: from fighting the *jihād* in the South (de Waal and Abdel Salam 2004) to creating the material conditions that would make possible a nation constantly in prayer (see Chapters 3 and 4). By justifying political participation on the basis of piety and by proposing that the desired end of political participation was a closeness to God and his prophet, the regime became vulnerable to rival claims. The functionaries of the state could not be the only legitimate owners of political sovereignty if they themselves saw sovereignty as deriving solely from one's relationship to God, since closeness to God was a status many claimed, from the *awliyāʾ* (saints) to the *ʿulamāʾ* (scholars).

And yet, despite this instability built into the Islamic state, there was a way in which the equation of political legitimacy with Islam meant not only the amorphousness of political power (because it could potentially reside anywhere "Islam" was found and not just in the formal state), but also the ubiquity of the state. Even at a time when the power of state institutions was receding in a landscape of international governance, the state, and in particular the Islamic state, came to be undeniable social fact. As Abdelwahab El-Affendi wrote of the situation in the mid-1980s:

> The language that the *Ikhwan* kept speaking in relative solitude [turned] into the language of the majority and even *Ikhwan* opponents started citing the classical Islamic texts. The prevailing atmosphere favoured the Islamists and a great number of secularist (and even left-wing) intellectuals started announcing their conversion to the path of Islam. . . . [The "anti-Islamization camp's"] weakness was [its] inability to state its case more clearly. As even the communists and Christians persisted in speaking of the "true spirit of Islam," their very discourse helped the Islamists maintain their grip on the political agenda. (El-Affendi 1991: 124, 136)

Indeed, while true in the mid-1980s, by the time of the "Salvation Revolution" the language of political discourse had irreversibly become an Islamic one, upheld both by the Islamists and their opponents. This is a process that has only solidified in the intervening years.

In an interview I conducted with a former Communist in which he explained his recent joining of a leftist Sufi movement, I saw in clear relief the staying-power of the Islamic state as a political ideal, appreciated even by staunch opponents of the regime. He recalled to me:

> The fact that [the Communists did not resist after the Islamist revolution] did not simply effect a political change in me. It effected a major personal change in me, in my lack of confidence in the leadership of the Sudanese Communist Party, to be frank. I mean in relationship to their responsibility as fighters (*munādilīn*) of the first degree. Because of [their guidance] we had become apostates to religion (*fī sabīlihum kaffarnā bi-l-dīn*). I was not an apostate to religion because I don't believe in it, but rather I was searching for the proper tools to bring about justice. . . . There is no [other] reason that I would be against the sound natural inclination of the masses, of the majority of all our people [in Sudan], which is mostly the Islamic religion. [But after joining the Communists] I was capable of sacrificing anything to implement justice. And on the other hand, I was thinking that the Muslim Brotherhood

> and other Islamic organizations do not represent Islam anyhow. In fact it was the opposite: they represent a parasitic (*ṭufayliyya*) capitalism. This is the reason that I paid attention to the [Communists]. But when [a group] doesn't have desire to realize the social revolution [which they talk so much about, by seizing the opportunity that the knowledge of the coming Salvation Revolution afforded], so how will they make it real? If the Communist Party was wrong or not able [to implement social justice, I thought that] I must then see what tools, in fact, are appropriate.

Such sentiments are not atypical of how politics had come to be imagined by the turn of the twenty-first century for many: what mattered was no longer choosing between Islam or secularism, but determining what kind of Islamic expression would best bring justice and peace to this long-suffering nation. Even for opposition members, the Islamic state was becoming less and less a deniable reality. They might reject the government in power and its vision of Islam, but the fact that there was and would remain a religious basis to the organization of governance and society became harder and harder to dispute.[14] As Yael Navaro-Yashin has written, "If the political survives critique and deconstruction, if the state endures, as it has, then the anthropologist must venture [into] other arenas and analytical frameworks for the study of the political. For the people who critique the state also reproduce it through their 'fantasies' for the state" (2002: 4). It is in this sense that, in Sudan, the Islamic state was truly everywhere, not merely as the encroachment of formal institutions of the Inqadh government into various sectors of life, but rather as the growing coherence of a political commitment to an Islamic political order to which individuals of a variety of political persuasions aspired, despite their multiple definitions thereof.[15]

The robust presence of the Islamic state in the political imaginary, even in a period in which its institutional instantiations were increasingly occupied by the liberal logics (and actual representatives) of international development and aid, created not only a conceptual dilemma for me but an empirical one as well. The individuals with whom I interacted and whose organizations I studied were often hard to locate: were they situated inside

14 Such an observation should not discount the importance of secularist movements in Sudan such as the Sudan People's Liberation Movement (SPLM), yet they are not the subject of this book.

15 It was in this sense that many would say to me, "No matter what one thinks about the Inqadh, no matter their corruption and disingenuousness, they have to be given credit for bringing *sharīʿa* to Sudan." (Note that despite the fact that the adoption of *sharīʿa* predates the 1989 coup by six years [as it was put in place by President Jaʿfar Numayri during his 1981–85 Islamization phase], the inqadh government and the National Islamic Front party that preceeded it are credited by most as both inspiring and sedimenting *sharīʿa* in Sudan).

or outside of the state? One example is the Sudanese Shaykh ʿAbd al-Rahim Muhammad Waqiʿ Allah, known as al-Buraʿi, whom you will meet on several occasions throughout the pages of this book. Al-Buraʿi was the kind of shaykh at whose *masīd*[16] one would find both regime figures and members of the opposition. This was not because he was apolitical, embracing all Sudanese (as his followers often presented him).[17] The reason instead was that, like me, Sudanese had trouble classifying him, or rather found ample evidence to classify him as either a supporter of or an alternative to the regime.

Al-Buraʿi was among the twenty-first-century Sudanese shaykhs and poets who benefited most from the Islamist coup of 1989. This was true both due to his direct access to media channels established by the regime and, more indirectly, to the way in which shaykhs like him became the beneficiaries of those looking to answer religious questions provoked by the state. Moreover, the massive population shifts that took place in the final decades of the twentieth century, as a result of the war the regime waged, served as the material path to his success. The distinctive shape of his life, from obscurity to superstardom, could not have occurred in any other era, as his name and fame were carried from his home in the vast deserts of Northern Kordofan to the capital by people from western Sudan who had migrated as a result of war, famine, and underdevelopment. Indeed, for this reason, this first and paramount media shaykh of the twenty-first century can be understood as a product, likely unintended, of the regime's military and urbanization programs. His popularity was further cemented by his ability to fulfill a kind of pastoral longing expressed by many Sudanese who had left the "simple life" of the village for the ravages of the city (al-Buni and

16 The term *masīd* likely derives from the Arabic *sayyid* (respected or holy man) and is akin to something like "the place of the holy man," and thus is not a bastardization of *masjid*, as is often assumed. (It took an Iraqi scholar, Omar Dewachi, to destabilize this Sudanist truism, and I thank him for pointing it out to me.) The word refers to a Sufi compound for retreat, study, and worship, which indeed is usually occupied by a great shaykh, his descendants, and the tombs of his forefathers.

17 His biographer, ʿAbd al-Rahim Hajj Ahmad (2006b), concurs with the understanding that al-Buraʿi was putting forward an Islam that was apolitical. The author tells the story of when he composed a poem praising the regime that he wanted to deliver on the occasion of a visit of President ʿUmar al-Bashir to al-Buraʿi's village of al-Zariba, and how al-Buraʿi told him that if he wanted to write praise poetry (*madīḥ*) he should praise the Prophet instead (2006b: 68–69). Hajj Ahmad depicts al-Buraʿi as at any given time having a circle of people who surrounded him, among whom there would be a member of the Democratic Union Party (*Ittiḥādī*), a member of the Umma Party (*Anṣārī*), an Islamist (*Islāmī*), a Communist (*Shiyuʿī*), and even a member of the adamantly anti-Sufi Ansar al-Sunna. Hajj Ahmad commented that al-Buraʿi unified them despite their political views being so divergent (Hajj Ahmad 2006b: 65). Further, the author presents al-Buraʿi as scrupulous in avoiding gifts from politicians and commanding his followers to ask nothing of them. For more details on al-Buraʿi's relationship to politics see Salomon 2010.

Saʿid 2000). And it was the media tools and networks of the urban space his poetry now occupied that quite literally enabled his immense popularity. The programs he supported, from group marriage to discouraging alcohol and excessive mourning (Hajj Ahmad 2006b: 28, 59, 61–63), were those the regime supported. He was celebrated on their radio and television stations; his poetry framed their events.

Al-Buraʿi represented a paradox: both sedimenting the values that the regime sought to spread in its Civilization Project (*al-mashrūʿ al-ḥaḍārī*, Chapter 2), while at the same time offering an alternative locus of spiritual power (Chapter 5) and a thinly veiled critique of the modernist variety of Islam and its accouterments that the regime supported (Chapter 4). Both enabled by state media projects and critical of the kinds of piety they represented, al-Buraʿi's work is evidence of the difficulty involved in conceiving of the public sphere as either inside or outside of the state. His fame was built on the architecture of the state, while his poetry simultaneously sought to destabilize the new moral geography the state presented. Instead, he claimed a much older vision that valorized the quiet rhythms of rural life, the *khalwa* (retreat) that has long been at the center of Islamic practice in Sudan. The public sphere that al-Buraʿi represented was thus both of the state—contributing to its agenda of using the aesthetic and ritual form of *madīḥ* to facilitate national Islamization—yet not reducible to it. The lines between the state and the public sphere were not easy to draw.

Moreover, the fact that the particular Islamic public sphere al-Buraʿi represents (one, of course, of many extant in Sudan) spoke in verse, rather than in the untheorized "talk" that characterizes the Habermasian public sphere, should not go unrecognized. In Chapter 4, I will present a full discussion of the distinctness of the communicative genre of poetry, and, in this case, of poetry accompanied by music. The transportability of poetry, both before and after recorded technology—the former due to its mnemonic characteristics and the latter to its ability to be heard by a wide public as a background substrate to any number of daily activities—meant that this genre reached different sorts of publics than did other forms of Islamic public criticism. Moreover, the tonal, affective, and even kinesthetic repertoire that accompanied these *madīḥ* had both communicative functions and an ability to inculcate certain kinds of pious virtues (Hirschkind 2006). Thus, what went on in this public sphere was not merely reasoned debate about the common good, but the actual shaping of good subjects through listening practices associated with *madīḥ*.

The public sphere of which al-Buraʿi was a part is both a space in which deliberation about and inculcation of the common good took place *and* a context organized by the state; it both reproduces state norms and rethinks them; it is both established by the state and seeks to undo many of the state's basic premises; it both challenges state adversaries and enables them. For this reason, it is problematic to think of the public sphere as either outside of the state or as a realm of unfettered deliberation. Moreover, the specificity of the genre of communication and performance that goes on in the public spheres I study exposes the provincialism of "talk" and calls attention to the unique characteristics of other modes of expression that both communicate ideas and form new kinds of pious subjects. This recognition raises the need, if not to look for a new term of reference beyond the "Islamic public sphere," then at least to rethink the concept, taking into account both the practices of deliberation and discipline that constitute it, as well as its inextricable intertwining with the state.

State of Conflict, State of Grace: New Models for the Study of Sudan

Regardless of its insides and outsides, its ubiquities or paucities, what the Sudanese state is most known for (at least in its current instantiation) is its fluent and brutal use of violence as a means of addressing the intractable problems it inherited from previous regimes. This reputation is not unfounded. The Sudanese government is perhaps not unique in its brutality, but it is prolific in it. From intensifying a war in the South for over a decade before eventually calculating a conclusion to it, to initiating a brutal "counter-insurgency on the cheap" (de Waal 2004) in Darfur that led to the massacre of an unknown multitude of civilians, to perpetuating a more recent war in the new South that has seen little distinction between noncombatant and soldier, this is a regime whose actions cannot be excused or explained away.

When I have delivered bits and pieces of this book as lectures or conference papers, almost invariably someone stands up with a perplexed look on his or her face and asks a pointed question. How does the Sudan I am describing in my work—one characterized by a robust culture of theological debate, by art and poetry, by intellectual exchange, creativity, and perseverance—mesh with the Sudan one hears about daily on the news, a place of war (or even genocide), religious fanaticism, poverty, and famine? The question is of course a valid and important one. I have also written on the civil war (Salomon 2004b, 2011), as well as national partition, and South Sudan's independence (Salomon 2013, 2014, 2015a), and I would not want to give the impression that what I describe here of my everyday experience in Khartoum, Kordofan, and Sinnar states (where I conducted the bulk of the research for this book) is divorced from the Sudan one hears about on the daily news. In fact these two stories are intricately intertwined. While in the more peaceful parts of Sudan one can lazily forget the misery hundreds of miles away (or even on the outskirts of Khartoum), it takes little searching to realize that the political situation in which Sudan found itself in the years bookended by the end of the North-South civil war and national partition, when I did the bulk of my fieldwork, weighed heavily on all aspects of life.

Sudan is a country in constant turmoil. Political instability, war, displacement, drought, and famine have afflicted the Republic of Sudan without respite for nearly the entire span of its sixty-year history. Since independence in 1956, the country has had eight constitutions, experienced five successful coups (and several more attempted coups), and witnessed two large-scale civil wars with the South and armed rebellion in the North, East, South, and West, as well as several famines and droughts that led to massive death and displacement. Further, in addition to having been one of the world's largest producers of refugees (war-afflicted, political, environmental, and economic), Sudan also has been one of the world's largest *recipients* of refugees, opening its borders to those escaping conflicts in Ethiopia and Eritrea, the Congo and Uganda, Chad and the Central African Republic. Despite the temporary boom in development due to the exploitation of oil reserves (Tisdal 2008), Sudan remains an extremely poor country, ranking 167th on the UNDP's Human Development Index of 2015, only twenty countries from the bottom.[18] In the time I lived in Sudan, I witnessed both the conclusion to the latest twenty-two-year chapter in the Sudanese civil war between North and South (at the time the longest-running civil war in the world) and the outbreak of massive new civil conflict in the western Darfur region,[19] a situation that brought massive international attention (and intervention) to a country that had previously been of marginal interest to international public opinion.[20]

Unsurprisingly, the vast majority of writing on independent Sudan has concentrated on these troubling events. Questions of conflict and peace, famine and drought, refugees and resettlement, treaties made and violated, the formation of successive governments and the intricacies of their successes and ultimate failures have been the focus of most of these studies.[21] While such works are crucial both to understanding Sudan and to thinking through possible solutions to its troubles, what has been neglected in this process is a sustained focus on the complex and intricate textures of the lives of individual Sudanese who have lived through these decades of political turmoil, particularly in more recent years. We are missing a key component to understanding Sudan (and potential solutions to its problems)

18 http://hdr.undp.org/sites/default/files/hdr_2015_statistical_annex.pdf.

19 A whole host of publications have come out on the Darfur conflict. Five volumes strike me as particularly useful: Flint and de Waal 2008, Hassan and Ray 2009, de Waal 2007, Daly 2010, and Mamdani 2009.

20 See Aidi 2005 for a persuasive account of why the conflict received so much attention in the US while other brutal African wars were virtually ignored.

21 See Johnson 2004 for a good summary of this literature.

when we pay attention only to the vagaries of macropolitics and ignore the intricacies of the cultural and religious life that goes on in their midst. In this regard, and perhaps most crucially, if book after book has blamed the woes of the contemporary period, at least in part, on the Islamization of the state that occurred after the rise to power in 1989 of the National Islamic Front government (NIF, *al-jabha al-islāmiyya al-qawmiyya*) and its rejection by diverse sectors of the Sudanese public (Idris 2005; Jok 2007), then it would do us well as scholars to provide a thicker description of what these policies meant to those who lived through them: how they were consumed and reworked by diverse publics on the ground. When we do so, we find that, in spite of state attempts at silencing opposition by any means necessary, a vast conversation is taking place in the space opened up by NIF political reforms, a conversation in which a variety of Muslim and non-Muslim actors participate that regrettably has been ignored by local and international policy makers alike.

This book offers an ethnographic study of the Sudanese experience with the Islamic state from its revolutionary establishment in 1989 to the present, with a particular focus on the years of National Unity, 2005–11, when I lived in Sudan for a prolonged period of time. The period of National Unity between the ruling National Congress Party (NCP) and the Sudan People's Liberation Movement (SPLM), representing the South, was particularly interesting because it constituted perhaps the first time since coming to power that the Islamists were compelled to grapple with religious pluralism as they sought to construct a state that did not give up on its Islamic aspirations, but might also appeal to non-Muslims. The project was unsuccessful to the extent that the SPLM came to argue that unity was not made attractive and in that its majority non-Muslim constituency voted overwhelming for secession, which occurred in 2011. But in terms of consolidating the Islamic state, one might argue that it was eminently successful, as the current regime remained in power even through these transitions, and Islamic political organizations that called for such a political model (albeit often in forms different from those the regime offered) seemed to gain strength and multiply following secession.

While a few important exceptions exist that will be discussed in more detail in the following (e.g., Nageeb 2004; Seesemann 2007; Willemse 2007), there have been few ethnographic attempts to study the changing manifestations of Sudanese Islamic modernity since Abdou Maliqalim Simone's (1994) and Victoria Bernal's (1994, 1997) important studies, fieldwork for which was undertaken in the very different political climate of the 1980s. Moreover, the majority of recent work on the Sudanese state (e.g., Collins and Burr 2003; Gallab 2008, 2014) has bequeathed to us a picture of Islamism in Sudan that focuses only on the official written policies of the ruling party, with very little attention to how Sudanese Islam was changing under the long shadows cast by these political developments.[22] Such a limited view obscures the fact that a variety of other Islamic forces exist in Sudan that have acted both in cooperation and conflict with the Islamic vision (and its subsequent rethinking) promoted by the ruling party. In neglecting the varieties of activist Islam in contemporary Sudan, scholars of Sudan have ignored the essential tension that lies at the heart of what they have termed the "Islamic revival": namely, that it encompasses not only an argument about what constitutes a proper society and a proper Muslim believer, but also about what constitutes Islam itself. It is this debate over the nature of modern Islam in Sudan—its epistemology (Chapter 3), its aesthetics (Chapter 4), and, finally, its politics (Chapter 5)—enabled by the changes brought about by the state, that will be the focus of the chapters that make up the heart of this book.

It is my hope that this book will make a significant intervention into the study of Sudan, a country not only of long-standing importance to scholarship, but also of great policy concern to the West, indeed one of the few African nations consistently in the headlines. Recent works on Sudan that have focused primarily on the architecture of conflict and the resulting situation of poverty and underdevelopment are of course crucial for our understanding of life in Sudan. But if we hope not only to understand Sudan's problems, but also to discover how Sudanese and their international partners might move forward from them, we cannot overlook Sudan's many resources. Such writings too often ignore the ingenuity of daily life, the intellectual and social production that goes on even in situations of extreme repression, and even in contexts that cannot be easily untangled from the state. They fail to listen to the people—their philosophies of life, their visions of the good, their dreams for the future—on whom, at least in part, the future of Sudan must be built. This tendency to focus on the political wranglings of the elite to the neglect of the great wealth of knowledge in other sectors is arguably one of the reasons that international engagements with Sudan have been such predictable failures. By exploring everyday efforts to maintain a social and political order inspired by an Islamic normative framework, under the challenges posed both by the horrors of war and the complexities of national unity, my work seeks to broaden our understanding of "ordinary ethics" (Lambek 2010) and their consequences in countries in and emerging from conflict. Building on other efforts in Sudanese ethnography (e.g., Bernal 1997; Boddy 1989; Kenyon 2012; Nageeb 2004; Seesemann 2007; Simone 1994) and intellectual history (El-Affendi 1991), as well as on critical approaches to the study of Muslim Africa more broadly (Şaul 2006; Seesemann

22 One exception to this is chapter 6 of Fluehr-Lobban 2012, which offers an interesting discussion of some of the social transformations wrought by Islamization around issues of marriage and sexuality.

2006), this book aims to put Sudanese interlocutors into conversation with key works on the place of Islam in the future of the African continent.

The Impossible State Made Possible

Countless works have analyzed the nature of the liberal state, the neoliberal state, the democratic state, and the authoritarian state. But how can we characterize *the Islamic state* as a modern political form? What makes it so attractive to Muslim intellectuals? And, most importantly, how does it function in our modern world, combining a nineteenth-century European political form, imposed on the Muslim world through colonialism, with a system of political and religious thought evolving from the seventh century onwards? Wael Hallaq's recent monograph *The Impossible State: Islam, Politics and Modernity's Moral Predicament* offers one potential answer to these questions. There he argues for the incompatibility of Islam, as a mode of subjectivation and governance, with the modern state. Where the former enshrines moral autonomy and a robust rule of law (a law outside of politics in the true sense), the latter is positivistic, its metaphysic "resid[ing] within its own boundaries as sovereign will" (2013: 157). While the former is interested in a project of moral retrieval, the latter has primarily rationalistic and materialistic concerns.[23] Though Hallaq relies on a massive telescoping through history and geography of both modern states and Islamic governance to arrive at these paradigms, his more general point is well taken: Islam and the modern state represent two incommensurable modes of governance and moral authority. It is for this reason that he calls the Islamic state an impossible state; it is a contradiction in terms. His argument is premised on his earlier work (Hallaq 2009), which traces the evisceration of *sharīʿa* by the colonial state, not only through processes of codification that limit its pluralism and interpretive flexibility, but also through attempts to shoehorn *sharīʿa* into a Western legal framework, thus isolating it from the larger regime of moral rearing (including ritual law) of which it was once an organic part. Outlining the key components of the modern state—from its abstract sovereignty (2013: 25–28) to its bureaucratic machinery (31–33)—Hallaq contends that the state is not a neutral vessel into which Islamists can simply pour their aspirations (155). Citing McLuhan (1964), one might say that for

23 Hallaq: "Whereas the Muslim subject strives for moral improvement, the state's subject strives to fulfill sovereign will, fictitiously a representation of the will of the commanding sovereign. The difference is a paradigmatic one between a continuous and unending moral struggle for the Ought and a continuous and unending worldly struggle for the Is. The subject of Is and the subject of Ought are two drastically different human subjects. They stand not only in diametrical opposition but in irreconcilable contradiction" (2013: 160–61).

Hallaq "the medium is the message." The state is in fact a rival moral order to Islam: "It comes with its own arsenal of metaphysics and much else. It *inherently* produces certain distinctive effects that are political, social, economic, cultural, epistemic, and, no less, psychological; which is to say that the state fashions particular knowledge systems that in turn determine and shape the landscape of individual and collective subjectivity and thus much of the meaning of its subjects' lives" (Hallaq 2013: 155–56).

Yet, incompatible as Islam and the modern state might be in their ideals, the Islamic state is a phenomenon that has come to exist in our world in spite of the tensions that Hallaq identifies. Not only this, but for Islamists—from ISIS to the Sudanese regime (despite their vastly different readings of the Islamic state)—the state form is not at all incidental to their goals. The ability of the state to assume its unique mode of power—through its abstract sovereignty, its bureaucracy, its monopoly over legislation, law and violence, and its cultural hegemony (Hallaq 2013: 19–36)—are precisely the elements that make Islamic statehood attractive to those who claim it. This is perhaps not obvious in theoretical formulations of the Islamic state (Belkeziz 2009; Brown 2000; Qutb 1953), where the state form itself is rarely elaborated, but it becomes clear in any attempt to examine how the Islamic state comes to fruition and how it makes use of the apparatus it has inherited from the colonial regime and previous postcolonial endeavors. Chapter 1 of this book will trace the establishment of the modern state in Sudan in the colonial period, according particular attention to how it attempted to undo the Islamic order that preceded it, the Mahdiyya. Chapter 2 will examine precisely how the Sudanese regime drew on the legacy of the Mahdiyya, the intellectual resources of the Islamic movement that it had built since the 1950s, *and* the political form of the colonial state to craft its unique mode of governance; in other words, how it attempted to make Hallaq's impossible possible. The remaining chapters will trace the life of this state, observing how both its mechanisms and its ideals have come to structure Sudanese society. These chapters serve as evidence that the Islamists in charge of the Sudanese state did not see that state as an empty vessel, but rather quite skillfully used its very characteristics (from its abstract sovereignty to its bureaucratic machinery) to propagate their vision. What are we to make of Hallaq's *impossible state* when it in fact becomes a practical possibility?

Despite the attractiveness of Hallaq's analysis of both the modern state and of Islamic law and governance, his conclusions about their incommensurability become increasingly difficult to uphold as they rely on a vision of both Islam and the state that seems to lie outside of history. As Hussein Agrama writes in his study of Islamic law within the Egyptian state, perhaps implicitly critiquing work like that of Hallaq, "The idea that muftis directly access the Islamic tradition, while judges do not because of a code, comes close to saying that the *Sharīʿa* has a traditional essence to which legal codification—a mark of modern law—will always be alien. Yet this idea of a traditional essence fundamentally alien to modern innovation is hard to sustain, both conceptually and historically" (2012: 128). Agrama's discussion of what happens to the *sharīʿa* in the modern state provides a unique intervention into the literature on the subject. Though Agrama offers a careful and sophisticated account of the techniques of moral inquiry and the sedimentation of virtues particular to the classical *sharīʿa* system that are lost through the restructuring of *sharīʿa* under civil law (2012: 54–55, 57), he does not thereby conclude that *sharīʿa* is lost in the modern state. Rather than offering a eulogy for an ideal *sharīʿa*, Agrama tells us about its transformation, along the way providing a careful appraisal of how modern legal subjects in Egypt are formed at the intersection of the liberal rule of law and Islamic jurisprudence. In describing how this happens, Agrama moves away from more speculative conclusions about the death of *sharīʿa*, showing precisely what becomes of it in the modern state and under the secular logics to which it has come to subscribe.

It is the goal of this book to unpack the political form of the Islamic state, exploring it in practice and from the ground up. While previous studies of Sudan have explored the vagaries of political developments in the period of Islamization (Collins and Burr 2003; Gallab 2008, 2011, 2014; Sidahmed 1996), freezing in print what has been rather ephemeral on the ground, this book will depict the character of the Islamic state as it appears in daily life, examining the lasting effects of state Islamization on Sudanese society through a study of the individuals and organizations that function in its midst. Presenting for analysis the results of several years of fieldwork in both urban and rural Sudan, the following pages will explore how, at the outset of a period that eventually brought about the dissolution of the country, a rapidly shifting historical context gave rise to a variety of answers to the question of the place of Muslim piety in the nation's future. The process of trial and error that produced these answers provides extremely valuable data not only for those who study Sudan, but also for scholars of public religion more broadly, not least for those interested in the fate of countries that are grappling with applied Islamic politics of the kind that Sudan has been experimenting with since its Islamist revolution of 1989. Though this book certainly does discuss *an* Islamic state, and a particularly unique one at that, my interest is in using this Sudanese example to make some broader observations about the political form of *the* Islamic state, which has become an increasingly popular one in the second decade of the twenty-first century, despite its purported impossibilities. How can we use the experience of Sudan to understand this influential paradigm, its accomplishments, and its challenges? The heart of this book provides the data needed to begin to answer this question. Its epilogue makes some speculative inquiries into the future of Islamic states in our fraught present and explores as well the difficulties presented by two recent attempts to transcend their problems.

Though it has taken the violence and bombast of ISIS for analysts to begin to take the idea of the Islamic state seriously as a mode of contemporary Muslim expression, twenty-five years ago a much quieter experiment in Islamic statehood (and of a totally different hue than that of ISIS) was attempted in Sudan. It is about time we come to understand it, and why the political form of the state, despite its genealogy in Europe and despite the loud rejection of the colonial past by Islamist thinkers, came to be the favored envelope in which Muslim political aspirations have been packaged from the mid-twentieth century onwards. Was the state simply inevitable as a political form following colonialism, as is often argued, or is there something about its mechanisms (its bureaucracies, its modes of wielding violence, its relationship to territory, its impersonal nature) that has been particularly attractive to contemporary Islamic movements?

By examining the micropolitics of individual and organizational struggles for new modes of Islamic modernity in Sudan under the "Islamic state" and in the interregnum between two periods of disunification (civil war and then national partition), a context of great political instability and thus experimentation, this book expands our understanding of how Islamic politics works as it faces the challenges of governing a diverse and dynamic population. By forcing us outside of models that see Islamic politics *either* as opposed to western political ambitions *or* as simply providing Islamic versions of the political ideals we hold dear (whether as celebrants or critics of modernity), Sudan's experience allows us to see an Islamic politics that proceeds on its own terms, in conversation with political trends sweeping the globe, but also reconceiving the scope of the political in ways that are rarely appreciated (Chapter 5 outlines this argument in more detail).

In the chapters that follow, we will examine the Sudanese Islamic state experiment through the lens of the ethnographic present, in a period when, due to the pressures of peace with the majority non-Muslim South, it was being rethought at many levels. Such a rethinking has given fuel to groups and thinkers that call for a revitalization and reform of Islam not in response to growing secularism, lax morals, or Westernization, as is the case in most examples of modern Islamic reform and revival (e.g., Euben and Zaman 2009), but in response to a problematic experience *with Islamism,* the twenty-plus year phenomenon of Inqadh rule. Interestingly, these responses do not come in the language of a rejection of Islamic politics or modes of social organization, but rather argue for a reworking of Islamic political theory, ritual praxis, and moral reasoning on a diverse set of foundations. These arguments do not emerge solely from the ideas of modernist Muslim intellectuals (such as the vanguard of the ruling regime), but instead encompass a multitude of Islamic intellectual and organizational trends. The rise of the NIF government led paradoxically *not* to the monopolization (or even success) in Sudanese society of the modernist Muslim Brotherhood-style Islamic activism that the NIF upheld, but instead built a scaffolding for the resurgence and the exponential growth of other trends in contemporary Islam, whose programs overlapped in often uncomfortable ways with those of the ruling regime and which came to engage the Islamic state in novel ways. The "Islamic revival," in the Sudanese case at least, seems to be neither a monolithic flood-stream sweeping away more secular ways of being, nor a global force blotting out local traditions,[24] but rather a space of contest in which questions about the nature of Islam and its place in modern articulations of state, society, and subjectivity are continually hashed out.

24 Victoria Bernal (1997), in one of the few studies of the Sudanese "Islamic revival" as a social phenomenon, came to the conclusion that the Islamic revival meant a homogenization of Islam, blotting out the diversity of local traditions through global forms of scripturalist Islam with which she associates the NIF ("The global Islamic revival is, among other things, a movement from local particularized Islams to Islam as a world religion" [p. 132]). Our evidence of the effervescence of a variety of Islamic traditions, reacting in creative ways to the complicated itinerary of the NIF project, proves that far from Islam being homogenized in modern times, the interaction with new global trends has created innumerable syntheses unimaginable in earlier decades.

Interventions

CHAPTER ONE

Of Shaykhs and Kings

The Making of Sudanese Islam

> The very life of the people of Sudan has rested on the efforts of the righteous and the good among the Islamic scholars, jurists, and Sufis who have served as a focus (*qibla*) for the people and been to them a refuge. Such righteous figures give knowledge and guidance to the people of Sudan and they provide them with abundant sanctuary in times of misfortune, war, and disturbance, presenting whatever nourishment they can in periods of drought and famine. Because of this, [these shaykhs] are exalted in the memory of the people and extolled in their emotions. But how many people remember any of the kings who have appeared across the length and breadth of Sudan?
>
> —ʿAwn al-Sharif Qasim (Qasim 2006: 8)

Histories of religion are plentiful in contemporary Sudan, both popular and academic.[1] In a country that has wavered between Islamism, communism, pan-Africanism, Arab nationalism, and World Bank-driven liberal capitalism, the question of the origins and the subsequent development of religions has had very real consequences within the continuing struggle over national vision (Deng 1995; Lesch 1998). The debates occasioned by

1 In addition to the critical editions of the canonical late-eighteenth-century work *Ṭabaqāt wad Ḍayf Allāh* (Ibn Dayf Allah 1975), the academic sources include: Zayn al-ʿAbidin and ʿAbd al-Rahim 2004; Johnson 1994; Karar 1992; Trimingham 1965; Qasim 1989; Warburg 2002. Contemporary academic summaries of the rise of Islam in Sudan owe much to the *Ṭabaqāt*, and the lack of earlier sources often leads to claims like that of Karar that only a "superficial" Islamization (of an unknown character) had been occurring since the seventh century, whereas "real" Islamization did not begin until the sixteenth century with the emergence of the Funj kingdom and the coming of the Sufi shaykhs to Sudan (Karar 1992: 13). Contemporary Sufis have latched onto the story told in the *Ṭabaqāt* of the bringing of Sufism to Sudan by traveling scholars during the early Funj period (c. 1500–1821), often leading to the proud comment made by many of my Sufi informants: "If it were not for Sufism, there would have been no Islam in Sudan" (*law mā kānat al-ṣūfiyya, mā bikūn fī islām fī-l-Sūdān*). As for the popular histories, they deserve a chapter of their own, though I don't have room to discuss them here. (For a Sufi perspective on this history, see Muhammad Khayr 2005; for a Salafi revisionist history of the development of Islam in Sudan, which sees the Sufis as corrupting an original pure Islam brought to Sudan by ʿAbdullahi ibn Abi al-Sarh in 651, see al-Badri 1995. I discuss both sources in more detail in Salomon 2010: 43, 163.)

this struggle are, however, in no sense new to Sudan, as since its first recorded history, religion has had a tense, if often productive, relationship with various political orders, giving the stories told about its origins—native or foreign, civilizer or conqueror—considerable stakes. Presently, in a period when the Islamic state project of the ruling regime is particularly unsettled, these histories seem again open for debate, as if the history of Islam in Sudan might help Sudanese to re-envision its future as a mode of national belonging. Notably, in such debates, the "state" in the Islamic state equation is taken for granted, or even understood to have an Islamic genealogy that predates what otherwise might be seen as an obvious colonial heritage. In such debates, it is only the manner in which the resources of the Islamic tradition—be they scriptural, ritual, or historic/paradigmatic—might fuel the progression of the existing state that is up for discussion. The state itself remains unanalyzed as an undeniable fact of political existence.

The debate over the "Islam" in the Islamic state is, in great measure, the subject of this book. In this chapter, however, I will take a brief look at the other half of this convenient phrase, the history of the state in Sudan, and in particular its myriad interactions with the diverse and plural religious landscapes into which it has intervened, and out of which it sought to manufacture a productive partner for its governing efforts. A history of the state, I will argue, occasions a new kind of history of religion, as the "Islam" that emerges as both the means and the object of the Islamist interventionist projects of the late twentieth and early twenty-first centuries has a clear genealogy in Sudan's political history, in particular in the colonial period when the first attempt at creating a modern nation-state was made. This version of Sudanese history is rarely recognized because twenty-first-century concepts of religion and state are often anachronistically projected onto the deep past where projects in Islamic state-building seek their legitimacy (as the postscript to this chapter discusses). Yet, the agenda of "religion-making" forwarded by the Inqadh regime has important precedents, ones that are both direct precursors to its project and heuristically useful parallels for our own understanding of the peculiar governmentality of the modern state when it comes to organizing religion, in Sudan and beyond. While histories of religion in Sudan often obfuscate or ignore political histories—those forgotten kings referenced in the quote with which I began this chapter—if we are to understand how religion developed and became such an important point of contention in contemporary Sudan, recognizing its emergence as a category of political intervention is crucial. While the present regime claims to offer a break with Sudan's recent past by constructing a "modern" Islam that will erase the scars of colonialism, in significant ways its project in managing religion is the continuation of an effort that began nearly one hundred years ago under a very different banner: as an attack on an Islamic political order rather than an effort to establish one.

Recognizing this fact raises the question of whether the distinction between Islamic and secular states is as sharp as is commonly alleged in the literature on politics in the Muslim world. By questioning such a distinction, I do not mean to call the Islamic state unremarkable, or disingenuous, using a mask of religion for political ends. The chapters that follow should allay such a suspicion, as the creative synthesis of state logics and Islamic moral authority is revealed. Rather, I seek to trouble this distinction because the materiality of the state is often forgotten in the over-determined arena of modern politics in which Islamists and secularists are understood to be upholding two polar-opposite political positionalities (Agrama 2011; Marzouki 2012; Zeghal 2013a).[2]

This chapter will examine the early efforts of British colonialism as it sought to undo the Mahdist Islamic political order that had taken over Sudan in the early 1880s and to replace it with the institutions of a modern secular state. By both institutionalizing its religion and "civilizing" (Boddy 2007) its population, the British hoped to pull Sudan into an emerging global order, one to which the Inqadh regime responded nearly a hundred years later, not by rejecting its categories, but rather by seeking to instill in them the ethical values of Islam. Highlighting Sudan's colonial past at the outset of this book deprovincializes the history of Sudan's Islamist present, locating it as part of a much longer struggle to define the relationship of religion to the modern state. This is a struggle that cannot be reduced to a secularism versus Islamism dichotomy, precisely because it spans them both.

2 In a short article posted to the Social Science Research Council's *Immanent Frame* blog, Nadia Marzouki (2012) productively destabilizes our understanding of the distinction between secular and Islamic parties in Tunisia. She writes of the al-Nahda Islamist movement that it has very little interest in speaking of religion, but rather focuses primarily on combatting despotism and corruption. "In fact, Islamists are, in some sense, more secular than secularist groups. They advocate a high wall of separation between religion and the state, while secularist organizations and parties demand a close monitoring of mosques and religious institutions by the state." For her, the secular-religious distinction not only lacks analytical purchase, but it falls apart on the ground as well. Divides between state and society, between young and old, between autocrats and democrats, seem to have more substance in the political context she studies than those between secularists and Islamists. Hussein Agrama (2011), moreover, describes the Egyptian protests that led to the overthrow of Mubarak as standing "outside the problem space of secularism," being uninterested in the question of where to draw the line between religion and politics, a question peculiar to state sovereignty in its multiple forms ("secular" and "Islamic").

Colonialism as Religious Reform

In many ways, the colonial project in Sudan that began with the British victory in Khartoum in 1898 could be read as an archetypal attempt at establishing secular governance. Indeed, it is often referenced by proponents of the Islamic state in the present as such a powerful episode of secular state-building that its legacy still poses a challenge to the success of contemporary Islamist projects in freeing religion from its limited domains. The British conquest came under the mandate of transforming the Sudanese state from an Islamic theocracy into a secular republic. The British had entered Sudan to rid it of the Mahdist regime, a seventeen-year period (1881–98) of rule by a messianic figure (and later his successor) who overthrew the Turkish-Egyptian overlords, shepherding Sudan into what then seemed to be a rapidly concluding eschatological drama (Holt 1958).[3] This figure, who called himself "the Mahdi" (the rightly guided one), was the bearded Muslim fanatic of the Western fantasies of his day, and the British not only feared for the fate of Sudan under his rule, but worried that his unique mix of religion and politics could spread to other countries in the region in which they had interests, in particular to Egypt.

Yet, the sudden takeover of the country by Anglo-Egyptian forces in 1898, though it successfully eliminated the Mahdist forces, did not herald the retreat of religion from politics. On the contrary, the British, fearing a repeat of the Mahdiyya, were greatly preoccupied with molding and reforming religion in their new territory, a process they saw as central to their governing strategy. Suppressing both neo-Mahdist and Sufi organizations—both of which the British understood as having potentially destabilizing effects, the former because they enacted the next scenes of the apocalypse, the latter because Sufism had been the breeding ground of the Mahdi in the first instance—became a priority of the British leadership, and they undertook this effort in several different ways. While the British did try to marginalize the influence of these groups over the Sudanese public through direct persecution (Ibrahim 1979), a more robust component of their project was an attempt to supplant their influence by importing and giving patronage to a class of Egyptian religious scholars and officials (Voll 1971; Warburg 1971: 95–106). The goal of this move was to establish something akin to an

3 Sunni eschatology holds that near the end of time God will send a *mahdī* (lit. "guided one") to earth to lead the entire Muslim community in installing justice and destroying tyranny. Following this *mahdī* will come *al-dajjāl* (the anti-Christ), and then the second coming of the prophet ʿIsa (Jesus). Many Sudanese saw the British as an embodiment of *al-dajjāl*. Therefore, in the years following the British conquest of Sudan, several individuals arose proclaiming to be the prophet ʿIsa, thus fulfilling the next step of the eschatological plan (Ibrahim 1979).

Islamic orthodoxy, or perhaps in British officials' minds even "Islam" itself, since they judged the Sufism and neo-Mahdism present in Sudan as debased forms of spirituality, quite distant from anything that could properly go by the name of religion.

The Islam of al-Azhar University that British officials had encountered in Egypt, and the scriptural tradition about which they'd read in their field training courses,[4] seemed a far cry from the kinds of spiritual practices that confronted them in Sudan. In a classic example of what religious studies scholars have referred to as "religion-making from above" (Dressler and Mandair 2011: 21–23; Peterson and Walhof 2002), the British sought to produce a singular Islam out of the crowded and diverse spiritual landscape of Sudan. Manufacturing a "civilized" religion that would not only play by the rules of the modern nation-state, but would also help Muslims respond flexibly to issues of public concern, became a major agenda of the colonial government. This is an agenda that we will see taken up again in 1989 with the coming of the Inqadh regime, which also saw the state as the most effective tool for modernizing Islam and the encouragement of an Islamic public sphere as the best way to do so. Both the colonial and Inqadh governments understood private religious practice and its institutions as detrimental: to the individual (for its ritual distractions from matters of import),[5] to the community (for its tendency to fragment allegiances),[6] and potentially to the state as well (for its ability to serve as an alternative locus of sovereignty).[7] Thus, in both the secular state-building project and the Islamic state, those in charge sought to force religion out of the shadows and to normalize it under the watchful gaze of the state.

4 Though I do not have room to discuss them in the body of this chapter, I came across some very interesting descriptions of the training courses to which British officials were subjected before embarking on their work in Sudan. In one account, I found the then Governer General of Sudan, Francis Reginald Wingate, during a holiday from his duties in Sudan in July of 1906, addressing the Committee on Oriental Studies at the University of London, trying to convince the reluctant professors to establish a program to train civilians for service in the Sudan like the programs that already existed at Oxford and Cambridge. Discussing these programs, as well as the curricula for civilian officers that were in place in the Sudan to supplement them, Wingate says, "All these young civilians now come out with a good knowledge of reading and writing, and know something of the history of the country, they have some acquaintance with the religious law, the Koran, the Shariah Mohammedieh and so on. They all have a smattering anyway of it. . . . Of course, the religion of the bulk of the Sudan, certainly half of it, is Muslim. It is very important that they should know something of the religion of the country, and more especially the religious law of the country; that is to say the Sharia Mohammediah" (SAD 283/1/30, 35). It is worth reflecting on what counted for the British as "the religion of the country" and what necessarily was left out, a task we undertake later in this chapter.

5 See Hasan al-Turabi's comments on page 167 of this text.

6 See the discussion of "sectarianism" (*al-ṭā'ifiyya*) on pages 61 and 69.

7 See the discussion of the promotion of ethical Sufism in Chapter 2.

While in the fields of law, government, and commerce the British administration aimed to replace a theological order with one based on the secular liberal tradition of common law, representative government, and market capitalism,[8] it did not thereby seek to marginalize Islam, as the much problematized secularization thesis might assume (cf. Calhoun, Juergensmeyer, and Van Antwerpen 2011). "If the secularization thesis no longer carries the conviction it once did," argues anthropologist Talal Asad, "this is because the categories of 'politics' and 'religion' turn out to implicate each other more profoundly than we thought, a discovery that has accompanied our growing understanding of the powers of the modern nation-state" (Asad 2003: 200). Indeed, in the case of the British in Sudan, secular governance is distinguished more for its promotion of certain modes of religiosity than for its separation of religion from government.[9] Such a concern with religion represents not a failure of secularism, or a tension inherent to its unfolding, but rather, in this case and others, seems to be the very paradox that sustains it (Agrama 2012: 71; Fernando 2014).[10] Indeed, here and elsewhere it seems clear that secularism relies on the production of a category of religion in order to ensure the conceptual distinctness of its domain, particularly when existing spiritual practices on the ground lend no respect for such boundaries (a process scholars of secularism have referred to as "differentiation" [Casanova 1994]).

Examining the case of Sudan from the year of its conquest by Lord Kitchener's Anglo-Egyptian forces in 1898 until the beginning of World War I affords a clear vision of the manner in which religion was produced and mobilized to support a form of governance that has lasted in Sudan until the present day, that of the modern nation-state. Though on the outbreak of the First World War, the British abruptly changed their strategy from one of reforming religion from above toward a favors-for-patronage model in which the only requirement was loyalty to the crown (Holt and Daly 2000: 111), the seeds they planted in these early years, in terms of the particular relationship between religion and state they established, reemerged at various points in Sudanese history and have seen their full flowering under the

8 See Gleichen 1905 for a fascinating account from a member of the administration of the British program for the "modernization" of the Sudan in the fields of commerce, military, government, and law.

9 Again, Asad: "It is easy to think of [secularism] simply as requiring the separation of religious from secular institutions in government, but that is not all it is. Abstractly stated, examples of this separation can be found in medieval Christendom and in the Islamic empires—and no doubt elsewhere too. What is distinctive about 'secularism' is that it presupposes new concepts of 'religion,' 'ethics,' and 'politics,' and new imperatives associated with them" (Asad 2003: 1–2).

10 My thanks to Mayanthi Fernando who pushed me on this point in regards to an essay I wrote on secularism in South Sudan (Salomon 2014).

present regime. While the partisans of the Islamic state claim to be offering a break with Sudan's recent past in manufacturing a "modern" Islam that will aid the progression of their state, in significant ways they are continuing a project that began nearly a hundred years earlier, but under a very different banner: as an attack on an Islamic political order rather than as its establishment. Understanding the history of the state in Sudan, in its myriad interactions with religion, is not only essential to any project that claims to be a study of the Islamic state, but will help us also to avoid the common tendency to overemphasize the Islamic side of that equation while ignoring the problems such a political model shares with myriad other efforts at modern state-based governance. comprehensive background matters

From Private Practice to Public Religion: Establishing Orthodoxy in Sudanese Islam

From the very first months of the British occupation, there was a concerted effort to cleanse Sudan of any trace of Mahdism and to reform the Sufi orders from which it had arisen. One of the first acts the British undertook was the destruction of the Mahdi's tomb. Shortly after the occupation of Khartoum, Lord Kitchener, the head of the British-led Egyptian army, and the first Governor-General of the Sudan, telegraphed Lord Cromer, the British Consul-General of Egypt (and Kitchener's direct superior since Sudan was officially under joint Egyptian and British "condominium" rule), to inform him of the decision and its execution. Kitchener wrote:

> I thought it was politically advisable, considering the state of the country, that the Mahdi's tomb, which was the center of pilgrimage and fanatical feeling, should be destroyed. . . . When I left Omdurman for Fashoda I ordered its destruction. This was done in my absence, the Mahdi's bones being thrown into the Nile. The skull only was preserved and handed over to me for disposal. No other bones were kept, and there was no coffin.[11]

The tomb was a major pilgrimage site in Sudan, for the Mahdi, like the founders of the Sufi orders, was revered in a manner similar to a saint. Kitchener's brutal disregard for the cult that surrounded the Mahdi can be read as the inaugural step in a sixteen-year campaign to stamp out Mahdism and encourage a new type of Sunni orthodoxy. (And I can't think that it is mere coincidence that the Muslim boogeyman of the late twentieth and early twenty-first centuries, Osama bin Laden, met the same fate as

11 PRO 30/57/14.

the Muslim boogeyman of the late nineteenth, his body likewise deposited in a watery grave to avoid the potential of religious fervor rising up around a terrestrial burial site. However, in the twenty-first century case, the souvenir of the Mahdi's skull, rumored to have sat on Kitchener's desk for many years thereafter, has been replaced by the more civilized stuff of DNA.)[12] In addition to destroying the tomb of the Mahdi, the British banned the Mahdist outfit, the patched *jibba* (a sign of membership in the Mahdist order and of ascetic poverty), and sent those caught wearing it into work gangs. Further, they disallowed Mahdist prayer meetings and public recitations from the *rātib*, the Mahdist prayer book (Daly 1986: 121). The British campaign used many different tactics to combat Mahdism, from physically crushing the active supporters of the Mahdi, neo-Mahdis, or other suspect Sufi groups (Ibrahim 1979; Warburg 1971: 100–106), to trying to install Islamic institutions that could produce a "truer" and, not coincidentally, more governable form of Islam (Warburg 1971: 95–106, 129–33; Voll 1971).

The British suppression of religious groups was not limited to the Mahdists. Sufi groups (except the Khatmiyya, which had directly opposed the Mahdiyya throughout its rule and therefore received special favor) were also considered a danger, and the British did everything in their power to discourage their reemergence ("*re*-emergence" because the Mahdi too had attacked Sufi orders, but in his case under the messianic conviction that his new order superseded and thus cancelled out all those that came before him [O'Fahey 1999]). Upon conquering Sudan, Lord Kitchener delivered a memorandum to the *mudīrs* (the new British directors of the provinces) on the proper method of rule when dealing with Islamic organizations. In it Kitchener lays out the policy toward Islam that his successor, Governor-General Wingate (r. 1899–1916), to varying degrees implemented until the beginning of World War I. He wrote:

> Be careful to see that religious feelings are not in any way interfered with, and that the Mahommedan religion is respected. At the same time, Fikis [*fakīs*][13] teaching different Tariks [Sufi orders], and dealing

12 For an intriguing story about the alleged severed head of Bin Laden's deputy (which turned out not to be his head after all), by an author who draws a direct parallel with Kitchener's treatment of the Mahdi's head, see H.D.S Greenway's *New York Times* piece "Meanwhile: The Curious Case of the Severed Head": http://www.nytimes.com/2007/04/03/opinion/03iht-edgreenway.1.5125683.html.

13 The term *fakī* is a Sudanization of the Arabic term *faqīh* (scholar of Islamic jurisprudence) that up until recently referred to Sufi leaders (who taught the law alongside the mystical sciences) and other "men of religion." More recently, following the integration of Sufi orders into global discourses of Islamic orthodoxy, Sufis have come to reject the term and it has taken on an almost pejorative sense, referring exclusively to "unlearned" practioners of traditional Qur'anic arts (divination, healing, etc.) who are not in the leadership of Sufi orders.

> in amulets, &c., should not be allowed to resume their former trade. In old days, these Fikis, who lived on the superstitious ignorance of the people, were one of the curses of the Soudan, and were responsible in great measure for the rebellion. Those among the people who desire to study religion should do so at the capital, where a school will be established under proper supervision. . . . Mosques in the principal towns will be rebuilt; but *private* mosques, takias [Sufi lodges], zawiyas [Sufi spaces of worship], Sheiks' tombs, &c., cannot be allowed to be reestablished, as they generally formed the centers of unorthodox fanaticism. Any request for permission on such subjects must be referred to the central authority.[14]

In this memorandum, Kitchener calls for respect of the "Mahommedan religion," but then instructs his subordinates to suppress the *fakīs*, and ban the reconstruction of damaged saints' tombs and places of Sufi worship, which were, by all accounts, the heart of Sudanese Islam prior to their suppression under the Mahdi. Kitchener instead advocates the establishment of a religious center in the soon-to-be-rebuilt capital of the Turco-Egyptian period, Khartoum. An Islam whose seats of authority and learning were spread throughout the villages and towns, and whose teachers were individual shaykhs of Sufi orders, was to be replaced by one central authority, one official seat of learning, in the capital, under the watchful gaze (and indirect administration) of the British authorities. In an interesting reversal of the common secularization thesis (cf. Van der Veer 2001: 14; Mcleod 2000: 3), wherein secular government is supposed to encourage the privatization of religion, leaving the public sphere open to secular logics only, Kitchener argues that it is "private" religious institutions that pose the deepest threat to Sudan. Private religious institutions were not only difficult for the state to monitor, but also were unaccountable to public norms and could easily devolve into a "fanaticism" to which the Arabs were understood to be naturally prone if untethered from the discipline of ordered prayer at a mosque under the leadership of a centrally appointed *imām*.

Such policies greatly complicate colloquial understandings of processes of secularization in that they seek not to marginalize religion from the public sphere, but rather to pull religion out of the private sphere not yet suffused with the regime's logics of governmentality. Here, the private sphere is imagined as a potential breeding ground for anti-state activities, while the public sphere is seen as something that can be monitored by the state. Thus the story of the secular state, in this instance and in many others (Sullivan, Yelle, and Taussig-Rubbo 2011), is less about the privatization of

14 FO 78/5022, my emphasis.

religion than the formation of new sorts of religious publics, ones that can function within and further the aims of modern statecraft.

"An Admixture of Cruelty and Sensuality": From "Fanaticism" to "Religion"

The British policy also relied on manufacturing a novel concept of religion in Sudan, a strategy they had attempted in earlier colonial efforts, such as their occupation of India, where they weighed-in on practices that they saw as abhorrent or "inauthentic" Hinduism (Mani 1998: 96). The determination of where "religion" lies—whether in scripture or everyday practice, in the commands of "authorities" or in the collective experience of believers—remains to the present day a conundrum for governing authorities (Sullivan 2005), and it was a major policy concern of the British regime as well (we will see in Chapter 3 that the Inqadh regime also adopted such a border-drawing strategy in their insistence on a scripturalist variety of Islam).

Such a strategy based itself upon a certain reading of the spiritual practices the British encountered in Sudan. If we are to understand some of the reasons behind the British attempt to install an Islamic orthodoxy, it will be useful to examine where they drew the line between religion (what they wanted to promote) and "fanaticism" (that which, of course, they wanted to discourage). Sudanese messianic and Sufi Islam were seen as the primary threats both to British rule in Sudan and to the development of the civilization the British were trying to promote more broadly (Boddy 2007). In the former case, this was because Sufism was understood to have the potential to fragment national allegiances, and because the power of its leaders was seen to derive from charisma rather than an ordered (and thus potentially co-optable by the state) hierarchy. Following World War I, the British came to realize that this understanding of Sufi authority was in fact incorrect (Sufis rely on an extremely rigid organizational structure [e.g., Chih 2007]), and thus sought to co-opt the Sufi orders in service of the nation, indeed as one of the few transtribal affiliations available. But, in these early years, the British saw Sufi orders as particularly threatening to the fulfillment of a nationalist agenda. On the other hand, in terms of Sufism's threat to civilization, British officials simply understood Sufism to be "backwards," distracting the individual with ecstatic worship when he should be spending his time on pursuits that would help advance his nation.

When British officials came into contact with Sufi Islam, so different from the Islam they had read about in their training courses and so radically alien to the Christian denominations of their home, their reaction was often extreme alarm. C. P. Browne, governor of Berber province in the 1920s and a member of the Sudan Political Service from 1902 onwards, jotted down some stories about his time in the Sudan during his early years in Blue Nile and Sennar provinces. Writing in the first person, Browne describes a Sufi *dhikr* that he observed:

> The ceremony, called 'zikr', is, I believe, unorthodox, but in this country it is the favored means of exciting joint religious enthusiasm; an evil and debased sight, with the admixture of cruelty and sensuality so often found in emotional religion, whereby a bestial, dehumanized excitement confounds itself with absorption in the deity, with that surrendering of the soul that gives its name to Islam.[15]

It is interesting to note that Browne begins by representing the *dhikr* using the paradigm of heterodoxy that we recall from our discussion of British officials' view of Mahdism. Again, it should be clear that the argument that the British were making is (or at least attempts to be) internal to the Islamic tradition rather than outside of it. While certainly the "emotional religion" that Browne encounters is distasteful to him for a variety of reasons, his comments that it is a heterodox practice foreshadows the way in which the British dealt with Sufism throughout the early years of their rule. Instead of condemning it outright, their argument was that it was aberrant by the measure of the Islamic tradition itself.

In Browne's mind, Islam, which he understands as a religion of surrender, became particularly dangerous when the Muslim submitted to what he saw as a wild emotional order. In delimiting the more official reasons for the British imposition of orthodoxy in the following pages, we must not forget the very real motivation of fear. Though British officials had read about the quiet and reserved Islam of the mosque, they most likely knew very little about the *dhikr*, and thus it must have seemed to them jarring and unpredictable when they encountered it for the first time.[16] As British officials like Browne were ruling over great masses of Sudanese people, unpredictability seemed especially threatening. This view, coupled with the memory of the Mahdiyya (which sprang from the Sufi orders), caused the British to see the Sufi orders as particularly dangerous. One hundred years later, Western policy makers would come to understand Sufism as "moderate Islam" and the scholastic Islam of the mosques that the British once sought to promote

concern comes from versions of Islam unfamiliar to British

15 SAD 422/14/15.

16 Though these officials seemed to be seeing the *dhikr* for the first time, the colonial administration must have encountered Sufi practices before in its endeavors in South Asia, the Middle East, and North Africa. How images of Islam were communicated across the diverse spaces of the British Empire would be an interesting topic to pursue. I thank Jeremy Walton for suggesting such an approach, even if I do not have the space to pursue it here.

in Sudan as hotbeds of fanaticism,[17] but in the early twentieth century their estimation was quite the opposite.

Another reaction to a Sufi *dhikr* is contained in S.S. Butler's memoirs of his time as a Camel Corps officer in Kordofan.[18] He writes:

> On all their faces is a sort of 'far away,' rapt expression, not a pleasant dreamy peaceful look, but a look that makes one picture them waving blood stained swords, as they hack their way through forces of 'unbelievers' to the cry of 'Allah Akbar. . . .' One almost begins to wonder if one is in the 20th century, an officer in the Hagana, in a well ordered little station and if that wild looking Arab swaying from side to side and chanting Islamic dirges is really your cook, who, an hour or so before, you had to tick off because the soup was cold! It made one feel in those far off days that one was sitting on the edge of a volcano.[19]

Here, in the opposition between the "well ordered" government station and that "wild Arab swaying from side to side and chanting Islamic dirges," we see clearly some of the threats that were merely implied in the passage from Browne. In his fantasy of the violence that these Sufis might commit, Butler's fear (and perhaps some guilty feelings toward those who serve him) rises to the surface. The metaphor of "sitting on the edge of a volcano" should not be taken lightly. The unease that mystical Islam aroused contributed to the strong-armed British policy to stamp out its more threatening manifestations and to put in its place an "orthodox Islam" with a leadership that would be more easily accountable to British rule and that would move Sudanese from their "wild" fanaticism to the contemplativeness of true religion.[20]

To be acceptable to the British administration, Sudanese spiritual practices needed to pose no danger to the kind of "well ordered little station[s]" that people like Browne and Butler were trying to make a model for all of Sudan.

17 See e.g., Rand Corporation 2003 and the myriad sources cited in *Markaz al-abḥāth wa-l-dirāsāt* 2013.

18 Butler spent most of his time in military intelligence in Khartoum, but for part of his early years, he was a military officer in the Camel Corps in Kordofan (Warburg 1971: 198). Warburg discusses some of the writings of both Browne and Butler in his account (1971: 99).

19 SAD 422/12/31.

20 It is interesting to compare these accounts of Sufi practice with how Browne characterizes the Islamic leaders appointed by the state. In his journal of October 12, 1911, Browne describes the representative of "orthodox" Islam as follows: "I've been in the intelligence department now about a month and have met quite an interesting lot of people. 1) The grand Mufti, by name [*sic*] Sheikh al Tayyib Hashimi—a most pleasant man—middle age, well [illegible word] + I believe broad minded Arab. He is [illegible word] quite loyal to the government + of assistance to us. He is the brother of 2) Sheikh Abdul Qasim, cadi of Wad Medani—a great friend of mine . . . a broad minded pleasant man" (SAD 400/10/3).

The civilizing project of colonialism needed a religion that could be its partner. If the modern state is unique, as Timothy Mitchell (1991) observed in his groundbreaking study of British colonialism in Egypt, for mobilizing a kind of "disciplinary power" (that is, the power not just to restrict individuals, but to produce certain kinds of individuals as well), then spiritual orders that engage not only in structures of discipline that are unfamiliar, but ones misrecognized as undisciplined, stirring the passions as we saw depicted in the above, become particularly dangerous. While the British were liberal in their application of violence, tracking and killing many Sudanese claimants to religious inspiration (Ibrahim 1979), they were equally eager to substitute a new brand of religious practice for what was common in Sudan, a form of practice that would play by the rules of the new structures of governance they were imposing. Thus, the official position the occupying powers took was not to condemn "Islam" but to argue that the Sudanese were not practicing it correctly.[21] Indeed, Wingate defined Mahdism not only as a revolt against "the recognised Government authority in the Sudan," but also as a "revolt against the orthodox Moslem religion" (Wingate 1968 [1891]: xxi). In those places where that orthodox religion could not be found, the occupying power sought to create it.[22]

Institutionalizing Orthodoxy: Councils, Courts, Courses, and Construction

Given the chaotic nature of the new occupation, it is surprising to note how many of Kitchener's early ideas about the British Islam policy were actually realized after Wingate took over his position as Governor-General of Sudan in 1899. During Wingate's tenure, the administration established three main institutions to implement its policy: a council of *ʿulamāʾ*, a

21 Note the parallel with the rhetoric of the twenty-first-century "War on Terror": e.g., George Bush's remarks at the Oval Office on September 28, 2001: "I have assured His Majesty [King Abdullah of Jordan] that our war is against evil, not against Islam. There are thousands of Muslims who proudly call themselves Americans, and they know what I know—that the Muslim faith is based upon peace and love and compassion. The exact opposite of the teachings of the al Qaeda organization, which is based upon evil and hate and destruction": http://georgewbush-whitehouse.archives.gov/infocus/ramadan/islam.html.

22 For a twenty-first-century analogue to this process, see Mahmood 2006, in which the author discusses US attempts to foster an "Islamic Reformation." In regard to how such a phenomenon impacts the way we might understand the secular identity of the US, she argues: "The political solution that secularism proffers . . . lies not so much in tolerating difference and diversity, but in remaking certain kinds of religious subjectivities (even if this requires the use of violence) so as to render them compliant with liberal political rule" (328). This observation applies nicely to the case of the British project in Sudan as well.

system of *sharīʿa* courts, and a *qāḍī* ("judge," in this case in Islamic law) training course at the newly established Gordon College in Khartoum. The British also constructed mosques, paid for their staff, financed Islamic primary schools to teach the Qur'an, and paid for Sudanese to go on the *ḥajj*, which had been outlawed by the Mahdi (Daly 1986: 123; Warburg 1971: 88), who, in his insistence on the immanence of the eschaton, saw such a ritual as too little, too late.

If their Islam policy was to succeed, British officials reasoned, Sudan would need a singular and stable authoritative structure that would not only represent Sudanese Muslims to the colonial government, but would shape them as well. The tactics the British employed will be quite familiar to students of the British Empire, as they exemplify a common British strategy, utilized in other colonial endeavors, of building up an elite class that could act as a (co-opted) intermediary between British officialdom and the general masses.[23] Yet here, indirect rule became indirect *iṣlāḥ* (Islamic reform). Kitchener proclaimed early in the British rule, "The task before us all . . . is to acquire the confidence of the people, to develop their resources and to raise them to a higher level. This can only be effected by the District Officers being thoroughly in touch with the better class of native, through whom we may hope gradually to influence the whole population."[24] Yet on matters concerning religion, the British soon found out that very few of this "better class of native" existed. The Mahdi had run out of the country or killed most of the Turco-Egyptian religious officials, and there were few people left in Sudan who represented the type of Islam that the British wanted to inaugurate. Therefore, in order to establish the desired orthodoxy, the British began a lengthy campaign of importing Egyptian scholars from al-Azhar University in Cairo to administer religious matters in the Sudan, as well as to train Sudanese in the proper functioning of "orthodox" Islam.

Announcing the establishment of a council of such scholars, one British official wrote, "The Arab Population is inclined to be fanatical; and to enable the Government to keep itself informed of the religious feelings of the people, a consultory board of Ulema (learned men) has been established at Omdurman" (Gleichen 1905: 11). The Cairene Islam of al-Azhar appealed to the British for many reasons. First and foremost, it represented a form of Islam in which leadership positions were granted on the basis of scholastic qualifications. A person could only become a leader through a lengthy course of university learning. The British, who misunderstood Sufism as a

23 Many Western actors working in the Muslim world have continued this strategy to the present day, often under the heading of "Religious Engagement." For a discussion of these efforts as an element of US foreign policy, see chapter 4 of Elizabeth Shakman Hurd's *Beyond Religious Freedom: The New Global Politics of Religion* (Hurd 2015).

24 FO 78/5022.

tradition with no clear order, in which a man became a leader simply by the fact of his charisma, felt confident that someone who had gone through scholastic training would be more amenable to the principles of rational state and civil society that they were trying to install. At the very least, they imagined, Azhar Islam, which had such a clear path to positions of status, would be much easier to administer than the decentralized system of rule that characterized Sufi Islam in the Sudan. Like the European university degree, the al-Azhar diploma established a common standard for assessing status, and the British hoped that it would save them having to deal with dangerous competing claims to "Islamic truth." A unified body, made up of Azhar graduates, would, they hoped, be able to enforce the distinction they wanted to uphold between orthodoxy and heterodoxy, fanaticism and religion.

However, it should be noted that the idea that the "Ulema" would act as a counterweight to the Sufi orders was based on a false premise, and that is perhaps one reason why the British attempt to promote an orthodoxy *distinct* from Sufism had limited success. Though certain practices of Sufism were deemed reprehensible by early twentieth-century reformers and traditionalists alike (Sirriyeh 1999), many Azhar scholars, including the great reformer Muhammad ʿAbduh, whom (as we shall see) the British ended up patronizing, were active in Sufi movements (De Jong 1999: 310). This was especially true among scholars in Sudan where, as a scholar of Islam who wrote during the colonial period observed, practically all Muslims belonged to a Sufi order of some sort (Trimingham 1965: 205). As Alexander Knysh has noted in a helpful interrogation of the category of orthodoxy among Western orientalists: "Eurocentric interpretive categories, when uncritically superimposed on Islamic realities, may produce serious distortions. Thus such distinctly Christian concepts as 'orthodoxy' and 'heresy' foster a tendency to disregard the intrinsic pluralism and complexity characteristic of the religious life of the Muslim community, leaving aside significant and sometimes critical 'nuances'" (Knysh 1993: 62).

Yet, as a principle of organization, rather than a scholarly category of analysis, orthodoxy seemed a helpful tool precisely *to eliminate* those "critical nuances" the British administration observed. The colonial government hoped that by marginalizing Sufi Islam and establishing new religious institutions it could create a centralized orthodoxy in a pluralistic religious scene where there was none. We will note in the next chapter that the Inqadh regime began with a similar agenda of marginalizing Sufism, though, like the British, it quickly realized that it would have to integrate Sufis into its reform project if it was to appeal to a wide spectrum of Sudanese.

The rationale behind the establishment of the *ʿulamāʾ* council in colonial Sudan was clear. This council would not only inform the government of the religious feelings of the people, but by appointing imams to mosques and sealing government crackdowns on various messianic and Sufi orders with a religious stamp, it would attempt to shape and domesticate religion in Sudan as well. The government needed a mechanism through which it could justify the many intrusions it would make into the religious sphere. Wingate wrote to Cromer on the 13th of June 1901:

> In order to deal with certain religious questions I have appointed a council of seven ulemas who have been more or less elected—governmental decisions in matters of religion will therefore in future have the [illegible word] of the council, and I hope the experiment will prove successful. Tarikas (religious sects) have been rather on the increase, but I hope with the aid of the council to quietly but firmly deal with them. Nothing [illegible word] will be done, but unless some steps are taken these sects are likely to become troublesome in the future.[25]

The British administration reasoned that, if the Azhar *ʿulamāʾ* were to point their fingers at the Sufi orders and call them "heresy," they might have a chance of stamping them out. In the absence of a single coordinating structure of this sort, no version of Islam could be deemed orthodox and none heterodox, and thus the potential for ever-expanding claimants to religious (and potentially political) authority seemed endless. The desire to create the categories of "orthodoxy" and "heresy," in order to lessen the threat of religious pluralism and of the political dissent that such nonconforming religiosities might engender, prompted the British to set up such a council.

In addition to the council of *ʿulamāʾ*, the other major mechanism the British created for establishing an orthodox Islam was the judiciary. The British legal secretary, Bonham Carter, appointed a "Grand Kadi" (chief judge) and a "Grand Mufti" (jurisconsult) to administer the system of courts under proper colonial supervision. While the British did allow customary law to rule in the more rural areas, *sharīʿa* courts, dealing with matters of personal status (marriage, custody, inheritance, and religious foundations), mostly with imported Egyptian judges, were set up in every major city and town (Warburg 1971: 124–36). While the British retained control of all criminal and commercial law, after establishing these *sharīʿa* personal-status courts, they ceded jurisdiction over them to the Sudanese and Egyptians. Yet the arm of the British state extended well into this "religious sphere" as well. Wingate and the legal secretary were in charge of appointing all judges and could overrule any decisions made by the *sharīʿa* courts. That said, the most important intervention they made was the formalization of Islamic law into a national court system. The changes they introduced had drastic consequences for the way that *sharīʿa* was practiced and mobilized, contributing to many of the

25 SAD 271/6/12.

present-day conundrums over its application (Ibrahim 2008; Salomon 2004b, 2011), since they did away with a key component of its judicial flexibility.

While the British imported Muslim scholars from Egypt to staff their new religious institutions, as the twentieth century rolled on, Wingate became increasingly nervous about Egyptian influence in the Sudan (Warburg 1971: 19–22). The first stirrings of nationalism and pan-Islamism were being felt in Cairo, and Wingate feared that Egyptian officials could spread these ideas to the Sudanese. Therefore, early on in his administration, Wingate tried to establish a mechanism by which Sudanese could take on the roles of *ʿālim*, *muftī*, or *qāḍī*, and established a *qāḍī* training course at Gordon College.[26] Despite Christian opposition to "Muslim theology" being taught at a college with British general Gordon's name,[27] the program was highly successful and by the end of Wingate's term in 1916, many of the Egyptians had been replaced by Sudanese (Warburg 1971: 88–93). While the British transitioned to a less interventionist model of governing religion following WWI, the institutions that they had established during those early years lived on and flourished, the precursors to some of the main scholarly Islamic institutions that persist in Sudan to this day. Thus, while to state that the British "created" the variety of modernist Islam in Sudan that has been embraced by

26 The name of General Charles George Gordon comes up often in histories of nineteenth-century Sudan, as well as popular literature on the period. Gordon, acting on behalf of the Egyptian Khedive (the representative of the Ottoman Empire, which hired many Europeans to administer its affairs in its later years), was acting as governor-general of Sudan in January of 1885, when the Mahdists seized Khartoum and killed him. There was a great sense of guilt on the part of the British following Gordon's death over the circumstances in which it occurred. Gordon had called for reinforcements from Great Britain, as he knew he would be no match for the Mahdi's forces. After much debate in Parliament, the British government finally sent out a fleet of ships to the besieged Gordon, which arrived down the Nile only a few days too late: Gordon was already dead. The horror of his death would haunt the British for a long time to come, and the conquest of the Sudan in 1898 was often framed as an attempt to avenge Gordon's killing. The last line of Wingate's *Mahdism and the Egyptian Sudan* spells out this justification: "That a new and better Sudan will be raised up over the ashes of Gordon, and all those brave officers and men who have perished in the loyal performance of their duty, is the fervent hope of every well wisher for the prosperity of Egypt" (1968 [1891]: 491). Additionally, we should note that here Wingate sees the British conquest of Sudan as returning Sudan to its rightful owners: the Egyptians. Yet the fact that the British ruled Egypt at that point makes such a statement somewhat less than straightforward. (The above biography of Gordon was gathered piecemeal from all of the histories of Sudan I mention in my bibliography, as well as from helpful e-mail exchanges with Prof. M. W. Daly; for a more complete history of Gordon, see Moore-Harell 2001).

27 Charles Watson, the corresponding secretary of the Board of Foreign Missions of the United Presbyterian Church of North America, whose group was doing missionary work in the south of Sudan, wrote Wingate on the 20th of May 1912 in regards to Gordon College, telling him of the "extremely widespread and deep desire of the Christian public that the memorial to Gordon's name should bear a closer relation to his religious practices and convictions" (SAD 181/2/191).

the intellectuals of the Inqadh regime would be an overstatement, the seeds they planted, which were watered and cultivated by a variety of individuals, have contributed greatly to its flowering, as even a cursory look at the CVs of Muslim Brotherhood leaders shows.[28]

Finally, in addition to establishing these three institutions, the British engaged in a lengthy campaign of mosque construction. On September 17, 1900, the acting Governor-General (replacing Wingate, who was on summer leave), wrote to the Khedive in Egypt concerning the celebration of the laying of the foundation stone of the Khartoum Mosque. Khartoum, which had been more or less destroyed and abandoned during the Mahdist uprising, was to be rebuilt as the capital of Anglo-Egyptian Sudan. The acting Governor-General gathered together the Grand Kadi of the Sudan, as well as the Grand Mufti and all the lesser *qāḍīs* (judges) from the cities and towns. The mosque was dedicated to the Khedive, the ruler of Egypt, in whose orbit the British had hoped to resituate Sudan. The acting Governor-General wrote to the Khedive (the nominal representative of the Ottoman Sultan in Egypt, now dislocated by the British occupation) about the celebrations that surrounded this mosque dedication: "Alms were distributed to thousands of the poor people, who all prayed for the prolongation of your Highness's life, and in honour of the day all Offices of the Government are closed."[29] In addition to attempting to ground the Sudanese back under the spiritual leadership of the Khedive, against whom they had revolted only nineteen years before, the Khartoum mosque project tried to supplant the influence of the Sufi *zāwiyas*, the traditional spaces of Muslim worship in Sudan, through the construction of the quintessential structure of what the British understood to be orthodox Islam, the mosque.[30]

When the British did not find an orthodox Islam in Sudan, they sought to create it, in great part through the four institutional devices discussed in this section. The modern state the British proposed—with its disciplinary power that sought not only to rule, but also to civilize—could not tolerate alternative loci of power and thus sought to order religion under its management and in its image. The political power of "otherworldly" religious affiliations was already quite clear to British officials, given what they knew about the rise of the *Mahdiyya*. By making religion a matter of public concern, and by limiting spiritual practices to a single model that they felt they could

publicize religion

28 See for example the discussion of Hasan al-Turabi's religious upbringing by a father who studied at the British-established *al-Maʿhad al-ʿIlmī Umdurmān* (Esposito and Voll 2001: 120).

29 "Celebration on the Laying of the Foundation Stone of the Khartoum Mosque," in the *Sudan Gazette* no. 15, 1–2.

30 For an interesting parallel from twentieth-century France, see Naomi Davidson 2012, Chapter 2.

more easily co-opt, the British established a blueprint for the relationship between religion and state whose indelible presence can still be felt today.

An English ʿĀlim

The British attempt to establish orthodoxy was not limited to an interest in its form alone, as an empty and easily co-optable mechanism capable of reaching the Sudanese public. Rather, the British were concerned that a particular interpretation of Islamic law be encouraged in Sudan, one that latched onto the modern revival of the concept of *ijtihād* (independent legal reasoning detached from the four traditional schools of Muslim jurisprudence). The British wanted Islamic scholars in Sudan to be taught "flexible" interpretations of their religious texts to help them meet the challenges of the modern age. Thus in addition to establishing an orthodox administrative body that might marginalize rival groups by deeming them heretical and pull Islamic practice into a public sphere that would be easier to monitor, the British sought to reform the kind of Islam that was promoted by these bearers of the new orthodox tradition.

When the British imported Azhar scholars to Sudan to do the work of establishing orthodoxy and discouraging "fanatacism," they particularly favored those who subscribed to the modernist ideas of the great Muslim reformer, and Grand Mufti of Egypt, Muhamad ʿAbduh.[31] Throughout the early years of the Condominium, ʿAbduh advised the legal secretary on appointments to the *sharīʿa* courts, and even visited Sudan on official government business in 1905, shortly before his death (Voll 1971: 214; Warburg 1971: 131). Since it was quite difficult to effect change in an old established bureaucracy such as that of Cairo, Khartoum was one of the first places where many of ʿAbduh's proposed reforms played out. In many ways, Cromer was a patron of ʿAbduh. He enjoyed ʿAbduh's thought because he believed that it would reform Islam in a direction that would enable it to uphold the values of the modern world that the British were trying to instill in the Sudanese. ʿAbduh called for a modernization of Islamic law in which no single school of jurisprudence would be slavishly followed, but rather in which all schools of thought and even new opinion could be combined to meet modern challenges (Hourani 1983: 152-53).

In subscribing to ʿAbduh's theories, Cromer began to act in a manner more befitting an *ʿālim* (Islamic Scholar) than a secular colonial administrator.

31 Though there is not the space to explore the issue thoroughly here, the symbiotic relationship between European orientalism and Islamic reformism in the late nineteenth and early twentieth centuries is a topic in need of further study. Michael Laffan does some of this work in regards to Indonesia in his recent *The Makings of Indonesian Islam* (Laffan 2011).

Instead of simply ceding personal status to the *sharīʿa* courts, the grand statesman did just the opposite: he weighed in with his own opinion on *ijtihād*, directly challenging the traditionalist interpretations of the Grand Kadi who was currently in power in the Sudan (due, he tells us, to the lack of any other suitable candidates). On the 11th of February 1907, Lord Cromer wrote Wingate concerning this "aberrant" Grand Kadi:

> I do not altogether like the tone of the kadi's report. He is evidently . . . very much opposed to the students learning anything but purely Mohamedan law. He wants them to 'clearly apprehend that Mohamedan law is founded on equity of all ages and all places, and does not require at any time any alteration or amendment, when it is accurately understood and properly acted on and applied to events and circumstances.' It is very natural that a conservative Mohamedan should hold these opinions. They are the views generally entertained by the class to which the Grand Kadi belongs. But, of course, they are sheer nonsense. Mohamedan law requires a great deal of alteration or amendment; and what, more than anything else, is keeping Mohamedans back, is the impossibility of altering or amending it. Some of the more enlightened among them see this. Mohamed Abdou saw it, or at all events pretended to see it.[32]

Cromer's letter, fascinating for its detailed and serious engagement with the intricacies of Islamic law and because it comes from one of the highest-ranking British colonial officials in the world, reveals a number of facets of the dominant British understanding of Islam. Cromer tells Wingate that it is precisely the stubborn adherence to tradition that "is keeping Mohamedans back." In order to modernize and civilize Sudan, Cromer reasons that religious law has to be reformed as well. ʿAbduh was directly opposed to those who said the gate of *ijtihād* was closed, and was in favor of creating an Islamic order in Egypt and Sudan based on a real engagement with the pressures of European modernity (Skovagaard-Peterson 1997: 65–68). From Cromer's letter, we see clearly the manner in which British officials involved themselves in attempting to reform every aspect of religious life in the Sudan. For Cromer, it was not enough that the British should do away with the multiplicity of Islamic practices present in Sudan; he also required that the orthodox Islam that he helped to impose should subscribe to his view of *ijtihād*. Instead of marginalizing religion from the work of governance, ceding the religious sphere to religious scholars, Cromer jumped into the debate himself. In doing so, he positioned the state as the engine of the modernization of Islam, a principle that, nearly a century later, the Inqadh would come to uphold as well.

32 SAD 280/2/83.

Postscript: The Genealogy of the Islamic State

In December of 2013, in the town of Qarri, north of Khartoum and east of the Nile, Sudanese President ʿUmar al-Bashir presided over a rally commemorating the five-hundred-year anniversary of the founding of what the organizers of the event called "the first Islamic state" in Sudan.[33] A large crowd gathered to welcome the president, holding up signs with slogans such as "The Qur'an Is the Constitution of the Nation (*umma*)" and "Youth of the Islamic Movement . . . A Burning Ember on the Path of *jihād*, and the Fruit of the Generations Contributing to Raising the Flag of 'There is no God but God and Muhammad is the Messenger of God.'"[34] After the performance of some poetry that praised both the Sudanese president and the ancestors of the ʿAbdallab people of Qarri—that is, the current patron of the Islamic state and the historical figures who were being resurrected as its pioneers—several speeches echoed out from the podium. Though one speaker took the president to task for his hypocrisy in claiming an Islamic state while failing to address the poverty and injustices prevalent across Sudan (before being ushered off the stage),[35] the rest of the opening speeches embraced the president's program, "stressing the necessity of returning to the glories of the [Islamic] state, placing the names of its founders on the streets of Khartoum, and rewriting history to make people aware of this period and to give it its rightful place . . . ."[36] With some traditional dance moves (for which the

33 I first learned of this event through Magdi El-Gizouli's wonderful blog, *Still Sudan*: http://stillsudan.blogspot.com/2013/12/president-bashir-historian-at-large.html.

34 These signs were observed in photographs of the rally in some of the articles I mention in the below footnotes and in "Hasahisa District Participates in the Celebrations at Qarri on the Occasion of the Passing of 500 Years since the Rise of the Islamic State" (*Maḥaliyyat al-ḥaṣāḥīṣā tushārik fī iḥtifāl qarri bi-murūr 500 ʿām ʿalā qiyām al-dawla al-islāmiyya*): http://www.hasahisa.gov.sd/news.php?action=view&id-454. See also: "al-Bashir to Attend the Celebrations at Qarri on the Occasion of the Rise of the First Islamic State" (*al-Bashīr yashhad iḥtifālāt qarri bi-qiyām awwal dawla islāmiyya*), http://www.alnilin.com/news-action-show-id-76699.htm.

35 Though from the reactions of the crowd on the YouTube video of the event (http://www.youtube.com/watch?v=4qSTLIY6ydY) it seems most were in support of the president's agenda, or at least playing along, a curious sign I noticed in the crowd questioned the president's historical conclusions: "Mahaliyyat al-Hasahisa: Arbaji District: It Is the Place from Which the First Islamic State Arose." In disputing the provenance of the first Islamic state, placing it in the Blue Nile town of Arbaji (which has an important place in Funj history), rather than the "Arab" town of Qarri, where the president was celebrating, the creator of this sign may be marking an ethnic tension that underlies al-Bashir's speech: while he speaks of the unification of Arabs and "others," he is celebrating a distinctly Arab version of Sudanese political history, thus potentially sidelining the importance of other ethnic groups in building the "Islamic state."

36 Ahmad ʿAliba, "The Gate of the Pyramids Was Here . . . a Trip with al-Bashir to Qarri . . . the Sudan Which No One Knows" (*Bawābat al-ahrām kānat hunāk . . . riḥla maʿ al-bashīr ilā*

president is famous) in sync with the music blaring over the sound system, al-Bashir began his speech:

> We are celebrating [today] an important historical event . . . the rise of the Islamic state in Sinnar (*qiyām al-dawla al-islāmiyya fī sinnār*). [This state] was the dividing point between two eras: the first era, classical history, and the new history that began with a pact between ʿAbdallah Jamaʿa and ʿAmara Dunqus. ʿAbdallah Jamaʿa gathered[37] together all the Arab tribes and ʿAmara Dunqas gathered together all the other tribes and they united and they created for us the new Sudan. And anyone who wants to talk about the "new Sudan," this is the Sudan that was founded by ʿAbdallah Jamaʿa and ʿAmara Dunqus, who unified the people of Sudan without force. There was no army that went and battled in another region, other than when [ʿAbdallah Jamaʿa and ʿAmara Dunqus] came together, and made a pact, and attacked the ʿAlawa state [the last Christian kingdom in Sudan] because it had become isolated. Because all of the inhabitants around it and all of the tribes around Soba [its capital] were Muslim. . . . And all of these tribes made a pact with their leadership to create for us a state that would be a model. And this is what has been founded now. . . . This is what founded for us this heritage of which each one of us is proud and that we are celebrating [today]. And everyone who says "I am Sudanese," the pride of this comes from a certain set of values, and morals and customs, [all of] which were established for us by the founders of the Sinnar state. And we have come today in order to remember our history, and to return to our roots, so that we look at our present and catch sight of the future. There are many attempts to splinter the people of Sudan and to foster differences between the people by reawakening regionalism and racism, which were manufactured for what? For impermanent worldly desires! We want this celebration to be for a new beginning, for the rewriting of the history of Sudan. . . . And this history of which we are proud [that of the first Islamic state], we want to build upon it the foundation of the new Sudanese state. On the same foundation and the same basis, around which ʿAbdallah Jamaʿa and ʿAmara Dunqus made a pact, we will revive and affirm it. . . . All of us face one direction in prayer, we believe in one God, and one prophet, and one book. [Inaudible, but something like: "Is there anything that should be getting between us, guys?"]

---

qarrī . . . al-sūdān alladhī lā yaʿarifhu aḥad), *al-Ahrām*, December 18, 2013. http://gate.ahram.org.eg/News/432087.aspx.

37 Al-Jamaʿa literally means "the gatherer," and ʿAbdallah was referred to by this title because he had gathered together the Arab tribes (Penn 1934: 60).

> There is no God but God! There is no God but God! There is no God but God! And if someone says, "There is no God but God," what else is there, guys? Is there racism? (Crowd: No!) Is there tribalism? (Crowd: No!) Is there regionalism? (Crowd: No!). And we want it [the state?] to turn toward God, and when we say it is for God, and use this new expression, it is for real. . . . And the people of Sudan are protected by the pious (*ahl allāh*) and are protected by the [inaudible "shaykhs?"] of Qur'anic Schools (*khalāwī*), and the people of Sudan are protected by the shaykhs of the Qur'an who are spread out everywhere. . . . [And the Islamic state] without any fighting or battles, people joined voluntarily, voluntarily and out of their own choice, this state, about which they were sure that it was a state for God (*swt*), a state for the *sharī'a*, and because of this the people joined it. And we say that this event that we are celebrating today should become a new holiday so that we can forget [the tribal, ethnic, regional] differences [among us], all of our differences, my friends. We have a nation that we are proud of, and we have a people of which we are proud.[38]

Several things are noteworthy about this speech. First, in addition to what I quoted above, al-Bashir also mentions the resignations of 'Ali 'Uthman Muhammad Taha, his erstwhile vice president and comrade in the Inqadh revolution of 1989, and of Nafi' 'Ali Nafi', his trusted advisor. Their departure marks the final migration of the old guard of the Islamist movement, a process that began in the late 1990s with the ouster of Hasan al-Turabi.[39] Though it is unclear whether al-Bashir's claim that they resigned to give a younger generation a chance to steer the movement is true, or if the retired aides were in fact part of a wider split in the Islamic movement[40] between those who support the president and those who wished to advance

38 http://www.youtube.com/watch?v=4qSTLIY6ydY.

39 Magdi El-Gizouli, "President Bashir: An Historian at Large," *Still Sudan*: http://stillsudan.blogspot.com/2013/12/president-bashir-historian-at-large.html.

40 The term "the Islamic movement" (*al-ḥaraka al-islāmiyya*) is in need of some clarification. In Sudan it both serves as a descriptor for Islamic political actors whose primary aim is the reform of the state, based on the model of the Egyptian Muslim Brotherhood, *and* as a proper noun ("the Islamic Movement"; e.g., http://www.has.sd/en/index.php). The latter refers to the branch of the Islamic movement (lower case m), that succeed the NIF, when the ruling regime dissolved it and founded National Congress Party (NCP) in 1998 in an attempt to transcend the revolutionary form of the "front." It is currently the closest branch to the ruling regime of the various Islamist movements in the country. Since the Islamic movement that has populated the regime since its founding in 1989 has gone by many names through its history, I refer to it and to the regime (as Sudanese often do) simply as *al-inqādh* (the salvation), the name that the regime proclaimed when it came to power *(thawrat al-inqādh al-waṭanī)*.

a reformist-Islamist agenda,[41] al-Bashir's Islamist credentials had certainly taken a hit in recent months. The new post-secession state, which the regime referred to as the "Second Republic," was thus trying to bolster its Islamic credentials by holding, for the first time, a celebration of the rise of the Islamic state in Sudan and promising a new distinctly Islamic path, a path made possible in part by the fact that the state no longer needed (in Bashir's mind) to grapple with questions of religious diversity now that the vast majority of Sudanese non-Muslims were no longer citizens of Sudan, having relocated to South Sudan.

Indeed, two years after the end of the "transitional period"—those five years when unity was to be made attractive, which preceded the secession of the South (and during which the bulk of the fieldwork for this book was undertaken)—Islam, in the mind of the president, could finally serve as an uncontroversial force for national unity, beyond "race," beyond "region," beyond "tribe." Ignoring the fact that, even after the departure of the majority non-Muslim South, Sudan was home to a significant non-Muslim minority, and that political positions among Muslims varied from secularism to alternative varieties of Islamization (and that several ongoing rebellions were being fought against the government by individuals who held these positions), the Islamic state was being repositioned here not as the cause of Sudan's fissiparousness but as its solution.

The reference the president makes to the "new Sudan" being a revival of the Islamic state created five hundred years ago by the pact between ʿAbdallah Jamaʿa and ʿAmara Dunqus is a direct jab at the SPLM-North. The newly marooned rebel movement based in the southern regions of post-partition Sudan continues to fight its battle under the banner of the "new Sudan" philosophy of the late Dr. John Garang, founder of the SPLM, who called for a Sudan free of ethnic and religious chauvinism, where citizenship would be based on national identity and not religion or ethnicity. While this vision was abandoned by the southern-based SPLM when they called for secession of the South rather than national reform, it remains the official position of its northern brethren who continue the fight in the margins of post-partition Sudan. Thus, in a key sense, the parallel between the Sinnarian Islamic state and the present one is spot on: both ʿAbdallah Jamaʿa (whose armies brought the last Christian kingdom in Sudan to an end in 1500) and ʿUmar al-Bashir (whose army's actions led to the secession of the Christian-majority South) indeed tried to fashion a "Sudan" (if you'll allow the anachronism in relation to the former case) where religious identity would be central to national belonging.

41 I am referring to the Reform Now Movement (*Ḥarakat al-Iṣlāḥ al-Ān*) of Dr. Ghazi Salah al-Din al-ʿAtabani and the Just Peace Forum (*Minbar al-Salām al-ʿĀdil*) of al-Tayyib Mustafa.

Yet, the parallel the president was trying to draw in his historical account strains at the seams in many other places. The "Islamic State" founded by ʿAbdallah Jamaʿa (r. 1500–1560), with its capital in Qarri was not a state at all in the sense meant by the phrase "Islamic state,"[42] a term popularized by anticolonial movements of the mid-twentieth century. Rather, ʿAbdallah Jamaʿa and ʿAmara Dunqus's pact constituted a very different sort of political arrangement. While ʿAbdallab leaders were certainly interested in promoting an Islamic social identity—though this seems only to have begun in earnest under the leadership of ʿAbdallah's son ʿAjib al-Manjilak (r. 1560–1611), who is noted as a patron of Islamic scholars and a promoter of *sharīʿa* (McHugh 1994: 39–41)—the ʿAbdallab dynasty was more properly a protectorate under Funj rule, with which they were constantly at odds over matters political and doctrinal (Penn 1934: 61–62). Their hostilities reached an apex at the battle of Karkoj in 1611, in which al-Manjilak was killed (McHugh 1994: 41; Penn 1934: 63–64). Thus the kind of unity under "there is no God but God" that al-Bashir promoted for today's Muslim Sudanese was not embraced by his predecessors in this "model state." Further, it is not clear that the ʿAbdallab were a recognized "government" in any clear sense of the word. Not only were they subject to the more powerful Funj, but their chronicles recall tribes in their domain "not subject to" ʿAbdallab leaders (Penn 1934: 62). Moreover, it goes without saying that none of the institutions we associate with statehood existed there. As so much scholarship on premodern Islamic jurisprudence elsewhere has shown (e.g., Hallaq 2009; Messick 1993), the *sharīʿa* they promoted was not a codified law implemented by a judicial system, but rather a set of ethical norms, enforced by the community, and embodied by believers. Bashir's choice of Qarri to stage celebrations for the First Islamic State is indicative of a kind of instrumentalist reading of history, anachronistically projecting the state he sought to establish back onto a deep Islamic past.

In his translation of the *ʿAbdallab Chronicles*, A.E.D. Penn tells a story that, even if apocryphal, clarifies the difference between the ʿAbdallab political system and anything approximating the modern state:

> One day [al-Manjilak] learnt that the chief of the Sobaha Arabs, who was not subject to him, was disobeying the tenets of Moslem law, in that he was putting persons to death, inflicting fines without religious

42 Note that the word *dawla*, which corresponds to "state" in English, can also mean "dynasty," and indeed is a term concerning political order that predates the establishment of the modern state. The term *al-dawla al-islāmiyya* ("the Islamic state"), on the other hand, refers clearly to a modern political formation, indexing the ambitions of contemporary Islamic political movements, which have used the phrase as their rallying cry in urging the Islamization of the modern state apparatus.

> sanction and allowing women to be divorced and married to another man on the same day. Sheikh ʿAgib [i.e., al-Manjilak] fought always in the good cause of religion and to further the word of God, so he gathered together a large force which he led in person against the Sheikh of the Sobaha. When he drew near his enemy, he went forward alone in the guise of a poor man seeking shelter and obtained lodging with the Sheikh. So, by a ruse he was able to verify for himself the truth of the reports and, having confirmed them, returned again secretly to his army. He then wrote to the Sheikh informing him that the poor man who had been his guest was Sheikh ʿAgib himself; that if he chose to submit to him and refrain from transgressing Moslem law, he would be appointed Sheikh of his tribe, but that if these conditions were unacceptable, he should prepare to fight. . . . [The sheikh of the Sobaha chose battle and was killed.] Sheikh ʿAgib appointed Nabit, the founder of Nabtab clan, ruler in their country after it had been subdued and bade him act justly, follow the ordinances of the true religion and build mosques over a province bordered by Suakin, Massawa, and Korosko towards the Red Sea. (Penn 1934: 62–63)

In this story about the leader of the ʿAbdallab, we can see clearly that Islamic governance in the sixteenth century played a very different role from that which it occupies in present-day Sudan. For al-Manjilak, there was neither a court system nor a police force charged with enforcing some codified Islamic law. There were no councils of *ʿulamāʾ* either, and no impersonal state that might have granted them their authority. The concept of limited jurisdiction (the very foundational principle of the community of states model) was lacking as well, as al-Manjilak is seen insisting on the applicability of Islamic law to an individual who *was not* subject to his rule. These institutions and concepts were creations of a much later period, as we saw in the first part of this chapter. Instead, al-Manjilak himself is seen as both inspector and enforcer of *sharīʿa*, the apparatus of a state appearing nowhere to help him.

The genealogy of the state that provides the foundation of Sudan's present governmental project has its roots not in the sixteenth century, but in the colonial period. Despite al-Bashir's grand gestures to the ʿAbdallab, it is the British project of managing religion that is most clearly cited in contemporary political practice. Both the colonial and the Inqadh regimes put the making of an Islam amenable to state governance at the center of their strategies. This said, the method by which Islamic sources are engaged in order to produce the present state, the way in which these sources inflect its politics in new directions unimagined by the state's colonial pioneers, and the results of state projects in religion-making as they intersect with diverse spiritual practices on the ground, certainly distinguish the contemporary

Islamic state from the secular colonial state and make the former worthy of serious engagement. That is the task of this book. Yet, in a tense political context in which secular and Islamic party politics are positioned as polar opposites, both nationally and on a global level, continuities between their projects are too rarely recognized (White 2013), and the problems with the authoritarian state too frequently neglected in favor of arguments over the color of its ruling ideology. What this means is that attempts to rethink the state that might offer new solutions to Sudan's woes are ignored, while both sides remain mired in a perpetual struggle over the nature of its identity.

CHAPTER TWO

Civilizing Religion

Observations on the Architecture of Late Islamism

Driving south on the airport road in Khartoum past the Turkish-built ʿAfra shopping mall and the heavily fortified main UN operations base, a rather stark, but beautiful, modern building rises on the horizon. Built in the style of an enormous Persian Gulf mosque complex, complete with copious domes and tinted windows, the *al-ḥajj wa-l-ʿumra* building has an air of religious sanctity. The building was constructed in the years directly following the "Salvation Revolution" with a large grant from the Saudi government and later became the property of the Ministry of Guidance and Pious Endowments (*Wizārat al-Irshād wa-l-Awqāf*). It was built with a specific purpose in mind: to be the place where major (*al-ḥajj*) and minor (*al-ʿumra*) Islamic pilgrimages to Mecca, which would leave from the nearby airport, were to be organized and funded. Attempting to bolster its religious credentials, the government of Sudan welcomed the Saudi gift and the *al-ḥajj wa-l-ʿumra* building quickly became one of the most talked-about structures in Khartoum, one of the first in a series of sleek Gulf-style buildings to be constructed in the capital. Yet, this feeling of austere religious sanctity that one gets on viewing the building from a distance is quickly shattered as one approaches it. Sitting on its walkway is a small sign announcing its new occupants: the Emirati-led phone and Internet provider Canartel.[1]

The Persian Gulf countries have been a source of both religious and capitalist inspiration for Sudan, and this was particularly so during the short-lived oil-boom years before the separation of the South. The Saudi funding of Salafi groups and contributions to new mosque projects by Sudanese expatriates returning from the Gulf (Bernal 1997; Kenyon 2004: 65–67) are examples of the former, while the chic new restaurants, car dealerships, and Dubai-funded construction projects are key examples of the latter. Canartel moved into the *al-ḥajj wa-l-ʿumra* building in 2005, a few months before it

1 This description covers the National Unity period (2005–11) on which the latter half of this chapter focuses. The UN Mission in Sudan (UNMIS) departed in 2011 with the secession of South Sudan, and then, just as this book was in its final stages, Canartel vacated the building to make way for a government investment body. The fact that the government itself was changing the purpose of the building from spiritual to material investment further bolsters the claims I discuss in the following about the ethos of the late Inqadh.

Figure 1. The *al-ḥajj wa-l-ʿumra*/Canartel Building. Khartoum, Sudan. Photograph by Osman Mohammed Attayeb

inaugurated its service in Sudan. It was offered a space in the building apparently in an attempt to raise revenue for the Ministry of Guidance and Pious Endowments, which had become somewhat neglected in the years of the late Inqadh, when the more robust projects of social reform devolved to other sites deemed more likely to initiate social change than a stodgy government ministry. With its chic air-conditioned offices and hip, youthful information-age employees, Canar transformed the building from a symbol of the early years of the austere Islamism of the Inqadh (when money was spent on public works that would assist individuals in their religious duties such as the *ḥajj*), to a quintessential symbol of the late Inqadh: that characteristic mix of Islamism and capitalism that Abdallahi Gallab has called the "Islamic Corporation" (2008: 79–81, 91–93). This capitalist blossoming was made possible in part by the signing of the Comprehensive Peace Agreement (CPA) with the SPLM and the prospects of stability that it afforded. The signing of the CPA encouraged Asian and Gulf-state investors to spend massive sums of money on the country, while the cessation of hostilities allowed for the exploitation of oil reserves previously off-limits due to instability.

In this climate, the appearance of what seemed to be a selling-out of some of the key elements of the Salvation Revolution was hard for the regime to avoid. "They goaded us into the mosques, while they entered the market" (*dakhkhalūnā al-masājid wa humma khashū al-sūq*), was a common popular refrain. Yet, not everyone saw a contradiction in the intermixing of capitalism and Islamism such as that which seemed to be exhibited by the *al-ḥajj wa-l-ʿumra*/Canartel building. Just a few months after the signing of the

CPA, an article entitled "Has the Salvation [Revolution] Ended and Has the Civilization Project Fallen Apart?" (al-Jundī 2005) appeared in an official magazine of the Sudanese army, *al-Jundī*. The writer expressed the anxiety faced by Islamists over a peace agreement and soon to-be-signed constitution that seemed to contradict the aims of their initial project by recognizing the validity of the claims on the state made by non-Muslims with the suspension of *sharīʿa* in the South. The unnamed (but photographed) author, apparently a military official of some sort, wrote that while the regime's Civilization Project (*al-mashrūʿ al-ḥaḍārī*, which I will discuss in more detail in the following) had as its purpose the linking of economics, society, law, culture, literature, and arts to the values of religion, it was important not to forget that it was also "about the unleashing of the energies of the individual Sudanese person to the greatest extent, so that he innovates in *this* life. . . . [And that due to this Civilization Project] the land [has] unleashed springs . . . and likewise springs of petrol. And [the political leaders of the Inqadh have] exploited the products of petrol, like gas that was not used in Sudan except among the bourgeois and the aristocratic classes. But now gas is available to all, and the poorest citizen with his [limited] abilities owns a gas cylinder" (2005: 14).[2] In looking back at the Inqadh revolution, the author argued that we should remember that moral salvation and the salvation of the national economy through exploitation of its resources were deeply intertwined. In a play on the common claim of the Islamists that they made no separation between religion and the state (*lā yafṣilū bayn al-dīn wa-l-dawla*), the author pointed out that the Inqadh didn't distinguish between religion and the livelihood of the people, their daily bread (*lā yafṣil bayn al-dīn wa-l-ʿajīn*), and that for this reason the regime should be praised.[3]

2 My emphasis. While the economic situation of the country as a whole had greatly improved by 2005, not everyone shared such rosy images of the NIF's project of economic liberalization. Some indeed saw liberalization and the privatization that came with it as merely masking the monopolization of the economy by the Islamist elite. Khalid Medani wrote of this period, "Economic liberalization has also impoverished the majority of the Sudanese population, including civil servants and those engaged in the private sector but not affiliated with the Brothers. . . . Only two sectors of society can meet the prohibitive cost of living: families receiving expatriate remittances and the NIF and their supporters" (Medani 1997: 174–75).

3 Haydar Ibrahim ʿAli, the director of the Center for Sudanese Studies in Khartoum and an opponent of the regime, analyzes the pronounced shift in the understanding of the Civilization Project in recent years in his book *The Collapse of the Civilization Project*, which is a good example of the position against which our unnamed soldier is arguing:

> [These days,] when the implementers of the Civilization Project enumerate [their] accomplishments they don't talk about the raising of the influence of religion (*iʿalāʾ kalimat al-dīn*) or implementing the *sharīʿa*, rather they boast about [the successes of the former state telephone company, now semi-privatized] Sudatel and [the exploitation of] new oil wells. This is not to diminish any material or economic accomplishment, indeed there is no doubt that we need such accomplishments, but this could be

Commerce has been a major portion of all civilizing missions and, despite the sentiments of those who see the mixing of religion with economic pursuits as somehow tainting the former, the Civilization Project proposed by the Salvation regime was no exception. As Janice Boddy reminds us in her insightful book on colonial Sudan, *Civilizing Women*, the British understood the "need for a host of commercially produced 'things' to sustain a civilized life" (2007: 35) as a necessary component of the moral reform they advocated. It was no coincidence that soap was one of their most highly touted imports, a product that might wash away the dirt of the barbarism they were trying to eradicate. The civilized life that the Inqadh imagined—wherein morally-reformed individuals would create a revitalized nation and thus a strong state—also required a roster of commodities to be realized. As an added benefit, the Inqadh reasoned, raising the standard of living would break the hierarchical economic ties rural Sudan still had to Sufi leaders (el Hassan 1993), the coordinators of previous political experiments in Islam, which the Inqadh argued had so failed the nation. In a sympathetic reading, a capitalist economy was not evidence of mere greed but was in fact necessary to interrupt the patronage-based system deeply embedded in the Sufi orders, and the Mahdi-family based Umma Party, that underlay the previous political order the Inqadh sought to interrupt. On a less sympathetic reading, the Inqadh itself simply desired new modes of patronage. In either case, it is clear that the Inqadh had the foresight to recognize that there was no *dīn* (religion, at least in the way they imagined it) without *'ajīn* (bread).

Such brute capitalism had been impossible during the civil war, when few countries were willing to invest in Sudan. It was the cessation of hostilities in 2003 and the signing of the CPA in 2005 that allowed Sudan to enter this new economic stage. Indeed it was economics that was said to be, at best, the glue that could keep Sudan together, or at least provide an incentive to maintain peace if the country should split, as it eventually did in 2011. Then, with the bulk of the oil fields in the landlocked South and the port in the North, both countries would need each other in order to enjoy the fruits of the natural resources that existed on their lands. The price of peace in a unified Sudan, however, was recognition of the political identity of religious minorities as integral to the identity of the state and the integration of the SPLM into a "government of national unity." Thus, not only did the period

---

done by any secularist revolutionaries at a lesser cost. So the question is: what is it that distinguishes the Civilization Project from the project of Numayri or 'Abud [two earlier presidents]? This is the starting point of the failure of the Civilization Project: when it turns its back on defending the high values of religion—such as justice, purity, and noble morals—to become a competition around [what are only] accomplishments [in the eyes of] the World Bank. . . . So [it turns out] that [the Civilization Project] is just a big fancy name for a comprehensive program of gradual transfer to economic liberalism (*al-infitāḥ*). ('Ali 2004: xx)

following 2005 raise the question of whether capitalism was possible alongside Islamism, but the question of the coexistence of multiculturalism and Islamism was also broached. The instability of the Islamist project in this period, never abandoned though constantly recalibrated as it grappled with these new challenges, was one of the reasons why the Islamic state became such an active site of debate and deliberation for Muslim organizations following the end of the Civil War, as the following chapters will show.

Today these debates over Sudan's future remain vibrant. New Islamic political movements, such as *Sāʾiḥūn*, made up of former Popular Defense fighters from the war in the South, and *Ḥarakat al-Iṣlāḥ al-Ān* (the Reform Now Movement), founded by Islamist intellectual Dr. Ghazi Salah al-Din al-ʿAtabani, have emerged as the Islamist project of the regime has entered into somewhat of a holding pattern while the government seeks to form a national consensus that might include other parties, Islamist or not.[4] Indeed, the sentiment expressed by the president that when the South and its diverse peoples seceded the regime would "fix the constitution of Sudan"[5] is a view shared by many who see the separation of the South, and the departure of religious minorities it occasioned, as a means to reinvigorate the Islamic state and not a mark of its failure.[6]

4 One result of this holding pattern is that the 2005 Interim Constitution, written in conjunction with the SPLM (the former partners in the Government of National Unity representing the South), remains in effect despite the separation of the South and the designation of the SPLM that remains in the North as a terrorist organization. Despite the government's explicit rejection of many of the principles of the Interim Constitution, it knows that any attempt to pass a new constitution before the national dialogue is completed would be viewed by the public as excessive unilateralism. Further, the government holds out the carrot of a negotiated new constitution as an incentive for parties to join the dialogue process and thus have a stake in shaping it.

5 "[T]here will be no room to speak of ethnic and cultural diversity. Islam will be the official religion and Islamic *sharīʿa* will be the principle source of legislation . . . and the Arabic language will be the official language of the state." http://www.aljazeera.net/home/print/f6451603–4dff-4ca1–9c10–122741d17432/436738a8–402b-4f8a-8e1f-48063bf63dbf.

6 The common assumption (e.g., Collins and Burr 2003; Gallab 2014) that Sudan moved into a post-Islamist phase after the expulsion of Osama Bin Laden in 1997, the split of the government with al-Turabi in 1999, or the signing of the CPA in 2005 (take your pick) thus results from a rather narrow vision of what Islamism consists of and how much tenacity it has as a political future for countries in the Muslim world. Carolyn Fluehr-Lobban begins her recent book *Shariʿa and Islamism in Sudan* by articulating her expectations of a "'post-Islamist' transition" (2012: 90), a "move away from sharīʿa" (96, by which it seems she means the implementation of *ḥudūd* punishments, giving a somewhat narrow read to this vast corpus of law), and a de-islamization of the country (96) due to the pragmatism occasioned by the flow of oil and the events of 9/11/2001. Yet, a little later on in the same volume, she is unsure whether to call the political transitions in Sudan post-Islamism or post-extremism (109), and by the end of the book she presents a very interesting picture of how government Islamists at *Majmaʿ al-Fiqh al-Islāmī* (the scholarly government body that evaluates policy according to *sharīʿa* standards) are "legitimizing a new social order" of sexual relations created as a by-product of earlier Islamization efforts (227) through their sanctioning of new forms of marriage with the mechanisms of

For now, however, we must try to understand how we got to where we are, to the era of late Islamism that characterizes the discursive landscape of the Sudan in which I arrived in 2005 to begin my fieldwork. We must understand where the Islamist coup began, into what problems it saw itself intervening, what solutions it offered to those problems, and how it recalibrated its vision as a result of realities on the ground. To do so, we need to turn our focus to an earlier era, to a time of unbridled optimism for the Islamic state project and to a landscape of open possibility.

optimism for Islamic state project

National Salvation

> The Revolution of National Salvation came to Sudan at a time of military and sectarian (*ṭā'ifiyya*) governments and found bareness and waste prevailing over the country, disagreements wasting away Sudan's people, rebellion that was diminishing the land from its margins, foreign encroachment plundering its security and its tranquility, and looting cutting off men from their brothers and terrorizing wayfarers. The coming [of the Salvation Revolution] was nothing but a spontaneous reaction to the imminent collapse wrought by the grave events that had befallen the body of the nation, exhausted by injuries. So the revolution came at its destined time, like the major events in the lives of societies that happen as definitive turning-points, [events that are like divers who have] probe[d] their depths and come up to the surface with pearls, banishing their evil nature. Thus the people hope, in the midst of this transformation, that this will be the end of the persistent political tension that has been circling this sick [nation], between deformed democracy and illegitimate militarism, so that hope can grow and so that it results in a national coming together around its program and the lofty goals it presents in its public discourse.
>
> —Jaʿfar ʿAbd al-Rahman, "Introduction," in *The Sudanese Islamic Project (1989–1992): Readings on Its Philosophy and Practice* (1995:3)[7]

The first years following the Inqadh revolution of 1989 were a time of undiluted confidence for its intellectuals, who projected a politics devoid of the kind of cynicism that often accompanies their pronouncements today. After

Islamic law. Thus by the end of the book it is hard for her to conclude with the post-Islamist thesis with which she began, instead contending, "after several decades of the *inqaz* regime and more than a quarter century since the September Laws, Sudan [*sic*] Islamism is experienced, mature, pliable and durable . . . it is clear that Sharīʿa has succeeded and its institutions and practice are now embedded in Sudanese society in myriad and unprecedented ways" (288). Indeed, as Fluehr-Lobban concludes, the Islamic state project, though reformed, appears alive and well in Sudan.

7 I offer a thousand thanks to Dr. Abdullahi Gallab of the University of Arizona who shared his copy of this volume with me.

spending their entire political life in opposition, Islamist intellectuals had gained control of the apparatus of the state and their writings from this period reflect a certain degree of giddiness, an excitement at finally getting to test hypotheses that their movement had been spouting for decades. Thus, at its height in the early 1990s—before the economy collapsed, before the war with the South accelerated its deadly and unrelenting pace, and before internal fighting left its ranks severely divided—the Government of National Salvation was eager to attempt some quite ambitious projects. Twenty-one years before the Arab Spring that would bring to power Islamists in Tunisia and Egypt (however briefly) and increase the sway of Islamic politics in countries from Jordan to Morocco, seventeen years before Hamas won overwhelming electoral victories in the Occupied Territories, thirteen years before even Turkey's Justice and Development Party had accomplished its victory in general elections, and many years before ISIS and the Taliban would come into existence, Sudan's NIF was ahead of the curve, transitioning from a movement of Islamic opposition to a governing force and establishing what one long-term Sudanese observer has called "the first Islamist republic" (Gallab 2008).

While much was new about the revolutionary project announced by Jaʿfar ʿAbd al-Rahman in the epigraph to this section, it was marked also by several important continuities with earlier projects in state-building. Ironically perhaps, and despite its claim to be inspired by the anticolonial impulse of the nineteenth-century Mahdist state that was aborted by British rule in 1898, the Salvation state exhibited most closely an affinity with the colonial state. This was true both of its bureaucracy, which copied, more or less unchanged, the colonial model, and of its grand ambitions. Indeed, despite the fact that the colonial state had the goal of secularization after years of Islamic rule, while the Salvation state championed Islamization after years of what it saw as secular rule, underlying both projects in state-building was the notion that a mastery of religion (in both an epistemic and political sense) was essential to the workings of governance. It is no coincidence, then, that both the colonial and the Islamic state projects spoke not in terms of social reform but of "civilizational" reform: both thought Sudan more or less devoid of such achievement, and both saw an unhealthy and irrational relationship to religion as a key reason why. The shared lexicon of "civilizational reform" is not incidental. Uday Mehta has argued that despite the disconnect between colonialism and liberal notions "such as tolerance, the right to representation, equality, and . . . consent and the sovereignty of the people" (1999: 81), the presumed lack of *civilization* among subject people can make what is essentially a despotic project palatable to liberal theory.[8] This was very much the case

8 Quoting Mill: "There are, as we have already seen, conditions of society in which a vigorous despotism is in itself the best mode of government for training the people in what is specifically wanting to render them capable of higher civilization" (Mehta 1999: 106).

in early-twentieth-century Sudan (Boddy 2007). Indeed, for both the British and the Inqadh, what Sudan lacked was civilization, and this made it an exceptional space for what otherwise and elsewhere would be an unacceptably despotic politics. So, whereas we see the mastermind of the Salvation Revolution, Hasan al-Turabi (d. 2016), arguing, in a much circulated essay, that "the freedom of the individual ultimately emanates from the doctrine of tawhid, which requires a self-liberation of man from any worldly authority in order to serve God" (2009b: 219), he is not advocating a kind of social libertarianism. Indeed he reminds us that "[t]he actual scope of government depends on society" (2009b: 218). In the paternalistic manner of the Salvation regime, this translated into the idea that society must reach a certain level of civilization before the retreat of the interventionist state.

Like the colonial state, the Islamic state too would go through massive reforms made necessary by the experience of governance. While it may have seemed to the Inqadh in the early 1990s that few obstacles stood between it and the realization of its projects, particularly given the space shared between the Salvation Revolution and the Islamic revival that had swept across Sudan prior to it (Ibrahim 2008; Nageeb 2004; Simone 1994), by the time of the signing of the CPA, which ended hostilities between North and South and that laid the blueprints for the eventual dissolution of the republic, the Islamic state had gone through a rather massive rethinking. While the several works I mentioned in the introduction that discuss the Islamization processes following the 1989 NIF coup have been interested in the legal, political, military, and educational ramifications of the early period of NIF rule, less attention has been paid to the relationship between this mode of reform and the society it aimed to reform, that is, on the calculations, revisions, and delicate balances the ruling Islamists made in response to the reality they encountered on the ground.[9] Indeed, in general, a diachronic exploration of Islamic rule is missing from the literature on Sudan (and elsewhere),[10] which tends too often to take government proclamations,

9 In her useful article "Political Islam in Sudan: Islamists and the Challenge of State Power (1989–2004)," Einas Ahmed (2007) offers the one other attempt I have seen in English-language scholarship to study the fate of Islamist political theory when faced with the challenge of governance. However, her article's time period stops before the signing of the CPA in 2005, which I argue below was the greatest challenge to the Islamist vision as conceived in its early years. Ahmed splits up the Islamist period of governance into three parts: "The period of revolutionary legitimacy" (1989–96) in which the boldest aspects of Islamization and social control were inaugurated; "The period of constitutional legitimacy" (1996–98) in which, due to a desire for international legitimacy, Sudan attempted to establish a constitutional republic and lessened the ideological rigor of its Islamism; and what she calls the "post-Islamism" period (1998–2004), a characterization with which I took issue above.

10 Recent work on Iran, such as Ghamari Tabrizi 2008 and Varzi 2006, constitute one important exception, though they focus on the very distinct world of Shiʿi politics in which a clerical system predominates, a feature absent in Sudan.

legal edicts, and institutional mission statements at face value, accepting without question their own bloated estimations of their power and influence. If the next three chapters are to present an ethnography of the state—that is, a study of the state as it is represented, experienced, and contested in daily life—a clear portrayal of what the state understood its priorities to be, how it institutionalized those priorities, and how it recalibrated them in response to a changing political landscape, seems necessary at the outset. Such a study offers a unique look at the Sudanese Islamist intervention into long-standing debates within Islamic thought and political practice, interventions that were revised and reworked not merely as a result of ideological disputes, but in response to the tangible challenges of governing a religiously and culturally diverse postcolonial state.

Locating Civilization

The initiative that the regime called the Civilization Project (*al-mashrūʿ al-ḥaḍārī*) took place both in the realm of political and legal institutions, where studies of Sudanese Islamization generally place their focus (Layish and Warburg 2002; Sidahmed 1996), and in less-studied areas, such as culture and the arts, science, architecture, language, and even in the promotion of certain forms of family and kinship. Indeed it was these latter arenas of intervention that made the NIF's project properly one that was "civilizational" in nature, rather than merely an effort at political or social reform. The Civilization Project was concerned with knowledge and the arts, religion and the body, language and literature, alongside politics and economics. New modes of knowledge production were inaugurated that rethought such modern scientific inquiries as genetics and immunology, sociology, and economics, through the Islamic fundamentals of Qur'an and Sunna, such as the *ta'ṣīl al-ma'rifa* ("fundamentalization of knowledge") project I discuss in Chapter 3. New endeavors in the revitalization of Islamic arts were created or supported, among them the projects to support the flourishing of *madīḥ* poetry and its extension to urban youth that I discuss in Chapter 4.[11] New mosques and Islamic public works buildings were erected at an ever-increasing pace, women's dress became heavily regulated, Arabization projects began in earnest, and Islamically sanctioned plural marriage (*taʿaddud al-azwāj*) and group weddings (Hajj Ahmad 2006b: 62–64) were initiated to combat what was derisively referred to as "spinsterism" (*al-ʿunūsa*).

That the foundations of this renewal of civilization rested on only one sector of Sudan (and a problematically monolithic portrait of it, at that),

11 Other Islamic arts initiatives are discussed in Abusabib 2004. On al-Turabi's theory of art, see Ibrahim 2008: 359–60 and Hamdi 1998: 63–64.

that to which the Arabic-speaking Muslim elite of the Islamic Movement belonged, was, in the first years of the movement's time in power, a fact seemingly ignored by its intellectuals. Though one gets the sense that the Civilization Project was "overlooking" Sudan's radical ethnic and religious diversity, perhaps T. Abdou Maliqalim Simone's argument about the NIF in its formative period in the 1980s is in fact a more apt characterization of its general posture. Simone argues that this refusal to deal with the problem of diversity was not due to the fact that the Islamists ignored it, but rather that they recognized it but hoped it could be assimilated away. If not, they would tolerate non-Muslims and non-Arabs as minority populations, while the Arab and Muslim majority they imagined (for in reality both "Arabs" and Muslims were far more diverse than they allowed) would alone define the official national character. Simone writes that, "instead of the undecidability of Sudanese identity inserting itself as a productive force in national life, it is engineered [by the NIF] as a problem that must be resolved, a problem on which the existence of the bulk of political life is dependent" (1994: 78). The NIF's relationship to minorities, however, was not always premised on the ideal of Arabization and Islamization, for the NIF also argued for respect toward minority cultures and noninterference in their affairs,[12] even while the application of its policy in this regard was inconsistent. Rather, and more significantly, the NIF's posture consisted of enforcing non-Muslims' *minority* status, denying them a stake in defining the nation.

The *Sudan Charter*, a party platform the NIF put together in 1987, two years before it came to power, argued less in terms of the classical legal categorization of *dhimmīs* (protected non-Muslim groups in an Islamic political order, [Emon 2012]) and more properly in terms of the minorities and majorities of modern democratic nation-states (Mahmood 2012). The Charter argued that while the minority non-Muslim opinion would be taken into account and respected, "the majority option" would be "determinative" (*Sudan Charter*: 3) in matters of state. This meant, for instance, that "Islamic jurisprudence" would be "the general source of law [as] it is the expression of the will of the democratic majority" (3), and that because Muslims were in the majority, they had "a legitimate right, by virtue of their religious choice, of their democratic weight and of natural justice, to practice the values and rules of their religion to their full range—*in personal, familial, social, or political*

12 See, for example, the Sudan Charter of 1987 (*Mīthāq al-sūdān: al-waḥda wa-l-tabāyun*, [*The Sudan Charter: Unity and Diversity*]), a blueprint for the establishment of an Islamic state that the NIF published two years before it came to power: "In the Sudan there are a large number of those who adhere to African religions, a substantial number of Christians, and a few Jews. These have their particular denominations (*milal*) and do not believe in Islam, and should in no way be prejudiced or restrained only for being in a minority. That is their due by virtue of their own creed, in concurrence with the Islamic *sharīʿa* and the fundamental rights of all men to freedom and equality" (2).

affairs" (2, my emphasis). This of course assumed monolithic support of the Islamist program by Sudanese Muslims, which has always been far from the reality. Moreover, the place of non-Muslims within the Islamic state was to be justified by a particular reading of their religious traditions in comparison to Islam, by which the restriction of their practices to the private sphere was not the violation of freedom of religion that it would have been for Muslims. The Charter continued, "Non-Muslims shall, therefore, be entitled freely to express the values of their religion to the full extent of their scope—*in private, family, or social matters*" (2, my emphasis). By "their scope," the Charter expressed the view that the non-Muslims' "creed" is "one that restricts religion to private life or morals only" (*alladhī taqṣir al-dīn ʿalā al-ḥayāt al-khāṣṣa aw al-akhlāq waḥdaha*)" (2) and is thus not relevant to public life as Islam must be. In doing so, the NIF imagined a kind of secularization for minority religions and thus a public sphere protected exclusively for Islam.[13]

The secularist African socialism that the SPLM proposed for governing Sudan's diverse populations in a "religion-blind" manner was seen by the NIF as an unacceptable solution to the problem of religious diversity. It deemed such a project "neither neutral nor fair, being prejudicial to [Muslims] in particular as it deprives them of the full expression of their legal and other values in the area of public life" (*Sudan Charter*: 2). While secularism might work for Christians, since they reasoned (incorrectly, of course) that their religion had no public implications, Muslims would always be straightjacketed in such a model, prevented from giving full and free expression to their religion. The only way for religious freedom to be guaranteed for all Sudanese, the vanguard of the NIF argued, was through an Islamic state, one that would encourage the application of Islam to matters of public concern and leave Christians and other non-Muslims alone to practice their religion in their homes and places of worship. For the Inqadh, the free fulfillment of Islam could only come about when public life and the life of the state were in unity with God. For regime supporters, law was not a force that constrains or enables religion, but rather was itself a mode of religious practice, its unfolding seen as the ultimate fulfillment of religious duty.

That the civilization to be revitalized through the Civilization Project was one that would be built solely on Arab and Islamic foundations was a key aspect of how the Inqadh regime described its project on coming to power. Amin Hasan ʿUmar, one of its key ideologues, characterized what he called the "comprehensive civilizational renaissance project" (*mashrūʿ al-nahḍa al-ḥaḍāriyya al-shāmila*) as follows:

> Perhaps we should reveal some of the features of the comprehensive civilizational renaissance project: it is a project for the renewal of the

13 I thank Jeremy Walton for this insight.

> essential nature (*tajdīd al-dhāt*) [of Sudan] and for its development and the raising of its effectiveness and the improvement of its abilities in order [for Sudanese] to achieve trust in [this essential nature] and reliance on it. It is at the same time a liberatory project (*mashrūʿ taḥarruri*) for the defense of this essential nature in confronting the dominance of the other that assaults its human dignity and its cultural identity and its material rights. Although a project with these characteristics could be found in any place across the world, we are concerned with it taking place in our Arabic Islamic region and therefore the renaissance project for this region must be Islamic and Arabic. (ʿUmar 1995: 26)

In short, the NIF was promoting a renewal of Sudanese civilization through national self-reliance, liberation from Western political and cultural imperialism, and a return to Sudan's essence, which it understood as Arab and Islamic culture in spite of the fact that Sudan is in fact home to many religions and even more languages and cultures.[14] In practice, this meant revising the apparatus of the state—from law, to education, to the economy, to the military—and doing so based on Islamic norms, or at the very least imbuing it with an Islamic inspiration, such as the language of *jihād* that propelled and justified the war effort in the South. Such a process, the NIF hoped, would free Sudan of the Western secular political and ethical norms that it had acquired through decades of colonial domination and postcolonial mimicry of European ideas, norms that held it back from its true and unique potential.

Yet, though the inspiration of the revolution was always stated to be Islam, the language in which it was justified was often more explicitly a populist one, with little attempt, for example, to hearken back to models for political action found in life of the Prophet, as Salafi-minded political theorists have done. Here the justification for the "renewed revolutionary return to Islam" was more often a quest for "liberty (*al-inṭilāq*), dignity (*al-ʿizza*), and progress (*al-taqaddum*)" (ʿUmar 1995: 29), than the imperative to follow the Sunna of the Prophet in its full range. The epistemological foundations of the NIF's political practice were thus entirely different from those of the Salafi movements that were also calling for an Islamic state, but that did so by mining classical texts that outlined political categories proper to the life of the Prophet. NIF intellectuals worked very much within the categories proper to the modern nation-state, filling them with Islamic content where necessary. Thus while the goal was an Islamic state, the justification was

14 The fact that Arabness was a relatively new and hybrid identity in Sudanese history (a fact recognized even by Sudan's most Arab-centric historians [e.g., Hasan 1967]) was not discussed in this literature. Instead Amin Hasan ʿUmar argues (1995: 30–31) that since the Arabic language had unified Muslims of many ethnicities in centuries past it is the appropriate means to unify Sudanese (presumably both Muslim and non-Muslim) today.

rarely Islam. Indeed, many state institutions took on populist names that harkened back to socialist experiments of the mid-twentieth-century Arab world, rather than to Islamic political models. Parliaments were supplemented by "popular congresses" (*al-mu'tamarāt al-shaʿbiyya*), in order to promote a participatory rather than a representative form of government and to transform local power from oligarchy to meritocracy. The professional army was complemented by "popular defense forces" (*quwwāt al-difāʿ al-shaʿbī*) on the understanding that all "Sudanese" (and here, Muslim Sudanese in particular) should have a stake in the defense of their nation. And in economics, while the Inqadh period initiated one of the more robust capitalist experiments of economic liberalization in Sudanese history, the regime argued for spreading wealth beyond the traditional postcolonial elite (al-Turabi 1995: 18).

This said, the masses themselves were always understood to be Muslims, and it was on this ground that the NIF justified the slippage between the state that belonged to the people and the state that belonged to God. Moving power out of the hands of the elite and into the hands of the people would, the NIF reasoned, almost automatically lead to Islamization. The system of popular congresses, for example, was described as "not just an administrative system, but rather a system that [could] . . . free the people from the margins of life and enable them to practice rule and thereby it [was a system that enabled] Islam and Muslims, since there [was] no conflict between Islam and the people" (Hamid 1995: 65). Or, as another regime intellectual put it:

> The project of modernization of the Westernized elite failed. There thus is nothing left among our choices except to return to the shores of the masses that remain holding onto religious authorities (*al-marjaʿiyya al-dīniyya*) in explaining life, and not letting go. If [one argues that] the religiosity of the masses is traditional and undeveloped, then [I respond that] it is a great duty for the elite in the Muslim world to develop it with a project of renewal of faith and religious thought, because faith and religious thought are the only things that can provide the vision and the incentive to move ahead on the road to civilizational progress (*al-taqaddum al-ḥaḍārī*). . . . [And because it is drawing on the resources of the masses], the Islamism of the Civilizational Project (*islāmiyyat al-mashrūʿ al-ḥaḍārī*) comes by intuition and needs no extreme effort. . . . And now, after the vision has become clear and the *daʿwa* that calls for the return to fundamentals (*al-ta'ṣīl*) and the return to the essence (*al-dhāt*) has become a motto for all who are loyal to the Arab Nation, the renewed revolutionary return to Islam opens the road toward liberty, dignity, and progress. (ʿUmar 1995: 26 and 29)

In passages such as these, we see traces of the battle for the hearts and minds of the urban sector that characterized the political landscape of the 1970s

(El-Affendi 1991: 81–84), in which university student unions often traded back and forth between the Communists and the Islamists. Both sought out the newly educated class and spoke on behalf of "the masses," and both forwarded an ideological program opposed to the traditional Sufi-based political organizations (which they both referred to as "sectarian" [*ṭā'ifī*]) that had dominated Sudanese politics for much of its postcolonial history (Warburg 1978, 2003). While the Left targeted the masses due to their class position, the Islamists did so on the basis of their religion, or at least what they supposed it to be. The masses were thus envisioned as both the object of civilizational reform and the origins of a civilization whose true flowering had been interrupted by years of ineffective rule.

When it was finally implemented, the Civilization Project aimed its efforts in three directions. First, it attempted to reform Sudanese political practice in a different direction from that taken by previous Islamic political experiments in Sudan, which it dismissed as sectarian in contradistinction to its own universalizing mission. Next, it undertook a massive effort for the moral reform of individual citizens and posed this reform as of paramount *strategic* value for the viability of the newly imagined Sudanese Islamic state. Finally, like the colonial regime we read about in the previous chapter, it attempted to reform the structure and focus of religious life and institutions in Sudan through a transformation of the traditional Sufi orders, which were then, and remain today, the foundation of Muslim piety in the country. Before turning to discuss how the Islamic state project was recalibrated through the signing of the CPA, I will examine each element of this project in turn.

New Models for Islamic Governance

Given the claims of exceptionalism of both the supporters and the detractors of the NIF project, it might otherwise be hard to recall that its assertion that it was practicing Islamic politics was not a particularly novel one in post-colonial Sudan. In fact, the claim to Islamic politics was one made consistently by leaders of varying allegiances. Indeed, with the exception of the Communists and various rebel movements (the SPLM, the SLA, etc.), no political party in power in Sudan has based their legitimation on anything but Islam. With the exception of some periods of military rule, the Sudanese state had, until the Salvation Revolution, changed hands between two parties, both of them Islamic: the Umma Party, led by the progeny and followers of the Mahdi (*al-Anṣār*), and the Democratic Unionist Party, led by the progeny and followers of the Khatmiyya Sufi order. Both parties continue to be led by the Sayyids (members of these "holy families") and understand themselves to be working toward a state with religious legitimacy, even though both have toyed with the idea of state secularism as a means of allying with other opposition parties. Thus the trumpet call that accompanied the NIF's announcement of the Islamic state was perhaps not quite as loud and distinctive as one might think, for it required a rejection of the Islamic legitimacy of many previous political experiments.

It was the NIF's exceptionalism, however, that served as the basis for outlawing such political organizations in the early years of its rule (the multiparty system was reestablished in the late 1990s). A 1994 directive issued by the government that justified the abolition of a multiparty system in Sudan was written in the interest of making a distinction between the Islamic politics of the Salvation Revolution and the Islamic politics that came before it. It stated: "Sudanese parties are not really political parties. They are only the political expressions of a Sufi order legacy whose objective is to monopolize power" (Ahmed 2007: 205). Following the failed experiment in eliminating the influence of the Sufi orders discussed in Chapter 1, the colonial authorities had concluded that the Sufis were the only successful pan-regional organization in the country and thus encouraged the building of political parties for the soon-to-be-independent nation-state on the foundation of their social capital (Warburg 1978, 2003). It was this political order that the NIF encountered when it came to power, and it was its influence that the NIF sought to undo.

Yet, it was not only the fact that the NIF claimed to be disrupting the traditional political organization of (northern) Sudanese society that made its intervention unique. Several other factors distinguished its Islamic program from those of its predecessors. The first was its embrace of the mechanisms of the state to do the work of the Islamization of society. For example, a defining factor for the period of Inqadh rule is the revitalization of *sharīʿa* as a system of state law and its extension into domains from which it previously had been excluded (Fluehr-Lobban 2012). Though the development of a *sharīʿa*-based criminal law preceded the Inqadh revolution by six years (Layish and Warburg 2002), and while the distinctness of the *Islamic* nature of Sudan's reformed laws is debatable, the intensified focus on law to do the work of governance is quite clear. Mark Massoud statistically demonstrates that since 1989, there has been an extraordinary flourishing of legal culture in Sudan, as evidenced by new courts, new lawyers, and new codes (2013: 140, 148–49), all the result of the regime's focus on the rule of law as a means of extending its power. Yet while the extension of Islamic law to non-Muslims was one of the chief obstacles to the signing of the CPA (Salomon 2004b), it was the intentionally inconsistent application of *sharīʿa* that became one of the means of securing social peace thereafter (Salomon 2011). Thus, while law was an important means of securing the Islamic state, it was a contested and instable one, and the regime therefore had also to look to other strategies if it was to consolidate its project.

Reforming Muslims, Producing the State

Perhaps the most controversial element of the Civilization Project was its explicit extension of what the regime called "governance" (*al-ḥukm*) to the reform of individual morals and moral action. While indeed some of this work was done through the law—codes on improper dress (*ziyy fāḍiḥ*), obscene actions (*afʿāl fāḍiḥa*),[15] and the drinking of alcohol (*shurb al-khamr*)[16] are the most commonly cited—the regime also undertook a productive, rather than solely repressive, program of individual reform. The argument of those who formulated this new model of politics was a totalizing one: in their minds, the strategic success of the state depended upon the ethical and cultural reformation of the individual. New men and women would need to be created who could adopt, and eventually help to form, the political and cultural models emanating from the state. In his contribution to *The Sudanese Islamic Project*, the agenda-setting book from which I have quoted above, Muhammad Mahjub Harun characterizes this novel political theory of the early years of the Salvation government as follows:

> Appearing on the table for research is the question regarding the project of change that the Salvation Revolution put out: is it a civilization project whose goal is the restoration of the structure of the individual and society and a restoration of the role of the state in relation to society, or is it a project for political change? . . . More than merely changing politics, the project of the Inqadh begins with the individual as the nucleus of society and the appropriate sphere (*al-majāl al-mawḍūʿī*) for the work of the state. The goal thus becomes the changing of individuals, purifying (*tazkiyya*) their desires [in order to instill in them] faith and goodness and righteousness and to weaken the tendencies toward compromised monotheism (*al-shirk*) and unbelief and ineffectiveness. The realization of this goal is entrusted to a program for the elevation of the soul and to training [individuals] as to what is moral and what is illicit (*al-taʾhīl al-akhlāqī wa-l-munhī*). (Harun 1995)

While most studies of Sudan have focused on the institutional reforms (the coming of *sharīʿa*, Islamic banking, etc.) that gave the NIF its early success, and on their repressive elements (e.g., Abusharaf 2009: 33, 64), Muhammad Mahjub Harun's statement suggests that the NIF was involved in a much more creative project as well. Its goal was not merely to Islamize the institutions of the state (he clearly says that the Civilization Project is not merely

15 See section 152 of the 1991 Sudanese Criminal Code.

16 See section 78 of the 1991 Sudanese Criminal Code.

"a project for political change"), but to reform the individuals who live in their midst. Harun argues that the Sudanese individual is in need of purification if Sudan is to achieve civilizational transformation and that this purification is the duty of the state.

The key agency in charge of reforming Sudanese individuals was the newly formed Ministry of Social Planning (*Wizārat al-Takhṭīṭ al-Ijtimāʿī*), headed by the future vice president of Sudan, ʿAli ʿUthman Muhammad Taha. It was in the halls of this ministry that what came to be called the Civilization Project was hatched and directed. One of its branches, a Sufi Council with the goal of reforming the Sufi orders to better serve the nation, published a particularly succinct description of the nature of this individual moral reform in the context of explaining why the regime was co-opting Sufism for its efforts. This account sought to make its readers understand why the reform of individual morals was not simply paternalistic meddling by the Islamists in charge of domestic policy, but was in fact of *crucial strategic importance* if Sudan was to become a viable modern state on the international scene. The document stated:

> From a strategic perspective, morals (*al-akhlāq*) are the framework in which the desired civilizational renaissance is realized for any nation. Not only this, but morals are nations and nations are morals. Nations remain firm when their morals are firm and they disappear when their morals disappear. How many civilizations that were founded by a nation or nations together disappeared and were obliterated through moral decline and decay that afflicted them? Thus the fission of the energies in Sudanese society for the purpose of the realization of the civilizational renaissance must focus on the latent power in this society, among which the most important thing is the moral values derived from its religion and its belief and its national tradition. And it is necessary that these values find encouragement from the official state for giving it strength to persevere and spread.[17]

With this understanding in mind, the morals of individuals began to take on *strategic* importance. If, as the above passage suggests, civilizational strength is based on moral strength, then the only way for Sudan to cope in the difficult climate of modern international politics was to revive and strengthen its moral foundations, a morality that the NIF understood to lie primarily in its interpretation of Islam. While the Inqadh was not the first government in Sudan to base its strength on Islamic legitimacy, never before had any government so comprehensively utilized the legal, law

17 Ministry of Social Planning, Republic of Sudan, Protocols of the National Council for Mindfulness of God and Those Who Are Mindful (November 12, 1995) (*Qānūn al-Majlis al-Qawmī li-l-Dhikr wa-l-Dhākirīn*).

enforcement, media, and military tools of a modern state in the service not only of governmental reform but of the moral reform of individuals as well.

Qur'an study groups were funded and encouraged in workplaces, television and radio took on the goal of *da'wa* (proselytization), grants were given to women who wanted to start "prayer upon the Prophet" groups, and the educational curriculum at the national level took on a distinctly Islamic tone. Despite the political discord in Sudan and varying opinions both for and against the government, it was this element of the Civilization Project that was most successful. When in 2007 I visited one of the burgeoning circles for "prayer upon the Prophet" (*taṣliya*) run and organized by women in Omdurman (Khartoum's sister city across the Nile), one of the leaders of the group put it to me this way:

> [In our mothers' generation] they also used to sing poems in praise of the Prophet, but there weren't structures that would organize their activities. . . . But here we have something organized: we founded a "house" (*dār*) called *al-ṣalā 'alā al-rasūl* (prayer upon the Prophet) from 1996. . . . We have to give the Salvation Revolution its due [in regards to making institutions like this possible]. I mean everything has good and bad qualities. And among its good qualities is that there were things we didn't know at all in religion, and praise be to God when this revolution came and opened the places for the study of the Qur'an [we came to know]. . . . And originally when this *dār* opened, it opened as a *dār* of Qur'an. Originally when we opened it we opened it as a *dār* of Qur'an and also a place for the sewing for the clothes of soldiers in the Popular Defense [who were performing *jihād* in the South]. It is when the Salvation Revolution came that it made this religious awakening. It is the one responsible for the awakening. . . . The religious awakening was started by Numayri when he closed the bars, and spilled out the alcohol. He is the one who started it, and that is before the Inqadh. But it was the Inqadh that encouraged and financially supported it.

From the establishment of Islamic universities such as Holy Qur'an University or African International University, to the funding of small circles for study or prayer, such as the humble Omdurman circle I visited in 2007, from the legal restrictions on dress, gender mixing, and personal comportment, to the *da'wa* camps established in war zones to train civilians in both Islamic knowledge and military skills (de Waal and Abdel Salam 2004: 91), the focus on the individual as the locus of Islamic renewal was clear in all that the NIF did. Yet Islamic renewal could not simply come in any color. The NIF insisted that in order for this renewal to have its desired effect, the Islam that people practiced was itself in need of serious revision.

Civilizing Islam

Another facet of the Islamist experiment with governance in its early years was an attempt to reform religious organizations so as to direct their energies toward the political goals that the regime had identified. One member of the Islamist vanguard framed the problem the NIF was trying to solve through such religious reform as follows:

> Sudan . . . has not created popular Islamic organizations that have the required skills to succeed in the long struggle and the continual *jihād,* so therefore it is the case that popular Islam (*al-islām al-shaʿbī*) has withdrawn from public life, surrendering to the leaders [who promote] internal reform (*al-iṣlāḥ al-bāṭinī*) who come from the pillars (*aqṭāb*) of Sufism and its saints. So there will be a continual dilemma for the enlightened Islamic Movement (*al-ḥaraka al-islāmiyya al-mustanīra*) in Sudan and it is: How is it able on the one hand to move these negative Sufi sentiments (*hadhā al-wijdān al-ṣūfī al-sālib*) to be positive revolutionary credit (*raṣīd thawrī mūjab*)? And how is it able, on the other hand, to forbid this credit from transforming into empty bubbles of air, and to make sure it is placed in a framework for disciplined civilizational building (*al-binā' al-ḥaḍārī al-munḍabiṭ*)? (Hamid 1995: 41–42)

The NIF answered this question by founding a key institution charged with transforming the enormous energy that the Sudanese people put into Sufi religious worship into the revolutionary Islamism of the NIF. It was called the National Council for Mindfulness of God and Those Who Are Mindful (*al-Majlis al-Qawmī li-l-Dhikr wa-l-Dhākirīn*) (NCMG). The NIF reasoned that because Sufi shaykhs were so widely beloved, they could perform a task that brute state power would never be able to achieve through coercion. Sufism was thus not to be abolished or transcended in the name of Islamism, but reformed, merged with Islamism in a way that is rarely appreciated in the scholarship, which too often sees these two trends as essentially opposed.[18] In the NIF's estimation, Sufism's energy should not be wasted but rather directed down new avenues. In its official magazine, the NCMG published articles with titles such as:

18 Rüdiger Seesemann's article "Between Sufism and Islamism: The Tijaniyya and Islamist Rule in Sudan" (Seesemann 2007), which I discuss below, is an exception to this rule and in fact clearly recognizes the way in which the NIF and Sufis often established a symbiotic relationship. That there were Sufi organizations who both supported and opposed the regime is an important point that frustrates political demographers' attempts to divide Sudan along sectarian lines.

- Qutbi [al-Mahdi, chief advisor to the president]: We Want to Activate the Role of the Sufi Center (*al-masīd*) and Sufi Qur'anic School (*al-khalwa*) for the Maintenance of Righteous Virtues (*al-qiyam al-fāḍila*)[19]
- Shaykh Wad Badr and Political Sufism[20]
- The Sufi Movement and Sudanese Independence[21]
- Popular and Political Action and the Sufi Orders Reject a Secular Capital[22]
- The People Who Are Mindful of God (*ahl al-dhikr*) and the Arenas of *jihād*[23]
- The Program of Sufi Proselytization in Strengthening and Deepening the Culture of Peace in Sudan: The Role of Sufism in Popular Diplomacy[24]

While the state created an Islam-oriented media by dominating content on television, radio, and newspapers, and while it imposed Public Order and Security of Society Laws and established a special police to administer them (to enforce, for example, the separation of the sexes at social events and modest dress for women), it also turned to religious organizations to do the legwork of social, moral, and political reform. Recognizing its own distance from the people, and recognizing the comparative irrelevance of the various *ʿulamāʾ* bodies it established (their personnel were rarely known to average Sudanese), the regime badly needed partners in the Islamic sphere who could help promote its cause. The most obvious choice was Sufi organizations, given their great public popularity. The only catch was that Sufi organizations, with their "inward-turning Islam" (in the eyes of the NIF, at least), promoted precisely the kind of Islamic piety that the NIF saw as leading to the defeat of Islam as a viable political alternative. The NIF thus set about trying to reform Sufis.

It is crucial to note that the Islamist critique of contemporary Sufism differed drastically from that waged by Salafi organizations, which were

19 September/October 2000.

20 June/July 2002.

21 March/April 2003.

22 Issue 13, August/September 2003, referencing debates concerning the status of Khartoum that were part of the peace negotiations leading up to the CPA.

23 Ibid. Or, capturing the same idea in reverse, another headline from the August/September 2003 issue: "The Inqadh, a Revolution for *dhikr*."

24 Ibid. Here indicating the ambivalence of the period that directly preceded the signing of the CPA, when the government was vacillating between mobilizing Islamic organizations for *jihād* and maneuvering them for "the culture of peace" that was to be promoted after the CPA's signing.

primarily concerned with correcting errors they perceived the Sufis committing in matters of doctrine. The Islamists seemed unconcerned with suppressing doctrinal innovation. The "enemy" for them was instead Western-style secularism, and thus they criticized the Sufis only to the extent that the Sufis did not direct their energies toward fighting it. Hasan al-Turabi, the intellectual mastermind of many of the early Inqadh's programs, argued that Sufi movements were in need of reform not because they did not follow Qur'an and Sunna, but rather because by turning inward to *tazkiyyat al-nafs* (the cleansing of the self) they ignored the great external enemy, secularism. He wrote: "For the trials of today, the Sufi movements are of no use, nor is scholastic theology (*ʿilm al-kalām*), nor the movements of doctrinal reform (*ḥarakāt al-iṣlāḥ al-ʿaqīdī* [i.e., Salafi organizations]), because the trial is with the school who has no religion (*al-madhhab al-lādīniyya*)" (al-Turabi 1995: 11). In contradistinction to the regime's parallel program of personal moral reform, al-Turabi argues here that spending time on the *jihād* against the self, on the details of Islamic theology, or on critiquing Muslims for doctrinal error, as the Salafis did, is a distraction from the true battle. By distinguishing the Islamic movement he led from these other trends in modern Islamic reform, al-Turabi marked its distinctness as an intervention that, uniquely, could respond to contemporary challenges.

The implicit argument being made by the choice of the name "National Council for Mindfulness of God and Those Who Are Mindful" should not be overlooked: in a government council on Sufi affairs, the word "Sufi" is not even mentioned. Sufi shaykhs and their followers were to be supported, but as pious men and women, *al-dhākirīn*, and not as Sufis (*al-mutaṣawwifīn*) per se. The name was also an attempt at creating a government agency with a title that no one in the Islamic coalition the NIF was trying to establish would oppose. By using a name with Qur'anic resonance ("Indeed regarding those men and women who are mindful of God: God will prepare for them forgiveness and great reward")[25] and by not mentioning Sufism explicitly, the Islamists dampened potential accusations of favoritism from the more Salafi-minded in their coalition.[26] The enormous encyclopedia, *Mawsūʿat ahl al-dhikr bi-l-sūdān* (al-Baqir et al. 2004) that the NCMG published in 2004 in-

25 *al-dhākirīn allāh kathīran wa-l-dhākirāt aʿadd allāh lahum maghfira wa ajran ʿaẓīman* (*Sūrat al-Aḥzāb* 35).

26 Confirming this impression, al-Turabi told me about the choice of the name: "If we had said [that we were establishing] a congress of Sufis, then the Salafis wouldn't have come. So because of this we called it *al-dhikr wa-l-dhākirīn* and no Salafi could say it was forbidden because the word *dhikr* is mentioned in the Qur'an so much. So we invited [the Salafi group] Ansar al-Sunna and all Sufis in Sudan. We talked to them and tried to convince them to participate with us in something. Any person who has a culture in which he is interested in the commandments of Islam (*thaqāfa fiqhiyya*), we bring him to us, for such a person gives large portions of his feelings to religion. And in the beginning they were all close to us, and this

cludes, in addition to hundreds upon hundreds of entries about Sufi shaykhs, a few entries on Salafi leaders such as Muhammad Hashim al-Hadiyya, the late president of Ansar al-Sunna. According to the philosophy of the Center, Sufis were a species (albeit the most populous one in Sudan) of the genus of *dhākirīn*, to which many belonged, including the Sufis' doctrinal opponents. By stressing the genus rather than the species, the NIF sought to overcome the internecine doctrinal strife in Sudan and create an Islamic front based on shared goals. It was through the formation of associations such as the NCMG, which dedicated financial resources to reforming Sufism, that the regime sought to make the discursive move of defining Sufis as *dhākirīn* into a tangible reality.

Discussing the conference of *al-dhikr wa-l-dhākirīn* that was convened in the year 1994 in order to establish the NCMG, its founding document recalls that the purpose of the council was "to establish an official mechanism to realize the strategy of lifting morals (*al-ruqī al-akhlāqī*) and to be a tool for activating the apparati of the state and popular social organizations (*muʾassasāt al-mujtamaʿ al-shaʿbiyya*) to push the Sudanese nation toward a complete civilizational renaissance, using its morals that derive from its religion and its beliefs and its national tradition . . . [and] to make values firm [in society] and to spread them and purify them from blemishes and foreign interventions (*al-dakhīl*)." Hasan al-Turabi was one of the key architects of the NCMG and described to me, in an extremely frank manner, the process of its founding:

> The NCMG was a project to fix the Sufis. And our goal was to create for them an institute and magazines . . . and lessons for their children. And in all of it would be *dhikr*. . . . We stand by them, and try to change their ideas. For if you leave them aside, they consider you alien. You enter slowly with their language and tell them the meaning of *dhikr*: what do the words mean, what do the religious rituals (*shaʿāʾir*) mean, what does the *rukūʿ* (bending over in prayer) mean, and the raising of the hands in prayer, what does it mean? . . . If we talk to [the Sufi] with nice words—not like Ansar al-Sunna who try to frighten them away—they accept what we are saying. And then they take their children and enlist them (*najannaduhum*) in the ranks of the modern Islamic movement (*al-ḥaraka al-islāmiyya al-ḥadītha*). And then when the father dies their children take the place of the father and they are registered in *al-ḥaraka* . . . And then we can effect *iṣlāḥ* (reform). If the shaykh was not corrected, when he dies we can work on his sons.

Given that the five-hundred-year-old Sufi tradition in Sudan has as its defining characteristic the idea of *dhikr* and that an elaborate theory of *dhikr* has

---

was a potential for us to make from them a front. We wanted to make one mass, which we called *al-dhikr wa-l-dhākirīn*, which until now is present."

been articulated in much Sufi literature, Sudanese and beyond, the claims that al-Turabi is making here might seem strange. But what he means is that there must be a new a way of thinking of *dhikr*, one that focuses on the spirit of *dhikr* and its potential meaning as a political force over the letter of its ritual significance alone.

For this kind of reform, the regime needed Sufi allies. A whole host of Sufi shaykhs and their followers readily engaged in projects sponsored by the NCMG, though they never quite resolved the tension between its critique of their practices and its support of their popular energies. The enthusiastic membership of many Sufi orders in this clearly Islamist project should dispel any illusions that Sufism is inherently opposed to political Islam, or that, as one analyst put it, "the Khatmiyya and Ansaar aside, the small Sufi orders have tended on the whole to be politically less active" (Mahmoud 1997: 190). Here was an arena in which many Sufis gladly joined the project of the Islamic state. However, as we will see in subsequent chapters, they did not thereby remain uncritical of the regime's articulation of it.

The NCMG's project in revitalizing Sufism was in serious tension with the organizational framework in which Sufi revitalizations of the past had taken place, that of the *ṭarīqa*, or "order." Indeed, on reading NCMG literature, it becomes clear that one of its main goals is spreading a new Sufi *ethic*, or what the founding protocols of the NCMG call "spiritual Sufism" (*al-taṣawwuf al-nafsī*)[27] over the Sufism of the *ṭarīqas*.[28] The council established a major office in Khartoum (and branch offices in the various states) that coordinated the disbursal of funds to Sufi *zāwiyas*, *daʿwa* efforts, and several publishing projects, and it organized a series of events celebrating Sufi heritage and the agenda the NIF had assigned to it. Such a promotion of a (reformed) Sufi *ethic* over the rigid hierarchical structure of the Sufi *order* served state interests—in that it promoted a certain kind of religiosity without threatening the state with an alternative bearer of authority (i.e., the shaykh)—and dovetailed nicely with a concept of religion in which religious commitment is deemed compatible with the voluntarist subject who does not submit himself to any human being in order to cultivate it.[29] The NCMG

27 Ministry of Social Planning, Republic of Sudan. *Protocols of the National Council for the Mindfulness of God and Those Who Are Mindful* (November 12, 1995) (*Qānūn al-Majlis al-Qawmī li-l-Dhikr wa-l-Dhākirīn*), 5.

28 Or, as Seesemann notes, "The designation of Sufi orders as *ṭuruq* . . . rarely appears in Islamist discourse, possibly because it implies several paths leading to God, whereas *ahl al-dhikr* suggests that the people of remembrance form a single group of devout and sincere Muslims in force with the Islamic movement" (Seesemann 2007: 34).

29 This state attempt to reform Sufism seems to me novel in comparison to other contemporary attempts of governments to reform and control Sufi orders. Both Valerie Hoffman (1995) and Julian Johansen (1996), writing on modern Sufism in Egypt at roughly the same time, pointed to the wide-ranging effects of the "Supreme Council of Sufi Orders" on suppressing

thus encouraged adherence to a principle rather than to a person, not so very distant from the NIF argument that Sudan was no longer to be ruled by a party, but the Islamic principles of the masses.[30]

I raise this example of the NIF's agenda to "civilize Islam" because it shows that rather than the Inqadh regime effecting a burst of Islam into a society that had fallen away from it, as their literature often claims, what it in fact did was intervene into already existing forms of Muslim religiosity. Thus its efforts take their place within a much longer lineage of theological debates about the relationship between religion and politics that had existed before the Inqadh and will continue to exist after it has passed into history. Unlike Egypt, where secular culture and ideology dominated the political scene from the late colonial period into independence (e.g., Lapidus 2002: 512–34; Wickham 2002), politics in Sudan, although it included a strong Communist party (Hale 1996: 151–79; Warburg 1978: 93–168),[31] was overwhelmingly religious in its orientation. Despite some fleeting attempts in the '50s, '60s and '70s to form popular secular parties, it was allegiance to the "sectarian" parties of the DUP and Umma that dominated during democratic periods. Thus the language of Sayyid Qutb in opposing secularization and Westernization (Abu Rabiᶜ 1996: 92–219), which inspired the early NIF, was a somewhat strange fit for the reality on the ground in Sudan, where Islamic politics dominated. John Voll, for example, notes that the modern period of Sudanese history has seen religious parties becoming more deeply entrenched rather than falling by the wayside, as a reading of the Islamist literature might otherwise suggest. It seems that at the very moment when Islamist language against secularism was reaching its highest pitch in Sudan, secular political programs were becoming harder and harder to find. Voll writes:

---

practices that were deemed beyond the pale of normative Islam. Yet, while both Hoffman and Johansen argue that the Egyptian government wanted to reform Sufism to meet certain normative standards, at no point did this government see Sufi organizations as strategically important to the implementation of a major component of their political agenda, as the Sudanese state so clearly did. For the Egyptian government, the Sufi orders merely needed to be kept in line. For the Sudanese government, on the other hand, reforms of doctrine and ritual practice were of less interest. More important was the issue of how to reform Sufism's relationship to politics, how to marshal the massive popularity of Sufi shaykhs so as to serve the political agenda of the NIF.

30 See pp. 67–69 above. Einas Ahmed cites a 1994 government directive outlawing political parties that makes the argument that the banning of parties is no major loss for Sudan in any case: "Sudanese parties are not really political parties. They are only the political expressions of a Sufi order legacy whose objective is to monopolize power" (Ahmed 2007: 205).

31 In addition to mentioning the communists, it is also important to note that a new movement of nonaligned Leftists called *al-Quwwāt al-Ḥadītha* (the modern forces) were agitating against the Umma/DUP coalition for the cancellation of *sharīᶜa* in the months prior to the NIF coup (see Medani 1997: 167).

> In contrast to many other parts of the Islamic world, relatively secularist radicals never came to dominate the political, social, or intellectual life of Sudan. . . . Throughout the twentieth century there has been a failure to establish urban secular organizations in the economic or political arena. When modern-style structures were created, they rapidly shifted from independent secular existence to coalition with the sayyids [i.e., the leaders of the Umma Party and the DUP] and large Muslim organizations. . . . Secularist programs and organizations had decreasing appeal among the educated and professional northern Sudanese Muslims by the 1980s. Even when the fundamentalist regime came to power in Sudan in 1989, the primary basis for opposition among northern Sudanese was provided by the organizations of the older Muslim groups and supported by the Mahdi and Mirghani [Khatmiyya] families rather than coming from radical northern secularists. (Voll 1997: 296, 289–90, 292)[32]

For the NIF, "the Islamic revival" (*al-ṣaḥwa al-islāmiyya*) was a chauvinistic name for what was in fact the initiation of a debate between two trends in contemporary Islamic politics: traditional organized Sufism and Mahdism and the political forms that emerged out of them, on the one hand, and NIF-style Islamic reformism, on the other.

A New Multiculturalism

> Those in service in the State and public life shall envisage the dedication thereof for the worship of God . . . and all shall maintain religious motivation and give due regard to such spirit in plans, laws, policies, and official business . . . in order to prompt public life towards its objectives, and adjust them towards justice and up-rightness to be directed towards the grace of God in The Hereafter. (Sudan Constitution of 1998, Article 1.18)[33]

> [Sudan will be] one nation gathering together religions and cultures, which are a source of strength, consensus and inspiration. (Sudan Interim Constitution of 2005, Article 1–3)[34]

32 A Westernized *affandī* (Effendi) class certainly existed in Sudan (see Ibrahim 2008: 330–31, 348–52), which al-Turabi, being a member of the elite, saw himself as up against, but the political salience of the class seemed minimal and they were never able to put together a secular Nasserist-style party of the sort that were organized elsewhere in the Arabic-speaking world (Numayri's fleeting attempts aside).

33 http://www.sudanembassy.ca/Docs/THE%20CONSTITUTION%20OF%20THE%20REPUBLIC%20OF%20THE%20SUDAN%201998.pdf. The Arabic version of the constitution can be found at www.aproarab.org/Down/Sudan/Dostor.doc.

34 *al-sūdān waṭan wāḥid jāmiʿ takūn fīhu al-adyān wa-l-thaqāfāt maṣdar quwwa wa tawāfiq wa ilhām.* One should note that earlier constitutions, such as that of 1998, from which I quote

The signing of the CPA with the SPLM (the representative of the majority-non-Muslim South), and the implementation of the Interim Constitution that emerged out of it occasioned a major rethinking of the Islamist project. This is an exercise that continues through today. The modern history of Sudan has been scarred by two massive civil wars with the South (1955–72 and 1983–2005) that claimed, most likely, millions of lives. While to call the most recent civil war a "religious war" is to ignore the political and economic factors that underlay it and to be deaf to the vocal claims of SPLM leader John Garang (d. 2005) that a broad sweep of Sudanese were marginalized regardless of their religious affiliations (Garang 1987), it is impossible to ignore religion as one important factor within the mix. Seemingly more consequential issues, such as protocols on power-sharing, wealth-sharing, and joint-military agreements, had been solved in the final stages of the peace negotiations that led to the signing of the CPA, but the issue that held up the successful conclusion of negotiations was the legal status of the Sudanese capital, Khartoum: was it to be governed by *sharīʿa*, by secular law, or by some combination of the two (Salomon 2004b)? Sudan's foreign minister at the time, speaking in the final stages of the talks, commented, "The issue of the national capital and the laws that govern it are the final obstacle [to peace] right now" (Kanina 2004).[35] Though President Jaʿfar Numayri's decision to divide the South administratively may be the main reason fighting between North and South resumed in 1983, his decision to impose *sharīʿa* law in September of that year added much fuel to the fire. The majority-non-Muslim peoples in the South saw the move as a major affront to the possibility of their political participation at the national level.

Though several moves throughout the early 2000s foreshadowed the reforms of the CPA, its actual signing in January of 2005 (coupled with the signing of the Interim Constitution a few months later) put into law the principle that Sudan should no longer be a state that merely governed religious minorities, but rather would have to integrate the diverse peoples of Sudan into

above, also had statements of "tolerance" of diversity. However, there, the Islamic character of the state was much clearer. Also under the heading of "The Nature of the Country," the 1998 attempt to define Sudan reads significantly differently from the 2005 Constitution, insisting on the dominance of Islam as the majority religion in spite of Sudan's diversity. Following an Islamic invocation that is absent in the 2005 Constitution, it reads, "Sudan is an inclusive nation in which races and cultures coalesce, and it tolerates [various] religions. Islam is the religion of the majority of inhabitants, and Christianity and customary beliefs have significant followers" (*dawlat al-sūdān waṭan jāmiʿ taʾtalif fihu al-aʿrāq wa-l-thaqāfāt wa titsāmaḥ al-diyānāt, wa-l-islām dīn ghālib al-sukkān, wa li-l-masīḥiyya wa-l-muʿtaqadāt al-ʿirfiyya ittibāʿ muʿtabirūn*). The 1998 Constitution can be found at: http://www.aproarab.org/Down/Sudan/Dostor.doc.

35 It seems that the 2004 negotiations were not the first Sudanese peace talks to be held up by the question of *sharīʿa*, however. Peter Kok recalls Jimmy Carter, after attending peace talks in Nairobi between the government and the SPLA in 1989, quoted as saying, "Talks broke down principally because of the government's failure to address the issue of Sudan's sharia laws" (*IHT*, no. 33, December 16, 1989, quoted in Kok 1991).

its very identity. The five-year interim period that followed the signing of the CPA was a careful, and in the end unsuccessful, effort to hold simultaneously to the ideals of the Islamic state and the principles of multiculturalism, the latter adopted so as to make unity attractive as the CPA stipulated. Though the reforms of the state required by the CPA were certainly implemented inconsistently, they nonetheless played out in important ways—politically, legislatively, administratively, and culturally as well. Their political impact was a consequence of what is probably the most radical federalist system in the history of the modern state (and I say this because the South was allowed not only a parliament, presidency, and much economic independence, but also a separate army independent of the national forces as well). Legislatively they operated through a system that created religion-based exceptions to the adjudication of Islamic law, administratively they functioned through affirmative action programs and the appointment of SPLM members to ministerial posts, and culturally they worked through the promotion of non-Arab African culture in education, on billboards, and by means of spectacles such as government-sponsored public street theater that sought to promote "the culture of peace" (*thaqāfat al-salām*). The CPA constituted a major turning point for the NIF from an idealist variety of Islamism whose goal was at times the destruction of cultures it saw as "backwards" (and at other times merely enforcing their minority status, their marginalization to the identity of the state), to an Islamism that was forced to take seriously the religious and cultural diversity of Sudan in reforming the state. Even if those who signed the agreement were not entirely convinced of its long-term feasibility, it is undeniable, as the following examples will show, that the spirit (or threat, however one saw it) of multiculturalism had trickled down to many levels of state and society, and both officials and regular citizens were actively grappling with its implications.[36]

The CPA and the Interim Constitution that emerged out of it clearly celebrated the religious diversity of Sudan. At the level of law, the symbolic hallmark of the Islamist movement, the new constitution states that "Islamic *sharīʿa*" *and* "popular consensus (*al-tawāfuq al-shaʿbī*) and the values and customs (*aʿrāf . . . wa taqālīd*) of the Sudanese people as well as its traditions and religious beliefs (*muʿtaqadāt dīniyya*), which come under the expression 'the diversity in Sudan' (*al-tanawwuʿ fī-l-Sūdān*), [are each] a source

36 Many skeptics have argued that the NCP's commitment to multiculturalism was solely rhetorical, a commitment in word, not in deed. I don't disagree that many things remained the same after the signing of the CPA: Sudanese TV was still overwhelmingly Arab and Islamic in character, the laws were never officially overhauled, the rhetoric of the state was still overwhelmingly an Islamic one. Nevertheless, the prospect of "multiculturalism" was still very much alive when I was in Sudan (even though its light weakened as the country moved towards dissolution in July of 2011) and both government institutions and private Islamic organizations took its prospects very seriously, as the following pages will show.

for legislation that is enacted at the federal level" (Article 5:2). Though this is flanked by a statement that *sharīʿa* and Islamic scholarly consensus (*ijmāʿ*) will be *the only* sources for legislation in the northern states, the regime's movement away from an insistence that *sharīʿa* be the only, or even primary, source of law at the federal level represents a major shift.

The CPA to which the government agreed set the tone for this shift in the Islamist project. It promised to "[e]stablish a democratic system of governance taking account of the cultural, ethnic, racial, religious and linguistic diversity and gender equality of the people of the Sudan" (CPA: 2). Under the heading of "Religion and the State," for example, the two parties agreed to recognize "that Sudan is a multi-cultural, multi-racial, multi-ethnic, multi-religious, and multi-lingual country" and confirmed "that religion shall not be used as a divisive factor," thereby agreeing that "religions, customs, and beliefs are a source of moral strength and inspiration for the Sudanese people" (CPA: 5). Laws were to be reworked to take this diversity into account,[37] the national capital was to be a meeting place for cultures rather

37 "There shall be a National Government which shall exercise such functions and pass such laws as must necessarily be exercised by a sovereign state at national level. The National Government in all its laws shall take into account the religious and cultural diversity of the Sudanese people" (CPA: 6). It should be noted that this issue of legislative reform almost entirely faltered in its actual implementation, however, and remained an extremely contentious issue for both parties. To prove this one only needs to follow the debates in parliament from those years. The daily *al-Ṣaḥāfa* reported in April of 2009 a vicious exchange between the NCP and the opposition that is worth recounting to show the roadblocks to actual legislative reform that appeared in the years following the CPA's signing:

> The parliamentary deliberations yesterday around the revisions of the Criminal Law turned into unprecedented sharp exchanges and arguments when one of the leaders of the National Democratic Alliance (NDA, *al-Tajammuʿ al-Waṭanī al-Dīmuqrāṭī* [an opposition coalition]), described the previous [criminal] law of 1991 as a backward document that was set down with an exclusionist (*iqṣāʾī*) mentality and he called for the establishment of a new law. And following him was the head of the SPLM block, Yasir ʿArman, who was calling for some of the punishments [required by the law] not to be applied to non-Muslims. The head of the [ruling Islamist] National Congress Party [NCP] block, Ghazi Salah al-Din [al-ʿAtabani], defended [the laws] in opposition to [their critics] with the warning that [these opposition party members] are taking the laws as a platform for attacks and withdrawal from the signed agreements [which stipulated that *sharīʿa* will remain valid in the North] and he refused the insinuations and suggestions that Islamic *sharīʿa* inflicts outrageous punishments. . . . [Faruq Abu ʿIsa of the NDP] pointed to the fact that the Comprehensive Peace Agreement (CPA) and the Constitution create a new environment [that defines Sudan on the basis of its diversity, not Islamic culture alone]. And he called for the setting down of a new law that adheres to the CPA and the Constitution and the present political environment. . . . And Yasir ʿArman said that his block [advocated for] the lack of application of the *ḥadd* punishments [punishments stipulated in the Qurʾan that are considered non-negotiable in orthodox jurisprudence, though their status in relation to non-Muslims is debated] on non-Muslims, insisting that they are indeed [being] applied, and [adding that] the

than an Arab capital in which Southerners were merely a minority,[38] law enforcement personnel were to receive sensitivity training in how to interact with diverse communities in a more equitable manner,[39] and even the design and the name of the Sudanese currency were now to reflect a religiously diverse Sudan, rather than one with an Arab or Islamic identity. This latter project was estimated to have cost 150 million USD,[40] a not insignificant investment for a country with a GDP (in 2006) of only 36.4 billion USD.[41] Figure 2 shows images of the currency established by the NIF in 1992 compared with the new currency released in 2006. The NIF's 1992 currency, called the *dīnār*, had replaced the old currency, the *jinayh* (pound), which the NIF felt had colonial connotations as it was the name the British had used, derived from the early modern English coin, the "guinea." However, in 2006, after the signing of the CPA, the currency was renamed the *jinayh* (this time glossed as the "new Sudanese pound") in response to the SPLM demand for a culturally neutral coinage. The images depicted on the currency released during the period of Islamic revolutionary fervor show a distinctly Arab and Islamic identity, while the later currency, implemented after the signing of the CPA, highlights peace, diversity, and national unity. Again, while it remains unclear how many of the promises of the CPA were in fact fulfilled, during my time in the field the implications of its promises were being grappled with at all levels of state and society and were causing a massive reassessment of the Islamist project.

In the period in which I did my research, when the virtues of multiculturalism were being celebrated in the words of top government officials and on billboards across the capital, a radical reappraisal was underway. It involved the reconsideration not only of the polity but also of the varieties of

---

punishment of flogging that is [applied for certain offenses actually is] not a *ḥadd* punishment and contradicts the Constitution which forbids torture in a general sense. And he touched on the subject of the crime of adultery (*al-zinā*) and [in this matter] he insisted upon consideration of the diversity of customs, traditions (*taqālīd*), and religions [that may not consider certain sex acts which are considered adulterous in Islam to be forbidden]. And [he argued] that we should include these cultures and customs and traditions in the [construction of the] Criminal Law. The members of the NCP strongly protested [the points] which Abu ʿIsa and ʿArman raised. (Hasabu 2009)

38 "Khartoum shall be the Capital of the Republic of the Sudan. The National Capital shall be a symbol of national unity that reflects the diversity of Sudan" (CPA: 23).

39 "Law enforcement agencies of the Capital shall be representative of the population of Sudan and shall be adequately trained and made sensitive to the cultural, religious and social diversity of all Sudanese" (CPA: 23).

40 "New Sudan Currency to Circulate from January 10 [2007]," on the *Sudan Tribune* website (http://www.sudantribune.com/spip.php?article19646).

41 From the World Bank Development Indicators: http://www.google.com/publicdata?ds=wb-wdi&met=ny_gdp_mktp_cd&idim=country:SDN&dl=en&hl=en&q=sudan+gdp.

Islamic ideologies that were compatible with it. Around the time of the late SPLM leader John Garang's arrival in Khartoum in July 2005, for example, the Islamic slogans and Qur'anic verses that festooned billboards around the capital began to take a marked turn toward highlighting tolerance and respect for diversity within Islam and away from mantras promoting *jihād* against a rebellious South, of the sort that earlier Islamic sloganeering had favored. Figure 3 shows one such billboard. It quotes the Qur'anic verse in which God exclaims, "Oh humanity! Indeed we created you as male and female and we made you into nations and tribes so that you may know one another."[42] The verse suggests a divine intentionality, and perhaps an inherent good, in diversity and calls on believers not to assimilate others but to learn from them. The context in which it was hung, namely the signing of the 2005 CPA and John Garang's imminent arrival to Khartoum, would have made its significance transparent to any viewer. Nevertheless, we should note that at the same time that the government was hanging signs celebrating tolerance and diversity, the ruling party was passing out stickers around the capital making it eminently clear that this turn to tolerance did not mean a turn away from *sharīʿa*. The constitution to which the NCP had agreed might stipulate a lessening of the role of *sharīʿa* at the federal level, but insistence that *sharīʿa* remain the sole source of law in the North meant that the NCP could still use it as a rallying cry. The stickers they handed out read: "Islamic *sharīʿa*: With the people it came and with the people it will remain" (see Figure 4). Thus tolerance and the granting of rights to minorities were positioned as elements of an Islamic program, which may have occasioned a new approach to *sharīʿa*, but never its abandonment.[43]

The changes enshrined in the Constitution and agreed to in the CPA led to a radical rethinking of the social engineering promoted by the Civilization Project. The ruling elite seemed to be questioning whether the coercive state measures characteristic of Islamization in earlier eras, such as those

42 *yā ayyuhā al-nās innā khalaqnākum min dhakar wa untha wa jaʿalnākum shuʿūban wa qabā'il li-taʿārafū. . . .* (*Sūrat al-Ḥujurāt*: 13). Note that this is the same verse US president Barack Obama used in his speech to the Muslim world in Cairo at the conclusion of his June 4, 2009 speech, flanked by the words, "The people of the world can live together in peace. We know that is God's vision. Now, that must be our work here on Earth. Thank you. And may God's peace be upon you." http://www.whitehouse.gov/the_press_office/Remarks-by-the-President-at-Cairo-University-6-04-09/. Thus the language of Islamic multiculturalism has truly become an international one.

43 It is the mid-twentieth-century South Asian scholar Sayyid Abu Aʿla Mawdudi, an extremely influential theorist to the ideologues behind the Salvation Revolution (often read by way of the works of Sayyid Qutb: see El-Affendi 1991: 13–22), who has made the strongest arguments for the compatibility of the Islamic state with the protection of religious minorities. Indeed he argues for the Islamic state's superiority in protecting minorities in comparison with other modes of politics, such as secular democracy, which he sees as essentially a tyranny of the majority. For this argument, see Maudoodi 1961.

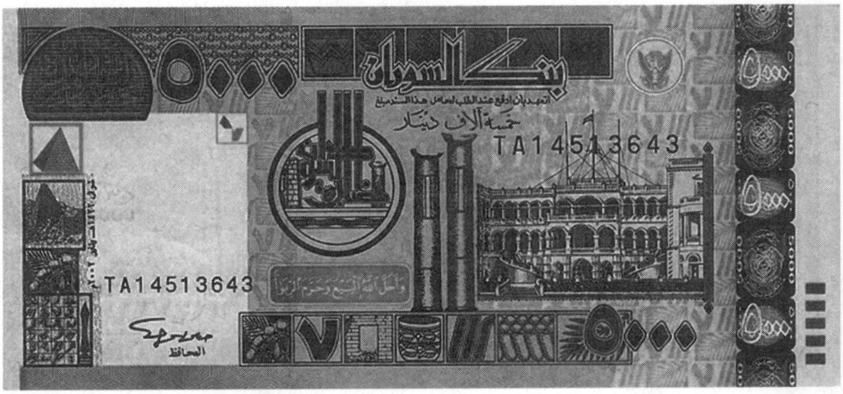

Figure 2. Sudanese currencies, 1992 v. 2006. *This p. from top:* The 1992 ten-*dīnār* note, depicting the famous Two Niles Mosque (*Masjid al-Nīlayn*); the five-thousand–*dīnār* note, depicting the Republican Palace, and various elements of northern Sudanese history: pyramids, Merotic script, etc. NB: While this note is part of the *dīnār* series, it was in fact released much later than 1992, following the currency devaluation when notes such as the ten-*dīnār* bill became nearly worthless. *Opp. p. from top*: The 2006 one-pound (*jinayh*) note, depicting peace (the doves) and prosperity (the Central Bank of Sudan Building); the 2006 two-pound note, depicting musical instruments from northern and southern Sudan; the 2006 ten-pound note, depicting the famous image of John Garang and ʿUmar al-Bashir joining hands in celebration of the signing of the peace agreement between North and South at the base of the tree, as well as a camel (the symbol of the desert Arabs) and the long-horned cow (the symbol of the dominant Dinka tribe in the South), walking side by side. The 1992 images are from http://3omlat.ahlamountada.com/montada-f32/topic-t418.htm.

بنك السودان المركزي
AJ51608712
٩ يوليو ٢٠٠٦ م
ورقة نقد قانونية
المحافظ
واحد جنيه سوداني
AJ51608712

CENTRAL BANK OF SUDAN
Legal Tender Banknote
July 9 2006
TWO SUDANESE POUNDS

بنك السودان المركزي
DN45228503
ورقة نقد قانونية
المحافظ
عشرة جنيهات سودانية
DN45228503

Figure 3. Two adjacent signs on a pole in Khartoum. Text in the sign on the left side of the frame: "In the Name of God, the Most Merciful and Compassionate: 'Oh people, indeed we created you as male and female and we made you into nations and tribes so that you may know one another' [*Sūrat al-Ḥujurāt*: 13]. God Almighty has spoken the truth (with greetings from the General Secretariat for 'Khartoum, the Capital of Arab Culture, AD 2005')." Text in the sign on the right side of the frame: "2005: the Year of Culture and Peace (with Greetings from the General Secretariat for 'Khartoum the Capital of Arab Culture, AD 2005')." Photo by the author.

we examined in the first half of this chapter, were possible in the current climate, wherein it was only the success of the CPA that would guarantee the kind of stability that had led to the end of the war with the South and would further advance the economic boom the country was undergoing.[44]

Examples of this rethinking can be found in the words of government officials once at the forefront of the Islamization efforts key to the Civilization Project. Take the response of the Minister of Guidance and Pious

44 According to the World Bank, after the signing of the CPA the GDP more than doubled, from 21.5 billion USD in 2004 to 45.9 billion USD by 2007. http://data.worldbank.org/indicator/NY.GDP.MKTP.CD.

Figure 4. Text in sticker: "Islamic *Sharīʿa*: With the People It Came and with the People It Will Remain (National Congress [Party], Khartoum State. With Greetings from the Media [sector] of the Congress)." Photo by the author.

Endowments (*Wazīr al-Irshād wa-l-Awqāf*), Dr. Azhari al-Tijani, to a row that erupted in al-Qadarif state (eastern Sudan) in 2007 over the proposed adoption by the state parliament of a new law entitled the Purification of Society (*Tazkiyat al-Mujtamaʿ*) Law. In the daily *al-Ṣaḥāfa*, Nahid Saʿid reported:

> The Ministry of Guidance and Pious Endowments proclaimed its innocence from the law . . . and assured its adherence to the text of the Constitution and the Comprehensive Peace Agreement, regarding the protection of religious, cultural, and ethnic plurality in the Sudan. The Minister of Guidance and Pious Endowments, Dr. Azhari al-Tijani . . . said that his ministry has no relationship to the Purification of Society Law whose passing is under consideration in al-Qadarif state. He revealed that [the] organization [by the same name] of the Purification of Society that is part of [his] ministry is [only] engaged in promoting virtuous values and morals in society, fighting against foreign values and morals that have come from outside, and bringing attention to

> the risk of moral transgression (*tanbīh ilā mukhāṭir al-ikhtirāq al-qīmī*) through [the means of] vocal admonition (*waʿẓ*), and consciousness raising (*tawʿiyya*), and through directing people gently (*tawjīh bi-l-rifq*) *and not through legal procedures or censorship* (*ijrāʾāt al-qānūniyya aw al-riqābiyya*). (Saʿid 2007, my emphasis)

Thus, while the state was certainly still involved in promoting its vision of Islam, many government officials were explicit in condemning the integration of such an approach into the legal or law enforcement apparatus that was a hallmark of the early Inqadh. Instead, they argued for a kind of gentle *daʿwa* (*bi-ālatī hiya aḥsan*), without state coercion and thus within the bounds of the CPA. Such a stance represented a major shift for the regime from the early 1990s when individual moral reform on an Islamic basis through repressive means was seen as a central strategy of its project. Attempting to please two constituencies at once, Dr. Azhari al-Tijani sought to uphold both the state as a locus of moral rearing for the citizenry, as the early Inqadh argued it should be, and the citizenry as free from state coercion on religion, as the CPA now demanded.

Another example of the adoption of multiculturalism by Islamist intellectuals comes in the writings of Dr. Ahmad ʿAli al-Imam, then advisor to the president on matters of *al-taʾṣīl*, an Islamist neologism that we will discuss at length in the next chapter that refers to a revision of the sciences and other intellectual pursuits to take into account Qurʾanic and other sacred knowledges. Interestingly, *al-taʾṣīl* was also up for revision in the late Inqadh. Below is Ahmad ʿAli al-Imam's 2003 iteration of the *taʾṣīl* project, written at a time when, though the CPA hadn't yet been signed, the negotiations on its contents were in full-swing and the spirit of the document that would later be signed already permeated the highest levels of government. In this quote we see the presidential advisor vacillate (in a somewhat self-contradictory way) between an Islamic and a multicultural version of *al-taʾṣīl*:

> *Al-taʾṣīl* is to return what has escaped from its fundamentals back to its fundamentals . . . in the judgments of *sharīʿa*. The fundament of [all] fundamentals is the Qurʾan and the Prophetic Sunna. [However, it is important to note that there] also enters into [the concept of] *al-taʾṣīl* the return to its origins [with the meaning of] going back to the noble deeds of morals from our *popular inheritance* (*mawrūthātna al-shaʿbiyya*) and our noble customs, that which is shared between us and between other religions, not in the fundamentals of doctrines about which they differ but in the programs of morals about which they agree. So finally, in other words, *al-taʾṣīl* is the return of all aspects of life, especially public life, to its Islamic origins (*uṣūlahā al-islāmiyya*) from which it has been cut off, not just because of negligence and the passing of the ages,

> but rather because of the deliberate action based on another civilizational [model]. (Muhammad Khayr 2008: 14, my emphasis)

Yet, while in 2003, Ahmad ʿAli al-Imam vacillated between multiculturalism ("going back to . . . that which is shared between us and between other religions") and Islamism ("the return of all aspects of life, especially public life, to its Islamic origins"), by 2005, following the signing of the CPA, he had published a revised version of the same paper that was even more clear as to the new multicultural stance the government was taking. Here is his revision of the last sentence of the above-quoted passage:

> In other words *al-taʾṣīl* is a return of all aspects of life, especially public life, to the fundamentals of the religious nation (*al-umma al-dīniyya*), and what is founded upon it in noble customs (*aʿarāf karīma*). . . . (al-Imam 2005: 6)

Like the proto-Christians Evans-Pritchard had discovered decades earlier when encountering "Nuer Religion" (Evans-Pritchard 1954), who worshipped the Holy Spirit without knowing its name, Ahmad ʿAli al-Imam was trying to conjure proto-Muslims out of the diverse religious stances of his fellow citizens from the South. The Islamic state did not need to go by that name to encourage the following of the "religious nation" and the "noble deeds and morals from [Sudan's] popular inheritance." These were shared by all Sudanese, regardless of their religious identities. Thus a state that recognized the political claims of non-Muslims did not, at least in this rendering, need to contradict its otherwise Islamic ambitions.

Postscript: A Society Left Unguarded

Despite the acrobatics of regime loyalists, many Islamist intellectuals began to evaluate the political experiment of the NIF in ever more bleak terms. Symbols such as the *al-ḥajj wa-l-ʿumra*/Canartel building were a daily reminder of the kind of concessions that the regime had made to its Islamist project, both in its attempts to appease minorities and to stoke the flame of capital. Yet, not only were capitalism and multiculturalism difficult for these intellectuals to harmonize with the Inqadh's earlier agenda, but the rise in popularity of both Sufi orders in their traditional arrangements and Salafi piety movements, especially among the youth, seemed to indicate a growing distance between regime efforts and the public. In an assessment of this phenomenon, Abdelwahab El-Affendi writes:

> One of the great ironies of the Islamist adventure in coup-making (leading to the creation of the National Salvation regime in June 1989) was that the move dealt a more serious blow to the Islamist movement

> than it [did] to any other political group. . . . The effect [of the inability to form a vital and independent Islamist movement with the specter of the Islamist failures in the administration of state looming over it] has been enhanced by the considerable fragmentation which hit the Islamist scene as a result of these policies [implemented by the NIF/NCP] and also due to other internal and external factors. For example, the *Salafi* trend has witnessed a remarkable resurgence in Sudan, as did its antithesis, *Sufi* revivalism. The *Salafi* trend, which is influenced by Saudi ulama, has remained a small and marginal presence in Sudan, and had traditionally allied itself with the Islamists in the 1960s and 1970s. That alliance also included some *Sufi* groups. Neither of these two tendencies had any significant presence within the universities or among the young. However, in recent years, both have been expanding their presence within the modern sector, and have emerged as strong competitors to the mainstream Islamists on university campuses, something that was unheard of until a decade ago. (El-Affendi 2008)

As we saw with the establishment of the NCMG, the encouragement of Sufi organizations and their newfound political relevance was at least in part a conscious strategy of the regime. The regime's insistence on the political relevance of Islam in all its forms was, however, a strategy that it could never fully control, as oppositional discourse also emerged from both Sufi and Salafi quarters, as we will observe in subsequent chapters. The Islamists' inability to control the theological ground they had laid out remained a bugbear for many Islamist intellectuals. Hasan al-Turabi argued in an interview I conducted with him in 2006 that the removal of the Islamists from traditional arenas of Islamic evangelism and reform (such as the mosque) and into government offices left society unguarded. Into this vacuum rushed the Sufis and Salafis. In al-Turabi's diagnosis, this revival of Sufism and Salafism was due to problems internal to the Islamic Movement in its new role in government. In a telling admission, he told me:

> [At the outset of the revolution] people became obsessed with politics. It was the new thing. Like when someone is about to get married he forgets everything else. We said that for the first time since the Righteous Caliphs [in the seventh century]: "Here comes the Islamic Government!!!" It had only appeared [previously] in the Shiʿa government of Iran. So because [we were pioneers in this regard, politics] became an obsession. We forgot culture. We forgot education. We forgot the mosques. There was no one among us who went and worked in a mosque. We worked in armies, embassies, police forces, government offices. And our children all of them we put in political positions and they were not prepared for this. We corrupted so many people! . . . And [in doing so] we left society [unguarded] and the Sufis came and worked

> in it, and the Salafis came and worked in it. The Salafis came because our work was over there, in public [political] life, without a base [in society]. When we looked back to our base we realized that it became full of Sufis and Salafis.

There was a real sense among al-Turabi and other Islamist intellectuals that it was precisely when the Islamists came to political power that the Islamist movement, as an evangelical (*daʿwa*) force, began to fail. The argument is not simply that "politics corrupts" and that one therefore cannot be a true Muslim and a politician at the same time, but rather that the Islamic movement's attempts at social reform through the mechanisms and institutions of the state alone (through "armies, embassies, police forces, government offices") left a void in matters of pious practice that was quickly filled by other groups whose activism took other forms and unfolded in other locales (mosques, *zāwiyas*, and lesson circles).

Yet, al-Turabi's self-criticism, while admirable in its frankness, elides a discussion of the way in which state-sponsored reforms such as the Civilization Project not only left certain religious spheres unoccupied and unguarded, but also in part *enabled* the kind of revivalism that Sufis and Salafis enjoyed. Sufis and Salafis enjoyed great success not simply due to the NIF's absence from society, as al-Turabi argues (for certainly the early Inqadh is remembered for an *invasion* of the government into areas that had previously been thought of as the protected domain of the social, such as comportment at public gatherings, dress, and the activities of private religious organizations), but rather due to the way in which the NIF changed the whole vocabulary of public life. Sufi and Salafi groups gained social and political salience in the time of the Inqadh precisely because the Islamists had insisted that all aspects of life—from politics, to social and family life, to the media—become a matter of religious concern. Sufi shaykhs who were able to speak to these contemporary concerns in an Islamic idiom benefited greatly from the Islamization that the Inqadh effected, whether they supported the state's formal program or not, for they were ready to fill the spaces that the Islamists opened up in their call for a return to Islam. What the NIF was not successful at doing was monopolizing the Islam that was said to undergird its state. The public turned to others to answer the questions the Inqadh posed, using its grammar to form other sorts of sentences. While it can perhaps be argued that state-sponsored Islamism was something of a "misfire," in the sense that it did not exactly hit the Islamist intellectuals' intended target of an "awakening," the shot it fired was nevertheless heard by Islamic movements across the country and they responded accordingly.

Itineraries

CHAPTER THREE

Rebuilding the Muslim Mind

Epistemological Enlightenment and Its Discontents

The more than two decades since the establishment of the Inqadh regime have been remarkable less for the changing modes of statecraft they present than for the space they opened up for specifically Islamic modes of deliberation. While the formal state structures the Inqadh employed look quite similar to those of the period before the Salvation Revolution, and even to those of the colonial state (as we saw in Chapter 1), the opening up of matters of public concern to Islamic discourse was unprecedented. To argue that the new modes of Islamic deliberation that resulted are merely the workings of an emergent Islamic public sphere (e.g., Salvatore and LeVine 2005) into which the state entered, and rather late in the game at that, is to ignore the explicit efforts at structuring and engineering this domain that have been a chief objective of the state. The Islamization of academic and intellectual culture through the establishment of think tanks, journals, fora, and even new universities, of print and televised media, of public space through mosque construction, dress codes and billboards, and of the workplace through Islamic associations and opportunities for Islamic learning, was a conscious effort by the regime to lay the basis for an intricate web of Islamic publicity. Even those who rejected major components of the regime's project (as we will see in the case of the Sufi groups we meet below), ended up getting caught in its web, unable to wiggle out of the discursive frame of the Islamic state even as they took issue with the particular iteration of it that the regime put forward. It is by training our gaze toward actors like these that we can begin to see the emergence of the public sphere that we identified in the introduction to this volume, a space that is neither of the state nor entirely distinct from it.

As a revolution of intellectuals, albeit instrumentalized by military forces, the Inqadh understood its project as taking aim at the very epistemological foundations of public culture. Its leaders argued that in order to build this web of Islamic publicity, its projects could not merely focus on the reform of public practice, but had to go much deeper, to reform the "Sudanese mind" as well. It was for this reason that the government began to promote a very particular epistemological stance, exploring what new ways of life could emerge out of a synergy between the methodologies of empirical science and the products of revelation. The regime instigated this project to further what it understood to be ethical practice, wherein it was the assumed valuelessness of the way scientific knowledge had been deployed that had led to the horrors of the modern age, Sudan's troubles clearly among them. From very early on in the Inqadh endeavor, state intellectuals argued that if the Islamic movement was to steer Sudan right, it must "put at the head of its priorities work on the rebuilding of the Muslim mind and the rebuilding of the Muslim nation, *as two inseparable operations*" (Hamid 1994: 7, my emphasis). With such a proclamation as its rallying cry, a project to reconstruct "the Sudanese mind," to instill within it certain knowledge derived from the fruits of science and within the ethical parameters of revelation, began in earnest. Though the project was relatively consistent in its efforts, it took on several names over the long duration of Islamist rule: fundamentalization (*al-taʾṣīl*), the Islamization of knowledge (*aslamat/islāmiyyat al-maʿrifa*), epistemological enlightenment (*al-tanwīr al-maʿrifī*).[1]

1 A few notes on translations seem necessary here to satisfy the reader with a knowledge of Arabic:

taʾṣīl: The term *taʾṣīl* literally means "bringing something to its root (*aṣl*)." However, to avoid the cumbersomeness of this phrase, I have chosen the term "fundamentalization" to define it. In doing so, I am referencing the English term "fundament," in the sense of "foundation" (both also attested meanings of *aṣl*), and not attempting to enter the debate over the appropriateness of the term "fundamentalist" to describe contemporary Islamic reform movements. However, there is ample evidence that those who coined the term were indeed embracing the notion of fundamentalism (*al-uṣūliyya*). Take the words of the Minister of Higher Education in the mid-1990s, Ibrahim Ahmad ʿUmar: "[I want] to say a few words on *al-taʾṣīl*. . . . The true fundamentalist (*al-uṣūlī al-ḥaqīqī*) is he who is able to devise or study thoroughly comprehensive issues with which he controls a field of knowledge or work. This is the general meaning of [fundamentalist] and in it are clear indications of the meaning of *al-taʾṣīl*" (ʿUmar 1998: 18).

maʿrifa: Note that *maʿrifa* was the term used for all varieties of knowledge in Islamist writings. The term *ʿilm* was either used interchangeably or limited to discussions of a disciplinary science (i.e., anthropology, *ʿilm al-insān*). If any distinction was made between the two terms, it seemed to be between *maʿrifa* as knowledge in the abstract and *ʿilm* as a particular field of knowledge. For example, the intellectuals I discuss were interested in Islamizing knowledge (*maʿrifa*) as a whole, with the Islamization of the sciences (*al-ʿulūm*, sing. *ʿilm*) being one facet thereof. Thus the distinction between *ʿilm* and *maʿrifa* in Sufi texts, which has been widely discussed in academic literature—the former being "discursive knowledge," or "acquired knowledge" from the study of Qurʾan and hadith, and the latter being "experiential, infused, intimate or mystical knowledge," gnosis, or "the flip side of normative Islam" (Renard 2004; Karamustafa 2004)—nowhere appears in the writings of the intellectuals with whom I worked. There *maʿrifa* can even refer to knowledge gained through empirical scientific observation of the world. For the development of various terms for knowledge (*ʿilm*, *maʿrifa*, *yaqīn*, etc.) within the Sufi lexicon, see Rosenthal 1970: 164–70, which argues that even within Sufism the *ʿilm/maʿrifa* juxtaposition is somewhat more complicated than a mere opposition between discursive and mystical knowledge and that at various times Sufis adopted both terms to describe their mystical acquisitions.

If the European Enlightenment had been about the shedding of the constraints of religious dogma and the triumph of secular reason, this new epistemological enlightenment was about shedding the constraints of secularism, inherited through colonialism, which, though British forces had left more than half a century ago, continued to lay claim to the Sudanese mind. While intellectuals across the Muslim world had debated the merits of such a project for several decades,[2] the political context of a state that devoted considerable efforts to support and implement it in the construction of its institutions makes the case in Sudan quite unusual.[3] Through the institutional reforms mentioned above, and by introducing the principles

---

al-tanwīr al-maʿrifī: Here I chose to go with the translation that the organization with this name uses on its website (www.tanweer.sd) and in its English-language publications, as awkward as it may sound. Note that the term used for epistemology in Arabic is generally *al-naẓariyya al-maʿrifiyya/naẓariyyat al-maʿrifa* (among more secular intellectuals it is also just referred to by its Greek-derived term, *ibistumūlūjiyyā*) and thus the adjective *al-maʿrifī* is commonly translated as "epistemological." The term *tanwīr* is also in need of explanation. Mona Abaza notes the term being adopted by Islamist intellectuals in Egypt as well (2002: 154–59). She observes, however, that before *tanwīr* was adopted by the proponents of the "Islamization of knowledge," it had generally been associated with a nineteenth-century movement of Islamic liberalism. This new *tanwīr* shared important characteristics with the earlier model (a struggle against Western hegemony, an attempt to reform thought based on Islamic heritage), but with no necessary commitment to liberal values.

2 See for example Stenberg 1996 and Ahmed 1995, as well as the copious debates contained in the multiple volumes of the "Islamization of Knowledge" series published by the International Institute of Islamic Thought (IIIT) headquartered in Herndon, Virginia. Mona Abaza (2002) discusses the work of this institute, particularly in its Cairo office, in her *Debates on Islam and Knowledge in Malaysia and Egypt: Shifting Worlds.* Abaza's work with advocates of the Islamization of knowledge project in Egypt and Malaysia differs significantly from the Sudanese case in that her subjects are on the whole non-state affiliated (often opposition) Islamist intellectuals and civil society organizations. In Sudan, on the other hand, the project emanated from the Islamizing state. This said, Abaza's observations on the *genealogy* of the Islamization of knowledge trend (in the work of nineteenth- and twentieth-century Arab intellectuals, contemporary identity politics, and the third-world encounter with Western academia), as well as her sociological observations about the identities of the intellectuals who steered the trend themselves (33–40), are instructive in understanding my own research context.

3 The uniqueness of this endeavor was signaled in an interview with the Presidential Advisor on Fundamentalization Affairs, Ahmad ʿAli al-Imam, in which the interviewer states, "Perhaps it may seem strange that you find in the palace of the presidency of a state a special wing devoted to the affairs of Islamic fundamentalization (*al-taʾṣīl al-islāmī*) right next to the other wings [of the palace] that are replete with other presidential advisors [working] on numerous other affairs: internal, external, media, and otherwise. The first thing that is strange to some is that we have not heard of an advisor who specializes in the affairs of fundamentalization present in [a] government palace . . . but he is present in Sudan, where Professor Ahmad ʿAli al-Imam, the president of the Academy of Islamic Jurisprudence (*Majmaʿ al-Fiqh al-Islāmī*), is entrusted with the tasks of the advisor to the president in the affairs of fundamentalization, a task which perhaps has no peer [in the countries of the world]" (Mawqiʿ al-Sūdān 2008).

of the Islamization of knowledge into the practice of Sudanese governance, the Inqadh regime placed Islamic knowledge at the center of a variety of modern disciplines and organizational practices that were not traditionally tied to it. In doing so, the regime took aim not only at modern institutions and disciplinary forms, but at Islamic knowledge itself, which was asked to perform all sorts of new kinds of work in order to serve as a firm and certain foundation on which these projects could proceed.

While the Islamization of knowledge has most often been studied as an oppositional discourse to a hegemonic secularity in the sciences (e.g., Stenberg 1996), in Sudan it *became* the hegemonic discourse to which a variety of parties responded. Sudan's twenty-five-year experiment with Islamic governance thus not only offers the researcher a unique site to observe Islamist interventions in practice, grappling with real-world challenges not imagined by theoretical models, as we did in the previous chapter, but also allows us to observe how these policies are consumed within the diverse publics to which they attend, which will be the goal of the present chapter. When discussing my research, I am often asked: Has the Islamic project of the Inqadh been a success? To what extent has the government of Sudan accomplished its goal of instilling its Islamic program in the citizenry? Are new Muslim subjects emerging out of the era of National Salvation, or was the Inqadh period largely one of slogans that bore little fruit among the masses? A study of the regime's project of epistemological enlightenment offers us one way of answering these questions. By tracing first the nature of the regime's Islamic epistemological project and then turning to observe how it was both inhabited and contested by the Sudanese to whom it was directed, we will get a better a sense of the impact of the Islamic state. In doing so, we will come to see both its indelible presence in Sudanese public life and its inability to be enclosed within the agenda of its makers.

Discourses of Certainty

> We have spoken for many years about the situation of all the many sciences—cosmic, social and human—in the frame of Islam. We were saying from the podiums of Sudanese universities since the 1970s that if we want to present to humanity a useful cosmic, human or social science, then it is necessary that this knowledge stems from the [Islamic] religion first and foremost. But the circumstances were not favorable [for the implementation of this project] at that time: Sudanese state and society and the foreign presence were the thing[s] with influence in Sudan, [and the people influenced by them] did not care about Islam, indeed most of them were hostile towards it. . . . As for the international

> community, it was going by the opposite of what we called for: [it was] dazzled by secularism and it was giving its intellectual leadership to it and increasingly abandoning religion. . . . [Yet today] the Islamic epistemological project (*al-mashrūʿ al-islāmī al-maʿrifī*) finds in Sudan a state that is convinced by it, and organizations that are implementing it and that are nourished by what it produces. So the state is opening all the doors of all its organizations so that the scholar (*al-ʿālim*) and the researcher can enter, [each] carrying his ideas and his theories that are emerging from the sources of Islamic knowledge—the Qurʾan, Sunna, and the [material] universe—in order to devote [him/herself] to its application and to reexamine it so as to fix it or increase its depth or comprehensiveness.
>
> —Ibrahim Ahmad ʿUmar, "Islamic Knowledge on the Path of Construction" (ʿUmar 1995: 1–2)

In the early 1990s, not long after its rise to power, the new Sudanese government established an office within the Ministry of Higher Education and Scientific Research with a rather curious name. The office was called the Administration for the Fundamentalization of Knowledge (*Idārat Taʾṣīl al-Maʿrifa*), and shortly after its founding an advisor to the president was appointed under the same heading, with the title Advisor on Fundamentalization Affairs (*Mustashār al-Raʾīs fī Shuʾūn al-Taʾṣīl*). The term *taʾṣīl* (fundamentalization) was a neologism, up to this point more or less unknown outside Islamist intellectual circles (al-ʿAlwani 1994). At once embracing the notion of "fundamentalism" (*al-uṣūliyya*), and referencing the classical mode of Islamic jurisprudence (*uṣūl al-fiqh* [Hallaq 1999]), the term is derived from the Arabic root *aṣl* (root, source, fundament), and means something akin to "going back to the sources." Both offices with this term in their titles were tasked with undoing what their creators called the "positivist epistemological domination" (*al-haymana al-maʿrifiyya al-waḍʿiyya*)[4] (Muhammad Khayr 2008: 11) of the human and natural sciences, law, economics, and government by secular principles and the subsequent degeneration of revelation as a valid source of knowledge encouraged by Western actors and those Sudanese who were said to be mimicking them. An intellectual writing in the project's chief journal contended:[5]

4 While the term *waḍʿiyya* means "positivist" in Arabic philosophical discourse, the more colloquial sense of the adjective *waḍʿī* was likely also being referenced here. That adjective means "man-made" as opposed to "divine" (or natural) as in *qānūn waḍʿī* (positive, man-made law).

5 I thank Rüdiger Seesemann, who first brought my attention to the *taʾṣīl* phenomenon and loaned me his copies of the journal *al-Taʾṣīl*, on which many of my conclusions are based. See also Seesemann 2007 for a discussion of the *taʾṣīl* paradigm.

> This simple premise under which a group of Muslim intellectuals have been proceeding since the beginning of this *hijrī* century [i.e., approximately 1979 CE]—which sometimes goes under the title of the Islamization of Knowledge (*islāmiyyat al-maʿrifa*) and sometimes under the name of *al-taʾṣīl*—was not born in an intellectual vacuum. [Rather,] it was born under the circumstances of an epistemological siege (*al-muḥāṣara al-maʿrifiyya*) that the Muslim intellectual feels when, every time he wants to listen to and comprehend revelation, the sensory empiricism (*al-tajrībiyya al-ḥissiyya*) and the logical positivist (*al-waḍʿiyya al-manṭiqiyya*) methodologies reject him on the pretext that there is an absolute division between the information of revelation and the facts of material reality. (Hamid 1994: 7)

The founders of the Islamic state project understood that their goal of reducing Western influence over Sudan could not be achieved solely by resisting the West's political priorities for the region or by standing up to the demands of the World Bank (indeed, despite their bombastic rhetoric, they did very little of either). Rather, they contended that Sudanese must confront the far more pervasive and effective domination that the West exhibits: its control over the Muslim mind.

This new administrative body at the Ministry of Higher Education was tasked with "building [both] the sciences and educational curricula on Islamic foundations . . . to effect a radical reform (*iṣlāḥ jidhrī*) [that can] pull [them] out of intellectual dependency and correct some of the secular trends that still rule over many educational issues" (al-Jazuli 1998: 37). With this goal in mind, the Qurʾan and Sunna were to be reexamined both at the upper echelons of research and in national educational curricula for what they revealed about the natural sciences (e.g., Taha 1994, "On the Foundation of Fundamentalization in the Field of Natural Sciences"), agriculture (e.g., al-Khalifa 1995, "Plant and Science Agriculture among the Muslims"), economics (e.g., ʿAbbas 1995, "Islamic Economics: A Psycho-Ethical Paradigm"), politics (e.g., ʿIlwan 1997, "Leadership Characteristics in the [Qurʾanic] Story of 'The Two-Horned One'"), philosophy (e.g., Imam 1996, "Toward the Fundamentalization of the Teaching of Logic in the Islamic World"), media studies (e.g., Musa 1996, "Towards a Vision of Fundamentalization for the Media"), historiography (e.g., Salih 1995, "The Writing of History among the Muslims"), and literature (e.g., Mahjub 1994, "[Religious] Commitment in Islamic Literature"), to name but a few of the disciplines this project boldly sought to reevaluate.

Although the Administration for the Fundamentalization of Knowledge section at the Ministry of Higher Education and Scientific Research was phased out prior to the signing of the CPA, the agenda of *al-taʾṣīl* has retained its importance at the highest echelons of government to this day. Until the latter years of his life, Prof. Ahmad ʿAli al-Imam (d. 2012) served as the Advisor to the President on Fundamentalization Affairs, counseling not only the presidency, but "all apparatuses of the government" (Mawqiʿ al-Sūdān 2008) on how best to bring the knowledge on which they rely, and indeed all of their activities, in line with the fundamentals (*al-uṣūl*) of Islamic jurisprudential reasoning (al-Imam 2005: 6). Today, governmental or quasi-governmental think tanks such as the Epistemological Enlightenment Center (*Markaz al-Tanwīr al-Maʿrifī*) and the Renaissance and Civilizational Communication Forum (*Muntadā al-Nahḍa wa-l-Tawāṣul al-Ḥaḍārī*), the latter run by former Minister of Guidance and Pious Endowments and current head of the government Fiqh Council of Sudan (*Majmaʿ al-Fiqh al-Islāmī*), Dr. ʿIsam Ahmad al-Bashir, continue its mission.

Though the framework of identity politics and cultural authenticity has been a common model for understanding interventions such as the epistemological enlightenment project, it is clear that the *ta'ṣīl* approach was not merely a rejection of Western sciences to be replaced with "Islam" as the only valid source of knowledge. Rather, something more complex was at stake than the "invoking of a disputed heritage" deemed misleadingly monovocal "for ideological and political purposes" (Abaza 2002: 23). For example, the advocates of the Islamization of knowledge accepted the Western taxonomy of disciplines, even as they critiqued their reliance solely on positivist empiricist knowledge: "The approach to the discipline more than the discipline itself needed to be cast in a more Islamic frame," argued one international proponent of the Islamization of knowledge (Ahmed 1995: 426). Western achievement was celebrated in this literature (and indeed often cited as an achievement that would never have been possible without Arab genius), but it was revised to take into account the lessons of revelation and their moral centering. Its intellectuals made the argument that if Sudan was to succeed, it could not return to some ideal past, but rather had to evaluate by Islamic standards those knowledges and disciplines that have been misidentified as exclusively Western.

"[Among] the culture that fills our brains [in the Islamic world]," wrote Iraqi-American intellectual Taha Jabir al-ʿAlwani in one of the first issues of *al-Ta'ṣīl*, "is Western knowledge that we find in the universities in the social sciences and the humanities. It is true [however] that much of 'Western knowledge' is [in fact] human heritage, but the Western man subjugates it to his [own] heritage and his intellectual and social standards" (al-ʿAlwani 1994: 55). With this understanding in mind, al-ʿAlwani's Sudanese colleagues attempted to deprovincialize Islamic reform, placing it within the collective project of humanity, heretofore hijacked by the West and its secularist agenda.[6]

6 Often carelessly lumped together with other contemporary projects of Muslim knowledge reform, such as those of Salafi organizations (see Salomon 2009, 2013), what distinguished

The argument stood that reliance only on goals that could be measured materially had led to a de-moralization of the sciences, which must now be reoriented to God's goals for humanity and the spiritual development of man. Positivism was thus critiqued not solely for ignoring revelation, but also for placing of objectivity over morality. The *taʾṣīl* project aimed at harmonizing modern "Western" regimes of knowledge, frameworks of understanding, and modes of governance (that "human heritage" whose origins were in fact plural) with the moral foundations of Islam. Dr. Hasan al-Turabi perhaps best defined this project when he wrote of the necessity for a "unification of Knowledge" (*tawḥīd al-ʿilm*) with the commands of God:

> And it is not possible for the scientific renaissance to be realized in our country unless we mobilize behind it faith-based concepts (*al-maʿāni al-īmāniyya*) and [unless] we [avoid] leaving [science] only [to] technical and positivist knowledges. . . . We can only guarantee that we don't use knowledge for the oppression of man or for evil if we employ natural science for piety toward God—*swt*—and link it with the precepts of *al-sharīʿa.* (al-Turabi 1995: 13–14)

For al-Turabi, positivism meant science without ethics, and the only way to liberate man from oppression was for Muslims to reclaim science, evaluating its successes and failures on the basis of its ability to fulfill the ethical goals of Islam.[7]

It is important also to recognize that projects such as *al-taʾṣīl,* and the epistemological enlightenment it was said to have sparked, relied on certain logics of circulation in order to achieve their results. This meant that certain publics had to be conjured if the Islamization of knowledge project was to achieve its desired results. Here the ability to extend Islamic knowledge to newly literate publics was critical. The very people whom the intellectuals I quoted above saw as having been hoodwinked by secular positivist knowledges would be indispensable to the epistemological enlightenment that the Inqadh promised. Hasan al-Turabi explained:

---

the *taʾṣīl* project of the Inqadh was not merely its instrumentalist readings of the Qur'an but its attempt to combine them within distinctly modern epistemological, bureaucratic, social, and political categories that emerged out of the secular scientific Enlightenment. Thus, for example, such ontological assumptions written into the notion of the division between the social and natural sciences are not questioned here, rather these categories are taken for granted, while the content thereof is "Islamized." Such a move, as we will see in Chapter 5, far from being embraced by other sets of "fundamentalists," often received rebuke, being accused of succumbing to the intellectual ordering of the West and thus blotting out the very unique epistemological categories provided by the Islamic tradition.

7 The fact that the period in which al-Turabi was in power was characterized by many as a time in which the government in fact flouted Islamic ethical norms (as al-Turabi himself recognized on pp. 92–3, above) while insisting on them for others, should not go unmentioned. I discuss local articulations of such criticisms in the story I tell at the beginning of Chapter 5.

> Today the *ʿulamāʾ* [elite scholars] in Islamic societies represent a class that monopolizes religion and stores it away. But knowledge of religion should be spread widely, even if people are of different abilities. In the society of the Prophet (*ṣlʿm*), one is not able to distinguish a group of companions of the Prophet who are the *ʿulamāʾ* class. Even the word 'scholar' (*ʿālim*) itself was used with a general meaning. Yet, today [it has taken on an] historical meaning [and] has come to describe a person who wears specific clothes and has arrived at a certain degree [of distinction] and has a delimited standard, isolated from the general Muslim public. (al-Turabi 1995: 16)

Although al-Turabi presents his thesis as revolutionary, in fact, democratization of access to knowledge and the reorganization of the hierarchies involved in its transmission had been occurring gradually throughout the nineteenth and twentieth centuries across the Muslim world, creating new kinds of religious intellectuals (and average Muslims as well) and transforming the public spheres that they inhabited (Abu Rabiʿ 1996). This said, the Islamist regime in Sudan spearheaded an especially massive project of augmenting access to higher learning that should not go unrecognized. This project resulted in higher levels of education and increased participation in the study and dissemination of Islamic knowledge, which was taken up not as a threat to the regime's firm control over theological interpretation, but rather as an opportunity to manufacture an Islamic public upon which its political projects could be built. Without denying the importance of skilled teachers, the Inqadh knowledge project contended that truth could only be arrived at through the efforts of individual actors engaged with the foundational texts of Islam. In this model, traditional scholars were seen as impediments to the activation of Islam among the masses. Much better suited to this task were the lawyers, engineers, and European PhD holders who understood how the world worked.[8] Though the sociological reality presents a far more complex picture, in which religious authority is not simply

8 The CV of Hasan al-Turabi, a Sorbonne-educated lawyer and PhD, is well known (Hamdi 1998). Figures like Ahmad ʿAli al-Imam, the Presidential Advisor on Fundamentalization Affairs, are less so, and yet his biography is quite typical of Inqadh intellectuals: an Islamic leaning, but Western educated, elite. Al-Imam had a traditional religious training as a young man (al-Imam 2003), but went on to higher education not in the Islamic world but at the University of Edinburgh in Qurʾanic studies, where he received his PhD (al-Imam 2006). The fact that none of the Inqadh intellectuals were traditional *ʿulamāʾ* did not stop them, however, from trying to found a *new* standard for Islamic interpretive authority in Sudan, despite al-Turabi's gestures towards the everyman. Ahmad ʿAli al-Imam, for example, was the director from 1990 to 1998 of the University of the Holy Quran (*Jāmiʿat al-Qurʾān al-Karīm*), one of the new Islamic studies universities in Sudan founded by the regime, whose goal was to produce new cadres of Islamic scholars. He later became the president of the government Islamic Fiqh Council (*Majmaʿ al-Fiqh al-Islāmī*), a body that is also trying to standardize Islamic authority in Sudan.

democratized but rather plays out in new and interesting ways in these new contexts, Inqadh intellectuals sought to present their program as an egalitarian and voluntarist approach to the attainment of religious knowledge. In this vision, since God and the Prophet have already acted in revealing divine knowledge, agency in attaining this knowledge is placed primarily in the hands of the Muslim individual. That individual needn't restrict him/herself to traditional curricula (indeed such curricula had isolated their students from the very world they were meant to reform): all knowledge, if read within the context of revelation, could be Islamic knowledge.

With this project, the regime quite consciously made use of the apparatus of the state—its abstract sovereignty, its bureaucracy, and its cultural hegemony (Hallaq 2013: 19–36)—not as an inconvenient assemblage into which it tried to squeeze an essentially incompatible Islamic moral framework, but rather as an effective tool for constructing the kind of moral society it envisioned. The unique ability of the state to project its sovereignty abstractly (i.e., *ta'ṣīl* as a *Sudanese* endeavor, in which all Muslims could participate regardless of sectarian affiliation), the placement of a knowledge reform project within a bureaucratic structure that citizens came into contact with on an everyday basis, and "the ability to work through the various units of civil society . . . [to] generat[e] the greatest sum of social and cultural consent" (Hallaq 2013: 35) were adopted as opportunities to produce the kind of epistemological enlightenment that only state power could conjure. The Islamic state here is neither an impossibility nor an oxymoron, but rather the perfect vehicle for establishing a vision of Islam that is voluntarist in its aspirations and ubiquitous in its spread.

In an era of deep political uncertainty, such as the one in which Sudan seemed constantly mired, the state sought to mobilize Islamic knowledge, to quote the Presidential Advisor on Fundamentalization Affairs, "to return what has escaped from its foundation back to its foundation another time . . . building methodologies of life for society or the *umma* on fixed fundamentals" (al-Imam 2005: 5–6). The various ruptures that are central to the nation-building process—chief among them the exclusions involved in the project of defining the citizens of the Sudanese nation as a Muslim "we"—were bridged through this discourse of certainty: fundamentals replacing failures, foundations grounding a state that was otherwise spiraling out of control. Yet the idea that Islamic knowledge could simply be reawakened, modernized, and spread to a ready public and that this would lead to a better future for Sudan left as many questions as it did answers. What exactly makes knowledge Islamic rather than secular? From where can we derive Islamic knowledge? What are the "fundamentals" to which we must return in doing so? Does knowledge lead inevitably to certainty and thus to a more prosperous future for the nation, or might an increase in knowledge open up new horizons of doubt, thus putting into question the instrumental relationship between knowledge and material success that the robust "corporate" logic of the Inqadh regime forwarded?

Finally, what is the relationship between Islamic authority and Islamic knowledge? Must its modes of circulation be egalitarian, or is its proper use contingent on its positioning within hierarchical social networks: teachers and students, cognoscenti and average Muslims? The undeniable thirst among the public to answer these questions, and thus to insist on the increased importance of Islamic knowledge as a reservoir upon which to draw for solutions to the nation's concerns, was a key mark of the success of the Sudanese Islamic state. The multitude of responses provided to these questions, however, serves to remind us that the solutions they elicited could never be fully determined by the agenda of those who sought to control it.

Evidence against Evidence

As we saw in the previous chapter, Sufi Muslims have both served as a ready public upon which Islamists staged their projects and often stood in oppositional or uncomfortable relationship to the eventual flowering of such projects. Studying Sufi publics in Sudan helps us to see the precise ways in which the Islamic state project of the regime has succeeded and where it has been reworked toward new ends. Examining Sufi engagement with the knowledge projects the regime put forward is one way to measure the effects of the Islamic state project on the populace it aimed to shape. Here we can observe a sector of Sudanese society that was both deeply influenced by the state's agenda in creating a public space for Islamic modes of discourse and reasoning, but deeply skeptical of the way it mobilized traditional Islamic knowledge to do so.

Franz Rosenthal's claim that "there is no other concept that has been as operative a determinant of Muslim civilization in all its aspects as *ʿilm* [knowledge]," that, as he put it, the story of Islam is the story of the "triumph of knowledge" and its "dominance over all aspects of Muslim intellectual, spiritual, and social life" to a degree unparalleled in other religions and civilizations (Rosenthal 1970: 2, 334, 335–40), has been a pervasive and relatively unquestioned understanding among scholars of Islam since at least the middle of the last century. Moreover, in the present-day world of mass-education, mass-literacy, and the burgeoning of new forms of media, knowledge is said to be even more readily available, and the transmission of the tools of the traditional Islamic sciences to a newly literate public as what most clearly distinguishes contemporary Islam from its predecessors. If knowledge was once triumphant among trend-setting elites, these scholars seem to argue, it has now triumphed among the masses as well.[9]

9 For one recent example of the thesis that Muslim modernity is characterized by an intensification of interest in Islamic knowledge among the Muslim masses, see the collection on Islamic schooling edited by Robert Hefner and Muhammad Qasim Zaman. In this volume

Yet, what such observations fail to take into consideration is that, contrary to the view of Islamist actors such as the Inqadh regime, knowledge is in fact quite often understood as a *qualified* good, which if mobilized outside of proper bounds has significant potential for causing damage. The "objectification of religion" (Starrett 1998) that such scholars invoke not only overlooks the fact that meaning can never truly be abstracted but is instead always situated within certain disciplines or the traditions that give them shape (Asad 2015), but also fails to notice that not everyone in the Muslim world is as swept away by the "democratization of knowledge" as scholars writing on Islamic renewal seem to suggest (e.g., Eickelman 1978, 1985, 1991, 1992, 1999). The various neo-*ʿulamāʾ* groups and arguments in their favor that have recently sprung up in the Middle East in response to the proliferation of Islamic militant organizations are one example of such skepticism (Hellyer 2015; Pierret 2013). Sudanese Sufis' recognition that knowledge must be situated within strictly structured networks of transmission to be effective is another. Such arguments not only force us to question teleological portrayals of "Islamic Awakening," but also force us to examine the ultimate impact of the reforms of the Islamic state project. Through tracing its itinerary as it trickled through Sudanese society, we can see how this project was reworked and repositioned by the new Muslim intellectuals the regime sought to fashion.

The recognition that a wide cross-section of Sufis maintained a relationship to knowledge that had not been entirely homogenized by projects in knowledge reform such as *al-taʾṣīl* should not blind us to the fact that Sufis were deeply affected by the new government-promoted forms of Islamic knowledge and their modes of circulation, even if they sought to bring attention to their limits. Indeed, through the work of organizations such as the National Council for the Mindfulness of God and Those Who Are Mindful (NCMG, whose formation I discussed in the previous chapter), Sufism itself was going through its own process of *taʾṣīl*, in which its knowledges were being brought in line with the "sources" (*uṣūl*) of Islam by a deeply interventionist government project.

Yet, the dense intertwining of Sufi and reformist logic that occurred in venues like the NCMG should not lead us to assume that the uniqueness of Sufi epistemologies was being sanded away, even if Sufis were provoked by the questions the government asked. In recognizing this, I hope to add to the recent conversation spearheaded by scholars such as Amira Mittermaier

---

Hefner notes that while "of course there have always been different carriers of religious knowledge in the Muslim world . . . plurality and contest of meanings acquired new intensity in the 1970s and 1980s, as debates over Islamic knowledge moved from elite circles into a restless and mobile mass society" (Hefner 2007: 33). Another iteration of this argument can be found in many of the essays included in Eickelman and Anderson 2003.

that looks at how imaginal realms—here that of the *sirr*, or "secret," the shorthand that Sufis use to discuss those higher realms of truth, off-limits to average Muslims—"constitute a vibrant aspect of the Islamic Revival," even if their practitioners remain "in a continuous if ambivalent dialogue with [a] reformism" that often critiques their foundations (Mittermaier 2011: 6). In Sudan, such dialogue pushed Sufis to devise creative ways both to respond to the reformists' critiques and to allow their own knowledge-ethics to flourish.

Reformists often dismissed Sufi categories of secret or inspired knowledge—*al-ʿilm al-ladunī, al-ʿilm al-mawhūb, ʿilm al-bāṭin, ʿilm al-ghayb, ʿilm al-kashf*[10]—as little more than hocus pocus having no clear basis in the textual sources of Islam. However, instead of arguing for an Islam beyond the texts, a knowledge of the heart in contradistinction to the knowledge of the book, Sufis in various contexts upheld both the idea of the existence of mystical, experiential knowledge *and* the idea that it must be founded in textual evidence. In other words, for Sufis scriptural "evidence" of the sort that the reformists demand was central even to the justification of those few modes of mystical knowledge that in themselves pose a deep challenge to the absolute necessity for scriptural evidence, since they derive from direct access to God, the Prophet, or a hidden realm.

To take but one example, in a polemical tract written against Salafi groups like the Sudanese Ansar al-Sunna, Hamid Ahmad Babikir, a Sufi intellectual and writer, tries to justify the idea that there is revelation to non-prophets (*waḥī li-ghayr al-anbiyāʾ*), and so by implication to the Sufi *awliyāʾ* (holy men, sing. *walī*) as well, in order to defend the notion that Sufi shaykhs have privileged access to secret realms of knowledge that the masses do not have (Babikir, no date: 48). In order to prove his argument, the author quotes several Qurʾanic verses that show God revealing knowledge to individuals who are not prophets, such as the bee (16:68: *wa awḥā rabbuka ilā al-naḥl)*, the mother of Moses (28:7: *wa awḥaynā ilā umm musā*), and the disciples of Jesus (5:111: *wa idh awḥaytu ilā al-ḥawāriyyin*). It would appear that even knowledge entirely without scriptural foundation (i.e., direct revelation based on personal communication with God) is justified here by textual evidence.

10 Though there is considerable overlap between these terms in practice, I will attempt a definition in the following: *al-ʿilm al-mawhūb* = "donated knowledge," a knowledge which is granted to the believer through the grace of God; *ʿilm al-bāṭin* = knowledge of the inner, deeper subtextual truths that go beyond superficial surface meanings of both texts and the material world; *ʿilm al-ghayb* = knowledge of that which is hidden in individual biography or history; *ʿilm al-kashf* = "revelatory knowledge," about the future, for example; *al-ʿilm al-ladunī* = "knowledge from our presence," knowledge that comes from God, a knowledge indicating access to a whole hidden realm, at times even an alternate universe, which intersects with this world in the biographies of a few select holy men who have passports to both realms, derived from the difficult to parse Qurʾanic verse *wa ʿallamnāhu min ladunnā ʿilman* (*al-Kahf*: 65).

Here we see clearly not the hegemony of one epistemological stance over another, but a creative use of both the notion of textual evidence and that of hidden knowledge to construct a nuanced position that constrains and enables its participants in very specific ways. The idea of revelation to non-prophets expressed in the Qur'an becomes for these Sufis "evidence" that a Sufi following a *walī* in fact *needs no evidence* in order to follow the latter's directives, since the evidence for such a practice has already been established. It is, in this sense, evidence against evidence. The fact that Sufis were writing such apologetic literature in the years of the Inqadh knowledge projects is indicative of the fact that the agenda of *al-ta'ṣīl*, of returning "what has escaped from its foundation back to its foundation another time," did indeed come to structure how Sufis understood their practices and how they justified themselves to a wider public. Yet these Sufis were also aware that the government's knowledge projects were changing the way in which Islamic knowledge circulated. In public and private fora, they criticized the intellectual foundations of the government project and presented their own epistemological position that stood in contradistinction not only to that of the present government but to the knowledge-centrism of twenty-first-century Islamic revivalist thought more broadly.

Secrets and the Perils of Knowledge

While pamphlets such as Babikir's clearly (though unstably) situate Sufis within the sorts of discourses of certainty prevalent in contemporary Sudan, the aspects of Sufi theories of knowledge that were not entirely normalized by government knowledge reform projects are less visible within their literatures. Instead, they are most keenly observed by the ethnographer who examines not only metadiscourse about knowledge, but the very process of attaining knowledge itself, "the cultural and social dimensions of epistemology" (Lambek 1993: 8) that play out in the everyday practices of the various religious groups s/he studies. Here we clearly see that the triumph of knowledge, and the attendant claims to its democratization promised by these government projects, are problematized by a Sufi epistemology that relies on the notion of restricted knowledge (the secret, or *sirr*) and a spiritual elite (the *awliyā'*) that has exclusive access to it. While government-allied Islamists saw the creation and dissemination of Islamic knowledge to a newly educated Muslim public as central to the rebirth of Sudanese society, and the process of freeing knowledge from the confines of the *'ulamā'* and spreading its benefits to the masses as a critical goal of their "Islamic revival," many Sufis with whom I worked problematized such modes of publicity that claimed Islamic rebirth could be achieved solely (or even primarily) through the production and transmission of knowledge.

For these Sufis, the transmission of knowledge imagined by the epistemological enlightenment project was crucial to one stage in the process of contemporary Islamic revitalization. Yet other practices based on the recognition that certain realms of knowledge were inaccessible to the average believer, and that therefore an ethic of disciplined submission to a shaykh was indispensable, were equally crucial to any contemporary reassertion of Islam in the public and private lives of Sudanese. Let us examine one such practice that can help us to identify the nature of the distinction that the Sufis upheld.

On the banks of the Blue Nile, a few hours south of Khartoum, there is a sizeable town called Jar al-Nabi,[11] widely known among Sufi Muslims as a holy city (*buqaʿ*), due to the burial of a line of shaykhs in its environs and the presence of an active *masīd* (center for Sufi fraternity, education, and worship [al-Tayyib 2005]) in its midst. A sleepy, beautiful little hamlet, flanked by banana and mango gardens on one side and the wide steppe of the Butana on the other, Jar al-Nabi is the kind of place where urban Sudanese take retreat, sometimes simply to escape the pressures of work and family life and other times for more pressing reasons, such as physical or mental ailments. A key activity that takes place in the *masīd* is what is referred to as "prophetic medicine" (*al-ṭibb al-nabawī*), in which a curative device called *bakhra* plays a paramount role. *Bakhra* consists of a sheet of paper on which is written the *basmala* ("in the name of God, the Merciful, the Compassionate") and several sections from the Qurʾanic verse *Sūrat Yūnus* 81: "Moses said [to the sorcerers], 'What you have come with is magic, and God will void it, for God does not encourage the work of the corrupt.'" The concept is that the power of God in voiding the magic of the sorcerers that Moses faced is transferred to the immediate situation of the patient and the illness from which he or she suffers, which is also thought to derive from "magical" causes. Also included on the *bakhra* are a set of two stars and symbols known as the Seal of Solomon (*Khātim Sulaymān*), and a set of numbers said to refer to Qurʾanic verses (the numbers refer to letters that begin these verses). The papers are stuffed with incense and burned, and it is reported that the fumes cure illnesses caused by curses and other forms of magic.

Once, while sitting with some writers of such *bakhra* under the shade of a *rākūba* (a lean-to-like structure), I inquired into the meaning of the set of stars and symbols shown in the *Khātim Sulaymān* and into the sources of its efficacy. A *bakhra* writer, whom we will call Hasab al-Rasul, answered as follows:

> The *khātim* is a private secret (*sirr khāṣṣ*). No one knows its true meaning except the shaykh . . . [the shaykh] gives you the form. But he is the

11 I use aliases for the name of this town and its residents in order to protect anonymity.

> only one who has the secret (*al-sirr ʿindu huwa*). And for the person who writes without permission, [the writing] is of no benefit. [One] only [can write] with *permission* from the shaykh, and [if] the shaykh has the permission from the chain of shaykhs [of which he is a part] . . . [I mean to say that] if your impact is to be strong, your shaykh must be strong, because the evil one will not leave [the individual he has possessed] except through what is done by the shaykh. If an evil one made a curse (*ʿamal*) over someone, and you read over that person a reading [of the Qurʾan in order to cure him, you should recognize that] if you have no ability, and you don't have a strong shaykh, the Satan will jump into you. It's a war and you are warring against the evil one. And if you are in such a war and don't have a shaykh with a strong lineage (*sanad qawī*), the Satan will jump into you [i.e., the person needing cure], or jump into your children. Because of this, it is necessary that your shaykh be of a high level. The closer he is to God, the stronger is his ability.

In his explanation of the *bakhra,* Hasab al-Rasul lays out a clear theory of knowledge. Indeed, three points in the above passage are worth noting. First, it is argued that the Seal of Solomon is representative of a realm of knowledge within Islam that is secret. There is no relationship between the profession of writing *bakhra* and having actual knowledge of the illnesses or the means to cure them. The writers remain mere functionaries, whereas the cure comes from the shaykh alone. Thus, the lay Sufi who writes the *bakhra* has access to the forms, but no access to the knowledge that underlies them. In order for the layman to heal effectively, he cannot merely pick up a book and read, instead he needs the explicit permission of one who has access to this knowledge; and even then he will have no understanding of it: it remains eternally secret.

The second point made is that this secret knowledge is passed down through a genealogy, the "strong lineage" and "chain of shaykhs" to which Hasab al-Rasul refers. We see here that the power to heal cannot come through a mastery of knowledge, spiritual aptitudes, or inculcated virtuous states, but only through one's genealogical relationship to other holy men, whether in terms of discipleship or blood relation.

The third point Hasab al-Rasul makes is that the popularization of this knowledge, its circulation beyond a restricted circle—that is, what happens when one uses this knowledge without the permission of the shaykh—is extremely dangerous. Not only could it be ineffectual, but using this knowledge incorrectly could cause actual harm: Satan possessing you. Thus, the higher realms of knowledge should not be accessed by the masses, and those who try to access this knowledge and use it incorrectly put themselves in great danger.

In making such claims, Hasab al-Rasul puts forward a clear critique of the idea that knowledge alone is sufficient to developing proper Islamic practice. The celebration of mass Islamic education, the penetration and indeed ubiquity of mass-mediated information about Islam in the life of the average Muslim that the Islamist vanguard embraced in its epistemological enlightenment project, is branded in Hasab al-Rasul's approach as a kind of arrogance. Here, an argument familiar from critiques posed by the traditional scholarly class ('ulamā') against the interpretive practices of a rising cadre of new Muslim intellectuals (Zaman 2002), untrained in traditional institutes of learning, is elevated to the level of the supernatural: Satan could possess one who uses knowledge for which he has no permission.[12] The redemptive status of knowledge, which we saw proclaimed above in the discourses of certainty embodied in terms like ta'ṣīl and the modes of mass circulation that accompanied it, is cast into grave doubt by this theology of secrets. For Sufis like Hasab al-Rasul, knowledge is only beneficial if emplaced within the web of social relations that God has established; it can never act alone to redeem us. If the social relations employed in an act of knowledge transmission do not map onto the ones that God has laid down for humanity, this transmission of knowledge has serious potential for harm. *knowledge = redemptive*

While many Muslims scoffed at Sufi insistence that some knowledge must remain secret, or otherwise restricted to a spiritual elite (often responding with the hadith: "The Prophet said: 'He who conceals useful knowledge will be bridled with bridles of fire [in the hereafter]'"),[13] for Sufis like Hasab al-Rasul, the dangers of misuse outweighed the promise of rebirth. Thus we can read the insistence on the "secret" as a direct challenge to the popularization of Islamic knowledge thesis put forward by the proponents of the ta'ṣīl project. While no Sufi would thereby argue that the Qur'an and Sunna, or the *fiqh* commentaries that actualize them, should be restricted knowledge, the argument that there are realms of nondiscursive knowledge that supplement the "fundamentals," attained through training or passed down through blood, was central to Sufi knowledge-ethics among the groups with which I worked. Thus the wide-armed embrace of "Islamic knowledge" as unproblematically central to enlightenment was cast into doubt by Sufis who recognized both the promise and perils of our information age. These Sufis contended that while Muslims had access to religious knowledge in unprecedented quantity in the twenty-first century, if this knowledge was not mobilized within a prescribed network of social relations, it had the potential to

religious knowledge needs to be applied to social context

12 The "evidence" for needing a shaykh in all endeavors of Islamic knowledge was often *Sūrat al-Furqān* 59: "He who created the heavens and the earth and that which is between them, and then stretched out on the throne, [He is] the merciful one! Ask an expert about Him (*f-as'al bihi khabīran*)." The shaykh, of course, was identified as this expert.

13 *qāla al-rasūl: man katama 'ilman nāfi'an, uljima bi-lijām min nār.*

do serious harm. It was the challenge that projects such as epistemological enlightenment posed to these time-tested networks of religious authority, and the idea that knowledge alone and unmediated could do the work of Islamic renewal, that seemed most troubling to my Sufi interlocutors.

Blood Knowledge and the Critique of *al-Ijtihād*

The revelation of secrets among the Sufis with whom I worked rarely took place, even through discipleship. Most often such knowledge was passed down within families, though not through any pedagogical process. Instead its transmission was said to come through the substance of the blood. One shaykh from Jar al-Nabi, whom we will call Shaykh Mustafa, explained this to me, again through the example of healing:

> The one who tries to cure through his own understanding of Prophetic Medicine (*al-mujtahid*) sometimes cures and sometimes does not . . . but the person who has inherited [the skill] from his father, from his family [will have a special ability to heal] . . . because the inherited thing[s] are secrets. . . . [Things] inherited are more secure because they are secrets, and secrets are what God has . . . *al-ʿilm al-ladunī*, [knowledge, which is] not academic. There are people who do healing through their own understanding (*bi-l-ijtihād*), with an academic approach. . . . But we learned by means of . . . the surroundings in which [we] live, of [our] family. . . . [Such knowledge] is inherited, like genes . . . it's in your blood. It is not a condition that the father must be present. Even if the father died and left you while you were in the stomach of your mother for only two months, it is still going to [be] present in your blood, the light [is still going to be present] because you are his progeny. . . . It is in the flow of the blood.

This theory of knowledge as something transmitted not through didactic means but through the blood of chosen individuals was central to Sufi epistemologies in Jar al-Nabi. It is interesting that Shaykh Mustafa puts his explanation in terms of *al-ijtihād*, a term that in Islamic thought is generally restricted to conversations in jurisprudence (*fiqh*), where it denotes an independent reappraisal of the sources of Islam uncoupled from the authority of legal scholars and the traditional schools (*al-madhāhib*) to which they belong, a notion that was key to the renewal advocated by Islamists in Sudan (El-Affendi 1991: 170–71).

In extending his critique of *al-ijtihād*, and the new configurations of knowledge and power that underlie it, to the issue of Islamic healing, Shaykh Mustafa's concept of blood knowledge gives birth to a notion of facticity that militates against the hegemony of projects in knowledge reform such as *al-ta'ṣīl* and its attendant claims of universal accessibility. Thus, while Sufis rely on evidentialist epistemologies (and thus even the practice of *al-ijtihād* itself in approaching the texts) to communicate their religious positions in many contexts, they also understand correct Islamic practice, in this case prophetic medicine, to be based on a knowledge that is inherited rather than disseminated through didactic means.

The Sufi critique of the egalitarian impulse at the heart of Islamist understandings of *al-ijtihād*, the notion that all qualified Muslims have equal purchase on their sacred texts, was seen nowhere more clearly than in my informants' discussion of the *walī*, the category of believer mentioned in the Qur'an (e.g., 10:62) as possessing a special closeness to God. For my informants, this figure could only be explained by relying on the episteme of the secret, in direct contrast to those who argued that such a station could be attained through proper displays of piety and by attaining the knowledge that makes that piety possible.[14] A Sufi adept in Jar al-Nabi explained this to me as follows:

> The status of being a *walī* does not come through independent striving (*al-ijtihād*) . . . There is knowledge then that cannot come through *ijtihād*, it is knowledge that God grants to whom he wants (*'ilm yahibuhu allāh li-man yashā'*). I could decide to seclude myself and become an ascetic, my fasting could be serious and eternal, and I could stay up

14 Though the following quote comes from a Sudanese Salafi tractate, and thus does not represent the knowledge project of the regime, note the contrast between the way in which the *walī* is described here and by the Sufi adept I discuss above:

> God in his majesty created all people equally. [As the hadith says]: "All of you descend from Adam and Adam comes from dust (*kullakum li-ādam wa ādam min turāb*)" . . . and [all people] came out from the stomachs of their mothers . . . and because of this [as the hadith says], "an Arab is not better than a barbarian except by piety" (*lā faḍl li-'arabī 'alā 'ajamī illā bi-l-taqwā*), just like a white man is not better than a black man or the opposite, or a rich man over a poor man or the opposite, except by piety. . . . Most people do not know that God commands all of them to become righteous *awliyā'* to him, and that the category of being a *walī* is open to all of them. Thus, God does not limit to [this category] a specific group or people, and God does not select an elite people as *awliyā'* from their birth and others as non-*awliyā'*. This is what [some] people imagine [him to do], and thus the categorizations of some people [as *awliyā'*] by others. . . . Allah created two signs or qualities that if they are fulfilled by the worshiper and he takes them on, then he can be a *walī* to God: they are faith and piety (*al-īmān wa-l-taqwā*). ('Abd al-Hamid 2005: 1–3)

Thus, for this Salafi author, the position of *walī* can be attained by any Muslim who remains pious in following the commands of Qur'an and Sunna. Here it is not at all a restricted spiritual station, as it is described by the Sufi adept above. Rather, the path to this spiritual station is a clear one, and it is achieved by human effort. Further, the language of social equality at the beginning of this passage is no coincidence, as many see Sufi hierarchies within the *ṭarīqa* as anathema to the egalitarian goals they understand Islam as expressing.

all night in prayer, and pray five times [per day] in the mosque. [But to do so] so that I become a *walī*? You don't become one [through such pious acts]. Only if God wants you to become a *walī* [do you become one]. . . . With *ijtihād* you can become *taqī* (pious), you can become *ṣāliḥ* (righteously upright), but not a *walī*, because there is a difference between the category of being a wali (*wilāya*) and that of being righteous (*ṣāliḥ*).

practical stipulations

Here it is clear that there is a practical impossibility in reaching certain realms of knowledge. Not only is *ijtihād* insufficient, but no manner of piety will help the Muslim attain them. Thus, in this instance, Sufism seems not about enabling access to *maʿrifa* (the secret knowledge to which these informants refer), as so much of the popular trade in Sufi literature in the West assumes, but rather about dealing with the existential reality of the impossibility that one faces in doing so. For these Sufis, such spiritual heights are exclusive, so in order to remain rightly guided, one must enter into a disciplined relationship with a shaykh—hence the common saying among Sufis, "If you have no shaykh, your shaykh is Satan."[15] Since knowledge can only get the adept so far, it is not knowledge but discipline in the face of one's ignorance that puts the adept on the correct path to proper piety (see also Silverstein 2007: 43).

Sufi Discipline and the Impossibility of Knowledge

If anyone in Sudan has access to the full palate of information technology available to a newly and well-networked capital, and if anyone might be expected to express confidence in knowledge of the Islamic fundamentals as a path to enlightenment, it would be the elite urban youth who make up the followers of Shaykh al-Amin ʿUmar al-Amin, whose *zāwiya* is located in the shade of his palatial three-story home in Omdurman.[16] Indeed, it was precisely to these upper-class youth that Islamist intellectuals were speaking, at least in their more highbrow writings calling for epistemological enlightenment. Well-educated, Internet-savvy, young, and well-traveled, this is a group whose confidence in the importance of *taʿlīm* (education) for righteous worship is evident in the fact that, uniquely in Sudan, their *dhikr* circle includes not only the singing of *madīḥ* poetry and rhythmic chanting,

educated youth- pivotal for social change

---

15 *law mā ʿindak shaykh, shaykhak shayṭān*, a somewhat international sentiment among Sufis that was expanded in rhyming fashion among Sufis in Sudan: *wa law ma ʿindak wird, inta girid! wa law ma ʿindak maḥabba, ma ʿindak ḥabba!* (And if you have no Sufi litany, you are a monkey! And if you have no love [for the shaykhs], you have nothing!)

16 See Willemse 2012 for further discussion of the shaykh and his followers.

but also a short sermon from their shaykh (referred to as *irshād*, guidance) after every *dhikr* cycle. Like many Sufi orders, they also hold *fiqh* lessons, but few are as adamant about their importance as Shaykh al-Amin, who holds them directly after the *dhikr* ceremony, and repeats again and again the famous hadiths: "Requesting knowledge is a duty on each Muslim, male and female" (*ṭalab al-ʿilm farīḍa ʿala kull muslim wa muslima*) and "The merit of knowledge is better than the merit of worship" (*inn faḍl al-ʿilm khayran min faḍl al-ʿibāda*).

Thus it was somewhat to my surprise that, on talking to Shaykh al-Amin's followers, I encountered a theory of secrets quite similar to the one I had found in the rural town of Jar al-Nabi, existing comfortably alongside an equal commitment to the *fiqh*-based knowledge that the *zāwiya* promoted. The idea that there is a part of religion that is private and off-limits to the average adept, the *sirr*, seemed to persist even among youth committed to the information age and to the idea of an ever more accessible religious public sphere.

A young university-educated man whom I befriended in Shaykh al-Amin's *zāwiya*, and whom we will call Faris, explained to me the kind of discipline necessary for the committed disciple and its connection to knowledge. He said:

> As for the *faqīr* (adept, lit. "impoverished one"), once he takes the *ṭarīqa* (way) from the shaykh to whom he has attached himself, it is incumbent upon him to implement the instructions [the shaykh gives] in their entirety. It's like the army: "Come!" He comes. "Go!" He goes. "Sit!" He sits. "Do the litanies!" He does the litanies. . . . Why? Because this arrangement is taken from the *Sunna* of what is said in *Sūrat al-Kahf* where *sayyidnā* Moses met Khidr. . . . [So like Moses to whom Khidr said "follow" (*ittabaʿ*)], the most important thing in the *ṭarīqa* is to follow (*takūn tābiʿ*), like a dead person between the hands of the washer (*ka-l-mayyit bayn yaday al-ghasāl*). If he turns you over this way, you turn. And you don't protest. . . . And Khidr told Moses not to question him . . . that he would have trouble being patient and this was a difficult and troubling way of doing things. [It is like the Sufi order:] a difficult path. . . . So . . . [we] are taking the whole thing about following [one's shaykh] from the story about Moses when he met the prophet Khidr. . . . As for the shaykh, God has given him knowledge (*rabbanā ʿallamū ʿilm*), the knowledge of the truth (*ʿilm al-ḥaqīqa*).

Here Faris refers to the famous story from the Qur'an (18: 65–82), wherein God shows Moses through an encounter with a mysterious sage (identified in later tradition with Khidr) that there is a knowledge that is off-limits even to the most renowned of men, and that one must therefore put oneself under the tutelage of a sage who knows. The counter-example of Moses, who failed to trust the knowledge of Khidr and did not understand that what appeared to be forbidden acts were actually beneficial under a higher wisdom, is seen as a warning by Sufi adepts. The kind of discipline Faris advocated requires one to be like a "corpse in the hand of the washer," passive to the will of one's shaykh. This is the posture the Sufi adept must cultivate in the face of his inability ever to reach the highest stages of knowledge. Here, in another example of "evidence against evidence," Faris argues that the story of Khidr and Moses from the Qur'an necessitates the Muslim's surrender not only to Qur'anic knowledge but also to one who knows, an obedience that comes about through the recognition of our existential ignorance. Such a use of evidence against evidence shows that Sufism, far from being a rejection of scriptural knowledge in place of mystical praxis, is a creative means of engaging both, a lived hermeneutics.

In this same conversation with Faris, I tried to understand how the shaykh's access to this inspired knowledge (and in turn the adept's lack of access to it) affected the kinds of moral reasoning in which adepts are involved. I asked Faris, pointing to a key issue about which there is much agreement "in the evidence": "If a shaykh told you to drink alcohol, what would you do?" He answered:

> I would drink it right away. Why? Because it possibly is not actually alcohol. It could be milk. . . . In the end it is about belief (*al-iʿtiqād*). So if I went to [my shaykh] and he said, "Hey you, drink this alcohol," I would drink it right away. But if someone else came and said, "Drink this alcohol," even if he was a shaykh and it wasn't [my shaykh], I wouldn't drink it. Because my belief is in one man . . . or also [his shaykh] and [his] successor. . . . If any of these people said to go to the top of [a] building and jump, I'd jump right away. Why? Because your belief is in that shaykh, that he doesn't want to harm you, that he wants what is good for you.

Here we see that despite the fact that Faris bases his relationship with his shaykh on evidence found in the Qur'an (the story of Khidr and Moses), the *specific choices* he makes in life (whether in worship, moral reasoning, or social relations) are not based on the collection of evidence from the Qur'an and Sunna, or even from a direct experience of mystical inspiration, but rather are determined from within an epistemological framework that recognizes the impossibility of accessing certain kinds of knowledge and thus requires obedience to a shaykh.

It is important to add here that not only is confidence in the redemptive power of knowledge, such as that promoted by the government's epistemological enlightenment project, shattered by a position like that of Faris, but that aspects of other globalized forms of public Islam are problematized as well. The question of, as Faris put it, "not any shaykh, but *my* shaykh" becomes central here. Though one can imagine a virtual means of discipleship, Faris puts forth a theory of Islam opposed to the idea of a universal knowledge applicable to all Muslims and promoted by delocalized media such as the Internet. Instead, truth is relative within the context of the particular disciplined relationship an individual Muslim has to his or her shaykh ("But if someone else came and said, drink this alcohol, even if he was a shaykh and it wasn't [my shaykh], I wouldn't drink it," compare Chih 2007: 26). Like the practices of knowledge transmission Brinkley Messick (1993) discusses—those face-to-face disciplines he sees as being swept away by the abstract authority of the bureaucratic state—Faris argues for a religiosity that requires human presence.

A Landscape of Unknowing

If, for these Sufis, the highest realms of knowledge come through the blood and through God's selection, then for the masses of lay adepts, this knowledge is, in the end, practically speaking, unobtainable. Such a position of course renders questionable the value of knowledge-based Islamic reform as propounded by government projects in epistemological enlightenment. Yet there is something more at play here than merely laying out a bleak landscape of epistemic loss in contradistinction to government triumphalism. Instead, this Sufi epistemology might best be analytically framed in the language of "unknowing." Michael Sells's work on negative theology, or what he calls "apophatic language" (1994), is instructive in this regard. Sells's work is unique in that instead of understanding such ways of talking about God and religious truths as a mere rhetorical strategy to evade a fixed answer (or simply the "problem of language to express the unexpressable"), he sees the tension as productive. He argues that what apophatic mysticism offers is "a radical critique of essentialism":

> Essentialism is the notion that we can define . . . the essence of something and can then tell you what that is. And by so doing, [we] can possess it intellectually, or possess it through . . . thought or through . . . language . . . the critique of essentialism [that apophatic language puts forth] doesn't deny the form, but it refuses to absolutize it, to freeze it into an unchanging reality that can be possessed. (Sells 2006a)

Sudanese Sufis' approaches to knowledge participate in a similar kind of apophasis, engaging in a series of truth claims, while at the same time leaving open the possibility of the transformation, transcendence, or even negation of such claims, through the mystery of what lies within secrets. Sufis are often pressed by their leaders to approach God with a recognition that there is darkness, a realm of knowledge to which they will never have access, thus necessitating their submission to spiritual guidance as part of a Sufi order. For the Sufis with whom I worked, knowledge was crucial to the development of their piety, but they were cognizant of its limits. Stressing doubt over certainty, and secrecy over publicity, they argued for a mode of piety that relied instead on embodied discipline.

This Sufi theory of knowledge constitutes a critique of the prevailing ethic of certainty that pervades public Islamic discourse in contemporary Sudan and is promoted by the *ta'ṣīl* project of the Sudanese government. The paradigm of secrecy is a model that embraces doubt and uncertainty as the practical conditions under which Muslims live their lives and thus rejects the redemptive theory of knowledge and its accessibility that projects such as epistemological enlightenment uphold. For Sufis like Faris, the highest realms of knowledge, which bring individuals closer to God, are practically speaking unobtainable, and thus he and other Sufis like him work hard to articulate both a theology of secrets and a program of practical action for those living in a world populated by them. Such a theory of restricted knowledge leads neither to an antinomian rejection of the law, nor to the kind of universalistic esotericism that the Western celebration of Sufism often attributes to it. What it does, on the other hand, is recognize the limits of such knowledge, or as Sells puts it, it "doesn't deny the form, but refuses to absolutize it." Qur'an and Sunna can tell us how to organize our lives and communities, how to worship, and how to relate to others, but given a world enchanted by secrets, it is not only knowledge that will help us reach the Islamic civilization for which government projects strive, but also a humble recognition that there is much we will never know.

Postscript: Rethinking the Islamic State

On June 22, 2005, a major gathering of Sufi shaykhs, government officials, tribal leaders, and other luminaries took place in the town of Umm Dawan Ban, roughly forty-five minutes by car southeast of Khartoum on the east bank of the Blue Nile. Umm Dawan Ban (popularly known by its original name, Umm Dubban)[17] is a major Sufi center of the Qadriyya *ṭarīqa*, or Sufi order, and houses a large and well-respected *khalwa* (Qur'anic School).[18] In

17 The story goes that the town used to be full of flies due to the stagnant water that gathered there during the rainy season, hence the name Umm Dubban, "the place of flies." After becoming a religious center for the study of Qur'an, notables thought the name unfitting and changed it to the similar-sounding (but semantically opposite) "Umm Dawan Ban" (*umm ḍawan bān*), "the place where a light appeared."

18 The wonderful film by ʿAli el-Mek and Geoff Dunlop *Ways of Faith* (el-Mek and Dunlop 1983) depicts the *khalwa* of this Sufi town. While in classical Sufi parlance a *khalwa* refers to a

the history of Sudan, the town is remembered as playing an important role in the Mahdist uprising. It was the place where, in January of 1885, the Sufi troops of Shaykh al-ʿIbayd wad Badr joined forces with the Mahdi to attack General Gordon's garrison in Khartoum, overthrowing the last bastion of colonialism and inaugurating a new regime of Islamic rule.[19] It was precisely this historical role as a site of Sufi collaboration with Islamic revolution that was being referenced on that June afternoon at this unprecedented gathering.

The purpose of the June 22 event was to found a new political movement (*ḥaraka*) that would warn the Muslim community in Sudan of the threats to its sovereignty posed by the concessions made in the CPA, which the government of Sudan had signed only five months earlier. Referencing the Qur'anic verse *Āl ʿImrān* 103 ("Hold together in solidarity to the rope of God, and do not separate"),[20] the Sufi leaders called the movement *Ḥarakat al-Iʿtiṣām al-Waṭanī*, the Movement of National Solidarity (MNS). Here *iʿtiṣām* meant the gathering together of Muslims around the idea of the Islamic state in order to stave off its potential dissolution, should Sudanese unity lead to the recognition of minorities as equal players in the identity of the state. The event's promotional material stated that the aim of the movement was "raising awareness in the Muslim *umma* of the political and social reality [that the nation now faced] . . . [and], in compliance with the will of God, striving to give advice to the *umma*—its leaders and its base—as to what will realize unity and the good life, and giving this *umma* advice that will keep it from the pitfalls of loss or disintegration." Here the unity for which the MNS strove was not the unity of the nation (not necessarily, at least), but the unity of the *umma* in protecting the Islamic character of the state.

While Sudanese Sufis held a number of positions on the subject of the Islamic state—from SPLM-aligned secularism, to NCP-aligned Islamism—few

---

place of retreat (and such places also exist in Sudan: the man-made caves and secluded rooms of ascetic shaykhs, which I visited on occasion), the word denotes a Qur'anic school (*kuttāb*) in the Sudanese dialect.

19 Despite the fact that a certain variety of Islamist Sufi describes the militancy of the Badrab in this manner, other Sufis more critical of the attempt to pose Sufism as an instigator of violent *jihād* told me that Shaykh al-ʿIbayd wad Badr had second thoughts about this battle after a dream that cast doubt on the authenticity of the Mahdi. He is said to have prayed, "*yā qayyūm mā aṣal al-kharṭūm!*" (Oh God, do not let me reach Khartoum!). His prayers were said to have been fulfilled when he died en route to Khartoum. P. M Holt, in his *The Mahdist State in Sudan,* recounts the events of the Mahdist overthrow of Khartoum, and the role of Sufis therein (Holt 1958: 88–92). While he does not point specifically to the forces of Umm Dubban playing a major role in the siege, one can assume the Badrab were one of the many groups that took part since they had given their allegiance to the Mahdi as early as 1884.

20 *iʿtaṣimū bi-ḥabl allāh jamīʿan wa lā tafarraqū.*

hesitated to present their vision of that state, particularly at this unique moment of political opening when the precise configuration of Sudan's future was again up for grabs (or at least so it seemed). The fact that Sufis made explicit claims on the state, in addition to critiquing the Islamic program that motivated it, as we saw above in their engagement with the epistemological enlightenment project, shows that their discomfort with the Islamist agenda was not mere theological disagreement, but only one part of a comprehensive program to rethink the Islam on which the political legitimacy of the state rested. The Islamic state in the model of Hasan al-Turabi and his Muslim Brotherhood-inspired ideas had been attempted and had led to the difficult impasse the CPA presented. Indeed, for many Muslims with a political orientation grounded in Islam, the CPA represented a lose-lose equation: if unity *did not* become attractive to the South, it would secede, and the oil-rich bottom third of the country would be lost; but in order for unity *to become* attractive to the primarily non-Muslim South, the Islamic character of the state would have to be compromised. For this reason the MNS proposed an Islamic state on a different model. One shaykh proclaimed:

> In this period we need to join our lines together, and be devoted to God. And we should do this is in the coming years until the Sufi state (*dawlat al-ṣūfī*) arrives. [If we maintain our efforts,] a Sufi state will come after these six years [of the interim period before the South votes on secession]. . . . But if colonialism comes [again] to this country . . . [these outside forces] will destroy all we have grown and all we have built.

For the leaders of the MNS, protecting the Islamic character of the state was a duty that rightly fell to Sufis since it was they who had protected Sudan's unique character from external threats for centuries. As one speaker explained:

> The shaykhs who were living in the deserts began by teaching people religion and devoted themselves to rearing individuals. If it weren't for these Sufis, we would have become Turkified (*nistatrik*) during the Turkish rule. And our tongue would have become barbarian (*taʿajjam*) during the rule of the English. But [the Sufi shaykhs] kept for us our identity and our language and religion. And Sudan is now at a very dangerous point, as the people who have spoken before me pointed out.

He went on to explain that the Sufi shaykhs must again resume their role as protectors of the Sudanese *umma*. It was the Sufis who had protected Sudan from becoming Turkified, it was the Sufis who had protected Sudan from becoming Anglicized, and again it must be the Sufis who would protect Sudan from becoming yet another secular African state as the SPLM was demanding. The Sufis who made up the MNS had embraced the ideals of the Islamic state and had formed sentences using its grammar, whether by embracing the notion of Islamic knowledge as a source of public reason (despite their colleagues' warnings about its limits) or by upholding the irrefutability of an Islamic identity for the Sudanese state and for society. Regardless of their stance on the policies of the regime in power, the Islamic state had become an indelible frame in which they organized their political ambitions.

It was not only the unique role that Sufism played in the history of Sudan that the leaders of the MNS sought to mobilize for contemporary political purposes. Sufis also felt that their particular mode of dealing with difference (ethnic, religious, and otherwise) offered a model for the Islamic state that might well be more successful than that of the NCP regime, which had led to tensions not only between Muslims and non-Muslims, but among Muslims as well, as the conflict that was raging then in Darfur made clear. It was for this reason that the leaders of the MNS proposed Sufism as the solution to the problem of gathering Muslims around a unified position, for they recognized that the greatest threat to the Islamic state was not secular political parties, but the inability of Muslim parties to agree with one another on a comprehensive program for political reform. As another speaker noted:

> There is no group in Sudanese society more appropriate for confronting the problems of Sudan than Sufis. . . . [I]f this putrid racism and tribalism is one of the elements that threaten Sudan, then Sufis alone are the ones who are able to enter among the lines of the people, and to unify the positions of the people, and to gather the people around the word of "togetherness," not giving the matter of ethnicity (*ʿirq*) importance among the people, but rather giving importance to the path [he takes] in which [to quote a famous aphorism] "the fact of your belief is more important than who came first to it" (*al-ṭarīq liman ṣadaq wa laysa liman sabaq*).[21] . . . And if Sudan's problem is [in addition to the racial problems just mentioned] the tearing apart (*tamazzuq*) between the elements of Muslims, and its groups and parties and orders, then Sufism can be the greatest denominator for mutual participation (*qāsim mushtarik*), because the Sufis do not give up on any Muslim. All the other [Islamic] groups [distinguish between Muslims], saying: "this guy is a worthwhile person and this guy is not worthwhile." But the Sufis do not give up on anyone. They fix even the drunks, the confused, and the sinful by their acceptance and wide open program.

Here, the classical Sufi method of rearing a Muslim from sin to salvation—rather than denouncing him as a sinner or unbeliever—is mined for its

21 This aphorism echoes the famous hadith that I mentioned in footnote 14, *lā faḍl li-ʿarabī ʿallā ʿajamī illā bi-l-taqwā*, "No Arab is better than a non-Arab, except through his piety": i.e., that it is belief and not identity that should determine one's standing in this world, as it certainly does in the next.

Sufi method → Politicized [handwritten margin note]

political potential as a way of confronting difference alternative to the method that the government promoted and as a foundation of the "Sufi state" that the MNS envisioned.

The CPA and the Government of National Unity that emerged out of it produced a unique space for reimagining the nature of political community in Islam, which groups like the MNS came to occupy. After almost two decades under the Islamist regime, which had culminated in a peace agreement that recognized Sudan's diversity as part of the identity of the state and thus seemed to question the very premise of the revolution, Muslims across Sudan began to rethink the place of Islam in both the political and the national order. The CPA raised the question of whether the Islamic state that had emerged as a result of the 1989 Revolution of National Salvation needed only revision, or whether, as a result of national unity, its ideals would have to be abandoned altogether in favor of a state based on multicultural foundations. Though certainly there were some Muslims who did not feel threatened by this latter possibility, who in fact welcomed a Sudanese future in which religion was immaterial to citizenship, many others felt distinctly disenfranchised by the possibility of the construction of a multicultural or secular state, and attempts at countering "the end of Islamic politics," such as the MNS, began in earnest.

By chipping away at the regime's knowledge reform projects and by questioning the theological basis of the Islam of its "Islamic state," Sudanese citizens engaged actively and creatively in the process of reimagining the political community in which they lived. While for some this meant reaching toward secular horizons, seeing in the regime's failures a failure of "political Islam," for many more it meant rethinking, revising, and reworking the Islamic state and its projects of reform. It is here, far from the ministries of central Khartoum, that we can begin to map the contours of the Islamic state, not as a set of fixed government institutions, but as the political horizons within which a significant sector of Sudanese Muslims strove. It was through careful attention to the territory (human and geographic) into which it intervened that the regime succeeded in enabling such a state. It is to a discussion of the technical means that it used to do so that we will turn in the next chapter.

CHAPTER FOUR

The Country That Prays upon the Prophet the Most

The Aesthetic Formation of the Islamic State

Among the thousands who returned to Sudan from abroad in the middle part of the last decade due to the economic improvements brought about by the exploitation of oil resources, many would note how different Khartoum seemed from the city they knew in the years of their youth. Not only had new roads and bridges been built, new multi-story towers in its increasingly glossy inner neighborhoods erected, but the quiet, village-like feel of Khartoum's past had been replaced by that of a booming metropolis. A far cry from the city whose streets were once rumored to be organized on the model of the stripes of the Union Jack, and where everyone knew their neighbors, Khartoum now had a labyrinthian, cosmopolitan feel. Ever more persistent power cuts and limited water indicated, however, that this booming metropolis was not exactly blossoming, but rather growing larger than the land beneath it could sustain. The days of yore when agricultural schemes and a functioning transportation system facilitated a healthy flow of goods and people between city and countryside had been replaced by a state of permanent displacement. Urban development with scarce resources meant the underdevelopment of everywhere else. Khartoum had simultaneously become both a refuge for those fleeing wars and famine and the origin of the difficulty Sudanese experienced in living anywhere else.

In a recent volume, memoirist Ahmad ʿAbd al-Wahhab Muhammad Saʿid bemoaned the city Khartoum had become: a place of anonymity and division, rather than one of community and solidarity between diverse publics as it had been in decades past.

> These ideas simmered in my mind a little while ago as I was walking by the railway station in Khartoum, and the whistle of the wind came from inside the workshops in which the bats now nested. [And I thought this too as I passed by] the office of the director on which a spider had built a web that hung from a now mute bell. . . . Where are those times when we would return from the countryside (*al-balad*) to Khartoum and our father would come to meet us [at the station], undulating with people departing and people picking up [their loved ones] and the drivers of taxis screaming "Bahri!, al-Daym!, Umdurman!"? Where is the scent of moist dates and lard? Where are the smiles of those receiving [loved ones] and the tears of those arriving? (Saʿid 2005: 97–98)

The now-mute bell of the once-bustling train station and the empty sounds of the wind and bats in the once-active railway workshop indicated to the memoirist not the abandonment of the city, but rather the rejection of the countryside, visible in this site through which people once flowed back and forth from Sudan's agricultural heartland. Due to decades of underdevelopment, war, and famine, no one had much to return to any longer. Besides the occasional spiritual retreat or holiday visit to one's ancestors (living or dead), people stayed in Khartoum, and the countryside was increasingly emptied of its occupants. And so it was that the bells and whistles of the trains of Khartoum had been replaced by new sounds: the glaring horns of automobile traffic, the blast of store and bus radios, the clank of construction, the ever-persistent sounds of the new and newly-amplified mosques that were springing up in every neighborhood, the cacophony of voices—selling, inviting, imploring—that made a simple stroll through the city overwhelming, the individual beckoned from every direction.

This rapidly forming urban space, its potentials and pitfalls, was not merely the interest of nostalgic memoirists, however, nor even the ever-expanding cadre of international aid workers, warning of the economic dangers of uneven development. Rapid urbanization also had significant religious implications for a country in which decentralized, often rural, Sufi organizations have throughout its history been the engines of Islamic renewal, resisting attempts at reform from the urban center. In the early years of the new millennium, the Sudanese elegist and Sufi Shaykh ʿAbd al-Rahim al-Buraʿi lamented the moral hazards and threats to piety and social cohesion brought about by urbanization. In "The Return, Oh Forgetful One," a much-cited poem that became the title track of a popular cassette by a youth group famous for bringing al-Buraʿi's poems to the masses, the poet wrote in mournful tones of the dangers to the Muslim posed by urbanization: the pious rhythms of home life and its ritual duties drowned out by the distractions of the city, the perpetual feeding of the *nafs* (ego self) through greed goaded on by the market, the dissolution of the family left behind due to the absence of migrant men. It was for this reason that his poem—clearly a salvo in a tense debate between Islamic intellectuals over what soil could nourish an Islam that would best serve Sudan's future—counseled return to those who had left the countryside and staying put to those who still remained there.

> The return, oh forgetful one (*al-ʿawda yā nāsī*): do it before death comes. Staying put is the best thing to do . . .
>
> And how many have [gone away] to gather money for themselves, becoming only the followers of their own suspicious desires. Thus staying put is the best thing to do . . .

> And there is benefit and blessing to those who are staying put, for our prayers are constant and at the right time. Staying put is the best thing to do.[1]

Yet, in spite of al-Buraʿi's diagnosis of the ills of urban migration, his voice was amplified by the very demographic phenomenon he decried. Al-Buraʿi's influence was made possible by the massive population shifts that took place in the final decades of the twentieth century. The distinctive trajectory of his life, from obscurity to utter ubiquity in Sudanese media and public space, could not have occurred in any other era, as his name and fame were carried from the vast deserts of North Kordofan that he called home to the capital on the backs of people from western Sudan who had migrated due to war, famine, and underdevelopment. Indeed this most prominent shaykh of the twenty-first century was a product of urbanization, his popularity further sedimented by the way he fulfilled the longing of many displaced Sudanese (and not just those from western Sudan) for the sacred space of the countryside and its *masīds*, while it was the media tools and networks of the urban space his poetry now occupied that quite physically enabled his remarkable fame. Al-Buraʿi's poetry thus represented a paradox, offering a sacred substrate to urban life through its mass dissemination in popular radio and cassettes, played on public transport and on street corners, while at the same time decrying the dangers of the urban space in which it was most often encountered.

In remaining wary of urban migration, al-Buraʿi directly challenged the moral geography of the ruling Inqadh regime and its Civilization Project in which it was precisely the urban that was being positioned as the space in which the desired "modernization" of Islam would take place. The vanguard of the Civilization Project promised that through the tools of urban institutions such as universities, councils, and think tanks, a practical Islam could be cultivated that might help answer the challenges of modernity and thus become useful to the project of Islamic state-building. Al-Buraʿi's poetry sought to destabilize this new moral geography with a much older one that valorized the quiet rhythms of rural life, the *khalwa* (retreat) that has long been at the center of Islamic practice in Sudan. Al-Buraʿi's immense popularity, even among the urban middle- and upper-class *affandiyya* (Abdel Rahman 2008) was evidence of what Islamist intellectual Hasan Makki bemoaned in an interview I held with him as the "ruralization of religion" (*tarayyuf al-dīn*), a shorthand for the revival of Sufism in the city, as these ways of faith spread from migrant villagers to the urban bourgeoisie who employed them. However, despite their initial disappointment, the

1 Translated from the cassette: *al-ʿAwda yā nāsī* (recorded by *Awlād al-Buraʿī*, Omdurman: *al-Rūmānī li-l-Intāj al-Fannī wa-l-Tawzīʿ*).

intellectuals at the heart of the regime came to embrace major elements of this "rural religion," incorporating them even within their reform projects that will be the focus of this chapter.

In light of the demographic and infrastructural changes described above, the national capital came to pose a twin danger to the fulfillment of the Islamic state. First, as we saw in Chapter 2, the identity of the capital as a symbol of the nation was being challenged by those who sought a capital representative of a broader spectrum of citizens, Muslim and non-Muslim, a capital that was not an ethnic homeland (*dār*), but the property of all Sudanese. Replacing billboards promoting Khartoum as "the Capital of Arab Culture,"[2] the new Government of National Unity (the partnership between the ruling NCP and the SPLM that was established in 2005 as a result of the signing of the CPA) promised that Khartoum would mark not only the confluence of the two Niles, but would also serve as a confluence of two cultures. It would be "where Arab and African culture meet," as new signs hastily posted across the city declared. Thus the national capital posed the same challenge to Islamic statehood that the nation as whole posed, only in microcosm: is an Islamic state possible in a highly plural society?

Second, the capital also posed a danger to the project of Islamic statehood in that, in the moral geography that underlay the relationship of many Sudanese with Islam, the urban space itself was constituted as a threat, a place in which the Muslim could be tempted and distracted away from a faith that required quiet space for contemplation uninterrupted by the turmoil of city life, a notion we saw so clearly expressed in al-Bura'i's poem. If the Islamic state was not to be lost in this period of great political and demographic upheaval, new projects were needed that would both help secure the Islamic identity of the capital, in spite of its demographic diversity, and secure the Islam of its Muslim population, in spite of (or perhaps due to) the hubbub of city life.

To make not just religious Sudanese, but Sudan religious, the Inqadh regime began to attend to the unique qualities of the physical space into which it intervened, and not just to the people who populated it. While in rural areas the regime often used blunt force to establish its Islamic state (*jihād* in the South, *daʿwa* camps in the Nuba Mountains [De Waal and Abdel Salam 2004]), at the urban center the regime engaged in a much more nuanced project, one increasingly tuned to the challenges and opportunities that such a space posed to the project of Islamic state-building. Recognizing that national belonging on an Islamic basis could not be cultivated by law and education alone—particularly at this moment in history when both

2 "The Capital of Arab Culture" is an annual designation the Arab League bestows on an "Arab" city in a bid to promote and celebrate Arab culture.

domains had become increasingly contested as a result of the CPA agreement with the majority non-Muslim South—the regime turned to artistic forms in order to develop the affective qualities it deemed necessary to the foundation of its state, those passsions that made people not only tolerate an Islamic state but desire one. It is to a discussion of one such project, a poetry revival program that the government encouraged and funded, that we will turn in this chapter, tracing its itinerary as it intervened into the existing poetic and religious landscapes extant in Sudan.

New Sounds

During the month of Ramadan of 2005, new sounds began blaring from radios across the capital. Standing at a distance, one would be forgiven for thinking that he was just hearing the reverb of another typical pop radio station, with its young male and female hosts bantering back and forth, its top-forty format, and its contemporary beats. Yet coming closer to these radios, the meaning of the words being sung begins to take shape *ḥabībī anā* (my love, in the secular sense), a ubiquitous phrase in the kinds of love songs that such tunes usually carried, slowly morphs into *ḥabīb allāh, al-muṣṭafā* (the beloved of God, the chosen one, the Prophet Muhammad), a key phrase in Sufi *madīḥ* poetry, one of whose goals is the cultivation of love of the Prophet (*maḥabbat al-rasūl*) in its listeners through his praise. Though the integration of the traditional Sufi religious poetry in which this music has its roots into pop music has progressed gradually over the past twenty years, it was the founding of Radio al-Kawthar during Ramadan of 2005 that gave it a firm place in the soundscape of urban Sudan. Radio al-Kawthar (*idhāʿat al-kawthar*) 92 FM was the culmination of a roughly fifteen-year process in the transformation of the classical Sufi musical and poetic genre of *madīḥ* (sing. *madḥa*, "praise poetry," but in Sudanese parlance referring to a wide range of chanted poetry with Islamic content) to meet the needs of Sudanese who came of age in the shadow of the Revolution of National Salvation. Al-Kawthar's emergence came to change the relationship people had to their radios—no longer bearers of amusement and news alone, but actual tools in the development of their piety—as well as drastically to transform the urban Sudanese soundscape, which now rang out ever more with catchy songs of praise to the Prophet Muhammad and on other Islamic topics.

The mission of the radio station was, simply put, *taʿẓīm al-nabī*, "the glorification of the Prophet," and this mission was achieved primarily through the broadcast of *madīḥ*. Over the next few years, al-Kawthar boomed in popularity, especially among urban youth, and its main financial backers, two state majority-owned companies, Sudatel and Omdurman National Bank,

Figure 5. Al-Kawthar Radio 92 FM, "For Glorification of the Prophet." From *al-Kawthar Radio Annual Report*, 2006.

kept pouring in funds.[3] Al-Kawthar radio was the culmination of a long process in the transformation of *madīḥ* audition from a ritual practice essential to Sufi worship and benediction to a new kind of ritual that I will argue did another sort of work in instilling the ethical and affective framework necessary for a new iteration of the Islamic state, which the regime was establishing after the failure of earlier experiments in Islamic politics.[4] A musical tradition previously understood as a pious technology for cultivating the virtue of love of the prophet in the individual *sālik* (or Sufi adherent) was mobilized by outlets like al-Kawthar to help achieve a distinctly *national* goal: to make "Sudan the Country That Prays upon the Prophet the Most" (*al-sūdān akthar balad yuṣallī ʿalā al-rasūl*), as its directors put it in a project they founded during al-Kawthar's second year, festooning the slogan on billboards across the capital. In this project, and through the broadcast of *madīḥ* whose subject was the Sudanese nation's special relationship to the

3 Though the exact nature of the funding of al-Kawthar and the organization that founded it (*munaẓamat al-mabarra*) was never fully disclosed to me, the first-year Annual Report of al-Kawthar Radio (c. 2006) states on the back cover that it enjoyed the support of Umdurman National Bank (in which the Sudanese Army has a major stake) and Sudatel, the now-privatized national phone company in which the state still retains a major (if not majority) stake. Though I don't have clear data on the inner-workings of these companies, they are clearly identified by supporters and detractors as arms of the NCP. I was told by an official at al-Kawthar that the monthly donation of each during the time I was in the field amounted to approximately $100,000. This number seems plausible (especially given the lack of commercial advertising in al-Kawthar's broadcast) given the elaborate offices, recording studios, satellite broadcasting, massive advertising campaigns, and large staff that al-Kawthar had while I completed the fieldwork for this chapter. This support, and the place of al-Kawthar on the national airwaves, was greatly reduced as the country limped towards national partition and the threat of rival claims to public space subsided.

4 Several recent works have focused our attention on the "affective" (rather than the much-touted "deliberative") dimensions of the public sphere and the way in which religious media can help to produce them (e.g., Eisenlohr 2011; Meyer and Moors 2005; Meyer 2009; Stolow 2010). Eisenlohr, for example, insightfully examines how a genre of mediated religious praise poetry very similar to the *madīḥ* I study produces a moral substrate among Muslim communities in Mauritius that makes possible the affective attitudes on which the thriving of Mauritian pluralism is based. While I am also interested in the affective and political results of poetry audition among Muslim communities, the present chapter serves as a reverse mirror image of what Eisenlohr observed in two ways: (1) while the Mauritian state focuses on cultivating "the authenticity and validity of religious traditions" (Eisenlohr 2011: 265) as a means of fostering pluralism, the Sudanese state specifically tries to disrupt these traditions, not supporting ancestral Sufism, but rather extracting its ritual technologies and repurposing them towards the goals of the state; (2) while the poems he studies seek to cultivate a moral attitude resulting in pluralism, the ones I study seek to respond to the *threat* that pluralism poses to successful fulfilment of the Islamic state. Nevertheless, the attention Eisenlohr pays to both the discursive and affective ways that this poetry helps to develop a moral stance parallels my own interest in destabilizing the notion of the creation of Islamic publics as a solely discursive process.

Prophet, the purveyors of this poetry attempted to craft a Sudanese public that embodied *maḥabbat al-rasūl* (love of the Prophet), a task that was understood to be particularly important at a time when other national expressions of Islamic piety (e.g., Islamic law and Islamic education) were being challenged in an attempt to define the state on a more secular foundation, as 2005's CPA appeared to require.

At the intersection of the newly forming political context of postwar reconstruction (i.e., the Government of National Unity and its institutions) and the technologies mobilized to shape and sustain the refurbished capital that would lie at its heart (new medias, new infrastructural schemes), projects such as al-Kawthar became key arenas in which Islamist intellectuals reimagined the Islam of the Islamic state and the citizens proper to it. Otherwise hobbled in their quest for the Islamic state by the rapidly shifting national political context, which made the legal and pedagogical projects of yesteryear exceedingly controversial, the arts, and in particular classical arenas of Islamic artistic production such as poetry, became an important site not merely for the expression of Islamist ideas but for the cultivation of proper Muslim citizens through the means of aesthetic experience. The sonic density of urban space, with the constant drone of traffic and crowds, was embraced not as a void into which piety might disappear (as al-Buraʿi had feared), but rather as a potential workshop in which a new urban Muslim could be produced. Even the name of the radio station—which both refers to a river in Paradise and literally means "abundance"—suggests the sort of repetitive twenty-four-hour urban piety that the project imagined.[5]

Perhaps disabled by a simplistic association of revivalist Islam with aniconism (cf. Flood 2002; Elias 2012), the aesthetic dimension of contemporary movements of Islamic reform is too often ignored in favor of a discussion of their ideological features.[6] Recent works in the anthropology of Islam,

5 The term *al-kawthar* has a dual meaning in the Islamic tradition. It appears once in the Qur'an (*Sūrat al-Kawthar*: 1) with the sense of "abundance" ("indeed we have given you abundance") for which the believer must be thankful. Yet in the *sīra*, hadith, and *tafsīr* traditions it serves as a proper name for a river in Paradise in which believers were said to quench their thirst. In some traditions the river and the pools into which it accumulated are said to be the possession of the Prophet, the spring of his beneficence from which one drinks, and are often seen as a symbol for his intercession (*shafāʿa*) (see Horovitz and Gardet 1978; Schimmel 1985: 87, 139). Al-Kawthar radio station, which focused energy not only on praise and prayers for the Prophet, but also on educating Muslims about his noble deeds, was thus said also to be a virtual *al-kawthar* from which listeners could drink to give them a taste of the deep beneficence that love of the Prophet could bestow on Muslims.

6 Artistic forms and their producers are often seen as entirely marginal to the story of the rise of conservative Islamic political movements, as at most the unlucky recipients of a new austerity promoted by Muslim reformers. See, for example, Michael Peletz's description of the banning of the traditional Malaysian art of shadow puppets in his *Islamic Modern* (Peletz 2002: 229–30) and David Commins' discussion of the critique of Sufi music by the Salafis he

however, have been attentive to the ways in which poetry, song, and even the art of sermon delivery and Qur'an recitation has, in new technological contexts, helped to produce new kinds of Muslim subjects through nondiscursive means (Hirschkind 2006; Larkin 2004; Schulz 2012). Such scholars have argued that this has taken place through the production of a certain kind of aesthetic experience that has served as the practical means for the cultivation of a set of ethical virtues that cannot be produced through didactic means alone. These scholars have also often paid careful attention to the technological means through which these religious forms have been communicated, contending that the formal qualities of these means (their iterability, their transportability, their use of the same formats as secular media) have allowed them to perform a certain kind of "work" that earlier media could not accomplish. Still others have focused on the intercession of new media technologies into Muslim *communities*, showing how, for example, newly mediatized Islamic poetry helps solidify communal identity across a diasporic landscape and reopens and reframes classic debates about religious authenticity and mediation in Islam, unsettling the notions of religious authority that undergird them (Eisenlohr 2006; see also Kresse 2007). Drawing from the insights of both sets of work, this chapter will seek to extend such observations to a study of the production of aesthetic experience as a technology of the state, one that seeks to transcend communal identities in service of new imaginings of the nation.

By the twenty-first century, the classical genre of Sufi *madīḥ* poetry had become both a literary space in which the nature of public Islam was debated and contested, as well as an item in a technological tool kit utilized by the Sudanese regime in fashioning the Islamic state. The very audition of this poetry, and the aesthetic experience of the listener in the various ritual and mundane contexts where it might be heard, became the object of much attention from partisans of the Islamic state looking for new ways to craft a public that might sustain that state. Here the density and technological

studies in Syria in their support of a more "sober" Sufism (Commins 1990: 74). An excursus on the aesthetic forms of the Islamic movements on which Peletz and Commins focus would be out of place in either of these works, and I cite them here merely as examples of the standard position art (Islamic and "traditional") is often assumed to occupy in conservative Islamic reform movements across the Muslim world. Recent works on the poetry of the Taliban (Van Linschoten and Kuehn 2012) and poems used by ISIS (Creswell and Haykel 2015) begin to address some of this imbalance. Notable earlier works that discuss aesthetic aspects of Islamic reform include Varzi's (2006) work on martyrdom memorialization in post-revolutionary Iran and Magnus Marsden's *Living Islam* (2006). Marsden discusses the cross-sectional nature of *mahfil* music parties in Chitral, Pakistan, which draw on a tradition of Sufi love poetry and are popular with Muslims of diverse stripes, from Islamists to proud hashish-smoking antinomians. This said, such works have not yet penetrated most scholarly discussions of Islamism, which focus primarily on its ideological dimensions.

capacity of urban space were embraced as an opportunity for the staging of new collective ritual endeavors that relied on the unique addressability of the urban subject, perpetually enmeshed in a clamoring sonic landscape. The ability of mass-produced *madīḥ* to cultivate pious attentiveness within this landscape, whether in the quiet of the private car or the blare of public transport, was embraced as an effective tool for creating the mass public the state desired, untethered from the ritual space (and thus from the authoritative networks) of Sufism, in which this poetry was traditionally encountered, and from the "pointless distractions" of Sufism's other ritual obligations.

The cultivation of pious sentiments such as love for the Prophet (*maḥabbat al-rasūl*), classically understood to be one of the virtues that loyal listening to such poetry instills in the adept, was transformed through such efforts from an an individual to a collective aspiration and projected onto the screen of the nation. In this way, aesthetic experience, and the particular modalities of listening associated with it, became an arena for nation-building. Poetry and song became the tools through which proper Muslim subjects could be constructed, reborn through the appropriation of classical ritual technologies associated with Sufism that were utilized to meet new kinds of national aims.

While studies of the political contributions of Sufism have explored the sociology of charisma as a means of attracting followers (Werbner and Basu 1998), the unfolding of authoritarianism in master-disciple relationships as a mode of power relations transferable onto the political realm (Hammoudi 1997), and the phenomenon of Sufi orders as a proto-civil society (Villalon 1995), in the following we will examine the theological and ritual/technological contributions of the Sufi canon to a new mode of Islamic politics emergent in Sudan in the early years of the new millennium. Moreover, through understanding Muslim political subjects as the results of a project, rather than as givens within pious Muslim societies, we can better understand the labor that goes into developing the Islamic state, as political sensibilities are inculcated through ever more creative means.

Reviving *Madīḥ*, Rethinking Sufism

> We have a great love for the Sufi orders and a great respect because they presented a message in its time to the extent of the possibilities that were available to them. And now with the developments of globalization we need new means. [While] the Sufi orders are one of the means . . . there was a need for something additional. So when we [at al-Kawthar] came, we did not want to go in the same line. We could not add anything to their program. Instead we wanted to enact our philosophy and our program in this area, using our means, being careful

> that we don't go out of the framework of religion, but we also have our means and our way and our understanding of these matters.
>
> —The Vice Director of al-Kawthar Radio, personal interview

A particular concern of the Inqadh, as we saw in Chapter 2, was disrupting the fealty Sudanese had to their Sufi shaykhs and reapplying that energy to the Sudanese nation as a whole. Such a strategy was a clear attempt to craft a new mode of Islamic politics, one that would transcend the "sectarian" parties model that ruled Sudan until 1989 and had been based on affiliations to religious brotherhoods. Such a disruption in the relationship between Sudanese and their shaykhs would be accomplished not by an attack on Sufism, a project doomed to failure given the great respect and reverence Sudanese had for the Sufi shaykhs, but rather by attempting to transform Sufism from a disciplined and exclusivist mode of social organization into a disembodied ethic, a hermeneutics of Islam that could exist comfortably alongside the Inqadh regime and not compete with it. One way the regime did this was by attempting to co-opt the vast storehouse of Sufi *madīḥ* that already existed in Sudan and enlist it in the Islamist project. While the modernist intellectualism of the journals, conferences, and monographs of the Islamist movement were rather slow in reaching the masses, religious song had already proven its popularity among the Sudanese public in earlier eras. Thus, at some point in the mid-1990s, those who held power within the National Islamic Front began actively to support the proliferation and distribution of *madīḥ* and their transformation into modern pop songs sung by the hottest of pop stars. The aim was to meet the tastes of the young generation of Sudanese whom the NIF was trying to attract, if not to their party itself, then to a certain sort of ethical norm based on the principles of their vision for Islam.

The relationship of the revival of *madīḥ* to Sufism was a complicated one. While the *madīḥ* one heard on al-Kawthar and elsewhere were often written by Sufi shaykhs (and sometimes performed by the sons of the *ṭarīqa*), the boom in *madīḥ* that was characteristic of the modern *madīḥ* movement cannot be read as evidence of a flourishing of Sufism, but rather exists in great tension with it. Sufi orders continued to flourish in Sudan, as the previous chapter showed, but projects such as these sought to disrupt Sufi publics and the authority on which they relied, and to replace them with a new mass public in which different modes of Islamic authority came into play and different types of religious subjects were the goal. At the same time, such projects recognized the success that Sufis and other brotherhoods, such as the Mahdist *Anṣār*, had experienced in transforming affective capital (love of the shaykh, love of the Prophet) into political capital (membership in one of the parties led by a leader of a brotherhood) in decades past. The formation of an Islamic public that would—if not today, at least at some point in the future—come to desire an Islamic state was a key goal of a movement that, although it had come to power through a coup, subscribed to the idea that full membership in the project would require encouragement in addition to coercion.

One of the hosts on Radio al-Kawthar (who was also an amateur scholar of *madīḥ*) described to me the transformation of *madīḥ* from an element of Sufi ritual practice into a kind of national cultural product as follows:

> When I was young, listening to *madīḥ* was restricted to visiting the places of the Sufis. And if you listened to *madīḥ*, many of the political parties and other youth would accuse you of backwardness and of being reactionary (*al-rajaʿiyya*). . . . [They considered *madīḥ*] something in which old people were interested and [an interest] of the people who have a shallow culture, [that it was] an expression of naiveté[7]. . . and it was from 1983 that this idea [began to change] and from that time on, the view became different. . . . From 1983, the beginning of [the reinstatement of] *sharīʿa* [under President Numayri], people [realized], in a spiritually satisfied way (*al-ishbāʿ al-maʿnawī wa-l-ruḥī*), that our country has taken a religious turn: an orientation that satisfies our ambitions "that I am Muslim and I want to be ruled by Islam. I am a Muslim and I want Muslim culture to be the dominant [culture]." Since a long time back and in all ages, culture and literature flourishes in the shade of politics (*fī ẓill al-siyāsa*). In the age of the Abbasids, the Caliph Ma'mun, when he glorified the *ʿulamāʾ* and raised their status within

7 Note that the pervasiveness of this view is very much corroborated by Qurashi Muhammad Hasan in his encyclopedia of *madīḥ*, *Maʿa shuʿarāʾ al-madāʾiḥ* (Hasan 1972–76). He writes:

> I recall that when I was presenting my analytical studies on [my radio] program "The Art of *madīḥ*" (*adab al-madāʾiḥ*), one of the people who was ignorant about the literary and artistic value in the poetry of popular *madīḥ* said to me, "You are trying to till an ocean" [i.e., that your efforts will produce no yield]. And others said to me, "You are a new kind of dervish" [a term that refers to a Sufi ascetic unconcerned with this world and here is used with derogatory intent]. Still others accused me of spreading trickery and magic. But I did not listen to what they said and for ten years I thoroughly examined this great land that sprouted great poetry. . . . Then I was convinced that I was not trying to till an ocean and that I had not become a dervish among the literary dervishes and I was not spreading trickery and magic, rather I was actually one of the trailblazers of truth. And I did not regret the years I spent in the study of popular *madīḥ*, for I uncovered in it a treasure that was lost over tens of centuries. With it, I opened new horizons for study and thanks to our discoveries Sudanese people knew the genius of their country. (Hassan 1972–76: V. 1, 10–11)

The same author has an excellent introduction to the study of Sudanese *madīḥ*: Hasan 1977.

> the state, [also created] the largest library in history, the library of Baghdad, an Islamic library.[8]

Yet the process of extracting *madīḥ* from Sufism and growing them into a national cultural form was not as effortless as the radio host claimed, a simple effect of the Islamization of politics. Several tactics were employed both to draw off the important capabilities of *madīḥ* and to reform them in order to make them accessible within the new kinds of urban spaces the regime had created, directing them toward the new sorts of national goals they sought to implement. First, the vanguard of al-Kawthar Radio composed new *madīḥ* on the subject of national piety, while also drawing on existing *madīḥ* that were compatible with the regime's agenda of social and individual reform. Yet, perhaps even more important than transformations in the semantic content of *madīḥ*, the modern *madīḥ* movement's nationalist project was enabled by the insistence that new styles of listening to and modes of engagement with *madīḥ* were necessary if the kinds of reforms they desired were to be achieved. Whereas traditionally *madīḥ* were aids to help the individual Sufi *sālik* on his journey toward spiritual enlightenment, and thus were consumed as one component in a broader Sufi ritual context, these new "modern *madīḥ*" needed to be heard in contexts in which all Sudanese could participate, regardless of their particular sectarian affiliations, thus emphasizing their abstract citizenship over their other associational ties. If *madīḥ* traditionally achieved their effects within the quiet of the sacred spaces of Sufism and the disciplines they required, in order for these new "modern *madīḥ*" to reach the nation, they needed to be readily accessible in that aural space of urban life that al-Kawthar's listeners occupied with its peculiar disciplines.

If *madīḥ* were to address those quintessential urbanites (or, at least the ideal thereof), those upwardly mobile youth whom the Inqadh wanted to bring into its program perhaps more than anyone else, they had to be attentive to the youths' particular circumstances, lest they risk *madīḥ* being seen as something in which only the "old" or the "shallow" were interested. Another al-Kawthar employee explained:

> I promote [Sufism] and support it, but living by these norms is difficult. For example, you must visit so and so, you must do the things they do,

8 It is interesting that my interlocutor recalls this library as an Islamic library, when in actuality the literary project of Ma'mun is notable for the translation of *non-Islamic*, Greek philosophy into Arabic, something that was *opposed* by traditionalists who thought an Islamic community should draw solely on Islamic cultural production. However, such a notion of cultural chauvinism is the very idea my interlocutor seems to be promoting, albeit citing an example that in fact serves the opposite agenda of the point for which he was arguing. For more on the "translation movement," see Gutas 1998.

> like you have to meet the shaykh and go with him to each occasion. *With our work* we are not able to live by these norms. . . . They have things that are difficult for a person our age, as young people.

Al-Kawthar had to make *madīḥ* speak to a cohort disciplined not by a Sufi program of *iltizām* (ordered commitment), but by the peculiarly urban demands of labor and bourgeois life. Harnessing both the sounds of the many regions of Sudan now resident in Khartoum as the result of urban migration and the technologies and networks of this newly forming cityscape itself, al-Kawthar's project mobilized *madīḥ* toward a national piety, one uniquely attainable in the urban spaces that were its key achievement. Indeed it was urban space that made possible new kinds of ritual (Hirschkind 2006): the repeated encounters with *madīḥ* (at the corner store, on the bus ride home, in one's own front yard) that engrained them in one's being, the very character that the English neologism "earworm" perhaps best captures.

Yet, as much as al-Kawthar drew on the affective qualities of *madīḥ* in staging its own ritual performances, the affective nature of Sufism was also something that al-Kawthar's vanguard saw as in need of reform, or at least of supplementation. The emotion of pious love that Sufi ritual is so adept at invoking, while it was an essential ingredient to al-Kawthar's ideal Islamic nation as well, could not be properly cultivated in the absence of knowledge, its leaders argued. Thus, in addition to drawing on the affective potential of *madīḥ*, the directors of al-Kawthar argued that *madīḥ* must be reformulated from "mere" ritual devices at play in Sufi worship into didactic tools that could teach the Muslim about the good qualities and noble deeds of the Prophet, as a model to be emulated as well as an object of praise. Love could not be merely a surge of endorphins in the believer. It must emerge from a reasoned encounter with the noble qualities of the Prophet. The passions were seen to be developable means, not merely excited unconsciously, but rather motivated through a dense intertwining of emotion and intellection that the didactic *madḥa* uniquely could achieve.[9]

9 Hasan al-Turabi, in an interview I conducted with him, characterized such an attitude clearly, drawing out the importance of the affective qualities of Muslim ritual but critiquing an approach that inculcated feelings alone. He said to me:

> [The Sufi focus on the inner, ritual life of Islam as opposed to the concerns of the *umma*] has gone far away from the truth. They are not doing anything, just [grunting] "*hā hū*" [Turabi is mimicking the sound of Sufi ritual]. Remembrance of God means that your whole life will be in remembrance of God. All these things that we say before biding someone farewell (*maʿ salāma, waḍaʿnak allāh*) or eating (*bismillāhi*), are part of an *adab* of remembering God. But [Sufis] exceed the bounds of this by holding onto "*yā laṭīf, yā laṭīf*" [i.e., repeating the names of God] and repeating them over and over, 7,777 times. . . . I speak to [the Sufis] nicely and say, "When you say any one of the names, say with it a supplicatory prayer right away." You talk to God with that particular name

Just Sound? The Poetics of Piety in Sufi *madīḥ* Audition

In order to understand the precise nature of al-Kawthar's intervention—that is, how new modes of state-supported *madīḥ* audition both built off classical ritual technologies and acted as a departure from their traditional goals—it will be useful to turn to a brief discussion of how those who engaged *madīḥ* in their traditional context understood these "modern" *madīḥ* that the state supported in contradistinction to what they presented. In a conversation with ʿAbd al-Rahim Hajj Ahmad, the founder and director of the Grandsons' Center for Media Production and Publication (*Markaz al-Asbāṭ li-l-Intāj al-Iʿlāmī wa-l-Nashr*), which is the main producer of cassettes of al-Buraʿi's *madīḥ*, I asked him what the difference is between the function and goals of mass-mediated *madīḥ*, such as those one might encounter on al-Kawthar, and those used in Sufi worship. We should note that ʿAbd al-Rahim is a first cousin of Shaykh al-Buraʿi (though junior to him by probably about forty years) and a very active participant in the daily life and ritual of al-Buraʿi's Sufi order in its Omdurman branch, attending *dhikrs* and organizing *madīḥ* nights and recitations of classical Sufi texts such as *Dalāʾil al-khayrāt*. Though the existence of a new national audience for *madīḥ* is due in great part to his efforts, ʿAbd al-Rahim is also well aware of *madīḥ*'s origins and indeed sustains an interest in both modes of audition. It was his unique position, at the cutting edge of the mediatization of *madīḥ*, but also deeply ensconced in Sufi tradition, that distinguished him from the staff of al-Kawthar and made him particularly well positioned to answer my questions.

> [that has a particular meaning] because you need what this characteristic [associated with the name] offers. So I try to give them names so they understand the meanings of the words, but they just repeat the words. And now this *rātib* [a form of ritual chanting of the Sufis and the Mahdists], it is just music. And even the Qur'an to them is just sound: like the symphony of Beethoven. [But] the correct *tilāwa* (style of recitation) makes the tongue read [not only] with sound [but also] with mind, the meaning, reading with [attention to] how it moves your life [and impressing upon you that] you must follow this guidance.

For al-Turabi, as for the staff of al-Kawthar, the Sufi preoccupation with ritual audition distracted them from the meaning of scripture and the religious teachings included in them. Though *tilāwa*, the music of recitation, was a necessary component of that ritual act, if it only inculcated emotion and did not further practical action, then its energy was wasted. In the above passage, al-Turabi expresses bafflement that the Sufis, to whom he's explained the names of God so that they can use them properly in supplicatory prayer, persist in repeating them over and over without any concern for their meaning, as if they had some sort of talismanic properties. "Even the Qur'an," he bemoans, "to them it is just sound." The whole postural, kinesthetic, and sonic aspect of the traditional realm of both Qur'anic and *madīḥ* audition is in this manner deemed only important to the extent that it facilitates understanding.

While his answer to my request to compare the two modes of audition is both lengthy and technical, I think it is worth quoting in full, as in it he reveals a whole rule-bound kinesthetic regime governing classical *madīḥ* audition that is lost in the context of recorded audition. He told me:

> The goal of *madīḥ* in *ḥalaqa*s (Sufi worship circles) is for people to listen and to remember God as well. Listening and remembrance of God (*dhikr*) at the same time [is the goal]. And when you are in a *dhikr* [ritual ceremony], you are going to have the disposition (*istʿidād*) to listen to *madīḥ* more than when you are in a car, restaurant, or public transport. You will be focused and living from inside, living the meanings of these *madīḥ*. They influence you more than if you were just listening to them in a car, or if you were listening to them in a fast food restaurant. . . . When you are in the *dhikr* you want to be satiated by Sufism. And according to the Sufis when you are in a *dhikr* there is a spiritual connection between you and your shaykh. The soul of the shaykh is present at the *dhikr*. And you will benefit from this spirit [of the shaykh], and it will give you a spiritual energy. We call it the *madad* (help) and we take from [the *dhikr*] this *madad*. . . . [Further, in order to achieve maximum effect, in the context of Sufi worship] every genre of [*madīḥ*] has its own mode of action [associated with it]. Poems of *waʿẓ* (admonition) are used with the accompaniment of the *nawba* [large bass drum] and in a *dhikr* in which you are standing. For *madīḥ* [on the subject of the Prophet] you need to be sitting, and the rhythm of the[se] *madīḥ* is from the *ṭār* [small hand drum] and not the *nawba*. And you thus listen to *madīḥ* [on the Prophet] sitting and in a different way than the way you listen to *madīḥ* of *iṣlāḥ* [social reform]. . . . And one of the goals of the poem [that is recited in the *dhikr*] is not merely listening, [but rather] the rhythm itself. Because you are in a rhythm and you have a specific set of movements. If the rhythm were not there, the movements would not be orderly. But when there is a rhythm [as with the *nawba* drum in the *dhikr*] your movements will be in sync (*muntaẓim*) with it. And this [*dhikr* of] "allah, allah, allah," you can't pay attention to it unless there is this movement.

Several things are present here that ʿAbd al-Rahim indicates are absent in the new culture of *madīḥ* audition. First, we learn that the place in which one listens to *madīḥ* is crucial to the forming of the dispositions necessary to absorb its effects. In the *dhikr* your ability to listen and pay attention is different from your ability to do so in a car or restaurant. Here it is clear that it is not just listening to *madīḥ* that matters, but cultivating a certain kind of attentiveness that allows the *madīḥ* to have their effect on you, helping you to remember God and the Prophet, is essential as well. Next, and in relation to this issue of place, we learn of the *madad* (supernatural assistance) that one receives from the physical presence of a shaykh when *madīḥ* are sung in *dhikr*. Though modern *madīḥ* in the urban spaces one encounters them are posed as important for the kind of emotional apparatus they excite and the didactic work that they do, concepts such as *madad* or *baraka* that require the physical presence of the listener as one among a community of worshippers remain unimportant. Or rather, regardless of their importance, they are unattainable.

Next, ʿAbd al-Rahim tells us that the kind of attentiveness necessary to achieving these goals of *madīḥ* listening can only be attained through certain kinds of kinesthetic procedures. For example, we learn that there are specific postures associated with listening to certain genres of *madīḥ* and different postures for others: standing in a communal worship circle if the genre is *al-waʿẓ wa-l-irshād* ("admonition and guidance"), sitting submissively on the ground if the genre concerns the Prophet. Such observations about the appropriate *adab* (formal manners) associated with *madīḥ* listening are not posed merely as a way of performing a virtue that is already interior, but are instead understood as essential to developing a particular mode of attentiveness that allows the listener to embody the virtues expressed in the various *madīḥ* genres. As anthropologist Saba Mahmood has argued, "bodily form in this view does not simply represent the interiority . . . but serves as the 'developable means' through which certain kinds of ethical and moral capacities are attained" (Mahmood 2005: 134–38). This concept of bodily practices seems to be what ʿAbd al-Rahim is referring to in his discussion of *adab*. Indeed, a whole set of movements dictated by rhythm are also essential to the kind of attentive listening that he describes: "If the rhythm were not there, the movements would not be orderly . . . [and] you can't pay attention to it unless there is movement." Here not only is the specific type of rhythm deemed essential to the ritual act of remembering God, but the involvement of the body in this process of attaining this "attentiveness" is also central. For ʿAbd al-Rahim, listening does not just involve the ears but also co-opts many other parts of the body that join in its proper performance. The argument is that when *madīḥ* are played in nonritual spaces (the car or the fast food restaurant, to which he refers above), they speak *not only* to a distracted ear that is listening as much to the cacophony of urban Khartoum as to *madīḥ*, *but to a distracted body as well*, in which the limbs are not involved in listening (but instead eating or driving a car), as they are in the *dhikr* circle. This loss of attentiveness of not just the ear, but of the entire body, means a change in what *madīḥ* are able to accomplish. As ʿAbd al-Rahim puts it, remembering God in such contexts becomes impossible: "You can't pay attention."

This notion of the importance of attentiveness to achieving the goals of *madīḥ* audition was also stressed to me by an elderly *mādiḥ* (chanter of *madīḥ*, pl. *mudāḥ, mādiḥīn*) whom I will call Shaykh Mukhtar. The issue of attentiveness, and a certain kind of skepticism that it could be achieved in the urban contexts that were al-Kawthar's workshop for constructing the pious citizen, was crucial to those who participated in the classical regime of *madīḥ* audition. For them, the inability to achieve such attentiveness meant that some of the benefits of *madīḥ* were unattainable. Shaykh Mukhtar was highly skeptical of the recent resurgence in *madīḥ*. He argued:

> When you listen to *madīḥ* live in front of you, you pay attention. But when you are listening to *madīḥ* in a car, perhaps, people will be talking and won't let you listen well. . . . Before, in the [19]60s, when we would sing *madīḥ* for the *ʿulamāʾ* of the Sufis, it was forbidden for anyone to talk because they were visualizing (*bistaḥḍirū*, lit. conjuring up) the presence of the Prophet (*ḥaḍrat al-nabī*). . . . For when you remember the Prophet, he is present.

The ban on talking that Shaykh Mukhtar recalls was yet another important aspect of *adab* that was lost in new regimes of audition: the silence that he sees as necessary to proper listening was unobtainable in the constant hum of urban life. Shaykh Mukhtar argues that when *madīḥ* are played as background music in one's car, where people may be distracted by conversation or other goings-on of life, visualizing the Prophet becomes impossible. Further, when *madīḥ* are taken out of their ritual context, there are no religious authority figures present to effect the ban on talking, and thus the styles of listening he remembers are no longer enforced.

Shaykh Mukhtar contended that it was not only the style of listening that was essential to the realization of certain goals of the classical order of *madīḥ*, but that the particular style of musical accompaniment was also critical. Here, something deemed inessential, interchangeable, and merely a means of "attracting youth" by the vanguards of the modern *madīḥ* movement—who used even tunes derived from pop music as sugar-coating for their *madīḥ* project—was understood to be integral to the accomplishment of *madīḥ* audition's goals. He argued:

> [If] the [traditional] *ṭār* [drum] disappeared [due to this focus by the youth on other musical accompaniment, such as the keyboard], the love [of the Prophet] would also disappear (*idhā al-ṭār inʿadam, ḥat inʿadam al-maḥabba*). The reason is that in the *ṭār* is the leadership (*qiyāda*) of the *madīḥ*. So, if you sing *madīḥ* with the *ṭār*, the *madīḥ* will be good and will show you the miracles and the good qualities of the Prophet and will help you understand it easily and with love. On the other hand, this [playing of *madīḥ* with keyboard] is [just] dancing (*raqṣ*). It is my opinion that people should therefore return to [playing] *madīḥ* with the *ṭār*. . . . Because the music of the *ṭār* is entertaining spiritually

> (*muṭriba rūḥiyyan*). So that you feel that you have a soul that harmonizes (*titjāwib*) with the words and tune. . . . The *ṭār* brings the soul to life and also makes people [so moved that they] get up and dance in appreciation (*yaʿriḍū*, i.e., perform the *ʿarḍa*).[10] . . . [The *ʿarḍa*] is more than just a dance though, because after one has gotten up to do it, the tears will start running and then he begins speaking in *tarjama* [glossolalia].[11] Where does this all come from? From the performance of the *ṭār*. . . . What has happened to [this man who begins to speak in *tarjama*] is that there is something called "spiritual presence" (*tawājud rūḥī*). And where does it come from? From the taste [that you exhibit in the manner] of your listening (*min al-dhawq bitāʿ al-samāʿ bitāʿak inta*). If you listen and comprehend the words that are sung [in the *madḥa*], this "presence" occurs, a spiritual drunkenness (*sakar rūḥī*). . . . There are many types of spiritual alcohol (*khamra rūḥiyya*): *al-ṭilla* (drizzle), *khandarīs* (old wine). That which makes someone scream and run around is the *ṭilla*, wherein you feel that rain has entered inside your heart. So the rain comes in your heart and gives you a feeling that makes you scream and ululate and run around and your tears run and after a little while it goes away. You feel like you did something without any conscious volition on your part. So this is what? This is the influence of your love of what you have understood from that to which you are listening. On the other hand this music [of the keyboard played by the youth], you dance to it but there isn't anything. . . . We have never seen anyone cry because of it . . . [and when someone cries it means that his insides are] breathing [*tanaffus*]. . . . And this elevates the soul (*fīhā tarqiya li-l-rūḥ*).

The above passage is fascinating for several reasons. In it, Shaykh Mukhtar explains his understanding of the necessity of the *ṭār* drum for reaching the emotional state of love of the Prophet (*maḥabbat al-rasūl*) and the various modes of spiritual drunkenness that he describes. While the difference between *madīḥ* put to the sounds of the keyboard and the *madīḥ* sung to the accompaniment of drums is today often thought to be simply a matter

10 Two modes of expressive bodily movement, which English does not have the semantic range to capture (thus I translate both as "dance"), are indicated by the concepts of *raqṣ* (above) and *ʿarda* (here). The former is understood to be uncontrolled, passionate movement that takes place as part of a celebration, while the latter is a formal mode of dance performed by members of the audience as a means of thanking the performers and showing their love of the music in Sufi (and other) musical contexts. The speaker is denigrating the former and celebrating the latter.

11 *Tarjama* (literally "translation") was the word used for the ecstatic modes of glossolalia in which some Sufis engaged during *dhikr* or in response to *madīḥ* audition. Though I never got a clear answer, it was my impression that the term refers to the translation of emotional impulse into speech.

of taste, the favored music of the older generation versus that of the young, a question of what "dressing" they prefer on top of what is actually important in *madīḥ* (i.e., the words), here Shaykh Mukhtar argues that the *ṭār* itself has a crucial ritual function. It produces "spiritual drunkenness" and a harmonious soul, which "musical" *madīḥ* (that is, *madīḥ* put to modern instrumentation, such as those broadcast on al-Kawthar) cannot deliver. The screaming, crying, *tarjama*, and the *'arḍa* dance are both signs of love of the Prophet and a means by which to achieve it, all of which drops out in modern modes of *madīḥ* audition. So, in addition to the locations of performance and the kinds of postures one assumes while listening, the actual instruments with which *madīḥ* are perfomed are deemed essential to their function in the classical regime of *madīḥ* audition in a way that they are not by the vanguard of the modern *madīḥ* movement such as the directors of al-Kawthar. Shaykh Mukhtar contends that when the musical context of drumming disappears, true love of the Prophet also disappears ("We have never seen anyone cry because of it"), thus casting in doubt the translatability of *maḥabbat al-rasūl* into the new musical genres and contexts of reception that projects such as al-Kawthar promote.

Another Kind of Attentiveness: Listening to Modern *madīḥ*

While the participants in classical Sufi regimes of *madīḥ* audition insisted that love of the Prophet is unobtainable in the new urban listening contexts of al-Kawthar and pined nostalgically for older models of audition, the vanguard of al-Kawthar argued that not only is it possible to achieve *maḥabba* through its new modes of audition, but that through utilizing urban infrastructure (its media, the busses and cars that ferry its mobile populace around town) it could both achieve such goals among a wider populace and repurpose *madīḥ* toward new ends. Anthropologist Charles Hirschkind has argued in his work on cassette sermons in Cairo that theories of modern disenchantment, such as that of Walter Benjamin (or, perhaps, our classical *madīḥ* chanters), do not adequately capture the kind of embodied disciplines that are also made possible by modern urban contexts:

> Benjamin suggests that the accelerated pace of such modern conditions renders the body inadequate to the task of learning. But acceleration also engenders its opposite, slowness, modern monotony with its distinct qualities of repetition, syncopation, dullness. The body as medium of experience is not transcended here but congeals to a specific rhythm, thickness and density.... What forms of experience might exist within the rhythms and textures of urban monotony? . . . Much like Benjamin's storytelling audience, the taxi drivers and shop owners in Cairo

who listen to recorded sermons also engage in a listening practice organized around rhythm and repetition, one that exploits moments of boredom and labor as a means to shape a self through a process of ethical sedimentation. (Hirschkind 2006: 26–27)

Like the Cairene listeners of cassette sermons, the Khartoumite audience of al-Kawthar was also both the object and subject of "a process of ethical sedimentation" achieved through aural experience. It was precisely through modern technology's ability to disseminate religious poetry into new contexts, and through the support given to the resurgence of *madīḥ* by the state, that this traditional Sufi ritual practice was reformulated in pursuit of new goals unimaginable in earlier eras, to spread the *maḥabba* not only more broadly than before, but also to new sorts of religious subjects. As Sudanese moved from the rural Sufi heartlands to Khartoum in ever increasing numbers, and as the intellectuals of the Islamist movement looked for new ritual technologies to sediment the kinds of piety that would be necessary for the flourishing of the Islamic state they imagined, they increasingly turned to *madīḥ* to do this work for them.

While the classical chanter of *madīḥ*, Shaykh Mukhtar, was interested in articulating the unique Sufi modes of listening provided by Sufi ritual contexts, the promoters of modern *madīḥ* were equally interested in elaborating a clear theory of the modes of listening that they were trying to provide for their listeners and its unique potential fruits. While the representatives of traditional Sufi *madīḥ* culture presented modern *madīḥ* audition in terms of loss ("we have never seen anyone cry because of it"), the modern *madīḥ* movement was confident that through the fluent use of modern technologies much was also gained. This idea was clearly expressed by the vice director of al-Kawthar Radio:

> There is surely a difference [between new mediated *madīḥ* and traditional *madīḥ* in Sufi ritual]. When one listens to *madīḥ* in a *dhikr* circle, he doesn't understand the words well. There is a spiritual environment and one is being mindful of God [in the *dhikr* ritual] (*bikūn fī jaw rūḥāni, wa bikūn bidhkur fī allāh*). In most *dhikr* circles a person is doing the ritual through which he remembers God, like when someone does the litanies with the *sibḥa*. Sometimes someone praises God with the *sibḥa* and sometimes someone does so through the performance of *dhikr*. But when someone is in his car, he listens to the words more than in the *dhikr* circle. . . . There are currently so many more means [for hearing *madīḥ*] available for people than there were in previous times . . . there is no comparison.

As we can see, the notion of attentiveness and its proper aim is brought up in the words of this promoter of modern *madīḥ* just as was the case with the Sufis who argued for traditional modes of listening. Yet, here it is not the distraction of daily life that is being bemoaned, as it was with ʿAbd al-Rahim Hajj Ahmad and Shaykh Mukhtar, *but the distraction of Sufi ritual itself.* While for Shaykh Mukhtar the purpose of *madīḥ* was to envision the Prophet and thus to fall in love with him through his presence, for this promoter of new *madīḥ*, the purpose is to understand the words, and thus to come to love his example, something that is deemed impossible to achieve if we listen to *madīḥ* in the midst of the hubbub of drumming, dancing, shouting, and ululating that is characteristic of the *dhikr* and *layālī* scene that Shaykh Mukhtar describes.

While for ʿAbd al-Rahim Hajj Ahmad proper attentiveness could only be attained through involving all parts of the body in the practice of listening, for the vice director of al-Kawthar, bodily movement like *dhikr* and *tasbīḥ* was seen as a distraction from the kind of reflection a modern Muslim requires to understand the words being chanted. When she is not subject to the distraction of Sufi ritual, perhaps when she is driving home from work in the quiet of her car, she can focus on the words and understand. The function of *madīḥ* as a means of envisioning the Prophet, of creating a level of *maḥabba* so great that one cries and speaks in tongues, is replaced by a didactic approach to *madīḥ* in which different forms of attentiveness must be cultivated for the edification of Islamic knowledge, *which only then* leads to the virtue of love. While the affective turn in the humanities has taught us much about how aesthetic experience works through direct appeal to the emotions (e.g., Gregg and Seigworth 2010), contexts such as these show a more complicated intertwining of the intellective and the affective in which emotion (love) and the virtues associated with it (being in love with the Prophet) are the results of both discursive and nondiscursive processes.

Additionally, for the vice director of al-Kawthar, urban space, seen by al-Buraʿi in the poem I quoted at the beginning of the chapter as a potential void into which piety might disappear, was envisioned as the ideal platform on which to create pious individuals, for it provided an abundance of contexts in which to encounter religious poetry ("there are currently so many more means available for people than there were in previous times"). According to the partisans of the new modes of *madīḥ* audition, the portable small radio, MP3, or cassette does not cause religious poetry to degenerate into an entertainment genre, as Shaykh Mukhtar feared, but instead allows each citizen to access the religious experience of the *madḥa* in the mundane contexts of his everyday life. While the vice director imagines listening occurring in a car, and thus projects a certain kind of bourgeois sensibility, other urban sites as well, such as the bus, the store, and the street, become not distractions from ritual duties performed at the right time and in the right place, but new spaces where ritual can take place, so that one's day is suffused with remembrance of God and the Prophet.

Al-Kawthar's project was thus parallel to the critique of the secularization of knowledge posed by the Islamist intellectuals we discussed in the previous chapter. There were to be distinct spaces for "secular pursuits" separate from places for remembering God. Sufis, they argued, had limited *dhikr* to private space. Al-Kawthar, like the project of the Islamic state itself, sought to make all spaces of life arenas for worship, and thus to make all (Islamic) religion public (and, thus, not coincidentally, under the watchful eye of the state). All space was potentially sacred space and the cosmopolitanism, technology, and sonic saturation of urban life made it particularly well-suited to produce the kinds pious citizens necessary for the Islamic state project.

Affective Citizen-Making

The new format of twenty-four-hour pop radio in which al-Kawthar couched its *madīḥ* attempted to create a whole new type of religious subject, abstracted from his former "sectarian" ties, and whose personhood entangled the discourses of both piety and citizenship. To do this, the al-Kawthar vanguard imagined an Islamic state built on a nation in love with the Prophet, a bold claim, especially given classical Islamic theology's insistence on the individuality of pious achievements. This agenda is visible in the opening words of the radio station's glossy Annual Report for its first year, which began with the famous hadith that grounds the concept of "love of the Prophet" (*maḥabbat al-rasūl*) in the canonical tradition:

> The Prophet (*ṣlʿm*) said:
>
> > "Not one of you is a believer until I am more beloved to him than himself, his son, his father, and all people combined."[12]
>
> Believe [the words of] the Prophet of God (*ṣlʿm*).
>
> Emerging from this honorable hadith, there arose the idea of establishing al-Kawthar Radio, which would specialize in glorification and praise (*taʿẓīm wa madḥ*) of the Prophet (*ṣlʿm*), as well as in increasing the knowledge of the people (*ziyādat maʿrifat al-nās*) with the most thorough [descriptions of] the details of the life of the noble Prophet and his family and descendants (*āl baytihi*) and his pious companions. It is known that the Sudanese people are among the peoples of the world who love and glorify the beloved Mustafa [one of the names of the Prophet] (*ṣlʿm*) the most, so therefore al-Kawthar found no difficulty in

12 *lā yu'min aḥadakum ḥattā akūn aḥabba ilayhi min nafsihi wa waladihi wa wālidihi wa-l-nās ajmaʿīn*. For one iteration of this hadith, see e.g., *Ṣaḥīḥ Muslim, Kitāb al-īmān*, 63.

> finding acceptance and welcome from all of the Sudanese people, [living] in and outside Sudan (the latter [who heard al-Kawthar] through the Arabsat Satellite). . . . And here we are now, the radio station having completed its [first] year and it has assumed a leading place among the other radio stations . . . glorifying and spreading knowledge about the upright Prophet through explaining [his] sweet-smelling biography . . . in various programs and also through what the musicians (*muṭribīn*) and classical singers of *madīḥ* (*mādiḥīn*) perform of the prophetic *madīḥ*, [played] to the [the traditional] *ṭār* [drum] and to music. (al-Kawthar Annual Report, c. 2006)

The idea that the "Sudanese people are among the peoples of the world who love and glorify the beloved Mustafa (*ṣlʿm*) the most" relied on a definition of the country that willfully ignored its non-Muslim minority, whose presence had just been reaffirmed in the signing of the 2005 CPA with the SPLM and the drafting of the new constitution only a few months later. However, the idea that it should be "love of the Prophet" that characterized Sudanese people's relationship to Islam in the period of the late Inqadh also represented a significant shift from the earlier relationship to Islam that the Inqadh promoted in such initiatives as the Civilization Project, discussed in Chapter 2, which was so deeply problematized by the principles of the CPA. The cultivation of virtues such as *maḥabbat al-rasūl* was a task that took on special importance at a time when an effort to define state institutions on a more multicultural foundation was challenging *other* national expressions of Islamic piety, such as Islamic law and Islamic education. There is thus no coincidence in the concurrence of the signing of the CPA in January of 2005 and the founding of al-Kawthar only nine months later.

The regime's recognition that, as Terry Eagleton has written, aesthetics "insert[s] social power more deeply into the very bodies of those it subjugates" (1990: 28, or perhaps "subjectifies" to extend Eagleton in a Foucauldian fashion that he would most probably reject), focusing as it does on the seat of the passions, made the attention that the regime paid to aesthetics far from incidental. As we recall from the discussion in Chapter 1 about the colonial state's project to transition Sudanese from "fanaticism" to "religion," the recognition that an ability to appeal to emotional capacities has a certain political fecundity has a lengthy history in Sudan. It is perhaps to this very type of attention to the emotions that the Islamist intellectuals we discussed in Chapter 2 were referring when one of them wrote, "More than merely changing politics, the project of the Inqadh begins with the individual as the nucleus of society and the appropriate sphere (*al-majāl al-mawḍūʿī*) for the work of the state" (Harun 1995). Indeed, in projects such as al-Kawthar, the regime seemed to recognize the individual in all her capacities, rational and emotive. Its attempt to train the latter toward a higher set of passions is in line with the work of the aesthetic science since its inauguration.[13]

Yet, more immediately, by recognizing the importance of the passions and the proper shepherding thereof, regime intellectuals were able to draw on a lengthy tradition in Islamic theology that speaks robustly on this topic. Islamic thought has long contemplated the relationship between the aesthetic dimensions of ritual acts and the development of pious virtues, a relationship that runs directly through the domain of the passions. In al-Ghazali's famous *Iḥyāʾ ʿulūm al-dīn*, for example, he discusses the call to prayer as follows:

> When you hear the call to prayer given by the Muezzin, let yourself feel the terror of the summons on Resurrection Day. . . . So review your heart now: if you find it full of joy and happiness, eager to respond with alacrity, you can expect the Summons to bring you good news and salvation on the Day of Judgment. (al-Ghazali 1983: 44)

The call to prayer here serves not merely as a reminder to perform one's ritual duty. It works at an affective level as well, instilling fear in its listener. That fear is then embraced not merely as an emotion or passion, but as a virtue, akin to piety itself (Mahmood 2005: 144–45), which that aesthetic experience has helped develop and which the Muslim then carries with himself throughout all of his daily existence. Such a feeling of fear (which, interestingly, al-Ghazali conflates with "joy and happiness" in the same passage) cannot be taught but must be awakened in the listener through an appeal to his emotions. The audition of *madīḥ* works in a similar manner for the Sudanese state seeking new means to cement its Islamic identity: by quickening the feeling of love for the Prophet in the hearts of Sudanese Muslims, it is hoped that Sudanese will not just assent to the Islamic state project (by hook or by crook) but will come to desire it.

Such feelings of love were not only awakened through vivid descriptions of the Prophet in *madīḥ*. A downright sultry set of "public service announcements" featured on al-Kawthar in heavy rotation as well. In these announcements, a breathy woman's voice encouraged pious acts and whispered love and praise of the Prophet. Many of the tunes of the *madīḥ* also

13 As Baumgarten (1714–62), the founder of the modern science of aesthetics, wrote long ago, perhaps echoing the regime's interest in, on the one hand, policing sexual ethics, and, on the other, exciting passions of another sort: "The lower faculties require control and not tyranny . . . aesthetics, as far as this can be achieved by natural means, in fact leads them toward this condition by the hand, as it were, and . . . the lower faculties, as long as they are corrupt, should not be aroused or strengthened by aestheticians, but rather directed by them, so that they should not become even further corrupted by inexpert practice, or lest the use of a talent bestowed by God be abolished on the easy pretext of avoiding its misuse" (Baumgarten 2000: 491).

had romantic associations; some tunes came from popular love songs, and many of the pop singers employed to sing them were known for songs of desire for the opposite sex rather than for the Prophet.[14] In relying on the context of love songs, al-Kawthar was not engaged merely in an attempt to attract listeners using hip cultural forms and figures. Rather, it sought to draw on the emotional register of these songs in order to instill love of the Prophet in its listeners, activating an affective apparatus that *only* secular forms can invoke to the average listener untrained in mystical heights. The Sufi borrowing of form, meter, and metaphor from secular poetry for its own literary output is nothing new. Medieval Sufis are famous for engaging in this practice, often getting themselves into trouble for extending such metaphors too far.[15] As Brian Larkin has cogently observed about a set of Sufi love poems from Nigeria that used Bollywood tunes as their vehicle:

> In the context of Hausa society . . . Indian films can be sexually transgressive, as their erotic display, their sexual intermixing, and the use of music for carnal and not religious purposes combine to keep them beyond the pale of orthodox Islam. For *bandiri* singers it is necessary to evoke these origins to set in motion the power of nostalgia and affect at

14 Interestingly this extractive process of using love songs and their singers for their affective capabilities (and then discarding their carnal refuse) did not represent a one-way relationship between Islamists and pop stars. In an article published in a secular culture magazine entitled, "Between *madīḥ* and Singing: Have the Characteristic Marks of [Pop] Singers (*fanānīn*) Been Lost?" (al-Imam 2007), the pop star Muhammad Hasan implied that he was not being duped by Islamists. Just as the vanguard of al-Kawthar found him useful for the romantic love his voice evoked, so he found *madīḥ* useful for the technical improvements they contributed to his secular singing (*ghinā*ʾ). He said, "*Madīḥ* have a positive influence on my artistic path (*masīratī al-fanniyya*) [in singing pop songs], indeed because of *madīḥ* I have improved the articulation of the words that I sing, for *madīḥ* need a longer breath, and they include difficult words, so when you overcome [such difficulties] it becomes truly easy to sing [pop songs] (*taghannī*)." Though he too enjoyed singing praise for the Prophet, he did not see his *madīḥ* chanting as taking the place of his flirtatious love songs. Rather, his participation in this religious art made his secular singing even more effective.

15 Michael Sells discusses the borrowing of secular love poetry in which Sufis like Ibn ʿArabi were engaged. For example, Sufis took the figure of *Majnūn* Layla (the one who was mad for his beloved Layla) from pre-Islamic poetry as a model on which to base their own divine love, even boldly keeping the feminine gender at times when talking about God as the beloved. Thus, like in present-day Sudan, in the medieval period, Sufi poetry owed a great debt to the secular tradition (Sells 2000: 20–24; see also 31, where Sells speaks of Ibn ʿArabi's debt to the *ghazal* love poet ʿUmar ibn Abi Rabiʿa). Sells also argues elsewhere that Qurʾanic verse spoke in a genre that would have appealed to its Arabian audience and thus included themes present in pre-Islamic Bedouin poetry, albeit with its values transfered toward Godly ends (Sells 2006b: 8–10). Thus the preoccupation of the tradition in distinguishing between sacred verse (from *āyāt* to *madīḥ*) and poetry (from *shiʿr* to *ghināʾ*) may be due to the tensions raised by the very subtle ways in which the former draws on the latter while rejecting many of its key premises.

> the same time as they must be rejected in order for the transformation from secular to sacred to occur. . . . *Bandiri* singers wish to maintain that intensity of emotion, to copy it, but then to divorce it from its original context, leaving only a heightened state of being. (2004: 104–5)

Some of the same techniques were employed by al-Kawthar as well, except here the target was not merely the individual Muslim, but the Sudanese nation as a whole, which it sought to form into being "[among] the peoples of the world who love and glorify the beloved Mustafa (*ṣlʿm*) the most."

"The People of Sudan Love You, Oh Messenger of God"

By dislocating *madīḥ* from their traditional home in the Sufi orders, the producers of modern *madīḥ* attempted to address Sudanese Muslims *in toto*, regardless of their associational affiliations, as well as to reach them where they were: in those spaces of labor and movement that are characteristic of the modern city. The ultimate goal was reforming the citizenry to create a national public "in love" with the Prophet, so as to define Sudan in Islamic tones at a time when rival definitions of its character (secular, multicultural, African) proliferated. The urban context of the national capital would be the geographic space in which that definition took place, exactly at the moment when its demographic identity was in flux due both to massive migration and a peace agreement and constitution that explicitly recognized the nation's diversity. Moreover, the urban context became a means to sustain this Islamic definition, specifically because its unique features of population and sonic density made mass-ritual projects possible there in a way that would be unachievable in any other geographic space.[16]

One particularly vivid example of this national project was the massive media campaign that al-Kawthar organized to make "Sudan the Country That Prays upon the Prophet the Most" (*al-sūdān akthar balad yuṣallī ʿalā al-rasūl*). As with *madīḥ*, al-Kawthar drew again on Sufi ritual practices, here that of *taṣliya*, to help constitute the idea of an Islamic Sudan at a time of great uncertainty. "Prayer upon the Prophet" (*taṣliya*) is a common ritual practice in Islam, though one particularly pronounced among Sufis, in which the listener prays to God that he extend his mercy on the Prophet.

16 Though of course they were well aware that certain Salafi groups, such as Ansar al-Sunna, saw *madīḥ* as forbidden in Islam—because instrumentation in worship (or elsewhere) was out of the bounds of *Sunna* and because the "excessive" praise of the Prophet and Sufi shaykhs in the poems themselves was, in their minds, akin to idolatry—the directors of al-Kawthar aimed at the vast majority of Sudanese who held no such bias. A key example of the Salafi critique of *madīḥ* can be found in Umar al-Tihami's *Shiʿr al-Buraʿī fī mīyzān al-kitāb wa-l-sunna* (*The Poetry of al-Buraʿi on the Scales [of Judgment] of Qur'an and Sunna*) (al-Tihami 2002).

The practice is most often stressed as bringing good fortune not on the Prophet (who, being the greatest of all God's messengers, has little need for Muslims' prayer) but on the believer herself, instilling in her the virtue of *maḥabba*, or love of the Prophet, and bringing good fortune (de la Puente 1999; Schimmel 1985: 92-4).[17] The prayer is unique in that, since it is supererogatory, and since the Prophet did not specify as necessary any particular formula (*ṣīgha*) for performing it, it can be uttered in any context, by any person regardless of his ritual purity, and in any form. It thus lends itself particularly well to informal contexts: driving a car, lying in bed at home, or walking down the street. While *taṣliya* is traditionally performed as part of an individual regime of piety, in the case of the project that sought to make "Sudan the Country That Prays upon the Prophet the Most," the Sudanese nation itself took on a central role in the theological imaginary of those who organized it.

Along with the words "Join Us!" (*ishtarikū maʿanā!*), in 2006 the phrase "Sudan Is the Country That Prays upon the Prophet the Most" was plastered on billboards across the capital and repeated often on al-Kawthar Radio, along with the rejoinder that in order to participate listeners should perform *al-ṣalā ʿalā al-rasūl* (prayer upon the Prophet) by repeating one of several stock phrases in front of their radios, in their cars, or at work at least ten times per day. If all of Sudan would do this, the project organizers suggested, the motto (whose empirical veracity many questioned),[18] could

17 In a famous hadith the Prophet says, "He who prays for me one time, God will extend upon him his blessings 10 times. And he who prays for me 10 times, God will extend upon him his blessings 100 times. And he who prays for me 100 times, God will extend upon him his blessings 1000 times. And he who prays for me 1000 times, God will not torture him with the fire [in the hereafter]." Though this practice is most often seen within the Sufi tradition, its permanence in the Islamic tradition as a whole is often stressed by pointing to the *āya* from the Qur'an (*al-Aḥzāb*: 56): "Indeed God and the Angels extend their blessings on the Prophet. Oh you who believe, ask for his blessings and good fortune" (*inna allāha wa malāʾikatahu yuṣallūna ʿalā al-nabī, yā ayyuhā alladhīn āmanū, ṣallū ʿalayhi wa sallimū taslīman*).

18 The title of this project caused much confusion, and even derision, among Sudanese who understood the verb *yuṣalli* as being in the present tense and read this phrase as an evaluation of Sudanese piety as greater than that of other countries ("How would one measure this?," they asked). Al-Kawthar's director for external relations explained the project to me as follows:

> And in the year 1428 [AH] we decided to do [a project called] "Sudan Is the Country That Prays upon the Prophet the Most." And around this name a lot of disagreement arose. There are people who say how does al-Kawthar Radio know that Sudan is the country that prays upon the Prophet the most? From where did you get these statistics? So we say to them, "My brother, if you checked the motto from the perspective of the Arabic language, '*al-sūdān akthar balad yuṣallī*,' *yuṣallī* is in the tense which includes both the sense of present and future (*al-muḍāriʿ*). It is continuing. I didn't say *ṣalla* [i.e., the past tense verb]! What it means is that al-Kawthar Radio wants, it hopes that this

become a reality: Sudan would indeed be the country that prays upon the Prophet the most. Piety was not to come about through the enforcement of the unpopular public-order laws of yesteryear, which regulated dress and public comportment, but through encouraging Sudanese to cultivate the virtue of *maḥabba*.

On the radio itself, advertisements for this project ran every fifteen minutes that year. They began with the words, "Oh kind listener (*ayyuhā al-mustamaʿ al-karīm*), indeed your prayer upon the Prophet (*ṣlʿm*) is the definite guarantee for the forgiveness of sins. Participate with us in the program 'Sudan Is the Country That Prays upon the Prophet the Most' (*ṣlʿm*), 1428 AH." Then it would be explained that one should repeat a certain litany ten times a day in the most simple of the *ṣīghas* (formats), the *anasiyya*: *allāhumma ṣallī ʿalā sayyidnā muḥammad wa ʿalā ahlihi wa sallim*. By means of the radio, a national ritual endeavor was inaugurated that sought to instill *maḥabba* as the defining characteristic of the newest stage in Sudan's Islamic present.

That love of the Prophet had become a national agenda for the modern *madīḥ* movement was reinforced by some of the *madīḥ* broadcast on al-Kawthar itself. The *madḥa* "*shaʿb al-sūdān yuḥibbak yā rasūl allāh*" ("The People of Sudan Love You, Oh Messenger of God"), written by the founder of al-Kawthar Radio, Khalid al-Mustafa,[19] seemed to suggest a definition of Sudan based on the virtue of *maḥabba*:

> The People of Sudan love you, Oh Messenger of God.
> (*shaʿb al-sūdān yuḥibbak yā rasūl allāh*)
> All of Sudan holds you dear, oh you of great position.
> (*kul al-sūdān yaʿizzak, yā ʿaẓīm al-jāh*)
> We are the people who love you the most
> and we challenge other nations in this matter [to prove better than us].
> (*u fīk nitḥadā li-l-ajnās*)
> Our love for you is firmly founded between our ribs, and the foundation stone [for our nation(?)], oh you of high position. . . .

---

year Sudan *will* be the country in which people pray the most for the Prophet (*ṣlʿm*). And this is actually what happened.

19 Khalid al-Mustafa is a key non-Sufi composer of *madīḥ* (by "non-Sufi" I mean that he did not represent a particular *ṭarīqa*, though he was clearly engaged in Sufism as a general religious program). He had a background in business and journalism, and only late in life started to compose *madīḥ*. Many of his *madīḥ* were performed on al-Kawthar, and an important *dīwān* of his work was published by al-Kawthar that came with a CD of his *madīḥ* performed by Sudan's most popular pop stars. He was widely said to be a regime activist or sympathizer, and judging by his political *madīḥ* and statements on his website (http://www.hashimoon.com) regarding the Sudanese president, as well as the fact of al-Kawthar's government support, this seems to be the case. In an interview with him published on his website, this sense was echoed by the interviewer who comments, "It is said that you are the sultan's poet."

The People of Sudan love you, Oh Messenger of God.
All of Sudan holds you dear, oh you of great position. . . .
Your love is a national resource (*tharwa qawmiyya*).
We pray [upon the Prophet and in so doing] renew our desire.
And the percentage that Taha [one of the names of the Prophet Muhammad] would get in votes is more than 100%, oh you of great position.
The People of Sudan love you, Oh Messenger of God.
All of Sudan holds you dear, oh you of great position.
The young and old in my country, our prayers and good wishes are in the thousands for you, who give support to the family of the Quraysh so that they may remain secure,[20] oh you of great position.
The People of Sudan love you, Oh Messenger of God.
All of Sudan holds you dear, oh you of great position.[21]

While the nationalist context of these lyrics is obvious to any listener, the specific historical context of Sudan in the post-CPA world was also being referenced in this poem: the prediction of election results overwhelmingly favoring the Prophet (or, obliquely, the parties who claimed to represent his way) came as Sudan was pondering its first national elections in twenty years, a contest in which the Islamic party was not certain of victory.[22] At a time when the fruits of one national resource (oil) were finally being harvested thanks to peace with the South, Khalid al-Mustafa reminded Sudan not to ignore its greatest national resource (*tharwa qawmiyya*), the love of the Prophet, which many argued was being ignored simply to perpetuate

20 Referencing *Sūrat Quraysh*: 1 (*li-īlāf quraysh*). The Quraysh is the tribe of the Prophet.

21 I recently came across a music video for this *madḥa* on YouTube (http://youtu.be/IQLUL_A-bo0). The *madḥa* is performed (as it likely was in the version I heard on al-Kawthar in 2006) by the pop singer Muʿataz Sabahi and alternates images of the song being performed live, Sufis deep in the throng of *dhikr*, and political leaders (such as the president and then vice president, ʿAli ʿUthman Muhammad Taha) celebrating at various public events. As if to stress Sudan's unity around the Islamic identity that is being invoked, the pop star Mahmud ʿAbd al-Aziz (who tragically died a few years later in 2013 at age forty-five), a member of the opposition SPLM who turned to *madīḥ* in his later years, is seen singing backup. Though Mahmud's reasons for singing this song was likely purely spiritual, the way his image was co-opted for this clearly political project is evidence of the way the government sought to unify all (Muslim) Sudanese around an Islamic national identity of which it then claimed to be the best representative. The tensions evident in Mahmud's new role as a *mādiḥ (*chanter of *madīḥ)* are on display in Ranya Faqiri's (2007) interview with him, which I discuss in more detail in Salomon 2010.

22 Only a few years before the then-expected April 2010 elections, in which the question of who really *does* want an Islamic state was to be put to the test for the first time since the 1986 democratic elections, the percentage that "Taha" (and those who claimed to be ruling according to his way) would get in the elections was an issue of great concern for the NCP. Though there were many accusations of vote-fixing, a plethora of parties participated in the elections, at least initially, suggesting that an NCP victory was not always a foregone conclusion.

peace with the non-Muslim South (where the oil was), through putting the Islamic program in abeyance. And, at a time when Sudanese who had returned home from the Gulf and Egypt to take part in the economic boom were questioning the idiosyncrasies of Sudanese Islam, Khalid al-Mustafa challenged all other nations to prove that their love for the Prophet was greater than that of Sudan.

On his website, Khalid al-Mustafa explains this poem (among others in his *dīwān)* as follows:

> There were poems on love that spoke about an individual who loves the Prophet (*ṣlʿm*) and then there came [my collection of poetry] . . . which spoke about the love of the [Sudanese] *umma* for the Prophet (*ṣlʿm*). We are a people who love and extol the Prophet (*ṣlʿm*). It would be a big shortcoming for poets not to speak of this love. And I have heard a lot about visions of the Prophet, even from non-Sudanese, [in which the Prophet] talks about the love of this great people for [him] (*ṣlʿm*). And this Sudanese nation (*hadhā al-shaʿb al-sūdānī*) needs to be proud of this and present its love and praise of the Prophet (*ṣlʿm*) on a platter of light to the whole world.[23]

Here Khalid al-Mustafa was clearly transferring the agenda of Sufi *madīḥ*, which called for the individual to cultivate and express love for the Prophet, to the Sudanese nation as a whole. It was the duty of Sudan to express this love, and Khalid al-Mustafa was ready to be the poet who would facilitate this national flourishing. In an era when some internal actors and the international community were pushing the Sudanese nation to understand itself in a multiculturalist vein, activists such as Khalid al-Mustafa were attempting to reimagine an Islamic identity for the nation through the powerful combination of classical Sufi poetry with a modern media technology that could broadcast such poetry to the nation as a whole and to its diaspora as well. Poems that had spoken about individual love for the Prophet had been written aplenty, he argued. Now was the time to reflect on and further the special affinity for the Prophet held collectively by the Sudanese nation.

The dual acts of cultivating *maḥabbat al-rasūl* in the nation through mass mediated collective ritual projects such as "Sudan Is the Country That Prays upon the Prophet the Most" and through the audition of nationalist *madīḥ* such as "The People of Sudan Love You, Oh Messenger of God" had important stakes. For al-Kawthar's founder Khalid al-Mustafa, it was through a national auditory project such as al-Kawthar that the nation could achieve the level of love for the Prophet that would help to ensure its Islamic character in this period of great national instability. In an urban space where people were

23 http://www.hashimoon.com/download/1.doc.

detached from their home-*zāwiyas* (small centers of Sufi worship), Khalid al-Mustafa sought to make the entire capital a place where pious training could occur. The future of the state, as Islamic, secular, or something else, depended in the mind of the Inqadh on the ability to create this public piety, a task that was facilitated in part by the modern *madīḥ* movement.

Postscript: Toward a Republic in Love

While revitalizations of Islamic aesthetic forms such as poetry might be understood as an effect of Islamic renewal, in contemporary Sudan we can clearly see that they are also mechanisms to bring such a renewal about. By examining the careful balance established by the promoters of "modern *madīḥ*," between a revival of certain Sufi practices (i.e., sparking love of the Prophet in listeners through poetry) and an Islamic reform agenda (i.e., transcending the limits of this poetry as Sufi ritual practice in order to use it to create new kinds of Muslim subjects), we greatly complicate our vision of the labor involved in establishing the Islamic state. Interventions like al-Kawthar are neither uncritical revitalizations of ancient modes of Islamic practice, as caricatures of Islamist movements such as the NIF/NCP often assume, nor attempts at an obliteration of "local Islams" in favor of a global norm, as others have argued about the emergence of such Islamisms on the African continent.[24] Rather, projects like al-Kawthar can be understood as creative reappropriations of highly effective classical ritual technologies, in this case within Sufism, in the service of new agendas, in this case ones that transcend the bounds of the Sufi orders in which they were developed, reaching for the much-broader mass public of the nation.

Islamist intellectuals recognized the changing face of urban Sudan as a dilemma due to its shifting demographics and its new modes of sociability, both of which challenged the Islamic identity of the republic. Projects such as al-Kawthar, however, sought to harness these challenges and turn them into opportunities, and in so doing rethought the nature of the Islamic state beyond the typical renderings of legal and institutional reform alone. Relying on the classical aesthetic form of poetry and the dense urban space of the unevenly developed republic, the government attempted to instill not only knowledge of Islam in the citizenry, as they had in their epistemological enlightenment project, but also an affective disposition: that of love for

24 An example of an approach that understands Sufism as "local" African Islam, and Islamism as a foreign imposition always in bitter conflict with it, is found in the introduction to *African Islam and Islam in Africa: Encounters between Sufis and Islamists* (Rosander and Westerlund 1997). See Rüdiger Seesemann's insightful critique of this volume on this very matter: Seesemann 2006.

the Prophet. Resisting the post-secular anachronism of dividing the shelves of Islamicate writings into law, literature, history, government, and poetry, in Sudan the Islamic genres that served as a wellspring of political ideas were much more varied than is often recognized in anthologies of "Muslim politics."[25] The full breadth of this political imagination will be on display in the next chapter.

25 Several works in the anthropology of art and poetics have made similar observations. Steven Caton's work on poetry resituated a topic most often studied as "mere aesthetics" in the political and social debates that propelled the Yemen in which he worked. Caton argues, "To suggest that one is doing an ethnography of poetry is to challenge one of the most serious shortcomings of Western poetics, namely, its failure to ground the theory of the poem and the literary institution in a theory of sociopolitical reality, no matter how it is represented ethnographically" (Caton 1993: 20). For Caton, poems are not removed flights of literary fantasy, but are deeply enmeshed in the social and political life of the communities in which they are written and performed, not only in the sense that they are expressive of it, but also in that their performance and consumption has a tangible effect on the social and political life of the communities in question. Jessica Winegar's *Creative Reckonings*, though it is not interested in questions of Islamic reform, also reminds us how an anthropology of art forms, such as the one I attempt in this chapter, is uniquely situated to restore art to the center of social and political processes in the Muslim world (Winegar 2006).

CHAPTER FIVE

Politics in the Age of Salvation

Reimagining the Islamic State

Late one night, during the height of the economically lean years of the Revolution of National Salvation in the early to mid-1990s, a small group of pilgrims straggled wearily off the back of a pickup truck that had just rolled into the holy town of al-Zariba. A small, sandy, but often-bustling village, tucked into an otherwise empty corner of the vast steppe that makes up Northern Kordofan, al-Zariba had only attracted visitors such as these in recent years. The town's renown had arrived on the national stage during the lifetime of its then-patron, Shaykh ʿAbd al-Rahim Muhammad Waqiʿ Allah (1923–2005), a Sufi shaykh of the Sammaniyya order, known by the nickname al-Buraʿi, after a fifteenth-century Yemeni elegist whose poetry the Sudanese shaykh's own verse resembled. A center of religious activity, al-Zariba included by that time several sites for worship, study, and contemplation, as well as all of the trappings of other sacred sites the world over, from traditional medicine to desert commerce.[1]

Tired, thirsty, and hungry from their unexpectedly long journey, the pilgrims were happy to find a small line of worshippers performing the nighttime liturgy (*rātib*) just inside the walls of the *masīd*, the area of the village that included the guest house for pilgrims (*takiyya*), the tomb of the founding father of this branch of the order (*qubba/ḍarīḥ*), the residences of the present shaykhs, the mosque complex, and the school for Qurʾanic

1 The main plot lines of the story I am about to relate were told to me several times during my stay in Sudan. The more literary details about the setting of al-Zariba and the supporting characters were not part of the fable as I was told it, but rather emerge from my field notes from my own travels to and stays in the holy town of al-Zariba, as well as from numerous interviews I conducted over the years with adepts who had spent time there. I took such literary license to add flesh to the bare-bones story I was told in the hope that it might bring the reader closer to the position of the Sudanese receiver of this story. To grasp the political intervention that occupies the central theme of the story's plot, one needs to be familiar with the broader context into which the story intervenes. The experiment in ethnographic fiction writing that follows is my attempt to provide such a context.

study (*khalwa*). The pilgrims stood somewhat shyly a few feet away from the worshippers who were rapt in their late night chants, the same chants that closed out every day in al-Zariba, asking for God's blessings on the Prophet, on his companions, and on the line of shaykhs (*silsila*) from whom al-Buraʿi and his father had received teachings and blessings. This night, however, the lilting chants took on a quickened pace as the worshippers noticed the out-of-towners, and were eager not to neglect their duty of unbounded generosity to guests (*karam*) simply due to the fulfillment of another.

On the conclusion of the last stanza, a young man among the worshippers, whose robes shone a resplendent white even in the dusty desert sand, and from whose eyes a distinct glow could be seen even in the darkness of night, snapped his fingers and mumbled something that the visitors did not quite catch. At that very moment, from the middle of the line, a tall man weighted down with rosary beads around his neck got up quickly and ran with his back arched in a posture of submission, returning only a minute later with a young boy, carrying cups of cold murky water in which sugar and fermented flat bread (*kisra*) had been dissolved. The group of out-of-towners heartily drank this refreshment (called *ʿukāra*, "the muddy drink"), its reputation as the fuel for late-night Qur'an study having followed stories of the shaykh himself to far-off corners of Sudan.

It had been an exceedingly long day for these pilgrims, from waking up at al-Buraʿi's outpost mosque in the state capital of al-Ubayd after a long night of being eaten alive by mosquitos, to finding a ride to al-Zariba in the market at a stall filled with posters depicting the great shaykh, to waiting in the hot truck until it filled up with passengers, to breaking down and losing the path several times in the desert, to sitting longer than they had planned with villagers in a desert hamlet who welcomed them in for a drink of camel milk and insisted that they stay a while. As the sun set that night, still hours from their destination, the women in the group broke into a chant of the *tahlīl*, the Islamic profession of divine unicity. Without pausing, the men had responded to this call with a rhythmic refrain of their own, a syncopated counting of two of the most efficacious names of God. The song that resulted seemed to propel the vehicle along its way: *"lā ilāha illā-llāh . . . ḥayy qayyūm, ḥayy qayyūm . . . lā ilāha illā-llāh . . . ḥayy qayyūm, ḥayy qayyūm"* (There is no God, but God . . . the living, the sustaining, the living, the sustaining . . . there is no God, but God . . . the living, the sustaining, the living, the sustaining). The voices of the passengers filled the empty desert with the presence of God and the pure intentions of his worshippers, strangers bonded in a unity of spirit, and provided a sense of place in what otherwise seemed an infinite expanse of darkness teeming with *jinn* and other misfortune.

After a short stop in the aptly named settlement of Wad al-Qamr (Son of the Moon) for some watermelon, which somehow grew abundantly in Kordofan's otherwise barren landscape in the months following the rainy season, the group continued on its way, dipping and diving over unseen hills, with the blanket of stars above them. From time to time they would catch a grazing camel in the headlights or a stray bush, but otherwise they saw nothing. One by one and then in chorus, the women began to sing *madīḥ* to pass the time, *madīḥ* written by al-Buraʿi as well as classic *madīḥ* written by composers of old, such as al-Hayati, Hajj al-Mahi, and al-Turayfi.

al-surāy, al-surāy
al-jāfū al-nawm wa ʿaqadū al-rāy
allīm mitayn yā mawlāy

The night travelers, the night travelers
Those who forgo sleep and speak in one voice
When will I gather with them, my Lord?[2]

Lulled into a half sleep by this moving prayer circle, all were awoken suddenly when the driver revved the engine and exclaimed his excitement at catching sight in the distance of a single green light, a neon beacon that could be nothing else than the top of the minaret that crested above the central mosque of al-Zariba, the one village with electric generators in this region. The women ululated in joy as the driver sped up, quickening his pace toward the light, which served a similar function to the glow of a lighthouse, or perhaps a modern North Star, the desert certainly as vast as an ocean.

Finally in al-Zariba, after their evening drink and after fending off more substantive offers, the group went off to bed, the men in the men's guesthouse, the women in the women's. They

2 This is a poem attributed to the classical composer of Sudanese *madīḥ*, Shaykh al-Turayfi. The night travelers referred to here are generally understood to be the saints—always awake in prayer and all representing the same path to God despite their varying manifestations—while the poem expresses the believer's longing to be with them.

slept deeply that night, not even noticing the 3 AM recitation of the Qur'an in the nearby boys' *khalwa* or the *fajr* call to prayer, and missing the customary morning tea. The men's sleep was not entirely peaceful, however, as they were awakened several times by the playful nudging of a pet gazelle that lived in the guest quarters. The animal served as a particularly vivid sign of the power of these shaykhs, who exhibited the ability to tame the desert not merely by domesticating wild animals such as this one, but in establishing this remarkable town in the first place. The group finally awoke to the clang of brethren bringing in a late morning breakfast: a small plate of broad beans with sesame oil sprinkled with salt and cumin, bread, some cooked eggs, and a bowl of sweetened sesame paste (*ṭaḥīniyya*). The person in charge of the guesthouse implored them to eat quickly and wash up, for the shaykh was ready to see them and the window for visitors was exceedingly narrow.

The pilgrims reconvened in a shaded area outside the structure known as "the building" (*al-ʿamāra*), the one house in the village that would have been at home in the upscale neighborhoods of the national capital, looking somewhat as if it had arrived by helicopter and been plopped down in the middle of the desert. They climbed the steps of the building until they reached a small *dīwān* on the top floor. There they saw a man whom they had encountered many times before, on television, on the ubiquitous stickers and posters that decorated the backs of busses and small shops in Khartoum, but whom they had never seen in person. Somewhat more frail than they had expected, and with a distinctly informal air about him, al-Buraʿi smiled at these guests, seeming to direct his attention on them, and only them, even though the room was filled with other guests—petitioners and supplicants alike. Though he never said so, the great shaykh made the members of the group feel that he had been expecting them and that he knew what they had come to ask of him.

Still, after they had been beckoned to approach him and were sitting on the floor as he reclined on a cot above them, they made their much-rehearsed plea. Times were tough financially. Their families back home had little to eat. Their sons were fleeing to far-off lands to find work so they could send home remittances, irreparably breaking up the fabric of family life in the process. The Revolution of National Salvation seemed to be turning into yet another of the ambitious projects proposed by successive governments and never completed, millions invested but no result, another failure, like the Jonglei Canal digger, the largest moving

machinery in the history of mankind, that now sat rusting and rotting in the great swamps of the South, foiled by successive bouts of political disarray.[3] And yet, though the pious peregrinations of the National Islamic Front had led to naught, this had not instilled in the pilgrims a sense of the powerlessness of Islam in the face of modern challenges, but only of the failure of some of its servants. Al-Buraʿi's closeness to God was in fact crucial to his this-worldly efficacy. His prayers brought his followers success, he appeared in visions directing people to choices that brought them good fortune, he called to people (and not just Sudanese) in their dreams and drew them to him from as far away as Syria and the Gulf. Like metal to a magnet, they found their way to Sudan and to him, to a better, more fulfilling, life. Al-Buraʿi was a man with power, and if anyone could solve their problems, it was he. Yet no one expected a miracle overnight. The pilgrims simply made the smallest of requests: they asked him to pray for their good fortune, for God to ease their financial woes. Given that his position was so close to God, they hoped that his prayers might have more effect than their own.

Al-Buraʿi met his petitioners' request. He raised his hands in front of his face, whispered his *duʿāʾ* (supplicatory prayer), and concluded it with a clap of his hands. If God willed it, his petitioners' fortunes would be improved.

Most hagiographies of al-Buraʿi, or any other Sufi saint, would have ended with one more line: the resolution of the pilgrims' problem and the recognition of the power of the saint. But this particular story was to turn in a rather different direction, unbeknownst to our protagonists, the weary travelers, who the very next day were likely back in the hull of a pickup truck on their way home. In Sudan in the 1990s, to engage Islam was to engage the state. As the self-appointed arbiter and guarantor of Islamic life, there was no escaping the state for pious Muslims, and this story, too, as we will learn in a moment, is about to become deeply entangled in its snares. Indeed, contrary to assessments that it was a failed project, the state was in fact ubiquitous in those days, the spiritual unable to fend off the grip of the political, no matter how hard it tried, even in Sufi retreats in the far off deserts of Northern Kordofan.[4] Through outfits like the National Council for

3 I thank Professor Justin Willis of Durham University for this metaphor for (and example of) the successive failures of ambitious projects for creating a new Sudan.

4 This was a fact I learned the hard way when I travelled to al-Zariba in July of 2005, trying to escape the riots that followed the death of SPLM leader John Garang. Thinking I'd dodged the country's troubles in this idyllic setting, I was stunned when suddenly the state governor

the Mindfulness of God and Those Who Are Mindful, the state extended its tentacles into ever more remote corners of Islamic life in Sudan. Islamic organizations could not avoid the state, their actions validating state projects or opposing them, often at one and the same time. Al-Buraʿi himself exhibited this phenomenon, for he was at once an agent of the state's Islamization process and an alternative fount of religious (and political) authority, as we saw quite clearly in the previous chapter. In such a context, hagiography, perhaps the primary genre of Islamic storytelling that touches on the intersection of Islam and earthly power[5] (to the extent that its chief literary device is the explication of miracles), became particularly fertile ground for political critique, as this story, which I have left *in media res*, clearly exhibits.

> **To return to our tale: that night, after his petitioners had gone, al-Buraʿi had a dream. Dreams, in the context of Sufism at least, are often a portal to some communication with God or the Prophet, a portent of things to come, or a warning or goad directing the dreamer toward or away from some action in which he or she should or should not be engaged. They are rarely understood as mere fantasy, but rather have an integral connection to the playing-out of waking life.[6] As al-Buraʿi was regarded by his admirers as having access to *ʿilm al-bāṭin* (hidden knowledge) due to his status as one of the *ṣāliḥīn* (righteously pure religious figures), his dreams took on special importance. Al-Buraʿi dreamt that night of a cosmic finger pointing at Hasan al-Turabi—the leader of the National Islamic Front, the ruling political party in Khartoum, the power behind President al-Bashir's throne, and the architect of the state Islamization program—as both the cause of the woes that his petitioners were**

---

and high-level security figures, guarded by several jeeps with machine-gun-toting lookouts, arrived in al-Zariba and were invited to take over "the building" in order to hold what seemed to be high-level meetings, complete with PowerPoint presentations assessing the crisis.

5 For excellent discussions on the topic of hagiography and saintly power in Islam, see John Renard's *Friends of God: Islamic Images of Piety, Commitment and Servanthood* (Renard 2008) and *Tales of God's Friends: Islamic Hagiography in Translation* (Renard 2009). Also see the discussion of Islam and power as expressed in hagiography in Scott Kugle's *Sufis and Saints' Bodies: Mysticism, Corporeality and Sacred Power in Islam* (Kugle 2007).

6 Or, as Amira Mittermaier has put it in her wonderful *Dreams That Matter: Egyptian Landscapes of the Imagination*, dreams "matter in the sense of having significance in people's lives and, more literally, in the sense of having an impact on the visible, material world. They matter because they complicate the notion of a monolithic Islam, and they matter because they destabilize conventional understandings of the 'real.' . . . [Dreams] place the dreamer in relation to the Divine, offer guidance, and enable a mode of being in the world that disrupts the illusion of the autonomous self-possessed subject, calling attention to in-betweenness and interrelationality instead" (2011: 2).

Figure 6. *Above:* A small wall-hanging with Shaykh al-Bura'i in the center above the words "Succor of His Era" (*ghawth zamānū*), surrounded by other important Sufi shaykhs. Such a tableau would be said to depict *al-qawm*, or the "nation" of Sufi leaders, often thought to have true powers over Sudanese affairs. NB: the shaykh wearing the sunglasses is in fact not al-Shaykh al-Shayqi, as identified, but rather al-Shaykh Dafa' Allah al-Sa'im Dima (lit. Dafa' Allah "Always Fasting") (d. 1992). *Opp. p. clockwise from top:* The way to al-Zariba; approaching al-Zariba; the *masīd* of al-Zariba; al-Zariba's resident gazelle; al-Zariba town; camels in the headlights. Photos by the author.

describing and as their potential solution. On awakening from his dream, al-Buraʿi did something rather unbecoming of a Sufi shaykh. While political leaders have a long history of going to Sufi centers to seek shaykhs' blessings and advice on political decisions,[7] it is rare for Sufi shaykhs, who like to maintain at least a veneer of political neutrality, to make trips to the halls of power. But that morning, al-Buraʿi disregarded precedent and headed directly for Khartoum and the office of the man singled-out in his dream, Hasan al-Turabi.

The next day, when al-Buraʿi arrived at al-Turabi's well-appointed office, al-Turabi welcomed him in a gregarious manner, apparently thinking he was interested in a small financial favor or wanted to discuss some sort of internecine strife he wished the politician to help solve, as would make sense given the sort of relationship Sufis have had with the government in Sudan for many decades.

But following the greetings and niceties, the conversation suddenly took a sour turn when al-Buraʿi explained the reason for his visit: he had dreamt that al-Turabi was the cause of the woes that the Sudanese people faced and he had come to request that al-Turabi respond with a set of policy changes. Al-Turabi was taken aback. Who was this uneducated Sufi shaykh from the western deserts to advise a Sorbonne-educated lawyer, such as himself, on policy matters? After hearing him out, al-Turabi fell silent, looking al-Buraʿi directly in the eyes. Then, suddenly, he cleared his throat and asked the renowned shaykh a question he likely was not expecting. "Were you ritually pure (*ṭāhir*) when you had this dream?"

In Islam purity is an essential condition for the successful performance of many ritual acts. While *duʿāʾ*, certain *adhkār*, and *al-ṣalā ʿalā al-rasūl*, for example, can be performed pure (*ṭāhir*) or impure (*nājis*), the five daily prayers and the truthful dream vision must be done when the believer is ritually pure. To suggest that such a great shaykh as al-Buraʿi might have been impure at the time of his dream was, of course, a great insult, not only because it projects dirt on a man who was widely regarded to be among the *ṣāliḥīn*, and perhaps even a saint (*walī allāh*), but also because it reflects al-Turabi's generally patronizing attitude toward the Sufis: his belief that their version

7 For example, on President Numayri's (r. 1969–85) relationship to the Sufi orders, see Sidahmed 1996: 122–23 and el-Hasan 1993. For an anecdotal discussion of Numayri's years as a famous drunkard and his conversion to Sufism at the end of the 1970s, see al-ʿAwad ND.

of Islam was a kind of hocus-pocus, with little basis in the sources of the tradition (*al-uṣūl*) and its rules (*al-aḥkām al-fiqhiyya*).

Though he rarely expressed such an attitude toward Sufism in writing, al-Turabi was not shy about airing his opinions of Sufi Islam when one asked him in person. In an interview in 2006, he said to me:

> And then there is the Sufi, and he wastes all of [his energy] with *hā, hū, hā, hū* [imitating scornfully the noises made in Sufi ritual], and all [his] energy is dissipated in it. . . . When the communists came the Sufis became more active, when [former President] Numayri came, they became very active, because the new Islamic movements [such as the Muslim Brotherhood] weren't permitted at this time because Numayri was cooperating with the communists. . . . Like the English,[8] he left [pious Muslims] in the *khalwa* (the Sufi retreat, the school for studying Qur'an) and *dhikr* (congregational worship), and left all their energy to be consumed [by that]. This is [an] intelligent [ploy] to divert all [of the pious Muslims'] energy to private ritual so that you will avoid a response or challenge as a political force.

Al-Turabi's question to al-Bura'i about his dream was borne out of these sentiments: Sufism, with its ostensible focus on "private" ritual acts, prevents the Muslim from applying his Islam to issues that really matter, those that al-Turabi sees as of public concern and that he describes with the adjective "political." As we saw in the previous chapter, in the post-Turabi era the state came to understand Sufi ritual not as the enemy of Islamist politics but rather as a resource for its fulfillment. Yet, during the Inqadh version 1.0, which al-Turabi certainly represents, Sufi ritual was still understood to be a distraction from issues of national concern.

The political categories of relevance to the NIF, as represented by al-Turabi, look quite familiar to the contemporary political scientist—state, society, citizens, majorities, minorities—though al-Turabi came to argue that such categories need to be filled with Islamic content if politics is to serve moral ends rather than material progress alone. For other Islamic actors, however, as this story of the encounter of the government shaykh and the Sufi from the Kordofani desert will show, political power emerged from different foundations and suffused other sorts of spaces. Here, political sovereignty went beyond the boundaries set by the model of politics borrowed from the colonial state on whose foundation the Islamists sought to build. Understanding these alternative political traditions—whose critiques are often found in genres outside the common "argument" of the public sphere

8 As we saw in Chapter 1, however, the English were perhaps not as shortsighted as al-Turabi assumes them to be. Rather, they understood that the *khalwa* could just as easily be a site for political agitation as the political party.

(e.g., in the lines of poems and the whispers of hagiographic fable)[9]—requires an empirical process that forces scholars out of the frameworks generally posed by the liberal political thought that has come to dominate conversations about politics in the Islamic world. In such alternative traditions, ritual practice, literary genres such as hagiography, and the intricacies of theological doctrine (*ʿaqīda*) are positioned not as distractions from politics, but as the essential ingredients upon which a true Islamic politics can be built, as well as under-examined spaces from which political critique can emerge. Non-state Islamic actors in Sudan sought to rethink not only how to Islamize politics, but also what counted as political in the first place, as clearly shown in the story to which I will now return.

> **After receiving such insult from al-Turabi, al-Buraʿi abruptly left the government office and returned to his home in al-Zariba. It might have seemed to those who accompanied him that day on his journey that his short foray into political lobbying had been unsuccessful. But back in Khartoum, al-Turabi was having problems of his own. After completing the ritual washing (*al-wuḍūʾ*) one undertakes before prayer in order to reach the state of ritual purity (*al-ṭahāra),* al-Turabi began uncontrollably to leak urine. As urine is one of the bodily substances (along with blood, semen, feces, vomit and flatulence) that in falling on one's garments invalidates ritual cleaning, al-Turabi was rendered *nājis* and unable to pray. Al-Turabi then went back and performed his *wuḍūʾ* again, so that he could reach the condition of *ṭāhir* and commence his prayer, but again he leaked urine. The strange problem persisted. Whenever he got ready to raise his hands for the *takbīr,* he felt it happening, the drip of urine soiling his clothes. This terrible state of affairs in which al-Turabi could not become *ṭāhir,* in which he was thus perpetually *nājis,* went on for several days, leaving him entirely unable to fulfill his most basic duty as a Muslim: ritual prayer. Al-Turabi went to several doctors, but none was able to solve this most perplexing problem. He then considered what might be the cause of his perpetual state of impurity, if**

9 Political theorist Jennifer London has an interesting article on the way in which political critique emerged in fable during the eighth-century Abbasid Caliphate, when direct political critique was not possible. We can see Sudanese tellings of the fable I have recorded in a similar light: "The term 'public sphere' has become a 'cue' that contemporary scholars use to locate critical debate. Yet the absence of recognizable Western institutions that characterize the public sphere should not lead us to overlook the existence of frank speech in non-democracies" (London 2008: 191).

> **not a medical condition. Islam has a long tradition of attesting to the powers of what is referred to as *al-ʿayn* (unintentional bad luck cast upon a person through such negative emotions as envy, *ḥasad*) or *al-ʿamal* (intentional black magic), and al-Turabi began to wonder who might wish misfortune upon him, particularly in the form in which it was being expressed. He then recalled his conversation with al-Buraʿi and determined that it was most likely him, or God acting through him, that was behind his own strange troubles. He had accused al-Buraʿi of being a charlatan, of proclaiming holy insight when he had not even fulfilled his most basic ritual duties. He had accused al-Buraʿi of not being a good Muslim and thus having no legitimate basis for political critique. Yet now al-Turabi, the man meant to be guiding Sudan to an Islamic future, was himself unable to perform those same basic ritual duties.**

That the Islamic state is led by a man who doesn't pray has always been the suspicion of those skeptical of the political uses of Islam, those who understand it as an opiate for the masses (*afyūn al-shuʿūb*), distributed by a dealer who does not himself partake. Here such suspicions were played out in the Sudanese imaginary in phantasmic form.

> **Al-Turabi then summoned al-Buraʿi back to his office in Khartoum and begged the shaykh for respite from his woes, promising in return to assent to al-Buraʿi's request for the unnamed policy changes that would ease the woes of the people of Sudan. On hearing him out, the shaykh asked God in a *duʿāʾ* to remove al-Turabi's troubles. Almost immediately, al-Turabi was cured.**

The Miracle of Sovereignty

By the end of the first decade of its rule, the Sudanese regime had come to realize that Islam was extremely unstable ground on which to build a state, since who represented Islam was an issue that was far from settled, despite myriad attempts by those in power to clear up the matter. If Islam was to be the foundation for politics, then all claims to Islam, even those seemingly of the most apolitical variety, attained significant political stakes, and figures like al-Buraʿi could emerge as alternatives, real or imagined, to the regime. It is due to the proliferation of claims to Islamic authority—rather than the incompatibility of some coherent and singular model of subjectivation called Islam and that of modern state-based governance, as some scholars have recently argued (e.g., Hallaq 2013)—that perhaps makes the Islamic state, if not an impossibility, then far more of a difficult entity to stabilize than rival modes of state-based governance. If the modern state is distinguished by its absolute sovereignty, and the Islamic state bases that sovereignty on closeness to God, then others who also make a claim of such closeness immediately threaten to participate in that sovereignty, as the miraculous tale recounted above has shown.

Through the means of hagiography, this tale makes an interesting set of claims about the nature of political authority in Islam. I heard the story several times in Sudan, often as a response to my professed interest in Islamic politics. It was meant to suggest that I was perhaps looking in the wrong place if I wanted to understand Islam's true political power. The story seemed to represent several things at once to the individuals who told it to me. First, it made the point that the notion of an intellectual vanguard that could awaken the Sudanese to their true responsibilities under Islam (and indeed show them *what* true Islam was) was deeply offensive, not just to Sufis, but to secularists and practicing Muslims of all stripes. Al-Turabi's arrogance in questioning a holy man's understanding of key principles of Islamic law was emblematic of the whole approach of the Inqadh, at least in its early years, when such key projects such as *al-daʿwa al-shāmila* (the Comprehensive Call) and *al-mashrūʿ al-ḥaḍārī* (the Civilization Project) suggested that Islam was dormant in or absent from Sudanese society and that there was thus a need to civilize and Islamize it. Al-Turabi once famously declared, "Islam is a large body of water, and we [the Islamist vanguard] are the cups [that deliver this water to the people]" (*al-islām huwa al-baḥr, wa naḥnu al-kayzān*), leading to the derisive nickname for the Islamists of "the cups" (*kayzān*, sing. *kūz*), and suggesting to the Sudanese public that the NIF understood them as a people in spiritual need. Yet in this tale the tables are turned: it is in fact al-Turabi who is in need of spiritual help. True power (earthly and transcendent both) lies with the Sufi shaykhs and not the political class, no matter how the latter may try to co-opt the aura of the former.

Next, it is important to recognize that in this story, just as in the political strategy of the Inqadh, al-Turabi uses Islam to disarm political critique. The story clearly shows the danger of such a strategy. Instead of addressing al-Buraʿi's critique of his policies directly, al-Turabi attacks his commitment to Islam by calling him *nājis*. This is precisely the strategy that the Islamists used with all opponents, equating any disagreement with their policies as an affront not just to those policies but to God. For example, to certain Islamists, disagreeing with the imposition of their version of a law based on *sharīʿa* was not merely a political issue, but evidence of apostasy. (Consider, for example, the arrest and execution of Mahmud Muhammad Taha in 1984, which was a direct response to his critique of the imposition of *sharīʿa* by President Numayri, but was decided under the banner of apostasy.) Armed rebellion against the Sudanese state was cast as a "war against Muslims."[10] Likewise, in this tale, al-Turabi turned a political-economic request made by al-Buraʿi into a matter of ritual concern by questioning whether al-Buraʿi had attained the requisite state of religiosity to make his political criticism viable. This was not a mere strategy to disarm. Rather, al-Turabi was making the claim that the ability to participate fully in the political system did not derive from the rights of man, as it would perhaps in a liberal model, but only emerged from rightly formed men, first the objects of pious training, and only then valid participants. Thus political critique coming from someone who was *nājis* was invalid in the first instance. Therefore, the fact that on the very next day al-Turabi was himself unable to meet the basic demands of religion in performing the required prayer was highly significant. Such a state of affairs, according to al-Turabi's own logic, had significant consequences not only for his status as a Muslim, but as a political actor as well. Without prayer, it is hard to imagine the Muslim, and without a Muslim leader it is hard to imagine the Islamic state.

Through miraculous acts (or by means of mobilizing hagiography about them, depending on how one wants to look at it), al-Buraʿi is positioned squarely in a context that both accepts the inextricability of religious and political authority and questions the way in which the Inqadh had tied the knot. With the failure of the Inqadh project to deliver on its promises, Sudanese were looking for new ways to think through the nature of Islamic politics, and posed often far more creative and innovative models than those available on the official stage. In the story we have examined, the miracle itself, or rather the telling of the hagiography, functions as a mode of political critique. The miracle is not used to gain a critical mass, which might then overthrow the state, but rather is mobilized to reset the balance between religious and political modes of authority that the state had so violently upset through its Revolution of National Salvation and its attempts

10 From the famous "al-Obeid *fatwā*," in which six pro-government *ʿālims* (religious scholars) in Kordofan (western Sudan) met to give religious justification (specifically in the idiom of *jihād*) to the war in the South and in the Nuba Mountains. The *fatwā* reads, "The rebels in Southern Kordofan [i.e., the Nuba Mountains] and Southern Sudan started their rebellion against the state and declared war against the Muslims. Their main aims are: killing the Muslims, desecrating mosques, burning and defiling the Qur'an, and raping Muslim women. In so doing, they are encouraged by the enemies of Islam and Muslims: these forces are the Zionists, the Christians, and the arrogant people who provide them with provisions and arms. Therefore an insurgent who was previously a Muslim is now an apostate; and a non-Muslim is a nonbeliever standing as a bulwark against the spread of Islam, and Islam has granted the freedom of killing both of them" (quoted in de Waal and Abdel Salam 2004: 73). De Waal and Abdel Salam point out that this *fatwā* was cited infrequently in Sudan and it is unlikely that al-Turabi himself had any say in it, but the logic behind it, that rebellion against the state amounted to rebellion against Islam, certainly reflects a sentiment prevalent among the ruling elite in the country at that time.

at civilizational reform on an Islamic basis.[11] There is no danger here that al-Buraʿi or his supporters will come to control the government. Rather, the hagiography itself functions to topple the notion that the government is the locus of sovereignty in Sudan and that studies of Islamic politics should therefore look primarily to the government if they want to understand their object of study, the very warning that my Sudanese interlocutors were giving me when they told me the story. Al-Buraʿi represents a mode of Islamic politics that refuses to be confined by the framework of the nation-state and the questions that emerge out of the political traditions that underlie it. It is a politics that celebrates the efficacy of ritual power, the salience of *ṭāhir* and *nājis* as qualifications for political participation, that sees the sovereignty of God and holy men over the earth as an undeniable fact of existence, and that envisions a mundane substance such as urine as having the power to gum up the machinery of the state. It is, in short, a politics that refuses to be corralled into the categories of Western political science.

Rethinking Islamic Politics

In her recent volume *Political Spiritualities*, anthropologist Ruth Marshall articulates a politics emerging out of the Pentecostal revolution in Nigeria that, she argues, has been misrecognized by political science and anthropology alike. Writing against the tendency in social scientific literature to downplay the unique contribution of religious activism to the political sphere, to explain religious revival as merely a translation of global processes into local idioms, a "domestication of modernity," an "African *bricolage* as opposed to western engineering" (Marshall 2009: 33), Marshall argues for an approach to religious revival that sees its discourse not as a set of symbols to be decoded but as a mode of performing and engaging power. She writes, summarizing the reductionist studies of religious revival that her work seeks to challenge:

11 The political salience of Sufism has been clearly recognized in the recent scholarship as an important corrective to those studies that promoted an understanding of Sufism as a kind of distant mystical praxis, disengaged from the world. For example, in the introduction to his edited volume *Sufism and Politics*, Paul Heck argues that spiritual discipline translates into sociopolitical capital in two ways: (1) through the saint's charisma, wherein he is viewed as a "mediator between divine authority and the created order"; and (2) in the Sufi order itself, "its membership and its material holdings" (Heck 2007: 8, 10). In this rendering, the miracle, the divine gift that serves as the sign of charisma, is primarily a means to attract the loyalty of followers, which then translates into sociopolitical capital. In the context of the story I just recounted, on the other hand, it is the miracle itself, or rather the telling of the hagiography, that functions as a mode of political intervention.

> What is left out of these studies—that irreducible element of faith that marks the frontier of what it is possible for social science to think, and which analyses circumnavigate, reduce or ignore—reveals another form of struggle and danger. In many vital respects, religious regimes today not only find themselves, but also *position* themselves in competition or confrontation with social scientific forms of knowledge. . . . They constitute, in this sense, distinct regimes for the government of conduct, and lay out different domains in terms of which the true and the false can be distinguished. For example, the idealistic voluntarism and self-consciously linear and progressive temporality implied in constructs such as development and modernization clash with religious ideas of historical agency and time, even if their interpenetration is more complex than may first appear. The economy of miracles . . . develops a complex, conflictive relationship with dominant notions of economic productivity and political agency. (Marshall 2009: 32–33)

Though Marshall focuses on the Pentecostal revival in Nigeria, her observations apply equally well to our subject matter, Islamic political action, for it has likewise been reduced to a set of familiar social scientific paradigms that do very little to help us understand the political imagination expressed in, to take but one example, the hagiographic tale we discussed above. The framing questions of studies of Islamic politics—Is Islamic politics a product of modernity or a revolt against it (Lawrence 1989)? Is authority held by the elite or the masses, traditional brokers or new Muslim intellectuals (Eickelman and Piscatori 1996)? Is sovereignty bounded by the nation-state or held within a global, nonterritorial community (Mandaville 2001)?—all raise important issues, but all share in a refusal to take many of the key categories of Islamic politics seriously. These categories enfold notions of time,[12] authority,[13] and space[14] that do not always map onto post-Enlightenment models. Frequently in studies of Islamic politics, the political discourse of Islam is abstracted to fit into familiar social scientific categories, translated into familiar post-Enlightenment political models that take the disenchantment of the world as an unquestioned starting point for analysis. While this impulse toward the familiar may emerge from a liberal desire to find common humanity in all, it relies on an imperialism of categories (Rudolph

12 For a discussion of the intricacies of nonsecular time in Islam that seeks to upset evolutionary models of time upon which categories such as the modern are based, see Deeb 2009. See also Chakrabarty 2000: 15–16.

13 For a nuanced discussion of sacred power in Islam that moves beyond the sociological categories common to academic studies of Islamic history, see, for example, Kugle 2007.

14 See e.g., Amira Mittermaier's "(Re)Imagining Space: Dreams and Saint Shrines in Egypt" (2008).

2005) in defining the human, and in doing so it necessarily distorts what it studies.[15] To understand Islamic politics, particularly those aspects of Islamic politics that lie outside of the official structures of modern governance in the postcolonial nation-state and thus needn't play by its rules, we must move from an analytics to a hermeneutics of Islamic politics. As described by Chakrabarty:

> Analytic social science fundamentally attempts to "demystify" ideology in order to produce a critique that looks toward a more just social order. . . . Hermeneutic tradition, on the other hand, produces a loving grasp of detail in search of an understanding of the diversity of human life-worlds. . . . The first tradition tends to evacuate the local by assimilating it to some abstract universal. . . . The hermeneutic tradition, on the other hand, finds thought intimately tied to places and to particular forms of life. (Chakrabarty 2000: 18)

It is through a hermeneutics of Islamic politics that we can come to understand its own ontologies, its own categories of understanding, and thus the life-worlds that Islamic politics makes possible.

The shortsightedness of existing studies of Islamic politics stems not only from conceptual limits, but from methodological ones as well. Given that the vast majority of these studies have been based on the writings of Muslim intellectuals, ignoring political practice, a rather limited set of data has come to define what is characteristic about contemporary Muslim politics (see e.g., Abu Rabi' 1996, 2010; Esposito 1983; Euben and Zaman 2009). Analyses of Islamic political movements, on the other hand, almost exclusively focus on the Muslim Brotherhood or groups that have emerged from it (e.g., Lybarger 2007; Scott 2010; Wickham 2002, 2013), or come out of a recent burst of literature on global jihadist organizations such as al-Qaʿida (e.g., Devji 2005; Lia 2008), many with explicit security concerns. So that, for example, while Euben and Zaman's extremely useful volume, *Princeton Readings in Islamist Thought*, gives us a good sense of the field of Islamic intellectual debate around political matters, focusing primarily on Muslim Brotherhood and Salafi-Jihadi affiliated individuals, we get little sense of how these politics actually function in the Islamic world. What are everyday practitioners of Muslim politics saying and

15 In Suzanne Rudolph's "The Imperialism of Categories: Situating Knowledge in a Global World" (Rudolph 2005), she argues that the attempt to universalize categories is at the heart of liberalism, which assumes a universal humanity. Yet this universalism is only one side of the coin of which the other is imperialism, for it misrecognizes Western particulars for universals and promotes its values absolutely, impervious to difference. Following Uday Mehta (Mehta 1999), Rudolph advocates instead an encounter with the other based on the ideals of Edmund Burke: "While the liberal assumption of human homogeneity eliminated the need to comprehend the meaning system of the other, Burke recognized and valued difference and made space for conversation and negotiation meant to bring strangers together" (Burke 2005: 8).

doing as they respond to the social realities they encounter on the ground, moving outside the grand theories of their leaders? The formal politics of political parties, intellectuals, and government is important, but an exclusive focus on them obscures the much broader field of political life taking place in the countries we study.[16] Understanding the Islamic state in Sudan requires studying not only policies from on high, but politics in the vernacular (White 2002), particularly in the moment of Sudanese history that I witnessed, when the specific form of the state was again up for grabs.

The gap in our understanding of these vernacular politics is sometimes due to technical barriers: the political actors who are ignored are people who tend not to publish, and thus access to their ideas requires lengthy fieldwork, interviews, and recordings of their public pronouncements. But another part of the problem is that many of them espouse ideas that Islamist intellectuals and the scholars who study them do not deem relevant to political life in the first place, in part because they often speak in a language that is difficult to translate into familiar political idioms—as the story about al-Buraʿi shows, couched as it is in the language of hagiography. For example, the still-common dismissal of Sufis as otherworldly (as if the otherworldly does not have a say in this world) and of *daʿwa*-centered Salafis as focusing on obscure matters of doctrine said to be irrelevant to the problems of the nation-state, suggests an inability to think through political categories other than those commonly posed by Western political theory.[17] The

16 The work of Farah Godrej is instructive here. She speaks of the tendency among scholars in comparative political theory "to gravitate un-selfconsciously towards a 'great books' or a 'history of political thought' version of political inquiry, in which emphasis is placed on the thinkers and texts that seem equivalent to canonical works in the Western tradition. . . . But little reflection occurs on *why* precisely these resources might be worthy of investigation or *what* about them might be valuable for the purpose of cross-cultural theorizing. Often, it is implied (rather than investigated or proven) that what is theoretically worthwhile is precisely the fact that these resources address questions that are recognizable to Western-centered political theorists" (Godrej 2011: 29). I am further grateful for the review article of Diego von Vacano (2015) that pointed me to additional debates in comparative political theory that parallel some of my own interests in the present chapter.

17 Political theorist Leigh Kathryn Jenco has also observed that Western political theory rarely takes the categories of non-Western political thought seriously. Indeed, she argues that postcolonial theorists and scholars in comparative politics are as guilty as their predecessors:

> [P]ostcolonial and comparative political theorists have called into question the "universal" applicability of Western liberal political norms, but their critiques are drawn most often from competing Western discourses (e.g., poststructuralism), rather than from the culturally diverse traditions of scholarship whose ideas they examine. In contrast, I suggest attending to these culturally situated traditions of scholarship, especially their methods of inquiry, in addition to their substantive ideas" (Jenco 2007: 741).

While Jenco's goal here of thinking with the traditions of scholarship of other cultures, rather than merely determining how they contribute to our own debates, is admirable, she

categories of these other interventions are beyond "the frontier of what it is possible for social science to think" (Marshall 2009: 32).

Our knowledge of Islamic politics, as evidenced by the standard books in the field I have cited, is not necessarily incorrect, but it is most certainly

---

nevertheless makes some significant missteps in this article that make her argument less persuasive than it might otherwise be. First, her polemic against critics of liberalism seems to be based on a serious misreading of their work: for example, Saba Mahmood and Dipesh Chakrabarty, both of whom she critiques for embracing a kind of Eurocentrism in situating their objects of study within poststructuralist thought, have at the heart of their projects a desire to bring the critical insight of the cultures they study to bear as *correctives* to Western social theory. Mahmood's subjects come to critique poststructuralist presuppositions (take Mahmood's debates with Judith Butler, for example) as much as they affirm them, not merely offering alternative answers to a set of questions posed in this literature, but asking new sorts of questions entirely. Moreover, as heirs themselves through al-Ghazali to the Aristotelean tradition, they are not perhaps as far removed from what is today called European thought as Jenco wants to believe. It is also worth mentioning that Jenco distorts Chakrabarty's argument significantly, a distortion she relies on throughout her article in order to further her argument, when she cites him as writing that it is "impossible to *think* of anywhere in the world without invoking certain categories and concepts, the genealogies of which go deep into the intellectual and even theological traditions of Europe." The full sentence is "The phenomenon of 'political modernity'—namely the rule by modern institutions of the state, bureaucracy, and capitalist enterprise—is impossible to *think* of anywhere in the world without invoking certain categories and concepts, the genealogies of which go deep into the intellectual and even theological traditions of Europe"(Chakrabarty 2000: 4). That is, Chakrabarty is making a fairly mundane comment here on the genealogy of the state in postcolonial polities and not the larger epistemological claim Jenco attributes to him and upon which she bases much of her critique.

Indeed, I fear Jenco's impulse to "supplant Eurocentrism" gets us dangerously close to a native/authentic versus "Western" dichotomy that is simply not sustainable, either for the Chinese scholars she studies or the postcolonies that are the subject of the works she criticizes. To close off "native" or "traditional" cultures (Jenco gives these terms scare quotes in her article, but seems to rely on them substantively in her argument, see 741, 745) entirely from Western social theory not only ignores the way in which these cultures are already embedded (by choice and by force) in the conversations we are having in the West (which in the postcolony are not as "parochial" as she assumes), but also results in furthering their exclusion from the global conversation about ethics and politics of which they certainly seek to be a part. Jenco imagines clearly delineated insides and outsides to the traditions she studies (753) and accuses a whole host of scholars whose project has been to take seriously the life worlds of non-Western societies of inadvertently forwarding a sort of Eurocentrism. All of this said, I share Jenco's interest in mining other traditions in order to offer a "means by which a theorist can formulate questions about political life . . . from within the framework constituted by other texts, practices and self-understandings" (742) that exceed the conversations we are currently having in the Western academy. I also find intriguing her idea that we should attend to regimes of practice and scholarly inquiry within the traditions we study and not merely to what various intellectuals from within them have said (744, 751) if we are to truly grasp what matters within these political traditions. However, I question whether her "methods-centered approach" is as radical a departure from that of the scholars she critiques as she seems to think. Or, alternatively, if it requires attaining a certain kind of "insider" privilege (as she seems to suggest elsewhere in this article), I wonder for whom that would be possible. For a discussion of the problems in reading scholarly epistemologies through an insider/outsider opposition, see Salomon and Walton 2012.

incomplete. While Robert Hefner may be right that there is "a struggle for the hearts and minds of Muslims taking place . . . around the world . . . [that] pits those who believe in the compatibility of Islam with democracy and pluralist freedom against those who insist that such values and institutions are antithetical to Islam" (Hefner 2004: 3), it is important to recognize that this is only one arena of debate. The "Islamists" and "progressivists" on whom these studies tend to focus are themselves almost universally members of the elite classes who were most deeply affected by the colonial encounter. It is thus no wonder that they are speaking in terms familiar to Western social science, the handmaiden of colonialism, which, if they could not defeat, at least they could attempt to nativize. For example, as we saw both in Chapter 2 and in al-Turabi's quote above, the Islamists share much with social scientific analyses of Islamic politics, agreeing with them on what constitutes relevant "political force." So it is no surprise that social scientific analysis has found familiar ground in Islamist writings and practice. Yet Islamic politics does not stop there.

While I find useful work like that of Roxanne Euben (1999), which seeks to show how Islamist political thinkers are in fact part of a larger conversation that includes Western critics of modernity, in that it serves as a corrective to those who view Muslim fundamentalists as irredeemably other, I worry that if we end the conversation there we fail to appreciate the register of Islamic political thought that is neither the West's other, nor its mirror image, but rather is holding an entirely different conversation in which "we" are not the reference point.[18] Though Euben's book does an essential service in

18 So I remain skeptical that, for example, Islamic politics is merely giving different answers to what are, in the end, a shared set of questions between Western political theory and that of the Islamic world. Euben argues that political theory in both liberal and Islamic models share "certain questions rather than particular answers":

> What is the good life? What is the nature of legitimate authority? Of justice? What is the right relationship of the individual to society? . . . Importantly, this possibility is not premised upon the existence of universal and perennial questions that arise by virtue of being human. . . . Rather, the possibility of such conversations is tied to the syncretism that is a hallmark of a world marked by extensive Western cultural influence: in a postcolonial world increasingly marked by neocolonial globalization, questions we take to be ours have ceased to be so exclusively (if in fact they ever were) because they have come to frame the sensibilities of non-Westerners as well. (Euben 1999: 9–10)

While what she writes here is persuasive, as it characterizes not a phenomenological universality, but one that has come to be shared as a result of history in the postcolony, it misses a whole set of questions that Islamic politics asks that are not shared by Western political theory, and that cannot be easily reduced to its terms. For example, in contrast with the questions she asks above, not *what is the good life*, but *what is the good death* (*ḥusn al-khātima*)—that is, not a life lived for its felicity in this world, but rather for its relationship with the next (e.g., Kane 1962)? What is God's role in shaping political order, and what is the general authority of superhuman or nonhuman forces in shaping sovereignty on this earth? How can God's rights best be upheld? What is the relationship between piety and political subjectivity? These are

comparative political theory, rethinking the relationship between Islamic political thought and that which holds sway in the West, too frequently we have assumed that we are the necessary interlocutors with Islamic movements, believing that they are as preoccupied with us as we seem to be with them. Though the Sufi and Salafi groups I focus on in this chapter cannot be thought of as islands, unaffected by the colonial encounter or Western dominance, they are not primarily concerned with the debates it has sparked and thus the categories of their political engagement are distinctly outside of them. For these Islamic organizations, the object of critique is not Western hegemony, secularism, or rationalism, as it was for Sayyid Qutb (the critic of modernity whom Euben introduces), but rather a lengthy experience with state Islamism in Sudan that has not borne its promised fruits.

An understanding of Islamic politics as primarily concerned with debates over democracy and freedom, pluralism and civic engagement, secularism and religious participation, Western hegemony and Muslim resistance was one that I carried with me when I went into the field, though it was greeted with much dismay when I raised the topic in Sudan. It was not that no one in Sudan was framing the conversation in such terms; indeed regime intellectuals were preoccupied with them. It was rather that the vast majority of Sudanese, for whom Islamic politics and the vision of the Islamic state was of crucial interest, nevertheless remained entirely outside the conceptual framework and presuppostions of these sorts of conversations. *Who had ever heard of the various think tanks whose journals I regularly read*, my friends would protest when I tried to bring their lofty insights into a conversation. When I first arrived in Sudan and told people of my interest in Islamic politics and that this interest would concentrate on the agenda of the ruling party, my interlocutors told me that I would be missing out not only on the true power players in the country, but also on the true objects of political contestation.

As evidence of my error, I was more than once provided with a version of the fable with which I began this chapter. Whether or not those who told me the tale believed that its truth lay in the events it recounted or in the lesson that those events conveyed, or in some combination of the two, was irrelevant to the fact that they presented the tale as a caveat for anyone claiming interest in Islamic politics in Sudan. For them, it revealed where the relationship between Islam and political power truly lay. The move of the ruling party to embrace aspects of Sufi ritual technologies in its political program in the post-CPA restructuring of the Islamic state that I discussed in the previous chapter is evidence that it was not only "the man on the street" who was thinking outside of these dominant political categories, but that at

also questions asked by Islamic political actors, ones that have less obvious correlates in the Western canon of political theory.

the highest levels of governance the conversation was shifting beyond the familiar terms of debate. What were the politics of love that we saw Inqadh intellectuals embrace in projects like al-Kawthar? On what violences did they rely and what crises could they transcend? For both "sides" in the story of the encounter between al-Turabi and al-Buraʿi, piety was a prerequisite for political critique, a piety that could only be achieved through ritual action that rendered the body pure (*ṭāhir*), and without which the body was not only soiled (*nājis*) but infelicitous as a political subject. What might it mean for us, as analysts of Islamic politics, to take *ṭahāra* and *najāsa* seriously as political categories, as my interlocutors certainly did, to think earnestly about their implications for understanding political action?

A truly cosmopolitan understanding of political theory that does not begin "its inquiries from the locus of [its] own conventions and seeking analogous things elsewhere" but instead "willingly engage[s] with ideas that defy settled understandings of 'the political' and makes explicit the resulting challenge to accepted presumptions about what constitutes political theory" (Godrej 2011: 32) seems necessary to understand such political interventions, such new imaginings of the reach and limits of the Islamic state. These shortcomings, however, are not unique to studies of Muslim politics, but rather must be viewed as central to the "problem of translation" more generally. As Dipesh Chakrabarty has written regarding the obstacles of social scientific knowledge when analyzing enchanted pasts:

> So it could be said that although the sciences signify some kind of sameness in our understanding of the world across cultures, the gods signify differences . . . Writing about the presence of gods and spirits in the secular language of history or sociology would therefore be like translating into a universal language that which belongs to a field of differences. . . . But on what grounds do we assume, ahead of any investigation, that this divine presence invoked at every turn of the *chakki* will translate neatly into a secular history of labor so that . . . the human beings collected in modern industries may indeed appear as the subjects of a metanarrative of Marxism, socialism, or even democracy? (Chakrabarty 2000: 76, 81)

Chakrabarty presents us with an important challenge. How can we animate the field of difference in Islamic politics in order to paint a more accurate picture of it? How can we get beyond the vanity of thinking it is always about us—a critique of Western hegemony or an assimilation of its political fruits—to come to appreciate what is important to its practitioners? As Jacques Rancière reminds us in his impassioned critique of the social scientific historiography of the *Annales* school (Rancière 1994), the violence we do through translation of our subjects' lives into social scientific categories, in our eagerness to understand "the people," often loses more of the character of their lives than does the classic narrative history of events and kings that our social history sought to replace. The unique and idiosyncratic ways people organize and understand their lives are left behind in the social scientific impulse to speak for the many: "To pass from the history of events to that of structures, one must separate the masses from their non-truth" (Rancière 1994: 22). What might it mean to leave Islamic politics untranslated?

The remainder of this chapter will attempt to answer this question by looking at a vision of the Islamic state that in Marshall's words "not only [finds itself, but *positions* itself] in competition or confrontation with social scientific forms of knowledge." Its debates are not with the West, nor is its critique concerning lax morals or secularization, as most Islamic politics is depicted in the literature that concerns it. Rather, its critique is directed at *pious Muslims* who, its proponents argue, have constructed an Islamic politics that is both inauthentic and infelicitous, in part because they have adopted such social scientific forms of knowledge as their own. In both the story with which I began this chapter and in what I will present below, the reach and limits of the Islamic state are explored in vivid form as it is reimagined in response to the lengthy tenure of the Inqadh and the particular challenges of the present. These responses do not take the categories of Western political science as starting points, but rather seek to reassess what resources and categories the Islamic tradition offers for thinking through the political. Ignoring interventions such as these, as I think the bulk of literature on Islamic politics has done, represents a failure to understand the breadth and scope of Islamic political action and its fundamental challenges to common conceptions of political theory. The desire to find an Islamic politics that acts as a counterweight to the "clash of civilization" thesis (e.g., Esposito 1999), while commendable in its intent, has ended up throwing out the baby with the bathwater, emptying Islamic politics of its own goals in conceptualizing the political and replacing them with our own. How can we avoid both the alarmist approach that sees the alterity present in Islamic political thought as a threat to Western values, as well as the (in the final analysis, distorting) impulse to redeem it by showing how much it looks like us?

The Salafi Critique of Islamism

As the last rays of sun dipped beneath the horizon and the evening call to prayer resounded over the densely-packed, mud-filled streets of Daym al-Jazuli,[19] an outlying neighborhood in Khartoum's urban sprawl, a friend and I shuffled into a small mosque affiliated with the Salafi proselytizing group

19 I have rendered the name of the neighborhood and the shaykh whose sermons I recorded as aliases due to the political sensitivity of the topic of discussion.

Ansar al-Sunna al-Muhammadiyya. Some months earlier I had begun attending the group's lectures and lesson circles in order to get a sense of the nature of Salafi teachings in Sudan. Ansar al-Sunna's primary interest is the proselytization (*daʿwa*) of Salafi doctrine.[20] Its influence has ebbed and flowed in Sudanese public life, but it has usually stood at the margins of both pious and political affairs, its variety of Islam characterized by a vocal opposition to the mode of religious practice of the Sudanese (mainly Sufi) mainstream. Recently, however, the group appeared to be gaining strength and adherents. Hundreds and sometimes thousands of people attended its lectures, and its mosques and education centers were spreading across the length and breadth of Sudan. Ansar al-Sunna interested me because throughout its history it had steadfastly advocated an Islamic political order and an Islamic constitution, often allying with—while at the same time clearly distinguishing itself from—the Muslim Brotherhood groups with which such causes are generally affiliated (e.g., El-Affendi 1991: 75). This said, I had rarely found anything in its lectures that I deemed of political relevance. Beyond critiques of Salafi jihadism, such as that of the al-Qaʿida organization (because it scared people away from Islam, and inviting people to Islam was Ansar al-Sunna's main agenda), the topics generally focused on issues of personal piety.

Speaking that night was a well-known Salafi preacher, Ahmad ʿAbd al-Raziq. Shaykh Ahmad is most often associated with the Salafi polemic against Sufism, and I had been collecting his writings and attending his lesson circles for the work I was doing on debates between Sufis and Salafis in Sudan, which were becoming particularly heated while I was in the field.[21] I was thus surprised when he began this lecture with a theme very different from most of his other sermons. After some rather standard commentary on the exclusive grasp on the truth that the Salafi understanding of Islam holds, he said the following: "The group (*firqa*) most dangerously in error in the Islamic world is the Muslim Brotherhood! Understand well what I am saying [and interpret] it as you like. The most dangerous group and the most corrupt group and the most deviant (*munḥarif*) program of thought (*manhaj*) is that of Hasan al-Banna the Egyptian, the thought of the Muslim Brotherhood, which calls for the acceptance of truth and error together (*al-jamʿ bayn al-ḥaqq wa-l-bāṭil*)." While I had heard Shaykh Ahmad speak critically of the Muslim Brotherhood the previous month in a lecture he gave as part of a week-long training course for Salafi missionaries (*duʿāt*), this was the first time I had heard him speak in such uncompromising terms. Indeed, Ansar al-Sunna remains in coalition with the ruling regime, though it claims to do so only as a means of increasing its influence and not because it has assented

20 For a history of Ansar al-Sunna, see al-Tahir 2004.

21 For an account of the violence into which these polemics have erupted more recently, see Maruyama 2013.

to the regime's policies.[22] Yet, Shaykh Ahmad's ominous "understand well what I am saying [and interpret] it as you like," left little doubt in the mind of his listeners as to whom he was referring: the Islamic movement that underlies the ruling cadre of leaders in Sudan.[23]

As we have seen in the previous chapters, the failure of the Islamist vanguard to maintain control of the program of social and religious reform it initiated, coupled with the relative degree of political freedom afforded by the signing of the CPA with the South, brought the political criticism of many actors to the fore. While the critique of the Islamist project of the Inqadh waged by Muslim liberals and secularists was to be expected, the critique that emerged from other proponents of conservative Islamic politics has been less well appreciated.[24] Some of the reason for this lack of attention

22 In an interview I conducted in 2013 with Muhammad Abu Zayd Mustafa, Ansar al-Sunna's chief liaison to the government, he described to me the on-again off-again relationship between his group and the regime. While they were working together initially, sharing an interest in establishing an Islamic state after the period of al-Sadiq al-Mahdi, when the government started dismissing people on no basis except their lack of allegiance to the NIF, Ansar al-Sunna started to have reservations. It was at this point that Muhammad Abu Zayd himself began serious protest, which landed him in prison for two months in the early 1990s. The disagreement reached a crescendo when the government decided for pragmatic reasons to side with Iraq in the first Gulf War, a state that clearly had no Islamic basis. Yet from the mid-1990s on, a reconciliation occurred and members of Ansar al-Sunna began to be appointed as district commissioners in various states and took on positions in ministries. Muhammad Abu Zayd Mustafa himself reached the level of minister in the ministries of education and culture and in 2015 became the Minister of Tourism. He stressed however that despite the practical cooperation, there was a major difference between the two groups around matters of doctrine. Using the gradual revelation of the Qur'an as an example of the fact that change cannot happen overnight, and Joseph's collaboration with Pharaoh as an example that getting involved in political systems is worthwhile even if such systems are corrupt, he told me that Ansar al-Sunna would cooperate with any government that could "increase the good, and lessen the evil" in the world, even if that government did not purport to be an Islamic one.

23 The Islamic movement that founded the Inqadh government is an offshoot of the Sudanese Muslim Brotherhood, which itself is an offshoot of the Egyptian organization by the same name. Despite nuances and differences, prominent among them over whether to ally or separate from the parent movement (el-Affendi 1991), the present regime is still understood to be ideologically attuned with the principles of the Muslim Brotherhood organization.

24 In her sophisticated and nuanced portrayal of the challenges state power has posed to Sudanese Islamists since their rise to power in 1989 until 2004, Einas Ahmed analyzes the accommodation that Ansar al-Sunna made with the NIF/NCP as evidence that the "boundaries between fundamentalists, Salafis, and Islamists have softened" (Ahmed 2007: 200). While the détente between the government and Ansar al-Sunna is significant—not least for the contrast it poses to *daʿwa*-oriented Salafi groups in many other Muslim countries that refuse involvement in the state—I do not believe that this represents any sort of new ideological softening on the part of Ansar al-Sunna as an organization. Even its involvement in state politics is nothing new, as Ansar al-Sunna was, for example, part of the various coalitions supporting an Islamic constitution following independence. Ansar al-Sunna shaykhs with whom I spoke stressed the *pragmatic* benefit in their alliance with the present government in the kinds of material

is due to the tendency of scholars to lump "Islamists" (i.e., those who agitate for the political relevance of Islam) into one undifferentiated category, when in fact they likely differ as much as they are alike. Yet another reason why these political programs have been ignored is that they often do not meet the standards of political relevance to which we are accustomed, as they speak neither in a language of *jihād* against Western values, nor in the language of civil Islam.

Though there were rare moments such as the one I describe here when Ansar al-Sunna shaykhs directly challenged the state, for the most part their politics spoke in a different language altogether, one that emerged directly out of their piety and that refused to be normalized by the mechanisms of a state that used religion as a means of shaping citizens. In this sense, theirs was a politics not unlike that of the piety movements Saba Mahmood discusses in her *Politics of Piety,* wherein "the political efficacy of these movements is . . . a function of the work they perform in the ethical realm" (Mahmood 2005: 35). In Ansar al-Sunna's model, theological doctrine (*ʿaqīda*) was not a means of translating power into a local idiom, or of rallying the masses, but was the object of political contestation itself, under the belief that establishing God's sovereignty on earth depends on humans embracing His commands correctly. Salafis' characteristic scholarliness, their promise not to rely on the scholarship of decades past but instead to reexamine the sources anew (for example reopening the hadith canon to criticism [Lacroix 2009]), made them particularly well suited to embark on this project. The task, which they referred to as the "purification of doctrine" (*tazkiyyat al-ʿaqīda*), was for them inherently political work, despite the fact that it made no mention of the state, civil society, rights, or justice, the common categories of our political vocabulary. That Ansar al-Sunna understood the ruling Islamists as construing their program too narrowly around issues of state sovereignty, and argued for a politics based on a program in which purified *ʿaqīda* and correct practice were front and center, is evidence that they had a clear agenda of not only rethinking Islam (as is commonly thought), but of reframing the nature of the political as well. The Islamist model could never successfully establish the Islamic state that it desired, figures such as Shaykh Ahmad argued. For this, another sort of political work was necessary, one that was rarely recognized as of political import, but that Salafis saw as essential to any successful political program in the name of Islam.

power (opening of mosques, access to media) they gained that furthers their *daʿwa*, in their ability to advise and reform the government to be more in line with correct Islamic doctrine, and to the degree that certain of their goals overlap. At the same time, these shaykhs remained vocally and often publically critical of the Islamist ideology that underlies the NIF/NCP political agenda and frequently stressed their independence. Salomon 2009 explains the distinction between Salafis and Islamists in Sudan in more detail than I have room to present here.

The Prophet in Mecca and the Politics of *daʿwa*

Salafis like those of Ansar al-Sunna understand that a key difference between their political agenda and that of the ruling regime centers on defining the nature of "the political." Ansar al-Sunna is an organization primarily concerned with the work of *daʿwa* or proselytization, the call to refining and reforming Islamic practice. As I mentioned above, someone attending Ansar al-Sunna lesson circles looking for "politics" in the form of debates over the nature of the state or over current hot-button issues would likely be severely disappointed. For the most part the subject matter covers such things as personal comportment and ritual practice—excluding a few moments of rupture such as those I discussed above. Yet, Salafis understood their work on *daʿwa* as inherently political and weighing heavily on the agenda of the state.

In Islamic political theory, political work is often linked to the model of the life of the Prophet Muhammad. Interestingly, while most Islamic political theory uses the Medinan period of the Prophet's life (when he founded an Islamic polity) as its source, for these Salafis political theory emerges, first and foremost, from the Meccan period (when the Prophet's role was primarily proselytization). As ʿAbd al-Rahman ʿAbd al-Khaliq argues in his treatise *al-Muslimūn wa-l-ʿamal al-siyāsī*, an important book for the Ansar al-Sunna members with whom I worked:

> The idea that the Prophet (*ṣlʿm*) did not practice politics until after the migration [to Medina] when he established a state is a grievous error. For [the concept of] "political work" (*al-ʿamal al-siyāsī*) is broader than just the idea of "governance" (*ḥukm*). The Prophet (*ṣlʿm*), from the first day that he began his call, called to a belief different from the prevailing belief, and he gathered people around [true] doctrine, and this is in reality political work according to contemporary understandings of the term. (ND: 4)

Salafis understand their project of the "purification of doctrine" as both analogous to the Prophet's initial call and as fundamentally political work. The Prophet's proselytization effort and the tortures his community endured on its account are thus held up as examples both of the political stakes one risks in spreading truth against "prevailing belief" and of the necessity of conducting *daʿwa* as a precondition to conversations about governance, as the Prophet did in his life. In other words, Salafi thinkers argue that God had a clear plan in placing the Meccan before the Medinan period of the Prophet's life, and that it is necessary that Muslims emulate the Prophet by following the same order of stages. Islamic politics, as ʿAbd al-Rahman ʿAbd al-Khaliq relates later in the same book, is about the rearing (*tarbiya*) of individuals out of the darkness of unbelief (*kufr*) and into the light of true faith (*īmān*), and about establishing the ascendancy of "the group that saves" the individual from damnation (*al-firqa al-nājiyya*) over all other claimants to religious truth (ND: 36). The life of the Prophet, he insists, shows that political work must include a serious focus on the kind of *tarbiya* and doctrinal reform exemplified by his life in Mecca. A study of Salafi political theory forces us to expand the category of "Muslim politics" beyond the sphere of debates about the implementation of Islamic law (on which most studies of the category have focused) to include the kind of political work undertaken in transforming the social body to assent to correct doctrine. Salafis like Ansar al-Sunna argue that it is only out of a doctrinally pure society that an Islamic state can emerge.

This stance often played out in the positions that Salafis took on key issues of the day. For example, the focus of Islamists on the oppression of Muslims in Palestine and Iraq became an object of critique for Sudanese Salafis. Their critique did not emerge from any variety of "liberal Islam," nor from collusion with the goals of Western imperialism; rather, it had a clear theological agenda, which included a rejection of political models whose primary points of reference were either the nation-state *or* the global *umma*. Here, the defense of God by upholding his religion seemed to militate against such worldly concerns. In the following comments from the course for Salafi missionaries, Shaykh Ahmad criticizes a group, the *Surūriyyūn*, which claims to present a balance between the approach of Salafis and Islamists. He argues:

> And additionally, among their other sicknesses is that in their speeches they repeat over and over, "Those who do not rule on the basis of what God revealed, they are unbelievers" (*man lam yaḥkum bi-mā anzal allāhu fa-ūlā'ika humu al-kāfirūn. Sūrat al-Mā'ida*: 44). And then they start shouting: "Palestiiiiiine!!!" The problems here [in front of us] are bigger than the problems in Palestine! So come here to die [meaning that, by being a martyr in Sudan, you will get more reward from God]. [The problems] that are happening here are bigger than there. Palestine! What is so important about it?! Solve our problems here: this one wears *ḥijbāt* [amulets, which are forbidden in the Salafi reading of Islam], this one has a [Sufi] doctrine, this one takes dirt in his pocket [from a Sufi shaykh's tomb because he believes it to be holy]. So what about Palestine?! Because of his obsession [with Palestine], he is not able to talk about the exclusive worship of God (*tawḥīd*), and this is a sickness.

For Ansar al-Sunna, a doctrine that focuses only on matters of governance is necessarily an incomplete doctrine (*ʿaqīda juz'iyya*). Promoting correct doctrine and getting rid of "superstitions" (*shirkiyyāt*) that turn one away from the worship of God, such as those mentioned in the above passage, are the essential grounds on which any righteous political community must be built. For Ansar al-Sunna, if the base is not strong, if Islam is not clean, then an Islamic polity will surely fall, for it lacks a sound foundation. The Islamists' notion that the creation of a Muslim society is the responsibility of the social-engineering state (e.g., endeavors such as the "Civilization Project") stands in stark contrast to Ansar al-Sunna's contention that it is only as a result of a reverent and doctrinally pure society that a true Islamic political order can emerge. Thus, for Ansar al-Sunna the social-engineering state of the early NIF and their "Civilizing Project" should be turned on its head: the Islamic political order cannot make Muslims righteous, rather it is only righteous Muslims who can make the political order Islamic.

The idea that Islam cannot be followed partially, that all of God's commands must be implemented in all things, from the most mundane to the most pressing matters of life (and besides, who are we to say what is mundane and what is pressing to God?) is a key characteristic of Salafi thought. It is why for Salafis matters of state and matters of ritual practice cannot be divorced from one another, why ignoring ritual details in favor of something you deem to be of greater importance to the *umma* amounts to *shirk*, to following an authority other than God, compromising the ultimate divine sovereignty. Ansar al-Sunna's focus on even the most (seemingly) minor details of doctrine as being equal in importance to the establishment of Islamic governance has earned its members the derisive nickname among some in the Islamist movement of "*ʿulamāʾ al-ḥayḍ wa-l-nifās*" (the scholars who are concerned with women's menstruation and issues of childbirth). In the view of these Islamists, Ansar al-Sunna concerns itself with minor details of ritual purity, while matters of great importance to the *umma*, such as its political status, are ignored. Yet, Salafis argue that if our goal is truly to establish God's sovereignty on earth, we need to be sure we are adhering to his commands in full. The sovereignty of God always trumps human sovereignty, in this world and in the next.

Contesting Categories

As an ethnographer working on groups like Ansar al-Sunna, I have become skeptical that the categories we use to understand Islamic politics capture the full range and goals of its proponents. And in this I am not alone. Yet another argument that Salafi scholars in Sudan level against government Islamists is that they have been too quick to embrace the categories of Western political thought in designing their program for the Islamic state. Taking on their acts of translation directly, Salafis argue that Islamists have let international norms and protocols set the agenda for the debate, busying themselves only with showing how "Islam too" can meet the standards set by the West. In particular, Salafi thinkers challenge the strategy of the ruling regime in responding to international condemnation over its human rights record by putting forward the idea that Islamic politics could be translated into an idiom that would satisfy Western human rights and governance norms, but with an Islamic color (e.g., "Islamic democracy," "Islamic human rights"). One area in which this criticism emerged was the debate around how to deal with the demands of the non-Muslim minority population, perhaps the key dilemma that occupied public Islamic debate about the state during my time in Sudan. This criticism came on the heels of the signing of the Comprehensive Peace Agreement (CPA) with the SPLM, the representatives of the majority non-Muslim South. Conversations between Salafis and regime Islamists over this issue were a means both of debating the issue at hand—how best to accommodate, or not, the demands of the non-Muslim minority—*and* of debating the nature of the Islamic state itself, which had certainly reached a crossroads after the signing of the CPA. It is for this latter reason that I find it instructive to reproduce here one such debate on religious minorities as a means of concluding this chapter.

On July 4, 2007, two separate but thematically related conferences were held in Khartoum, one throughout the day and one in the evening, both of which tried to address the vexing topic of governing religious diversity. Yet, although the subject of the two conferences was the same and although they gathered nearly equal attendance, they couldn't have looked more different. The daytime conference was supported by the governments of Sudan and Jordan, held at the gleaming new five-star Rotana Hotel in Khartoum, and featured guests from across the Arab world and East Africa, Sudanese VIPs, and a keynote speech from the Sudanese president, ʿUmar al-Bashir. The conference in the evening was held on the front lawn of a crumbling building with a makeshift stage and was attended by Muslim Sudanese from all walks of life. It featured speeches by a variety of leaders of Ansar al-Sunna. At neither of the conferences was there explicit mention of the other, but the evening event was obviously organized in response to the government-sponsored daytime gathering, as a people's version of the government's VIP event.

The conference held during the day was organized by the Sudanese Ministry of Guidance and Pious Endowments (*Wizārat al-Irshād wa-l-Awqāf*) and sponsored by the independent (but government-supported) Sudanese Council for Religious Coexistence (*Majlis al-Taʿāyush al-Dīnī al-Sūdānī*) and the Royal Institute for Religious Studies of Jordan (*al-Maʿhad al-Malakī li-l-Dirāsāt al-Dīniyya, al-Urdun*). It was titled the International Conference for Christian-Islamic Dialogue: For the Continuance of Peace and the Strengthening of National Unity.[25] The event featured Sufi drumming, Christian and

25 *al-Muʾtamar al-dawlī li-l-ḥuwār al-islāmī al-masīḥī ḥawl istidāmat al-salām wa taʿzīz al-waḥda al-waṭaniyya.*

Muslim benedictions, and several speeches by government officials, allied Islamists, and Christian and Muslim religious leaders, local and international.

The event opened with some words from the Sudanese president, 'Umar al-Bashir. It may come as somewhat of a shock to hear this man, who only a year later would be indicted by the International Criminal Court in the Hague for massive crimes against humanity in Darfur, speak in the very language of the international human rights community that later condemned him. But it is a testament to the power of such language (or perhaps to its banality, which is itself a mode of power) that the leader of a government that has secured its rule precisely through the flaunting of human rights law, speaks also in the language of human rights. Though government officials spoke the language of a *jihād* against a rebellious South quite fluently during the civil war, in those later days, in the spirit of national unity, they articulated their programs in the language of multiculturalism. The president began his introductory remarks to the conference attendees as follows:

> Welcome to Sudan, which has remained [over the years] a bridge for contact between peoples. Welcome to this country, which is like a continent with various climates, beliefs, and cultures, and languages and dialects. It is unique in its coexistence (*taʿāyush*) and tolerance (*tasāmuḥ*). Many cultures have contributed to the formation of the nation of Sudan (*ahl al-Sūdān*). . . . And we have not witnessed in the history of Sudan any confrontations or struggles between the Christians and Muslims. The unitary Sudanese family includes the Muslim and the Christian in perfect harmony, and likewise in the neighborhoods there is a mixture of Christians and Muslims. The environmental situation, struggle over resources, and political struggles, these are the real reasons behind the tribal struggles and wars that have ailed Sudan and its family from the time of independence in the 1950s. . . . And [today] we are committed in [our agenda of] implementing the Constitution, and the dispersal of freedoms and the peaceful exchange of power, and the protection of rights on the basis of equality, citizenship, and human rights, and extending [to all] the freedom of belief (*ḥurriyyat al-muʿtaqad*), and the freedom to proselytize (*al-daʿwa*) and to do missionary work (*tabshīr*) in a gentle way (*bi-llatī hiya aḥsan*) . . . [and we call on you who are gathered here] to direct the work in which [Christians and Muslims] participate (*al-ʿamal al-mushtarak*) to support social cohesion (*tamassuk al-mujtamaʿ*) and to bring together the social fabric, and to call for tolerance and moderation, and to close the road in front of religious extremism and those who accuse others of heresy (*al-fikra al-takfīriyya*), and [to promote] tolerance between the social groups. In so doing, we can begin to create peace between social groups, values that are characterized by religious brotherhood and against extremism.

Here, in a carefully worded mixture of the language of the war on terror ("against extremism") and international human rights norms ("protection of rights on the basis of equality, citizenship, and human rights"), the president of Sudan encapsulated both the promise and the perils evident in the global consumption of human rights norms such as rule of law, tolerance, and freedom. To anyone who knows the history of Sudan, the president's speech represents a unique reading of the nation's recent past. The origins of the conflicts he mentions may indeed lie in the lack of resources available to the people of Sudan, but the argument that religion is entirely epiphenomenal to the conflict is difficult to sustain. The speech remains, however, an interesting artifact of the period of "national unity" (the six-year interim period of NCP-SPLM cooperation in the federal government before the South voted to secede) and perhaps was a harbinger of its eventual failure. The term "tolerance," as used by the president, was clearly meant to depoliticize the conflict, and to promote peace and harmony between peoples with little concern for examining the present and historical injustices that had brought them to war in the first place. It offered little promise of effecting reconciliation, for that would depend on an ability to address the difficult issue of the violence that was in fact perpetrated in the name of religion.[26] The notion that religion was epiphenomenal to the conflict, merely a language in which grievances over the real issues (oil, power, land) were expressed, was a common tactic used by the ruling regime to downplay the very significant complaints that non-Muslims (and Muslims on the Left) had regarding the Islamization of the state.

The evening conference Ansar al-Sunna held at its headquarters in the Sajana neighborhood of Khartoum—entitled "The Manner of Treating non-Muslims as Revealed in the Life of the Prophet"[27]—addressed the very same question as the government's event: how could Muslims and non-Muslims

26 I am reminded in reading ʿUmar al-Bashir's speech of the critique of the discourse on tolerance offered by political theorist Wendy Brown. Al-Bashir's masking of the often-violent politics of religious identity that have been waged in Sudan through an appeal to tolerance seems to exemplify the very sort of appeal to tolerance that Brown critiques:

> When the ideal or practice of tolerance is substituted for justice or equality, when sensitivity to or even respect for the other is substituted for justice for the other, when historically induced suffering is reduced to "difference" or to a medium of "offense," when suffering as such is reduced to a problem of personal feeling, then the field of political battle and political transformation is replaced with an agenda of behavioral, attitudinal, and emotional practices. . . . [S]ubstituting a tolerant attitude or ethos for political redress of inequality or violent exclusions not only reifies politically produced differences but reduces political action and justice projects to sensitivity training, or what Richard Rorty has called an "improvement in manners." (Brown 2006: 16)

See also Walton 2015 for an excellent ethnographic account of tolerance as depoliticization.

27 *Manhaj muʿāmalat ghayr al-muslimīn fī-l-sīra al-nabawiyya.*

live together in Sudan? Yet the solution posed by the Salafi shaykhs at this event was quite different from the one offered in the daytime conference. Here, instead of relying on principles such as "religious coexistence," "tolerance," the "freedom of belief," and "equality," Ansar al-Sunna shaykhs mined the life of the prophet Muhammad for what it offered to how Sudanese Muslims should confront non-Muslims in their Muslim-majority society. Though Ansar al-Sunna's critique of the government conference was never explicit, its leaders problematized the notion of religious tolerance put forward by the government as not only incredibly naïve, but also out of sync with the proper way in which a Muslim polity should treat its minorities. It should be stressed that it was neither Ansar al-Sunna's goal nor its expectation to establish an antagonistic relationship to religious minorities.[28] Indeed, its members prided themselves on maintaining positive relations with minorities under its policy of conducting gentle proselytization that does not scare off potential adherents.[29] Rather, its point is that Muslims should envision the relationship between Muslims and non-Muslims using a set of organizing principles that emerge from Islamic doctrine as derived from the life of the Prophet, rather than using the principles bequeathed by the

28 See, for example, the story I tell about the president of Ansar al-Sunna's interactions with John Garang in Salomon 2009: 152, fn 19.

29 Ansar al-Sunna's approach to religious minorities is a key distinction between its program and that of other contemporary Salafi groups across the Muslim world. Ansar al-Sunna prides itself on maintaining a critical distance from the classic Salafi doctrinal principle of *al-walāʾ wa-l-barāʾ* (the principle of loyalty to Muslims and disassociation with non-Muslims or heretical Muslims), arguing that this principle should subordinated to its goal of *daʿwa*, proselytization, through which Ansar al-Sunna has been particularly successful at attracting non-Muslims and Sufi Muslims to its cause. Thus, while the great bulk of Salafi conversations about relationships between Muslims and non-Muslims center on interpretations of the principle of *al-walāʾ wa-l-barāʾ*, at this conference the phrase received only passing mention and no elaboration in the review of Qurʾan and Sunna to determine the proper relationship of Muslims to nonbelievers. For example, nowhere did Ansar al-Sunna shaykhs employ those verses of the Qurʾan that scholars like Ibn Taymiyya use as the foundation for advice to Muslims on how to deal with nonbelievers, verses such as *Sūrat al-Māʾida*: 51, which discusses Muslim relations with Christians and Jews ("Oh you who believe, do not take Jews and Christians as friends [*awliyāʾ*], for they are friends of one another. For he who befriends them is one of them. And God does not guide the people who are wrong-doers") and *Sūrat al-Mumtaḥana*: 4, which discusses the necessity of true believers distancing themselves from those who are not proper believers ("Indeed, you have had a good example in Abraham and those who followed him, when they said unto their [idolatrous] people: 'Verily, we are quit of you and of all that you worship instead of God: we deny the truth of whatever you believe; and between us and you there has arisen enmity and hatred, to last until such a time as you come to believe in the One God!'" [Muhammad Asad's translation]). (See Joas Wagemaker's [2009] discussion of the centrality of these verses in a well-researched history of the term *al-walāʾ wa-l-barāʾ* that explores the term from its origins in pre-Islamic Arabia to the writings of present-day Salafis, who consider it not only legitimate but a central matter of doctrine.)

liberal language of human rights upon which the government conference relied.[30] For Ansar al-Sunna, Islamic politics could not be couched within a set of epistemological frames derived from the West ("Islamic Human Rights," "Muslim pluralism," etc.), for these frames necessarily distorted the political intervention of Islam.

Interestingly, it was not only the arguments made in the government conversation about regulating religious diversity that posed problems for the Salafi speakers that night, but also the very categories used in making them. When one of the speakers observed that the organizers of their event had adopted one of these problematic categories in the very title of their gathering (that is, the term "non-Muslims," which appeared in the Ansar al-Sunna conference title), he took his brethren to task for such carelessness:

> A matter that demands my attention is the technical term "non-Muslim" (*ghayr al-muslimīn*) [that dominates the conversation about religious diversity in Muslim states and that appears in the title of this conference]. In my estimation it is a term that is not precise and also it is a term that is not fair (*munṣif*), and perhaps it internalizes a kind of defeatist condition. Yes, it is a term that is used by some modern people these days, but it is a term that is new in regards to the terms of Islam that preceded it. So in the insistence on repeating this term, as I see it, there is a kind of pushing forward of concepts such as these which we don't want to have a place in fora like these, fora of *ahl al-sunna wa-l-jamāʿa*.[31] So what is required for us is to be specific, to use the terms that are used in the Qurʾan and Sunna in relation to these groups that are now called "non-Muslims." The Qur'an and Sunna use clear and frank expressions that carry clear references. God said, in brief:
>
>> Those who believe (*alladhīn āmanū*) and those who are Jews and the Sabeans and Christians and Mageans and those who worship idols, [indeed God will separate them out (to render

30 Much interesting literature exists on the topic of how liberal human rights discourse is produced, challenged, and assimilated in the Islamic and Arab world. A particularly useful survey of the breadth and variety of approaches appears in Kevin Dwyer's *Arab Voices: The Human Rights Debate in the Middle East* (Dwyer 1991). However, I have yet to see any work that analyzes what seems to be the rather unique Salafi approach to this debate, which focuses its opposition not in terms of an "Islamic approach to human rights," as many liberal Muslim thinkers have attempted (see, for example, Sachedina 2009 and Abou el Fadl 2003), but rather rejects the very categories in which liberal discourse proceeds (as we will see below).

31 Literally, "the people of the *sunna* and the community," but used by Salafis today to refer to Muslims who uphold the Salafi understanding of Islam.

> judgment on who is wrong and who is right) on judgment day. For God is the witness of all things]. (*Sūrat al-Ḥajj*: 17)[32]
>
> Indeed this is a clear documentation that God gave each of them clear names, for among them are major essential differences. So the term "non-Muslim" is a term [that can be] criticized from this standpoint or vantage. . . . Anyhow, it may be appropriate to say that these words [in this verse from the Qur'an] call your attention to the fact [that we need] more specificity, especially when the matter concerns technical terms that have shadows. Playing with these terms harms the issues of Muslims at the intellectual level, at the theoretical level, and, as we said, the pushing forth of such impressions could even be defeatist.

For this speaker, the terms of engagement that framed the conversation about religious diversity in Muslim lands were highly inappropriate. The term "non-Muslim" lacks the necessary specificity to be a proper object of jurisprudential reasoning (*fiqh*). Instead, the speaker rightly recognizes that it is a category that is a product of modern Sudanese identity politics and has little to do with the traditional Muslim taxonomy of humanity. He contends that it is by adopting the language of human rights norms, the language of "the rights of non-Muslims," that Sudanese Muslims have lost what is unique about their own model of dealing with religious difference and entered a situation that he describes as "defeatist." The issue of terminology is so important, the speaker stresses, because these terms do not just effect how we *talk* about non-Muslims, but "have shadows" in Sudanese political practice as well.[33]

In addition to the conclusion arrived at by Salafi shaykhs such as these—i.e., that there are a whole host of relationships to God ("those who believe," "Jews," "Christians," "Sabeans," etc.) and thus that rights should never simply be extended generically to (or withheld from) those who don't accept Islam—it is the Salafi refusal to accept the terms of debate that makes their contribution a unique one within the scheme of Islamic politics in Sudan, as it very explicitly refuses to be translated. It asks the question: can we imagine a conversation about interreligious coexistence that does not rely on the liberal categories bequeathed by internationalist human rights discourse, a discourse that we have seen (as in the case of ʿUmar al-Bashir's speech) to be so inadequate for furthering peace and stability in Sudan? What might

32 Note that the expectation was that the Qur'an was known so well that quoting merely the first few lines of a verse would indicate the remaining lines, which I have put in brackets.

33 Indeed such language was codified in the establishment of the Commission for the Rights of Non-Muslims (*Mufawiḍiyyat Ḥuqūq Ghayr al-Muslimīn*) that was founded in Sudan as a result of the CPA, following its promise to provide such a mechanism to protect the rights of non-Muslims who were living in a capital in which *sharīʿa* was in force.

discourses about coexistence look like that emerge out of other political traditions?

It is significant to observe that in order to make his argument the speaker from Ansar al-Sunna focuses on *Sūrat al-Ḥajj*: 17 to speak about religious diversity, rather than on the much-celebrated *Sūrat al-Ḥujurāt*: 13 ("Oh people, we have created you all out of a male and a female, and have made you into nations and tribes so that you may know one another"), which we saw government agencies highlighting on billboards erected to celebrate tolerance (Chapter 2). The focus of *al-Ḥajj*: 17 is not on the necessity for cooperation in spite of difference ("know one another," as *al-Ḥujurāt*: 13 commands), but rather on humanity's *division* into clearly marked categories. This is not a language of *human* rights (or even of the rights of "non-Muslims"), but rather one in which the specificity of each religious category is recognized and engaged with in a manner appropriate to it.

The speaker continued:

> The legislative actions (*al-taṣarrufāt al-tashrīʿiyya*) of the Prophet were diverse regarding those people [that liberal human rights language has lumped into the single category of "non-Muslim"]. He didn't treat them on a single model. So the Prophet acted with each of these various and diverse sects each according to its situation. He differed in his treatment of these people. It can be observed that [such treatment] ranges between a warm welcome (*al-ḥafāwa*) in some of the behaviors of the Prophet, to perhaps a kind of apprehensiveness (*tawajjus*), to at certain times expelling and displacing and kicking out of the country [some groups].

Here, the category "non-Muslim" is rejected for its lack of specificity; its one-size-fits-all model cannot respond to the multitude of ways of being in the world that Salafis recognize, or to each of the ways in which they, as Muslims, might want to relate to difference in their midst. The Qur'an makes no recognition of non-Muslims per se, but rather recognizes Jews and Christians, idol worshippers and hypocrites, who, *crucially*, are afforded different status within the law laid down by the Prophet not only on the basis of their specific creed, but also depending on their relationship with Muslims at the point of history in question (at war, at peace, under treaty, etc.). Here, groups are engaged not on the basis of a roster of rights (universal human rights *or* those given to the minority as *dhimmī* within some notions of the Islamic polity [e.g., Maudoodi 1961]), but rather with a form of adjudication that examines the situational criteria of the individual (or the group of which he is a part) in relation to the Muslim community and its goals, then compares it to analogous cases in the life of the Prophet, and decides accordingly.[34] By

34 Though I would certainly not argue that Ansar al-Sunna has solved the problem posed by religious diversity in Sudan, its intervention has certainly opened up new space for

rejecting the terms of the debate (tolerance, extremism, and even the category of "non-Muslim" itself), Ansar al-Sunna refuses to translate Islamic politics into a standardized language of international norms and instead seeks a political discourse in the terms of Qur'an and Sunna. Its argument that the categories through which one understands and performs Islamic politics matter greatly to its ability to engage the world is one that needs to be taken seriously if we are to understand the full force of its intervention.

The Shadows of Salvation and New Horizons

The debates I observed in Sudan lend themselves particularly well to the task of rethinking Muslim politics beyond the common models utilized in the Western academy. Whether it was the imaginal confrontation between al-Bura'i and al-Turabi with which we began this chapter, or the very tangible debate between Ansar al-Sunna and the regime in the religious coexistence conferences we have just discussed, it is clear that many Muslims in Sudan who are thinking through the political relevance of their tradition are keen to think outside of the categories of contemporary global political engagement. Examining these multiple engagements with the Islamic state suggests that political discourse was not a one-way street in Sudan, imposed by an overbearing state and either embraced or rejected by the public. Nor did Sudan's experience with the Islamic state spark a teleological liberalization in Islamic political practice ("emphasizing rights instead of duties" [Bayat 2013: 8]), as proponents of the post-Islamism model have predicted. Rather, new political actors put forward novel articulations of foundational politics that were neither reducible to previous revolutionary models nor compatible with their liberal alternatives. The reforms that the Inqadh has

---

conversation. As Ussama Makdisi has taught us in his discussion of the transitions in models of governing diversity adopted by the Ottoman Empire from the early to the late nineteenth century, liberal models of equal citizenship are not always a guarantor of stability, and indeed the opposite might also be the case. He writes:

> [By the late nineteenth century,] the Ottoman Empire had dramatically reinvented itself as a "civilized" and "tolerant" state [in the eyes of the liberal West]. . . . In place of an *imperial toleration* premised on the superiority of Muslim over non-Muslim, but which also recognized and afforded a space for [Christians] to thrive . . . imperial authorities scrambled to propose a new order of things that would at once preserve imperial sovereignty and also win the approbation of the "civilized" world. Religious difference between the inhabitants of the empire was no longer to be emphasized and managed but rather neutralized and transcended by a reforming state that now actively claimed to represent all subjects equally. (Makdisi 2008: 182–83)

The failures of this attempt at transcending difference, and the way in which it spiraled into sectarian violence in the Mt. Lebanon Makdisi studies (2008: 159–60), should serve as ample warning that liberal models of tolerance are not necessarily more conducive to social stability than solutions offered by groups that reject liberal categories.

undergone in its twenty-one years in power, from revolutionary Islamism to thinking through a state that could integrate the diversity of identities included in the populace into its own identity, have by no means injured the political prospects of Islam as a solution to Sudan's continuing woes. Indeed, it is precisely the Inqadh's framing of political discourse in Islamic terms and its failure to maintain hegemony over the definition of those terms that has encouraged other Islamic groups to enter the conversation in a serious manner. The failure of the Inqadh to establish an Islamic state on its initial model has been seen by Islamic groups less as a cue to retreat from the public scene than as a challenge to create another Islamic future for Sudan that both upholds what they understand to be Islamic principles and responds to present political realities. Thus it seems to the contemporary observer that the shadows that the Salvation Revolution cast over Islamic activism in Sudan come not at the twilight of Islamism, but at a new dawn, in which new actors are opening up new horizons for the public and political role of Islam in Sudan's uncertain future.

Postscript: Finding the Islamic State

With the secession of South Sudan in 2011, the Sudanese Islamic state project is both on firmer ground and as unstable as ever. While the Interim Constitution of 2005 had made concessions to Sudan's diversity ("Islamic *sharīʿa*" *and* "popular consensus and the values and customs of the Sudanese people as well as its traditions and religious beliefs, which come under the expression 'the diversity in Sudan' [are each] a source for legislation which is enacted at the federal level"),[35] many imagined the secession of South Sudan and the demographic shift that would come with it as a solution to the tricky problems of religious pluralism that had plagued the full flowering of the Islamist project even before it rose to power (Simone 1994). As President al-Bashir famously stated a few months before secession, "If the South chooses separation, then we will fix the constitution of Sudan. And at that time there will be no room to speak of ethnic and cultural diversity. Islam will be the official religion and Islamic *sharīʿa* will be the principle source of legislation . . . and the Arabic language will be the official language of the state."[36] With the main element of the forces in support of a secular government now part of a different political entity, namely the new state of South Sudan, and with a great majority of non-Muslims now citizens of this state, one might imagine that the Islamic state project would be more easily implemented. Indeed this was the hope of the rarely acknowl-

35 Sudanese Interim Constitution (*Dustūr jumhūriyyat al-Sūdān al-intiqālī*) of 2005: 5:1–2.

36 http://www.aljazeera.net/home/print/f6451603-4dff-4ca1-9c10-122741d17432/436738a8-402b-4f8a-8e1f-48063bf63dbf.

edged *northern* movement in favor of national partition, active in the years following the signing of the CPA.[37] This group argued that the main obstacle to the realization of the Islamic state was the problem of religious minorities, since despite their demographic weakness they sat within a robust international regime of religious freedom and thus were able to stymie the Sudanese government's attempts to establish an Islamic state at every turn. Yet in the years since al-Bashir made that famous statement, we have not seen the government follow through on his promises.

Still working with the Interim Constitution that emerged from the CPA, the government seems hesitant to put anything into writing, maintaining alliances just long enough not to commit to anything or to miss the possibility of appeasing some more powerful party. Yet, the maneuvers and machinations of the particular government in power do not tell us much in the end about the fate of the Islamic state in Sudan, since, as several scholars have observed (Fluehr-Lobban 2012; Gallab 2008), the political survival of the al-Bashir regime has always overridden policy consistency. Indeed, as I mentioned at the outset of this book, in my first visit to Sudan around the time of the signing of the CPA, I found government officers more often discussing UN priorities than the dictates of the Islamic state. Instead, it is the itinerary of the Islamic state, as a "social subject in everyday life" (Aretxaga 2003: 395), as the political form within which citizens live, strive, and imagine their futures, more often than not unleashed from the vagaries of the al-Bashir government and its institutions, that should garner the attention of the researcher interested in the nature of Islamic politics in contemporary Sudan.[38] It is here, in how the Islamic state project has transformed the relationship between knowledge and truth, aesthetics and the virtues, politics and piety, that we can find the lasting effects of the National Salvation regime's twenty-five years in power. It is by tracing the itineraries of these relationships as they wind through the space of the everyday that we begin to see the elusive Islamic state in Sudan coming quite prominently into view, structuring the landscape of discourse and debate on which diverse expressions of contemporary Sudanese life take place. It is here, outside of the never-ending arguments about the relative Islamic character of the present Sudanese regime (both by theologians and those who recognize its debt to Western political forms), that we can truly find the Islamic state.

37 The most vocal spokesperson for this position was al-Tayyib Mustafa of the Just Peace Forum (*Minbar al-Salām al-ʿĀdil*).

38 Here I remain inspired by Yael Navaro-Yashin's observation of republican Turkey: "The political was not just a product of public discourses as fabricated in the obvious social institutions. As in the multiple garbs and guises implied by the metaphor 'faces of the state' the political was precisely unsitable. There were no institutional or other boundaries that could ...alyzed around it; no site, as such, for it" (2002: 3).

Inquiries

EPILOGUE

Escaping the Islamic State?

In March of 2015, nine students disappeared from the University of Medical Sciences and Technology in Khartoum.[1] Four months later, twelve more vanished. From their social media accounts and reports of friends, it quickly became clear that the students had escaped their homes and families and fled to Turkey with the intention of joining the self-proclaimed Islamic State, which occupies territory in Iraq and Syria (ISIS).[2] Though all of Sudanese origin, the students were said to hold Western passports, making their travel to Turkey far easier than it would have been had they only held Sudanese nationality, since Sudanese passport holders need visas to travel almost anywhere. While the fact of their dual nationality may have been merely the practical means that allowed them, and not others, to travel, most commentators in Sudan saw their foreign upbringing as evidence of something else. The consensus they arrived at was that, due to their time in the West, the students had not properly assimilated true Islamic values, which would have shown them the error of "extremists" such as ISIS (e.g., Siddiq 2015: 31). The university they attended, popularly known as Ma'mun Humayda University, after its founder, a regime loyalist and former state health minister, is known as a place that caters to the sons and daughters of the wealthy and well-connected,[3] the new elite that has emerged out of the regime's artful mix of Islamism and capitalism (Gallab 2008).[4] Yet, despite what their parents' allegiances might be, these are students whom Sudanese refer to as *hanākīsh*: Westernized, comfortable, and

1 Reports are conflicting as to how many of them were actually currently enrolled in the university; however, all were current students or recent graduates. See http://www.alsudani.sd/news/?tmpl=component&print=1&option=com_content&id=27896. Also, some initial reports had put the number at eleven students, but this was later reduced to nine.

2 According to the media reports I cite below, the students were quickly posted to hospitals in Mosul where their skills would best be put to use.

3 One of the students is the daughter of the director of the Soba Teaching Hospital, while another is the daughter of Sudanese Foreign Ministry spokesperson ʿAli al-Sadiq (the latter, it was reported, traveled to Turkey on her diplomatic passport). http://www.alarabiya.net/ar/arab-and-world/2015/06/30/ابنة-المتحدث-الرسمي-للخارجية-السودانية-تلتحق-بتنظيم-داعش-.html. (NB: The Arabic word order is inverted in this URL and in the URLs below).

4 One commentator notes that the university is not only famous for teaching in English in this era of higher-education Arabization, but that it charges exorbitant prices that must be paid in dollars, further cementing its elite status (Siddiq 2015: 30).

interested more in the latest fashion fad than in Islamic political action. Part of the shock that analysts expressed about these students joining ISIS was that these *flaneurs* were the last people anyone would imagine being attracted to Islamic extremism.[5] Yet, surprised or not, the fact of Sudanese students joining ISIS caused great anxiety among the Sudanese intelligentsia, and among none more than those who had envisioned an Islamic state for their country.[6]

One of the key members of that cadre, active in the Islamic movement that called for an Islamic state in Sudan since his student days, is Mustafa ʿUthman Ismaʿil, former Sudanese minister of foreign affairs (1998–2005) and current president of the political sector of the ruling NCP. In an interview with the press, he revealed that he was "requesting an investigation into the reasons that led the students to join ISIS," adding that "it is necessary that the apparatus of the state pay attention and be prepared to respond to any indication of recruitment for the benefit of ISIS in the country." He further noted that once the students were (he hoped) back in Khartoum, they would have access to the perfect antidote, the regime's school "for curing extremism through conversation," which had been very successful up to now.[7] While Dr. Mustafa's comments could be read as yet another instance of counterculture radicals becoming establishment and then critiquing the youth for their present rebellions, something more significant was going on as well. Sudan, the first country in the Arabic-speaking world to experience the coming to power of proponents of *an* Islamic state, was being eclipsed by a new claimant to *the* Islamic State, at least in the minds of these few students and of the international community, which has come to see Sudan as a partner in the war against such adversaries. Though the numbers of Sudanese joining ISIS seems to be extremely small, the attention the path of these students has garnered in Sudan signals growing concern among the Sudanese public, particularly on the part of those who are sympathetic to Islamic political ideals.[8]

As we have seen throughout this book, the question raised by the Inqadh regime when it came to power—how do we establish a moral and political order based in Islam?—has been an extremely attractive frame for the

5 For an interesting account of the biographies of each of the students in the March group, see: http://www.alsudani.sd/news/?tmpl=component&print=1&option=com_content&id=27896.

6 See: http://www.reuters.com/article/2015/03/27/uk-mideast-crisis-sudan-students-insight-idUSKBN0MN1C920150327 and http://www.alaraby.co.uk/society/2015/3/20/خاص-داعش-جند-11-طالبا-من-جامعات-سودانية. See also Siddiq 2015.

7 http://www.alaraby.co.uk/politics/2015/3/22/السودان-إعادة-9-طلاب-قبل-التحاقهم-بـ-داعش-قريبا.

8 One example of such an anxiety can be found in the psychopathological reading of students who join such an organization, i.e., the notion that joining the group is due to some sort of malaise rather than motivated by a conscious political choice. Such a reading is on display in an interview cited in Siddiq 2015.

aspirations of countless Sudanese, both pro- and anti-regime. To think of the Islamic state as a series of aspirations with undetermined instantiations (Khan 2012) and unlinked to any particular regime (for a parallel, consider the "democratic ideal" of the United States), is to destabilize the notions of Islamic politics, proposed both by Western scholars and Islamic political actors themselves, that see their becoming as an archeology of sorts, a process of uncovering the principles of *siyāsa* (politics) from the time of the Prophet and applying them to today. Not only is God's rule never so transparent—as the very theory of *al-siyāsa al-sharʿiyya*, the central principle of Islamic jurisprudential thought on politics, reveals (Emon 2012: 177–88; Vogel 1997) with its recognition of a sphere for the ruler's discretion along with the dictates laid down by God—but many of its proponents do not even aspire to such an ideal (think of the framing of what we understand as Western political and epistemological categories as "human heritage" in the *ta'ṣīl* project discussed in Chapter 3).

If we begin to evaluate the success of the Sudanese Islamic state project based not on the staying-power of the particular doctrines the Inqadh regime imposed or on the institutional forms it assumed, but rather on the questions it continues to provoke and the aspirations it engenders, we will better be able to explain why groups like ISIS have become attractive to Sudanese students such as these, living in the era of the late Inqadh. As we have seen throughout this book, the Islamic solutions put forward by the regime did not result in the prosperity or autonomy that the regime promised (at least not for most Sudanese), but led instead to continuing poverty, the proliferation of civil wars, and the loss of the southern third of the country. Moreover, the regime's Islamic project is certainly less bold in 2016 than it was in the 1990s, or even in the years during which the bulk of the fieldwork for this book was completed, sitting as it is in the holding pattern I described at the conclusion of the last chapter. But though the regime's attempt to answer the question "How do we establish a moral and political order based in Islam?" seems to be on ice, there are others rising to the provocation. They range from disaffected former members of the Popular Defense Forces (PDF, the military units mobilized to fight *jihād* in the South during the Civil War) called the *Sā'iḥūn* ("the wanderers in the way of God") Group,[9] to Islamist intellectuals who are now on the sidelines of the government, such as Ghazi Salah al-Din al-ʿAtabani and his Reform Now Movement (*Ḥarakat al-Iṣlāḥ al-Ān*), to dissident figures such Muhammad ʿAli al-Jazuli and his One Umma Current (*Tayyār al-Umma al-Wāḥida*).

The fact that the renegade students felt they could not fulfill Islamic political aspirations in Sudan but needed to make the radical move of traveling

9 See *Sūrat al-Tawba*: 112 for the Qur'anic reference that this movement was citing.

across the world to join an organization vilified both at home and internationally suggests not only that the definition of an Islamic state remains as contested as ever, but that, contrary to some predictions (Roy 1994), the failures of the Islamic state model in Sudan have led not to the eclipse of Islam as a viable political foundation, but rather to an even more active search for its true embodiment. Given the failures of the Sudanese Islamic state project, one can certainly see why ISIS could have appeared an attractive alternative for someone seeking an Islamic political order. As Andrew March and Mara Revkin note in their recent analysis of the ISIS phenomenon, "In the long run, the ISIS legacy will be not only its gruesome record of sadistic violence, but also its profound challenge to existing Islamist thinking. It is a rebuttal to the long-standing Islamist view that modern, centralized states can be 'Islamized' within their existing institutions merely by substituting codified positive laws with codified 'Islamic' laws" (March and Revkin 2015).[10] By boldly rejecting the nation-state model altogether, ISIS, with its "state of the Islamic Caliphate" (*dawlat al-khilāfa al-islāmiyya*), is clearly attempting something quite different from what the Sudanese Islamists enacted.

Embracing some of the key principles of ISIS, Dr. Muhammad al-Jazuli, the leader of the aforementioned One Umma Current, has used its successes to bolster his own critique of the Sudanese regime, to which he juxtaposes ISIS in his rhetoric.[11] Al-Jazuli is said to have been a possible inspiration for the escaped students, who may have been motivated by lectures presented by his organization on the campus of the university they attended. Platforms such as his, which critique not only Sudan's application of its Islamic state project, but the entire framing of it within the constraints of the nation-state model, pose a particularly troubling threat to the monopoly that the regime aspires to hold on Sudan's political future.

10 Again citing March and Revkin 2015: "ISIS leaders appear bent on avoiding some of the problematic features of modern Islamic lawmaking—namely, the ubiquitous tendency to issue codes of law and formal constitutions. Instead, the group has refused to codify any but the most widely known Islamic legal rules in order to avoid the emulation of modern nation-states."

11 In an interview with *al-Sūdānī* newspaper in 2014, al-Jazuli explained his support for ISIS:

> We support [ISIS] from four basic starting points. First [since] it is a libratory project against colonialism, second [since] it is an Islamic project against secularism, third, [since] it is an Islamic Sunni project opposing the Shiʿa (*rāfiḍī*) project, and fourth [since] it is an umma project opposing Sykes-Pikot. . . . The Islamic State will fight until it liberates the entire Islamic world, from Indonesia to Andalusia. It is necessary that you know that now is the appointed time for the caliphate. . . . An Islamic Spring will happen, but it will happen with ammunition boxes instead of ballot boxes. . . . Everything that [ISIS leader] al-Baghdadi does is an application of [Qur'anic] *āyas*, and we support him and support the application of the revealed *sharīʿa* and the revitalization of the jurisprudence of revelation.

In a harshly worded video released by his supporters following his imprisonment by security services for anti-state activities,[12] al-Jazuli offers the Sudanese president ʿUmar al-Bashir "advice" (*naṣīḥa*), as he feels is his duty as an Islamic scholar, on how best to put the Islamic state he established back on track. A full-scale rebuttal of the Islamic credentials of the Sudanese state from an Islamic scholar is rare, and al-Jazuli offers a particularly comprehensive critique of the government's program.

Posted on the Facebook page of the Organization of Lovers of the Young Intellectual Dr. Muhammad ʿAli al-Jazuli, the video is entitled "Urgent Letter to ʿUmar al-Bashir after the Inauguration[13] from the Imprisoned Shaykh Dr. Muhammad ʿAli al-Jazuli (May God Free Him)." It bears the production date June 2, 2015.[14] The video begins with the name of al-Jazuli's organization, the One Umma Current, splashed across the screen, flanked by a Qurʾanic verse in which the notion of a unified *umma* that his organization's name cites, is situated ("Indeed your *umma* is one *umma* and I am your Lord so fear me," 23:52). Then a reproduction of the now famous "ISIS map" of the Islamic world (the proposed caliphate that would encompass historical Islamic lands in disregard of the borders drawn by colonial powers) emerges on the screen. The map stays in a corner of the screen throughout much of the video, as both a testament to the allegiances of this shaykh and a reminder of the juxtaposition of Sudan's nation-state model with the caliphate to which ISIS gestures.

After some meditative humming that accompanies the above-described scene, a loud crackling sound jolts the viewer from his contemplations. The face of ʿUmar al-Bashir suddenly appears on one side of the frame and that of Shaykh al-Jazuli on the other, as if engaging in some sort of simulated campaign debate. Next al-Jazuli's voice, already in animated crescendo, implores:

> We face a catastrophe, and there are six Islamically legitimate (*sharʿiyya*) steps that if we do not apply them . . . not even one house will be free of the fire (*al-ḥarīq*). (A fire burns loudly on the screen for dramatic effect.) And no organization will be safe from it (sound of a gunshot), nor any tribe (sound of a gunshot), nor any political party (another gunshot). [These are the] decisions the president of the republic must take. This or the fire!
>
> The first principle: to make the major ablution with the water of repentance (*ightisāl bi-māʾ al-tawba*) and to make a confession of all

12 According to press reports, al-Jazuli was first arrested in late 2014, then released in late June of 2015, only to be rearrested a few days later. See http://sudantribune.com/spip.php?article55488, http://www.alriyadh.com/1061446.

13 ʿUmar al-Bashir was reelected in a sweeping and uncontested victory in April 2015.

14 https://ar-ar.facebook.com/loversdr.algzouli.

the errors and crimes that were committed in the name of religion.[15] This or the fire!

The second step: The government that is accused of ethnic cleansing, I allege that it needs another kind of cleansing: cleansing with the tool of *sharīʿa* (*al-taṭhīr al-sharʿī*) of all of the leftovers of the Naivasha Accord in the Constitution and all of the leftovers of secularism in the country.[16] This or the fire!

Three: Apply the Islamic *sharīʿa* in a complete and clear manner, not the truncated *sharīʿa*. This or the fire!

Four: Throwing out international law and all the foreign organizations from Sudan. This or the fire!

The fifth curative treatment: Cancel the federalist system that has been the reason for ethnic and provincial talk in each individual's heart. This or the fire! (At this point an image of Sudan appears on the screen in which Darfur and the eastern provinces dramatically split off, leaving a new map of a much smaller Sudan . . . a fantasy not so farfetched when one considers what happened to Sudan in 2011 with the secession of the South.)

Six: Announce *jihād* and complete mobilization, a *jihād* under a clear Islamic banner. (At this point in the video, images appear of Sudanese fighters in the bush marching and firing automatic weapons, pictures of martyrs, and the sounds of a *jihādī* anthem: *an oath we've taken [to protect] the lions' lair, always going forward and we never soften.*) . . . And if you have realized these five, ʿUmar al-Bashir, then we will fight [the *jihād*] alongside you, all of the *umma* will fight alongside you. . . .

Oh brothers, we are in a critical situation (a map appears with a picture of Ethiopia with a red crucifix in the center and threatening-looking red arrows moving from it into Sudan, as if predicting a Christian invasion from the east), a critical situation that cannot be solved except by the revealed book [i.e., the Qurʾan]. And man-made cures get us nothing except more burdens (*rihq*). (A picture appears of

15 Thinking back to the story of al-Buraʿi that we encountered in Chapter 5, we can see here that it is not only the Sufis who equate political status with ritual purity. The political salience of *najāsa* (ritual impurity) that is implied here—making politics akin to the conjugal act that also requires the *ightisāl*—is worthy of further reflection.

16 One might assume that al-Jazuli is referring to the remnants of colonialism, or to the pre-Inqadh system more generally, when he says "from all the remnants of secularism." However, at this point in the video a picture of a gathering of the commanders of the SPLM-North flashes across the screen, suggesting that instead he may be speaking about ridding Sudan of the SPLM-North that continues to fight a war in Sudan's new (post-partition) South. Though the SPLM that now makes up the government of South Sudan claims no further ties with their former comrades, now marooned in the "old Sudan," the latter claim to be fighting for the original agenda of John Garang, who wanted not partition but a new Sudan organized around secularism.

> the South of Sudan splitting off from the pre-2011 map of the country, and then the South turns into an Israeli flag, which grows in size until it covers the entire region, from Sudan to North Africa. Next a picture appears of a meeting between Salva Kir and some Israeli officials, after which we see al-Bashir meeting with John Garang, with Salva Kir, and then with the anti-Islamist Egyptian President, ʿAbd al-Fatah al-Sisi. Finally, we see a picture of the dome of the US Capitol Building.) *And there were persons from mankind who used to seek refuge in persons from the jinn, but all that was increased in them was burdens* (*rihq*) (*Sūrat al-Jinn*: 6).[17] . . . The curative treatments that do not come from the *sharīʿa* will not increase anything for us except burdens!

In three short minutes, al-Jazuli presents a critique of the state and its Islamist project that is without clear precedent. Al-Bashir is accused of applying a partial *sharīʿa* and of seeking refuge in man-made cures rather than those of Qurʾan and Sunna in order to stay in power. It is for this reason that Sudan faces a crisis: the southern third of the country has split off (and then made agreements with Israel, thus putting that enemy literally at Sudan's borders), rebellion continues in the West and the new South, and Christian neighbors in the Horn of Africa are ready to invade Muslim Sudan at any moment (notwithstanding that the latter fear has little basis in reality). The crisis can be solved, al-Jazuli argues, not by attempting to achieve harmony between Islamic ideals and outside agendas, but rather by returning to Qurʾan and Sunna, purely and fully.

Interestingly, in addition to speaking in a familiar Islamist idiom, al-Jazuli also mobilizes the critiques the Left has aimed at the regime, appropriating them to serve his own interests. Al-Bashir has committed crimes in the name of religion from which he needs to repent, al-Jazuli tells us. The government has been busy committing ethnic cleansing when quite another kind of cleansing is necessary: that of the remnants of the CPA (here referred to by the framework agreement that preceded it: the Naivasha Accords) and the compromises to the Islamic state that it required (which remain part of the Constitution of Sudan even after the South has seceded and the president has promised to nullify previous concessions). Al-Jazuli seems to suggest that we must move beyond the Islamic state model that the regime established, one that compromised with the West (both through treaties and in terms of adopting its epistemological categories), that appeased minorities in the Naivasha Accords, and that ended up seeking remedies

17 Clearly the parallel that is being drawn here is between two instances of seeking refuge from something other than God: in the former case from international law and agreements, and in the latter from the *jinn*. In both cases, those seeking refuge in something other than God lose out.

not from the Qurʾan, but from international mechanisms. For al-Jazuli, the choices are stark: this or the fire, ISIS or the secular state.

In posing the alternatives so starkly, al-Jazuli forces us to ask an important question: Is a modern nation-state that both adheres to international law and draws its domestic laws and policy from Islamic sources possible? Or must Islam always be compromised in an era when state sovereignty, although it may be invoked as an absolute, in fact applies differently to weak and strong states? Is it perhaps *this* clash that makes an Islamic state impossible, rather than any inherent incompatibility between the moral frameworks on which the state relies and "Islam"? Sudan does not offer us a clear answer. Its failures are as robust as its successes, and its integration into the community of nations is far from stable. Moreover, the events of the Arab Spring and its aftermath, in particular the coup in the summer of 2013 that overthrew the Muslim Brotherhood government of Mohamed Morsi in Egypt, foreclosed on our ability to address this question with any precision, as experiments were interrupted before they even began. What is clear, however, is that many are searching for a fulfillment of Islamic aspirations elsewhere, outside of the nation-state model that was bequeathed to the Islamic world at the end of European colonialism.

Despite the force of such trends, Sudanese regime supporters are not so quick to cede their claim on the Islamic state, even if their reasoning has become increasingly difficult to untangle. Shortly after news broke of the students' escape, the Organization of Sudanese ʿUlamāʾ (*Hayʾat ʿUlamāʾ al-Sūdān*), an independent body strongly allied with the government and made up of many current and former government officials, issued a *fatwā* condemning the actions of Sudanese who join ISIS. Speaking to the Sudanese daily *al-Mijhar al-Siyāsī*, Professor Muhammad ʿUthman Salih, the president of the Sudanese *ʿUlamāʾ* Council, explained the basis of his *fatwā*:

> It is clear that the Islamic state has a series of conditions if it wants to be fulfilled. And among them is that there must be a general allegiance [to it expressed among Muslims] and there must be a leader who applies [the] conditions [necessary for its fulfillment], that the state rules with what God laid down and what came on the tongue of the Prophet and that there is agreement among a great number of believers. . . . As for the behaviors that we have learned of perpetrated by ISIS, they are all reckless behaviors from which it is necessary that one repent and [then] review his actions and commit to the program of the Qur'an and Sunna. Because killing oneself is not permitted except under legitimate circumstances. Likewise I say that the pictures that appear of them killing people here and there and of them blowing up mosques are matters that don't have even a smidgen of Islam in them.[18]

18 http://almeghar.com/permalink/29116.html.

Groups like ISIS, and the horror of Sudanese youth being attracted to its program, made the Sudanese Islamist elite want to rescind the radical egalitarianism in Islamic authority that they had once promised. It was the thorough decentering of Islamic authority evident in groups like ISIS that made scholars like Professor Muhammad ʿUthman Salih want to put on the traditional turban of the *ʿulamāʾ*, despite the rather nontraditional training he had received in the form of an MA and PhD from the University of Edinburgh in Comparative Religion.[19] In what appeared to be a set-up question, after the professor offered a full-throated defense of the role of the *ʿulamāʾ* in Islamic society as a way of reining in "reckless" groups like ISIS, the interviewer gave him the opportunity to qualify what sounded like a major revision of the key Islamist goal of upsetting the *ʿulamāʾ*'s monopoly over the transmission of Islamic knowledge. Citing the language of the Islamists' own critique, the interviewer asked pointedly, "But do we find in Islam a concept of men of religion (*rijāl al-dīn*), like we find in the church?" The professor answered, "There is no such concept in Islam, but there is a concept that there should be scholars (*ʿulamāʾ*), and such persons may be totally devoted to knowledge and to studying the *sharīʿa* or they may be doctors or engineers or whatever [in addition to being scholars]. The only condition is that they know enough of religious matters to talk about them. In our Islamic tradition it is clear that the scholar of religion can have another profession at the same time."

Despite his attempt to redefine the nature of a "scholar," there is of course an irony here. The Islamism of the regime was founded on a critique of the *ʿulamāʾ*. But, when you give power to the people to interpret and become religious authorities, it is quite possible that you may end up with groups like ISIS. Thus Muhammad ʿUthman wants some scholarly control over the dissemination of Islamic knowledge, but he is clearly hesitant to support the notion of a traditional *ʿulamāʾ* class and thereby to renege on prior commitments entirely. The questions the Inqadh provoked were acquiring answers with which its intellectuals were increasingly uncomfortable. The Islamic public sphere they had enabled was turning out phenomena they could not control.

As a response, while figures such as al-Jazuli accused the Sudanese Islamic state project of having been corrupted by its relations with the West and thus compromising the purity of its Islamic program, regime supporters accused ISIS of being a Western by-product of another sort, only able to attract Muslims who were frustrated by their time in the West and did not know much about Islam in the first place. Summarizing an interview with the Dean of Student Affairs at the University of Medical Sciences and Technology, *al-Sūdānī* newspaper reported his view that: "[ISIS's] ability to

19 http://oiu.edu.sd/fic/show_page.php?page_id=2780.

attract the students was due to the fact that [the students] come from Western countries and perhaps their religious knowledge is not strong, this is the entry point that the extremists use." In other words, those who knew Islam well would never be drawn to a program like ISIS. Or, as Organization of Sudanese *'Ulamā'* president, Professor Muhammad 'Uthman, put it in his interview in *al-Mijhar al-Siyāsī*:

> All of [the students] are those who came from the West . . . and they were filled with frustrations that they faced because of racial discrimination in the West, and from the oppressions that fall on the Muslim community there.
>
> *You said that all who escaped came from the West. Does this mean that Sudanese youth are immune to [the appeal of] these organizations?*
>
> > I would say yes. I myself was the director of one of the universities [Omdurman Islamic University, 2001–2009] . . . that had more than sixty thousand male and female students and not even one student defected [to join an extremist organization]. Rather, they were all moderate people because they took legitimate and correct [Islamic] knowledge from the mouths of scholars.

For regime supporters, the antidote to ISIS is Islam, at least that which comes from "the mouths of scholars." It is due to insufficient knowledge of Islam that students are joining ISIS. Epistemological enlightenment on an Islamic basis, such as that which the regime sought to enact, is thus posed as a cure to the kind of radicalization that emerged out of the secularism and minoritization that Muslims are experiencing in the West.

The Sudanese state's eventual concessions on the purity of its Islamic character—to religious minorities in signing the CPA, to the Sudanese opposition in order to remain in power, and to the international community in keeping troops off the ground—coupled with the absence of the redistribution of economic resources and political power that the regime has long promised, have led to a malaise among young Sudanese Islamists of a variety of colors. ISIS, by suggesting a *dawla* (political entity) that is more authentic, a *khilāfa* outside of the European state-sovereignty model (Nielsen 2015), offers these youth the image of an escape from the problems of Islamic (nation-)state-building by relying on a different political tradition. Indeed, to call this *dawla* a "state" may be a mistranslation, at least in terms of ISIS's political ambitions. The problems that the Sudanese state ran into are seen by ISIS supporters as not merely the mistakes of the regime, but a problem with the nation-state model as a whole: the placement within a system of states (the very notion of *an* versus *the* Islamic state), the notion of popular sovereignty and the demographic challenge to Muslim unity it poses, the kind of truncation required of the *sharīʿa* when placing it within a codified system of law that adheres to the international order. Moreover, the compromises to its initial vision that the Sudanese regime offered as a result of the peace agreement with the South, which remain in effect even after partition, have inspired such activists to wonder: if the Sudanese regime is not able to answer the question it posed when it came to power—how do we establish a political order based on Islamic foundations?—perhaps someone else could.

Yet, as visually arresting as the smashing of the Sykes-Picot border may be,[20] and as interesting as the ability to pull Muslims from across the world into a new political order that rejects the current equation of their geographic location with their political identity ("there is no nationality, we are all Muslims, there is only one country"),[21] it is unclear that ISIS has escaped the model of modern state-based governance entirely. As one *New York Times* reporter wrote: "While no one is predicting that the Islamic State will become steward of an accountable, functioning state anytime soon, the group is putting in place the kinds of measures associated with governance: issuing identification cards for residents, promulgating fishing guidelines to preserve stocks, requiring that cars carry tool kits for emergencies."[22] Experts recognize that it is precisely the merging of the skill sets of the aterritorial jihadists (Devji 2005) with those of "former Baathist officers under Saddam Hussein with expertise in organization, intelligence, and internal security" (and, clearly, also in bureaucracy) that has made "the organization such a potent force"[23] (see also Mecham 2015). The ahistorical reading of ISIS that sees the movement as merely going back to the sources and putting them into action (Wood 2015) obscures the fact that not only is ISIS reliant on those who have expertise in the mechanisms and organizational strategies of state power (not to mention their equal reliance on new media technologies [Atwan 2015]),[24] but that, as they establish themselves, they

20 See "The End of Sykes-Picot," a production of ISIS's media-wing, *al-Ḥayāt:* http://www.liveleak.com/view?i=d43_1404046312.

21 Ibid.

22 http://www.nytimes.com/2015/07/22/world/middleeast/isis-transforming-into-functioning-state-that-uses-terror-as-tool.html?hpw&rref=world&action=click&pgtype=Homepage&module=well-region&region=bottom-well&WT.nav=bottom-well&_r=0.

23 http://www.nytimes.com/2015/07/21/world/middleeast/isis-strategies-include-lines-of-succession-and-deadly-ring-tones.html?hp&action=click&pgtype=Homepage&module=first-column-region&region=top-news&WT.nav=top-news.

24 In the *New York Times* article I cite in the previous footnote, we find the words of one intelligence analyst on this point: "Baghdadi is to a certain extent a religious figurehead designed to grant an aura of religious legitimacy and respectability to the group's operations, while the real power brokers are a core of former military and intelligence officials."

come to look more and more like other states that populate(d) the Middle East, despite their expanded borders. The Islamic state and the problems it raises are perhaps not so easy to escape after all.

• • •

The twenty-one medical students from Khartoum are not the only ones who have tried to escape the Islamic state in Sudan in the past decade. In addition to the thousands of economic migrants and political dissidents who have left, the entire southern third of the country defected from the Islamic state in 2011, declaring independence and setting up a political model that aimed to rearrange the relationship between religion and governance (Salomon 2014).

While there were multiple motives for this secession, it cannot be taken for granted that one of the key contributing factors to it was the injustice Southerners experienced as "second class" citizens in their own country. In pre-partition Sudan, Southerners were not only ethnically marginalized from networks of political and economic power, but also as predominantly non-Muslims within an Islamic political order that offered neither communal autonomy nor recognition within the identity of the state. Many Southerners argued that an Islamic political system was, by its nature, unable to accommodate the aspirations of minorities. Some concluded that state secularism would govern religious diversity far more justly than an Islamic ordering, based as the former is on a notion of legal equality rather than on a taxonomy of difference, as is the latter. With the founding of the South Sudanese state in 2011, SPLM political actors championed state secularism as a means of redeeming the nation from decades of religious excess in which full citizenship was only possible within an Islamic idiom. And yet, secularism, as an alternative, this-worldly soteriology to the regime's *inqādh*—a secularism that contended that it is only through a nonalignment of the political and the religious that the state could be saved from interreligious strife—quickly became an object of contention itself, read by many South Sudanese as anything but neutral.

South Sudan's secular project—whose development I had the chance to witness first-hand during fieldwork in Juba and Malakal during 2011 and 2012 (Salomon 2013, 2014, 2015a)—was propelled by a logic that strove for two incommensurable goals. On the one hand, the category of the "secular" indicated to South Sudanese political actors a state that expressed neutrality in regard to the religious confessions of its citizens. Such neutrality was said to be the ground on which religious freedom could best be cultivated.

This professedly universalist definition of the secular draws primarily on the American model (evidence that all secularisms, like "languages," are in fact vernaculars), wherein nonestablishment is said to enable a public sphere in which freedom of religious expression is guaranteed. Yet, on the other hand, political actors also understood the secular as a historically specific device through which they could erase a painful and violent past in which the political space had been forcibly "Islamized" through the actions of conquerors from the North, a means of escaping the legacy of the Islamic state.

Despite assurances from government officials that it was "Islamism" (that is, an insistence on the political relevance of Islam) and not Islam that was the target of secular purges, the category of the secular was read by many, particularly members of Muslim communities, as a veiled particularism. One informant I met on a trip to Juba, a young Muslim activist, challenged the secular premise of the government that one could be a believer at church on Sunday and a citizen uninfluenced by religion Monday through Friday, or that one could oppose Islamism, but not Islam. He put it to me this way: "The [government] announced the secularism of the state, but the president of the South prays in a church. All of those in power pray in churches. They put the churches in power and announce publicly that they are secularists. . . . This is not secularism but pure Christianism, masquerading as secularism in order to attack Islam." Statements like these highlight a controversial assumption about religion that is relevant not only to South Sudanese secularism but to secularism of all forms, namely, the concept of differentiation (Casanova 1994): the idea of religion as a bounded discipline, which secularism requires in order to protect the conceptual distinctiveness of its domain. My interlocutors asked: Are real people able to compartmentalize their lives in the way that the imagined citizens of state secularism do? Or do such claims perpetuate a fiction about the lived character of religion? Is secularism merely a sly way of allowing for one form of religious politics (i.e., that of the majority), while denying another?

For South Sudan, secularism was not merely a means to produce political equality after decades of living in a system where citizenship was marked according to religious identity. It was also a means of cleansing the physical marks of the Islamic state, institutionally, architecturally, and culturally. For example, while mosques in the centers of South Sudanese cities remained unmolested, those on government properties, built during an era in which the government was trying actively to convert Southerners and lay claim to public space as Islamic, were repurposed for "secular pursuits." The rationale was that, in order to protect the secular character of the new state and to reverse decades of forced Islamization, the mosques should be closed. With this goal in mind, mosques at military installations were transformed into army barracks, while, to take one example, the mosque at the Malakal airport was repurposed as a restaurant. Such repurposing of these active sites of worship was read by many South Sudanese Muslims as nothing short of a desecration of sacred space and a curtailment of freedom of worship. For them it called into question the state's commitment to the principle of religious neutrality. Given that large numbers of Muslims serve in the army and make use of public spaces like the airport, many Muslims read the closure of mosques not as an attack on past Islamization, but as an attack on Islam. *Was the process of de-Islamization of the state also a process of writing Muslims out of South Sudan's future*, they wondered.

Yet secularism in South Sudan, as elsewhere, was not merely a destructive intervention into religion. As countless studies in the burst of literature on secularism have shown, secularism is not only the purging of religion from the public sphere (as projects in mosque repurposing might initially suggest); rather, it is the constant management of religion in order to fashion it in such a way as to serve diverse projects of governance (e.g., Sullivan, Yelle, and Taussig-Rubbo 2011). The South Sudanese case illustrates this thesis very clearly. On the one hand, the state is obliterating marks of past Islamization from the land quite literally in order to create secular space. On the other hand, the state is constructing distinctly religious public spaces as a means of managing the diverse religions in its midst. An example is the South Sudan Islamic Council, which the state has established as an official forum where Muslims can organize their affairs and represent themselves within the apparatus of the state. This Islamic space that the state has created (and which it closely manages) is, however, an extremely toxic one.[25] There is much disagreement over whether the Council is a true channel for Muslim opinion or merely an attempt to co-opt potential Muslim dissent. Moreover, the very notion that Muslims could no longer exist in plurality, but were being told to choose a single roster of leadership, which would then report to the state, caused much consternation. Not only did the Council disrupt previous structures of authority within the community, it forced Muslims to question the nature of their "demographic" in the first place:

25 This toxicity was illustrated by the fact that I was picked up and detained by security agents during my last visit to the branch of the Council in Malakal, seemingly out of fear that I was documenting the tensions I describe here. Moreover, a vicious exchange between the Council's secretary general and some Muslims in Juba over the former's letter to the security services (a copy of which I obtained, though I was unable to verify its authenticity) accusing some members of the Muslim community of planning terrorist activities "with the coordination of Islamic extremist groups from Iran, al-Qaʿida, and the Sudanese Islamic Movement" further exhibits how this Council has become the site of considerable struggle.

Are we *a* Muslim community given our diversity? And even if we can be understood together as Muslims, who can represent us? Moreover, providing a new structure of authority within the Muslim community that reports to the state is controversial because it challenges the identity of those Muslims who do not seek recognition on the basis of religion, but instead wish to be politically engaged solely as South Sudanese.

Ironically, in order to conjure Muslims whose Islam would be irrelevant to their citizenship, the state felt it needed to involve itself actively in Muslim affairs—particularly, officials contended, after decades of "brainwashing" under the Islamic state, which emphasized to Muslims that their religious identity was essential to their position as citizens, and that religion was essential to the proper workings of the state. Organizations like the South Sudan Islamic Council were a means of producing these new sorts of Muslims.[26] Indeed, the state seemed to feel that it needed an officially sanctioned Muslim minority in order to protect itself from the threat of political Islam. And yet the very recognition of Muslims as a public with particular interests seemed to contradict the egalitarian model of equal citizenship (in which there were no minorities, only South Sudanese) that was supposed to stand as a counterpoint to the Islamic state. As an imperative of "religious freedom," the Islamic Council created the very community whose interests it was said to protect, its eventual impossibility indexed by its members' mutual accusations of extremism and disloyalty to the state.

These two examples from South Sudan—the Islam that the state sought to destroy and the Islam it sought to produce—illustrate the difficulties the modern state faces in disentangling itself from religion, even in an explicitly post-religious state such as South Sudan.[27] The results of South Sudan's secularization process force us to think critically about what exactly was escaped in the secession of South Sudan, since indeed many of the problems of managing diversity that arose in the Islamic state have been reproduced

26 Saba Mahmood argues that the political category of "religious minority" is not an object for, but rather a product of, the international discourse of religious freedom, thus upending the logic that sees religious freedom as merely a palliative to already existing religious division (Mahmood 2012; see especially p. 419: "Viewed from this perspective, 'religious minorities' do not just signify a demographic entity that are accorded a space of freedom and immunity by the institutionalization of religious liberty, but are also produced through the process of the legal codification of this principle. One of the key questions that guides this essay is that of how the discourse on religious liberty has participated in the production of 'the minority problem' in international law, and how this 'problem' has unfolded in the history of the modern Middle East").

27 Of course, South Sudan is not alone among self-professed "secular states" in seeing some version of religious establishment as a means of managing religious diversity. See, for example, Dressler 2011; Fernando 2005; Zeghal 2013b.

in the new state, and with tragic results. As recent events in South Sudan have shown,[28] the problem of difference (religious, political, ethnic) is no simpler to solve outside of the Islamic state than it was within it.

...

In both of the escapes that we have discussed here—the escape from the failures of the Sudanese Islamic state project to other Islamic political solutions and the escape from the Islamic state to the secular state—we see that the myriad dilemmas posed by the Islamic state in Sudan are extremely difficult to transcend.[29] This is perhaps because we have been misrecognizing the source of the problem. The problem lies not in Islam or in secularism, but rather in the particular organization of states and how they project sovereignty onto the communities that they govern (Kalmo and Skinner 2010; Steinmetz 1999). Too often problems with the state's exercise of power are neglected as objects of analysis in favor of arguments over the color of its ruling ideology, thereby reproducing the same dilemmas of pluralism and its limits, no matter if the state is secular, socialist, liberal, or Islamic. As a result, attempts to rethink the state that might offer new solutions to Sudan's woes are ignored, while combatants remain locked in a perpetual struggle over its identity.

As the preceding chapters have shown, regardless of the successes or failures of the regime in power in Sudan, the aspiration to an Islamic state has become an indelible presence in the imaginaries of countless Sudanese. In this sense too, no matter the desires of secularists, the Islamic state is inescapable, unless one imagines the kind of violent purging of Islamists on display in post-Morsi Egypt, a liquidation of the opposition. Thus all of us, Islamist, secularist, or otherwise, must take seriously the questions the Islamic state poses, the challenges it presents to the existing world order, and the challenges it has failed to take up in envisioning how Islamism can

28 I am referring to the civil war that began in December of 2013 in which fighting often took place along ethnic lines. See, for example, the African Union report on the South Sudanese Civil War (http://reliefweb.int/sites/reliefweb.int/files/resources/auciss.final_.report.pdf) as well as commission member Mahmood Mamdani's "Separate Opinion" (http://reliefweb.int/sites/reliefweb.int/files/resources/auciss.separate.opinion.pdf). See also the epilogue to Salomon 2015a.

29 Another way we might frame these two escapes from the Islamic state is that while the first group (the students) tries to escape the *political form* of the state and the compromises to its vision of Islam that it requires, the second (South Sudan) tries to escape the state's *religious character* as a means of fulfilling political equality. We have seen the difficulties each encountered in achieving either goal.

become a political order that is something other than authoritarianism in religious garb. To accomplish this latter task, modes of thinking are needed that explore possibilities of political order beyond state sovereignty, that imagine a politics of communal autonomy, and that draw critically from premodern political traditions—not as a means of resurrecting the past, but as a tool for destabilizing the naturalness of the present (Asad 2015). Though such a task might seem quixotic in the international order in which we live, the crises that have befallen both Sudan and its African and Middle Eastern neighbors may leave its citizens with no other choice than to explore such a process of inquiry.[30] Indeed, it is in those spaces outside the halls of power, and at the margins of official discourse, those spaces where Sudanese are imagining the Islamic state anew in a dizzying kaleidoscope of ways, that we can see that this process has already begun.

30 For in what sense can we speak of a functioning system of states in significant parts of Africa and the Middle East any longer?

Bibliography

Abaza, Mona. 2002. *Debates on Islam and Knowledge in Malaysia and Egypt: Shifting Worlds*. London: Routledge.

Abbas, Abdel Rahman. 1995. "Islamic Economics: A Psycho-Ethical Paradigm," *al-Ta'ṣīl*, issue 2, May 2.

ʿAbd al-ʿAziz, Muhammad (interviewer). 2014. "al-Munasiq al-ʿām li-Tayyār al-Umma al-Wāḥida d. Muḥammad ʿAlī al-Jazūlī li-l-Sūdānī: lam ubayʿ Dāʿish, wa lakin . . ." (The General Coordinator for the One Umma Trend, Dr. Muhammad ʿAli al-Jazuli, to *al-Sūdānī*: "I have not made a pledge of allegiance to ISIS, but . . ."). *al-Sūdānī*, June 7, 2014. (Newspaper clipping found online at: http://sudaneseonline.com/board/470/msg/سودانيون-حاربوا-مع-داعش!...ارهابي-انا-يقول-والجزولي-1404632768.html.) (NB: The Arabic word order is inverted in this URL).

ʿAbd al-Hamid, ʿAbd al-Qadir ʿUthman. 2005. *Ḥubb al-awliyāʾ wa-l-ṣāliḥīn* (Love of the *awliyāʾ* and the Righteous). Khartoum: Markaz al-ʿAfrāʾ li-l-Khadamāt.

ʿAbd al-Khaliq, ʿAbd al-Rahman. No date. *al-Muslimūn wa-l-ʿamal al-siyāsī* (Muslims and Political Work), no publisher listed.

Abdel Rahman, Amani Mohamed El Obeid. 2008. *Middle Class and Sufism: The Case Study of the Sammaniyya Order Branch of Shaikh al-Burʾai* [*sic*]. PhD Dissertation. University of Khartoum.

Abou el Fadl, Khaled. 2003. "The Human Rights Commitment in Modern Islam," in *Human Rights and Responsibilities in the World Religions*, edited by Joseph Runzo, Nancy M. Martin, and Arvind Sharma. Oxford: One World Press.

Abu Rabiʿ, Ibrahim, ed. 2010. *The Contemporary Arab Reader on Political Islam*. Edmonton: University of Alberta Press.

——. 1996. *Intellectual Origins of Islamic Resurgence in the Modern Arab World*. Albany: State University of New York Press.

Abusabib, Mohammed. 2004. *Art, Politics and Cultural Identification in Sudan*. Uppsala: Acta Universitatis Upsaliensis.

Abusharaf, Rogaia Mustafa. 2009. *Transforming Displaced Women in Sudan: Politics and the Body in a Squatter Settlement*. Chicago: University of Chicago Press.

Agrama, Hussein Ali. 2012. *Questioning Secularism: Islam, Sovereignty, and the Rule of Law in Modern Egypt*. Chicago: University of Chicago Press.

——. 2011. "A Secular Revolution," *The Immanent Frame: Secularism, Religion and the Public Sphere*, http://blogs.ssrc.org/tif/2011/03/11/asecular-revolution/.

Ahmed, Akbar. 1995. "The Islamization of Knowledge," in *The Oxford Encyclopedia of the Modern Islamic World*, ed. John Esposito, vol. 1. Oxford: Oxford University Press.

Ahmed, Einas. 2007. "Political Islam in Sudan: Islamists and the Challenge of State Power (1989–2004)," in *Islam and Muslim Politics in Africa*, ed. Benjamin Soares and René Otayek. New York: Palgrave Macmillan.

Aidi, Hishaam D. 2005. "Slavery, Genocide and the Politics of Outrage: Understanding the New Racial Olympics," *Middle East Report*, no. 234 (Spring 2005).

ʿAli, Haydar Ibrahim. 2004. *Suqūṭ al-mashrūʿ al-ḥaḍārī, al-juzʾ al-awwal: al-siyāsa wa-l-iqtiṣād* (The Collapse of the Civilization Project, Vol. 1: Politics and Economics). Khartoum: Markaz al-Dirāsāt al-Sūdāniyya.

ʿAliba, Ahmad. 2013. "Bawwābat al-ahrām kānat hunāk . . . riḥla maʿa al-Bashīr ilā Qarrī . . . al-Sūdān alladhī lā yaʿarifhu aḥad" ("The Gate of the Pyramids Was Here . . . a Trip with al-Bashir to Qarri . . . the Sudan That No One Knows"), *al-Ahrām* (http://gate.ahram.org.eg/News/432087.aspx), December 18.

al-ʿAlwani, Taha Jabir. 1994. "al-Aslama wa-l-taʾṣīl" ("Islamization and Fundamentalization"), *al-Taʾṣīl*, issue 1, December 1994.

Anderson, Jon. 2003. "New Media, New Publics: Reconfiguring the Public Sphere of Islam," *Social Research* 70:3 (Fall).

Aretxaga, Begoña. 2005. *States of Terror: Begoña Aretxaga's Essays*. Reno: Center for Basque Studies.

——. 2003. "Maddening States," *Annual Review of Anthropology* 32:1.

Asad, Talal. 2015. "Thinking about Tradition, Religion, and Politics in Egypt Today," *Critical Inquiry* 42:1 (Autumn).

——. 2003. *Formations of the Secular: Christianity, Islam, Modernity*. Stanford: Stanford University Press.

Atwan, Abdel Bari. 2015. *The Islamic State: The Digital Caliphate*. London: Saqi Books.

al-ʿAwad, Yahya. No date. *al-Ṭarīq . . . li-ittijāh wāḥid: Al-Surbūn, Karkūj, al-Zarība, qabsāt min mujāhidāt al-shaykh Bashīr al-ṣāmit* (The Road Goes in One Direction: The Sorbonne, Karkoj, al-Zariba, Images from the Trials of Shaykh Bashir "the Silent One") Khartoum: Dār al-Qawm.

Babikir, Hamid Ahmad. No date [post-2001]. *al-Ḥaraka al-Wahhābiyya fī-l-mīzān wa munāqashat afkārahā ʿalā ḍawʾ al-kitāb wa-l-sunna, wa yalihu al-iṭāḥa bi-afkār akbar zuʿamāʾ al-Wahhābiyya fī-l-sāḥa: Muḥammad Muṣṭafā ʿAbd al-Qādir, Musāʿid al-Sidayra wa ʿUmr al-Tuhāmī.* (The Wahhabi Movement on the Scales [of Justice] and an Examination of Its Ideas in the Light of Qurʾan and Sunna: As well as Discarding the Ideas of Its Biggest Leaders in the Field . . .) No publisher.

al-Badri, Hashim Muhammad al-Amin. 1995. *Talāʾiʿ al-fikr al-islāmī, 651–1504m* (Vanguards in Islamic Thought, 651–1504 CE). Khartoum: Dār al-Falāḥ li-l-Ṭibāʿa wa-l-Nashr.

al-Baqir, Taha and Yusuf Fadl Hasan, ʿAbd al-Hamid Muhammad Ahmad, eds. 2004. *Mawsūʿat ahl al-dhikr bi-l-Sūdān* (The Encyclopedia of the People in Sudan Who Are Mindful of God), 6 vols. Khartoum: al-Majlis al-Qawmī li-l-Dhikr wa-l-Dhākirīn.

Baumgarten. Alexander. 2000. "Aesthetics," in *Art in Theory, 1648–1815: An Anthology of Changing Ideas*, eds. Charles Harrison, Paul Wood, and Jason Gaiger. Malden: Blackwell.

Bayat, Asef. 2013. "Preface," in *Post-Islamism: The Changing Faces of Political Islam*, ed. Asef Bayat. Oxford: Oxford University Press.

Belkeziz, Abdelilah. 2009. *The State in Contemporary Islamic Thought: A Historical Survey of the Major Muslim Political Thinkers of the Modern Era*. London: IB Tauris.

Bernal, Victoria. 1997. "Islam, Transnational Culture, and Modernity in Rural Sudan," in *Gendered Encounters: Challenging Cultural Boundaries and Social Hierarchies in Africa*, ed. Maria Grosz-Ngate and Omari H. Kokole. New York: Routlege.

——. 1994. "Gender, Culture and Capitalism: Women and the Remaking of Islamic 'Tradition' in a Sudanese Village," *Comparative Studies in Society and History* 36:1.

Bernal, Victoria and Inderpal Grewal, eds. 2014. *Theorizing NGOs: States, Feminisms, and Neo-Liberalism*. Durham: Duke University Press.

Boddy, Janice. 2007. *Civilizing Women: British Crusades in Colonial Sudan*. Princeton: Princeton University Press.

——. 1989. *Wombs and Alien Spirits: Women, Men and the* Zār *Cult in Northern Sudan*. Madison: University of Wisconsin Press.

Brown, L. Carl. 2000. *Religion and State: The Muslim Approach to Politics*. New York: Columbia University Press.

Brown, Wendy. 2006. *Regulating Aversion: Tolerance in the Age of Identity and Empire*. Princeton: Princeton University Press.

——. 1995. *States of Injury: Power and Freedom in Late Modernity*. Princeton: Princeton University Press.

al-Buni, ʿAbd al-Latif and ʿAbd al-Latif Saʿid. 2000. *Al-Buraʿī rajul al-waqt* (al-Buraʿi: The Man of the Age). Khartoum: Qāf li-l-Intāj al-Fannī wa-l-Iʿlāmī.

Calhoun, Craig, ed. 1992. *Habermas and the Public Sphere*. Cambridge: MIT Press.

Calhoun, Craig, Mark Juergensmeyer, and Jonathan VanAntwerpen, eds. 2011. *Rethinking Secularism*. Oxford: Oxford University Press.

Casanova, José. 1994. *Public Religions in the Modern World*. Chicago: University of Chicago Press.

Caton, Steven. 1993. *"Peaks of Yemen I Summon:" Poetry as Cultural Practice in a North Yemeni Tribe*. Berkeley: University of California Press.

Chakrabarty, Dipesh. 2000. *Provincializing Europe: Post-Colonial Thought and Historical Difference*. Princeton: Princeton University Press.

Chih, Rachida. 2007. "What Is a Sufi Order? Revisiting the Concept through a Case Study of the Khalwatiyya in Contemporary Egypt," in *Sufism and the "Modern" in Islam*, ed. Martin van Bruinessen and Julia Day Howell. New York: IB Tauris.

Collins, Robert O. and J. Millard Burr. 2003. *Revolutionary Sudan: Hasan al-Turabi and the Islamist State, 1989–2000*. Leiden: Brill.

Commins, David. 1990. *Islamic Reform: Politics and Social Change in Late Ottoman Syria*. Oxford: Oxford University Press.

Creswell, Robyn and Bernard Haykel. 2015. "Battle Lines: Want to Understand the Jihadis? Read Their Poetry," *New Yorker*, June 8.

Cromer, Evelyn Baring (Earl of). 1916. *Modern Egypt*. New York: Macmillan.

Daly, M. W. 2010. *Darfur's Sorrow: The Forgotten History of a Humanitarian Disaster*. Cambridge: Cambridge University Press.

——. 1986. *Empire on the Nile: The Anglo-Egyptian Sudan, 1898–1934*. Cambridge: Cambridge University Press.

Davidson, Naomi. 2012. *Only Islam: Embodying Islam in 20th Century France*. Ithaca: Cornell University Press.

De Jong, Frederick. 1999. "Opposition to Sufism in Twentieth Century Egypt (1900–1970): A Preliminary Survey," in *Islamic Mysticism Contested: Thirteen Centuries of Controversies and Polemics*, ed. Frederick De Jong and Bernd Radtke. Leiden: Brill.

de la Puente, Cristina. 1999. "The Prayer upon the Prophet Muhammad (*Taṣliya*): A Manifestation of Islamic Religiosity," *Medieval Encounters* 5:1.

De Waal, Alex, ed. 2007. *War in Darfur and the Search for Peace*. Cambridge, MA: Global Equity Initiative, Harvard University.

——. 2004. "Counter-Insurgency on the Cheap," *London Review of Books* 26:15.

De Waal, Alex and A. H. Abdel Salam. 2004. "Islamism, State Power and *Jihad* in Sudan," in *Islamism and Its Enemies in the Horn of Africa*, ed. Alex de Waal. Indianapolis: Indiana University Press.

Deeb, Lara. 2009. "Emulating and/or Embodying the Ideal: The Gendering of Temporal Frameworks and Islamic Role Models in Shiʿi Lebanon," *American Ethnologist* 36:2.

Deng, Francis. 1995. *War of Visions: Conflict of Identities in Sudan*. Washington: Brookings Institution.

Devji, Faisal. 2005. *Landscapes of the Jihad: Militancy, Morality, Modernity*. Ithaca: Cornell University Press.

Dressler, Markus. 2011. "The Religio-Secular Continuum: Reflections on the Religious Dimension of Turkish Secularism," in *After Secular Law*, ed. Winnifred Fallers Sullivan, Robert Yelle, and Mateo Taussig-Rubbo. Stanford: Stanford University Press.

Dressler, Markus and Arvind-Pal S. Mandair. 2011. *Secularism and Religion-Making*. New York: Oxford University Press.

Dwyer, Kevin. 1991. *Arab Voices: The Human Rights Debate in the Middle East*. New York: Routledge.

Eagleton, Terry. 1990. *The Ideology of the Aesthetic*. Oxford: Blackwell.

Eickelman, Dale. 1999. "Islamic Religious Commentary and Lesson Circles: Is There a Copernican Revolution?" in *Commentaries—Kommentare*, ed. Glenn W. Most. Göttingen, Germany: Vandenhoeck and Ruprecht.

——. 1992. "Mass Higher Education and the Religious Imagination in Contemporary Arab Societies," *American Ethnologist* 19:4.
——. 1991. "Traditional Islamic Learning and Ideas of the Person in the Twentieth Century," in *Middle Eastern Lives: The Practice of Biography and Self-Narrative*, ed. Martin Kramer. Syracuse: Syracuse University Press.
——. 1985. *Knowledge and Power in Morocco: The Education of a Twentieth-Century Notable*. Princeton: Princeton University Press.
——. 1978. "The Art of Memory: Islamic Education and Its Social Reproduction." *Comparative Studies in Society and History* 20:4.
Eickelman, Dale and Jon Anderson, eds. 2003. *New Media in the Muslim World: The Emerging Public Sphere*. Bloomington: Indiana University Press.
Eickelman, Dale F. and James Piscatori. 1996. *Muslim Politics*. Princeton: Princeton University Press.
Eisenlohr, Patrick. 2011. "Religious Media, Devotional Islam, and the Morality of Ethnic Pluralism in Mauritius," *World Development* 39:2.
——. 2006. "As Makkah Is Sweet and Beloved, So Is Madina: Islam, Devotional Genres, and Electronic Mediation in Mauritius," *American Ethnologist* 33:2.
El-Affendi, Abdelwahab. 2013. "Islamism in Sudan: Before, After, in Between," in *Post-Islamism: The Changing Face of Political Islam*, ed. Asef Bayat. New York: Oxford University Press.
——. 2008. "The Future of the Sudanese Islamist Movement," *Making Sense of Darfur, Social Science Research Council blog*, http://www.ssrc.org/blogs/darfur/2008/04/13/the-future-of-the-sudanese-islamist-movement/.
——. 1991. *Turabi's Revolution: Islam and Power in Sudan*. London: Grey Seal.
El-Gizouli, Magdi. 2013. "President Bashir: An Historian at Large," *Still Sudan* (blog), http://stillsudan.blogspot.com/2013/12/president-bashir-historian-at-large.html.
el-Hasan, Idris Salam. 1993. *Religion in Society: Nemeiri and the Turuq, 1972–1980*. Khartoum: Khartoum University Press.
Elias, Jamal. 2012. *Aisha's Cushion: Religious Art, Perception, and Practice in Islam*. Cambridge: Harvard University Press.
Elsanhouri, Taghreed, dir. 2008. *All about Darfur*. California Newsreel.
Emon, Anver. 2012. *Religious Pluralism and Islamic Law: Dhimmis and Others in the Empire of Law*. New York: Oxford University Press.
Esposito, John. 1999. *The Islamic Threat: Myth or Reality*. New York: Oxford University Press.
——, ed. 1983. *Voices of Resurgent Islam*. New York: Oxford University Press.
Esposito, John and John Voll. 2001. *Makers of Contemporary Islam*. New York: Oxford University Press.
Euben, Roxanne. 1999. *Enemy in the Mirror: Islamic Fundamentalism and the Limits of Modern Rationalism*. Princeton: Princeton University Press.
Euben, Roxanne and Muhammad Qasim Zaman. 2009. *Princeton Readings in Islamist Thought: Texts and Contexts from al-Banna to Bin Laden*. Princeton: Princeton University Press.
Evans-Pritchard, E. E. 1954. *Nuer Religion*. New York: Oxford University Press.
Faqiri, Ranya. 2007. "Maḥmūd ʿAbd al-ʿAzīz (al-jadīd) li-Awrāq jadīda: anā ṣāḥib lawniya tatanāfa maʿa al-taqlīd . . . wa man lā yabdā min (al-ḥaqība) yukhṭiʾ fī ḥaqq al-fann!" ("I Am of the Position That Goes against Imitation . . . He who Doesn't Start with *al-ḥaqība* Violates the Right[s] of Art!") *Awrāq jadīda*, issue 15 (July).
Fernando, Mayanthi L. 2014. *The Republic Unsettled: Muslim French and the Contradictions of Secularism*. Durham: Duke University Press.
——. 2005. "The Republic's 'Second Religion,'" *Middle East Report* 235.
Fischer, Michael. 2003. *Iran: From Religious Dispute to Revolution*. 2nd ed. Madison: University of Wisconsin Press.
Flint, Julie and Alex de Waal. 2008. *Darfur: A New History of a Long War*. New York: Zed Books.

Flood, Finbarr Barry. 2002. "Between Cult and Culture: Bamiyan, Islamic Iconoclasm, and the Museum." *Art Bulletin*, 84:4: 641–59.
Fluehr-Lobban, Carolyn. 2012. *Sharīʿa and Islamism in Sudan: Conflict, Law and Social Transformation*. London: IB Tauris.
Foucault, Michel. 2010. *The Birth of Biopolitics: Lectures at the College de France, 1978–1979*. New York: Palgrave Macmillan.
——. 1997. *Ethics: Subjectivity and Truth* (Essential Works of Foucault, vol. 1). New York: The New Press.
——. 1990. *The History of Sexuality*, vol. 2: *The Uses of Pleasure*. New York: Vintage.
Fraser, Nancy. 1992. "Rethinking the Public Sphere: A Contribution to the Critique of Actually Existing Democracy," in *Habermas and the Public Sphere*, ed. Craig Calhoun. Cambridge: MIT Press.
Gallab, Abdullahi. 2014. *Islamism in Sudan: From Disintegration to Oblivion*. Burlington: Ashgate.
——. 2011. *A Civil Society Deferred: The Tertiary Grip of Violence in the Sudan*. Gainesville: University Press of Florida.
——. 2008. *The First Islamist Republic: Development and Disintegration of Islamism in Sudan*. Burlington: Ashgate.
Garang, John. 1987. *John Garang Speaks*. New York: Kegan Paul International.
Ghamari-Tabrizi, Behrooz. 2008. *Islam and Dissent in Postrevolutionary Iran: Abdolkarim Soroush, Religious Politics and Democratic Reform*. London: IB Tauris.
al-Ghazali, Abu Hamid. 1983. *Inner Dimensions of Islamic Worship*. Trans. Muhtar Holland. Leicester: Islamic Foundation.
Gleichen, Lieutenant-Colonel Count, ed. 1905. *The Anglo-Egyptian Sudan: A Compendium Prepared by Officers of the Sudan Government*. 2 vols. London: Harrison and Sons.
Godrej, Farah. 2011. *Cosmopolitan Political Thought: Method, Practice, Discipline*. Oxford: Oxford University Press.
Göle, Nilüfer and Ludwig Amman, eds. 2006. *Islam in Public: Turkey, Iran, and Europe*. Istanbul: Bilgi University Press.
Gregg, Melissa and Gregory J. Seigworth, eds. 2010. *The Affect Theory Reader*. Durham: Duke University Press.
Gutas, Dmitri. 1998. *Greek Thought, Arabic Culture: The Graeco-Arabic Translation Movement in Baghdad and Early ʿAbbasid Society (2nd–4th/8th–10th centuries)*. New York: Routledge.
Habermas, Jürgen. 1996. *Between Facts and Norms*. Cambridge: MIT Press.
——. 1991. *The Structural Transformation of the Public Sphere: An Inquiry into a Category of Bourgeois Society*. Cambridge: MIT Press.
——. 1974. "The Public Sphere: An Encyclopedia Article (1964)," *New German Critique* 3 (Autumn).
Haj, Samira. 2009. *Reconfiguring Islamic Tradition: Reform, Rationality, Modernity*. Stanford: Stanford University Press.
Hajj Ahmad, ʿAbd al-Rahim. ed. 2006a. *al-Shaykh al-Buraʿī: badr aḍāʾ al-dujuna* (Shaykh al-Buraʿi: A Moon That Lightened the Darkness). Omdurman: Markaz al-Asbāṭ li-l-Intāj al-Iʿlāmī wa-l-Nashr.
——. 2006b. *Buraʿī al-Sūdān: waqfāt ʿalā shāṭiʾ irthihi wa ḥarthihi* (Buraʿi of Sudan: Stations on the Shore of His Legacy and Its Tillage), 2nd ed. Khartoum: Markaz al-Asbāṭ li-l-Intiāj al-Iʿlāmī wa-l-Nashr.
Hale, Sondra. 1996. *Gender and Politics in Sudan: Islamism, Socialism and the State* Boulder: Westview Press.
Hallaq, Wael B. 2013. *The Impossible State: Islam, Politics, and Modernity's Moral Predicament*. New York: Columbia University Press.
——. 2009. *Sharīʿa: Theory, Practice, Transformations*. Cambridge: Cambridge University Press.

——. 1999. *A History of Islamic Legal Theories: An Introduction to Sunnī Uṣūl al-Fiqh*. Cambridge: Cambridge University Press.

Hamdi, Mohamed Elhachmi. 1998. *The Making of an Islamic Political Leader: Conversations with Hasan al-Turabi*. Boulder: Westview Press.

Hamid, al-Tijani ʿAbd al-Qadir. 1995. "al-Sūdān wa tajribat al-intiqāl li-l-ḥukm al-islāmī" (Sudan and the Experience of Transition to Islamic Rule), in *al-Mashrūʿ al-islāmī al-sūdānī: qiraʾāt fī-l-fikr wa-l-mumārasa* (The Sudanese Islamic Project: Readings in Its Philosophy and Practice), no editor listed. Khartoum: Markaz al-Dirāsāt wa-l-Buḥūth al-Ijtimāʿiyya.

——. 1994. "Taṣdīr" (Foreword), *al-Taʾṣīl*, issue 1 (December).

Hammoudi, Abdellah. 1997. *Master and Disciple: The Cultural Foundations of Moroccan Authoritarianism*. Chicago: University of Chicago Press.

Harun, Muhammad Mahjub. 1995. "al-Mashrūʿ al-islāmī al-sūdānī, 1989–1992" (The Sudanese Islamic Project, 1989–1992), in *al-Mashrūʿ al-islāmī al-sūdānī: qiraʾāt fī-l-fikr wa-l-mumārasa* (The Sudanese Islamic Project: Readings in Its Philosophy and Practice), no editor listed. Khartoum: Markaz al-Dirāsāt wa-l-Buḥūth al-Ijtimāʿiyya.

Hasabu, Ismaʿil. 2009. "Mulāsanāt fī-l-barlamān bisabab al-qānūn: taʿdīlāt ʿalā al-qānūn al-jināʾī tashmal jarāʾim ḍidd al-insāniyya wa-l-ibāda al-jamāʿiyya" (Sharp Exchanges in Parliament Due to the Law: Revisions to the Criminal Law include Crimes against Humanity and Genocide), *al-Ṣaḥāfa*, April 22.

Hasan, Qurashi Muhammad. 1977. *al-Madkhal ilā shiʿr al-madāʾiḥ* (An Introduction to *madīḥ* Poetry). Khartoum: ʿIdārat al-Nashr al-Thaqāfī.

——. 1972–76. *Maʿa shuʿarāʾ al-madāʾiḥ* (With the *madīḥ* Poets). 4 vols. Khartoum: al-Dār al-Sūdāniyya li-l-Kutub.

Hasan, Yusuf Fadl. 1967. *The Arabs and the Sudan: From the Seventh to the Early Sixteenth Century*. Edinburgh: Edinburgh University Press.

Hassan, Salah, and Carina Ray, eds. 2009. *Darfur and the Crisis of Governance in Sudan*. Ithaca: Cornell University Press.

Hefner, Robert W. 2007. "Introduction: The Culture, Politics and Future of Islamic Education," in *Schooling Islam: The Culture and Politics of Modern Muslim Education*, eds. Robert W. Hefner and Muhammad Qasim Zaman. Princeton: Princeton University Press.

——, ed. 2004. *Remaking Muslim Politics: Pluralism, Contestation, Democratization*. Princeton: Princeton University Press.

Hellyer, H. A. 2015. "This Stupidity Needs to End: Why the *Atlantic* and *NY Post* Are Clueless about Islam," Salon.com, February 20.

Hirschkind, Charles. 2006. *The Ethical Soundscape: Cassette Sermons and Islamic Counterpublics*. New York: Columbia University Press.

Hoffman, Valerie. 1995. *Sufism, Mystics and Saints in Modern Egypt*. Columbia: University of South Carolina Press.

Holt, P. M. 1981. "The Genealogy of a Sudanese Holy Family," *Bulletin of the School of Oriental and African Studies* 44:2.

——. 1958. *The Mahdist State in the Sudan, 1881–1898: A Study of Its Origins, Development and Overthrow*. Oxford: Clarendon Press.

Holt, P. M., and Martin Daly. 2000. *A History of the Sudan: From the Coming of Islam to the Present Day*. 5th ed. New York: Longman.

Horovitz, J and L. Gardet. 1978. "Kawthar," in *The Encyclopaedia of Islam*, 2nd ed. Eds. P. Bearman, Th. Bianquis, C. E. Bosworth, E. van Donzel, and W.P. Heinrichs, vol 4. Leiden: Brill. http://www.brillonline.nl.proxy.uchicago.edu/subscriber/entry?entry=islam_SIM-4043.

Hourani, Albert. 1983. *Arabic Thought in the Liberal Age, 1798–1939*. Cambridge: Cambridge University Press.

Hurd, Elizabeth Shakman. 2015. *Beyond Religious Freedom: The New Global Politics of Religion*. Princeton: Princeton University Press.

Ibn Dayf Allah, Muhammad al-Nur. 1975. *Kitāb al-ṭabaqāt fī khuṣūṣ al-awliyā' wa-l-ṣāliḥīn wa-l-ʿulamā' wa-l-shuʿarā' fī-l-Sūdān* (Book Regarding the Classification of Holy Men, the Righteous, Scholars and Poets in Sudan). Ed. Yusuf Fadl Hasan. Khartoum: University of Khartoum Press.

Ibrahim, Abdullahi ʿAli. 2008. *Manichean Delirium: Decolonizing the Judiciary and the Islamic Renewal in Sudan, 1898–1985*. Leiden: Brill.

Ibrahim, Hasan Ahmed. 1979. "Mahdist Risings against the Condominium Government in the Sudan, 1900–1927," *International Journal of African Historical Studies* 12:3.

Idris, Amir H. 2005. *Conflict and Politics of Identity in Sudan*. New York: Palgrave Macmillan.

ʿIlwan, ʿAli Muhammad. 1997. "al-Maʿālim al-qiyādiyya fī qiṣṣat dhī al-qarnayn" (Leadership Characteristics in the [Qur'anic] Story of 'the Two-horned One'"). *al-Ta'ṣīl*, issue 5 (April).

al-Imam, Ahmad ʿAli. 2006. *Variant Readings of the Qur'an: A Critical Study of Their Historical and Linguistic Origins*. Herndon: International Institute of Islamic Thought.

——. 2005. "al-Ta'ṣīl: manāhij al-iṣlāḥ wa-l-tazkiyya" (Fundamentalization: Methodologies of Reform and Purification) in *Taqwīm mafāhīm wa taṭbīqāt al-ta'ṣīl al-islāmī fī-l-Sūdān* (Reforming the Concepts and Application of Islamic Fundamentalization in Sudan), no editor listed. Khartoum: Markaz al-Tanwīr al-Maʿrifī.

——. 2003. *al-Khalwa wa-l-ʿawda al-ḥilwa* (The *khalwa* and the Sweet Return). Khartoum: Hay'at Riʿāyat al-Ibdāʿ al-ʿIlmī.

al-Imam, Nashat. 2007. "Bayn al-ghinā' wa-l-madīḥ: Hal ḍaʿat malāmiḥ al-fannānīn?" (Between Songs and *madīḥ*: Have the Characteristics of the Singer Been Lost?), *al-Ijtimāʿī* (January).

Imam, Zakariyya Bashir. 1996. "Naḥw ta'ṣīl tadrīs al-manṭiq fī-l-ʿālam al-islāmī" (Towards the Fundamentalization of the Teaching of Logic in the Islamic World), *al-Ta'ṣīl*, issue 4 (April).

al-Jazuli, Al-Tijani Ismaʿil. 1998. "ʿArḍ Idārat Ta'ṣīl al-Maʿrifa" (Presentation of the Administration for the Fundamentalization of Knowledge), in *Kitāb buḥūth nadwat tansīq juhūd al-ta'ṣīl wa islāmiyyat al-maʿrifa* (A Book of Research from a Symposium on the Coordination of the Efforts of Fundamentalization and the Islamization of Knowledge), ed. ʿIsam Muhammad ʿAbd al-Majid Ahmad. Khartoum: Ministry of Higher Education and Scientific Research.

Jenco, Leigh Kathryn. 2007. "What Does Heaven Ever Say? A Methods-Centered Approach to Cross-Cultural Engagement," *American Political Science Review* 101:4.

Johansen, Julian. 1996. *Sufism and Islamic Reform in Egypt: The Battle for Islamic Tradition*. Oxford: Oxford University Press.

Johnson, Douglass. 2004. *The Root Causes of Sudan's Civil Wars*. Oxford: James Currey.

——. 1994. *Nuer Prophets: A History of Prophecy from the Upper Nile in the Nineteenth and Twentieth Centuries*. Oxford: Clarendon Press.

Jok, Madut. 2007. *Sudan: Race, Religion and Violence*. Oxford: Oneworld Publications.

al-Jundī. 2005. "Hal intahat al-Inqādh wa hal inhār al-mashrūʿ al-ḥaḍārī?" (Has the Salvation [Revolution] Ended and Has the Civilization Project Fallen Apart?), *al-Jundī: majalla ʿaskariyya, taṣdur shahriyan ʿan Idārat al-Tawjīh al-Maʿnawī* (The Soldier: A Military Magazine Issued Monthly by the Moral Guidance Administration), April (No author listed).

Kalmo, Hent and Quintin Skinner, eds. 2010. *Sovereignty in Fragments: The Past, Present and Future of a Contested Concept*. Cambridge: Cambridge University Press.

Kanina, Wangui. 2004. "Sudan Talks Stalled over Sharia Laws in Capital," *Reuters Wire*, April 10.

Karamustafa, Ahmet. 2004. Preface in *Knowledge of God in Classical Sufism: Foundations of Islamic Mystical Theology*, ed. John Renard. New York: Paulist Press.

Karrar, Ali Salih. 1992. *The Sufi Brotherhoods in the Sudan*. Evanston: Northwestern University Press.

Kenyon, Susan. 2012. *Spirits and Slaves in Central Sudan: The Red Wind*. New York: Palgrave Macmillan.

——. 2004. *Five Women of Sennar.* Long Grove: Waveland Press.

Khalid, Mansour. 1990. *The Government They Deserve: The Role of the Elite in Sudan's Political Evolution.* London: Kegan Paul International.

al-Khalifa, Kamal Fadal al-Sayyid. 1995. "ʿUlūm al-nabāt wa-l-zirāʿa ʿind al-Muslimīn" (Plant Science and Agriculture among the Muslims), *al-Taʾṣīl*, issue 2 (May).

Knysh, Alexander. 1993. "'Orthodoxy' and 'Heresy' in Medieval Islam: An Essay in Reassessment," *The Muslim World* 83:1.

Kok, Peter Nyot. 1991. "Conflict over Laws in the Sudan: 'From Pluralism to Monolithicism'" in *Sudan: History, Identity, Ideology*, ed. Herve Bleuchot, Christian Delmet, and Derek Hopwood. Reading: Ithaca Press.

Kresse, Kai. 2007. *Philosophising in Mombassa: Knowledge, Islam, and Intellectual Practice on the Swahili Coast.* Edinburgh: Edinburgh University Press.

Kugle, Scott. 2007. *Sufis and Saints' Bodies: Mysticism, Corporeality and Sacred Power in Islam.* Chapel Hill: University of North Carolina Press.

Lacroix, Stéphane. 2009. "Between Revolution and Apoliticism: Nasr al-Din al-Albani and His Impact on the Shaping of Contemporary Salafism," in *Global Salafism: Islam's New Religious Movement*, ed. Roel Meijer. New York: Columbia University Press.

Laffan, Michael. 2011. *The Makings of Indonesian Islam: Orientalism and the Narration of a Sufi Past.* Princeton: Princeton University Press.

Lambek, Michael. 1993. *Knowledge and Practice in Mayotte: Local Discourses of Islam, Sorcery and Spirit Possession.* Toronto: University of Toronto Press.

——, ed. 2010. *Ordinary Ethics: Anthropology, Language, Action.* New York: Fordham University Press.

Lapidus, Ira. 2002. *A History of Islamic Societies*, 2nd ed. Cambridge: Cambridge University Press.

Larkin, Brian. 2004. "Bandiri Music, Globalization, and Urban Experience in Nigeria," *Social Text* 22:4.

Lawrence, Bruce. 1989. *Defenders of God: The Fundamentalist Revolt against the Modern Age.* San Francisco: Harper and Row.

Layish, Aharon and Gabriel Warburg. 2002. *The Reinstatement of Islamic Law in Sudan under Numayri: An Evaluation of a Legal Experiment in the Light of Its Historical Context, Methodology, and Repercussions.* Leiden: Brill.

Lesch, Ann Mosley. 1998. *Sudan: Contested National Identities.* Bloomington: Indiana University Press.

Lia, Brynjar. 2008. *Architect of Global Jihad: The Life of al-Qaida Strategist Abu Musʿab al-Suri.* New York: Columbia University Press.

London, Jennifer. 2008. "How to Do Things with Fables: Ibn al-Muqaffa's Frank Speech in Stories from *Kalīla wa Dimna*," *History of Political Thought* 29:2.

Lybarger, Loren. 2007. *Identity and Religion in Palestine: The Struggle between Islamism and Secularism in the Occupied Territories.* Princeton: Princeton University Press.

Mahjub, ʿAbbas. 1994. "al-Iltizām fī-l-adab al-islāmī" ([Religious] Commitment in Islamic Literature), *al-Taʾṣīl*, issue 1 (December).

Mahmood, Saba. 2012. "Religious Freedom, the Minority Question, and Geopolitics in the Middle East," *Comparative Studies in Society and History* 54:2.

——. 2006. "Secularism, Hermeneutics, Empire: The Politics of Islamic Reformation," *Public Culture* 18:2.

——. 2005. *The Politics of Piety: The Islamic Revival and the Feminist Subject.* Princeton: Princeton University Press.

Mahmoud, Mohamed A. 1997. "Sufism and Islamism in the Sudan," in *African Islam and Islam in Africa: Encounters between Sufis and Islamists*, eds. Eva Evers Rosander and David Westerlund. Ohio: Ohio University Press.

Makdisi, Ussama. 2008. *Artillery of Heaven: American Missionaries and the Failed Conversion of the Middle East.* Ithaca: Cornell University Press.

Mamdani, Mahmood. 2009. *Saviors and Survivors: Darfur, Politics and the War on Terror.* New York: Pantheon.
Mandaville, Peter. 2001. *Transnational Muslim Politics: Reimagining the Umma.* London: Routledge.
Mani, Lata. 1998. *Contentious Traditions: The Debate on Sati in Colonial India.* Berkeley: University of California Press.
March, Andrew and Mara Revkin. 2015. "Caliphate of Law," *Foreign Affairs*, April 15. https://www.foreignaffairs.com/articles/syria/2015-04-15/caliphate-law.
Marsden, Magnus. 2006. *Living Islam: Muslim Religious Experience in Pakistan's Northwest Frontier Province.* Cambridge: Cambridge University Press.
Marshall, Ruth. 2009. *Political Spiritualities: The Pentecostal Revolution in Nigeria.* Chicago: University of Chicago Press.
Maruyama, Daisuke. 2013. "Clashes, Conflicts and Contradictions: The External Policies of Sufi Tariqas in Contemporary Sudan," *Journal of Sophia Asian Studies* 31.
Marzouki, Nadia. 2012. "Nahda's Return to History," in *The Immanent Frame: Secularism, Religion and the Public Sphere, Social Sciences Research Council* blog, http://blogs.ssrc.org/tif/2012/04/30/nahdas-return-to-history/.
Massoud, Mark. 2013. *Law's Fragile State: Colonial, Authoritarian and Humanitarian Legacies in Sudan.* Cambridge: Cambrige University Press.
Maudoodi, Sayed Abul ʿAla. 1961. *Rights of Non-Muslims in an Islamic State.* Lahore: Islamic Publications.
Mawqiʿ al-Sūdān. 2008. "Ḥiwār maʿa al-ustādh Aḥmad ʿAlī al-Imām" (Conversation with Prof. Ahmad ʿAli al-Imam), on *Mawqiʿ al-Sūdān al-Islāmī.* http://sudansite.net/2009-06-21-20-02-15/-mainmenu-72/911-2008-04-09-07-54-34 (No author listed).
McHugh, Neil. 1994. *Holy Men of the Blue Nile: The Making of an Arab-Islamic Community in the Nilotic Sudan, 1500–1850.* Evanston: Northwestern University Press.
Mcleod, Hugh. 2000. *Secularisation in Western Europe, 1848–1914.* London: St. Martin's Press.
McLuhan, Marshall. 1964. *Understanding Media: The Extensions of Man.* Cambridge: MIT Press.
Mecham, Quinn. 2015. "How Much of a State Is the Islamic State?" *Islamism in the IS Age, POMEPS Studies* 12. Washington, DC: Project on Middle East Political Science.
Medani, Khalid. 1997. "Funding Fundamentalism: The Political Economy of an Islamist State," in *Political Islam: Essays from Middle East Report*, ed. Joel Benin and Joe Stork. New York: IB Tauris.
Mehta, Uday Singh. 1999. *Liberalism and Empire: A Study in Nineteenth-Century British Liberal Thought.* Chicago: University of Chicago Press.
el-Mek, ʿAli and Geoff Dunlop, dirs. 1983. *Ways of Faith.* Falls Church: Landmark Films.
Messick, Brinkley. 1993. *The Calligraphic State: Textual Domination and History in a Muslim Society.* Berkeley: University of California Press.
Meyer, Birgit, ed. 2009. *Aesthetic Formations: Media, Religion and the Senses.* New York: Palgrave Macmillan.
Meyer, Birgit and Annelies Moors, eds. 2006. *Religion, Media and the Public Sphere.* Bloomington: Indiana University Press.
Mitchell, Timothy. 2006. "Society, Economy, and the State Effect," in *The Anthropology of the State: A Reader*, ed. Aradhana Sharma and Akhil Gupta. Malden: Blackwell.
——. 1991. "The Limits of the State: Beyond Statist Approaches and their Critics," *American Political Science Review* 85:1.
Mittermaier, Amira. 2011. *Dreams That Matter: Egyptian Landscapes of the Imagination.* Berkeley: University of California Press.
——. 2008. "(Re)Imagining Space: Dreams and Saint Shrines in Egypt," in *Dimensions of Locality: Muslim Saints, Their Place and Space*, eds. Georg Stauth and Samuli Schielke (Yearbook of the Sociology of Islam 8). Bielefeld: Transcript Verlag.

Moore-Harell, Alice. 2001. *Gordon and the Sudan: A Prologue to the Mahdiyya, 1877–1880.* London: Frank Cass.

Mottahedeh, Roy. 1985. *The Mantle of the Prophet: Religion and Politics in Iran.* New York: Simon and Schuster.

Muhammad Khayr, ʿAbd al-Karim Ibrahim. 2005. *Awliyāʾ Allāh ʿalā arḍ al-Sūdān* (The *awlīyāʾ* of God in the Land of Sudan). London: Dār al-Tuhāma li-l-Thaqāfa wa-l-Nashr wa-l-Tawzīʿ.

Muhammad Khayr, al-Tayyib Ibrahim. 2008. *Masārāt al-taʾṣīl wa taṭbīqātuhu fī-l-Sūdān: ʿarḍ wa taqwīm tajribat al-taʾṣīl fī-l-taʿlīm al-ʿālī* (The Trajectories of Fundamentalization and Their Applications in Sudan: Presenting and Reforming the Experience of Fundamentalization in Higher Education). Khartoum: Markaz al-Tanwīr al-Maʿrifī.

Musa, ʿAbduh Mukhtar. 1996. "Naḥw ruʾya taʾṣīliyya li-l-iʿlām" (Toward a Vision of Fundamentalization for the Media), *al-Taʾṣīl*, issue 4 (April).

Nageeb, Salma. 2004. *New Spaces and Old Frontiers: Women, Social Space and Islamization in Sudan.* Oxford: Lexington Books.

An-Naʿim, Abdullahi Ahmad. 2008. *Islam and the Secular State: Negotiating the Future of Sharīʿa.* Cambridge: Harvard University Press.

Navaro-Yashin, Yael. 2002. *Faces of the State: Secularism and Public Life in Turkey.* Princeton: Princeton University Press.

Nielsen, Richard. 2015. "Does the Islamic State Believe in Sovereignty?" *Islamism in the IS Age,* POMEPS Studies 12. Washington, DC: Project on Middle East Political Science.

O'Fahey, R. Sean. 1999. "Sufism in Suspense: The Sudanese Mahdi and the Sufis," in *Islamic Mysticism Contested: Thirteen Centuries of Controversies and Polemics,* eds. Fredrick de Jong and Bernd Radtke. Leiden: Brill.

Peletz, Michael. 2002. *Islamic Modern: Religious Courts and Cultural Politics in Malaysia.* Princeton: Princeton University Press.

Penn, A.E.D. 1934. "Traditional Stories of the ʿAbdullab Tribe," *Sudan Notes and Records* 17:1.

Peterson, Derek and Darren Walhof, eds. 2002. *The Invention of Religion: Rethinking Belief in Politics and History.* New Brunswick: Rutgers University Press.

Pierret, Thomas. 2013. *Religion and the State in Syria: The Sunni Ulama from Coup to Revolution.* Cambridge: Cambridge University Press.

Qasim, ʿAwn al-Sharif. 2006. "Taqdīm" (Introduction), in ʿAbd al-Rahim Hajj Ahmad, *Buraʿī al-Sūdān: Waqfāt ʿalā shāṭiʾ irthihi wa ḥarthihi* (Buraʿi of Sudan: Stations on the Shore of His Legacy and Its Tillage). Khartoum: Markaz al-Asbāṭ li-l-Intāj al-Iʿlāmī wa-l-Nashr.

——. 2002. *Qāmūs al-lahja al-ʿāmmiyya fī-l-Sūdān* (The Dictionary of the Popular Dialect in Sudan). Khartoum: al-Dār al-Sūdāniyya li-l-Kutub.

——. 1989. *al-Islām wa-l-ʿĀrabiyya fī-l-Sūdān: dirāsāt fī-l-ḥaḍāra wa-l-lugha* (Islam and Arabic in Sudan: Studies in Civilization and Language). Khartoum: Dār al-Maʾmūn.

Qutb, Sayyid. 1953. *Social Justice in Islam.* Trans. John Hardie. Oneonta: Islamic Publications International.

Rancière, Jacques. 1994. *The Names of History: On the Poetics of Knowledge.* Trans. Hassan Melehy. Minneapolis: University of Minnesota Press.

Renard, John. 2009. *Tales of God's Friends: Islamic Hagiography in Translation.* Berkeley: University of California Press.

——. 2008. *Friends of God: Islamic Images of Piety, Commitment and Servanthood.* Berkeley: University of California Press.

——. 2004. *Knowledge of God in Classical Sufism.* New York: Paulist Press.

Rosander, Eva Ever and David Westerlund, eds. 1997. *African Islam and Islam in Africa: Encounters between Sufis and Islamists.* Ohio: Ohio University Press.

Rosenthal, Franz. 1970. *Knowledge Triumphant: The Concept of Knowledge in Medieval Islam.* Leiden: Brill.

Roy, Olivier. 1994. *The Failure of Political Islam.* New York: IB Taurus.

Rudolph, Suzanne. 2005. "The Imperialism of Categories: Situating Knowledge in a Global World," *Perspective on Politics* 3:1.

Sachedina, Abdulaziz. 2009. *Islam and the Challenge of Human Rights*. Oxford: Oxford University Press.

Sa'id, Ahmad 'Abd al-Wahhab Muhammad. 2005. *al-Kharṭūm ayyām zamān: dhikrayāt wa khawāṭir 'an sinīn al-Injlīz wa-l-Amrīkān fī-l-Sūdān* (Khartoum in the Old Days: Memories and Reflections on the Years of the English and the Americans in Sudan). Khartoum: Manshūrāt al-Kharṭūm 'Āṣimat al-Thaqāfa al-'Arabiyya.

Sa'id, Nahid. 2007. "al-Ḥaraka bi-l-Qaḍārif: tazkiyyat al-mujtama' ashbah bi-Qawānīn Sibtimbir; Wizārat al-Irshād tabarr'at minhu" (The SPLM in al-Qadarif: Purification of Society [Law] Resembles the September Laws [i.e., the September 1983 laws that imposed *sharī'a* on Sudan]; the Ministry of Guidance Proclaims Innocence from Them), *al-Ṣaḥāfa*, May 17.

Salih, Muhammad Mustafa. 1995. "Kitābat al-tārīkh 'ind al-muslimīn" (The Writing of History among the Muslims), *al-Ta'ṣīl*, issue 3 (October).

Salomon, Noah. 2015a. "Freeing Religion at the Birth of South Sudan," in *The Politics of Religious Freedom*, eds. Winnifred Fallers Sullivan, Elizabeth Shakman Hurd, Saba Mahmood, and Peter G. Danchin. Chicago: University of Chicago Press.

——. 2015b. Review of Hussein 'Ali Agrama's *Questioning Secularism: Islam, Sovereignty and the Rule of Law in Modern Egypt*, *Islamic Law and Society* 22:3.

——. 2014. "Religion after the State: Secular Soteriologies at the Birth of South Sudan," *Journal of Law and Religion* 29:3.

——. 2013. "Evidence, Secrets, Truth: Debating Islamic Knowledge in Contemporary Sudan," *Journal of the American Academy of Religion* 81:3.

——. 2011. "The Ruse of Law: Legal Equality and the Problem of Citizenship in a Multireligious Sudan," in *After Secular Law*, eds. Winnifred Fallers Sullivan, Robert A. Yelle, and Mateo Taussig-Rubbo. Stanford: Stanford University Press.

——. 2010. *In the Shadow of Salvation: Sufis, Salafis and the Project of Late Islamism in Contemporary Sudan*. PhD dissertation, University of Chicago. Ann Arbor: ProQuest/UMI.

——. 2009. "The Salafi Critique of Islamism: Doctrine, Difference and the Problem of Islamic Political Action in Contemporary Sudan," in *Global Salafism: Islam's New Religious Movement*, ed. Roel Meijer. New York: Columbia University Press.

——. 2004a. "Undoing the Mahdiyya: British Colonialism as Religious Reform in the Anglo-Egyptian Sudan, 1898–1914." *The University of Chicago Divinity School Religion and Culture Webforum*. http://divinity.uchicago.edu/martycenter/publications/webforum/052004/.

——. 2004b. "The Khartoum Dilemma: Religious Diversity and the Law in Contemporary Sudan," *Criterion* 43:2.

Salomon, Noah and Jeremy Walton. 2012. "Religious Criticism, Secular Critique, and the 'Critical Study of Religion': Lessons from the Study of Islam" in *The Cambridge Companion to Religious Studies*, ed. Robert A. Orsi. New York: Cambridge University Press.

Salvatore, Armando. 2007. *The Public Sphere: Liberal Modernity, Catholicism, Islam*. New York: Palgrave Macmillan.

Salvatore, Armando and Mark LeVine. 2005. *Religion, Social Practice and Contested Hegemonies: Reconstructing the Public Sphere in Muslim Majority Societies*. New York: Palgrave Macmillan.

Şaul, Mahir. 2006. "Islam and West African Anthropology," *Africa Today* 53:1.

Schimmel, Annamarie. 1985. *And Muhammad Is His Messenger: The Veneration of the Prophet in Islamic Piety*. Chapel Hill: University of North Carolina Press.

Schulz, Dorthea. 2012. *Muslims and New Media in West Africa: Pathways to God*. Bloomington: Indiana University Press.

Scott, James. 1998. *Seeing like a State: How Certain Schemes to Improve the Human Condition Have Failed*. New Haven: Yale University Press.

Scott, Rachel. 2010. *The Challenge of Political Islam: Non-Muslims and the Egyptian State*. Stanford: Stanford University Press.

Seesemann, Rüdiger. 2007. "Between Sufism and Islamism: The Tijaniyya and Islamist Rule in Sudan," in *Sufism and Politics: The Power of Spirituality*, ed. Paul Heck. Princeton: Markus Weiner.

——. 2006. "Islam in Africa or African Islam? Evidence from Kenya," in *The Global Worlds of the Swahili: Interfaces of Islam, Identity and Space in 19th and 20th Century East Africa*, eds. Rüdiger Seesemann and Roman Loimeier. Berlin: Lit Verlag.

——. 2002. "Sufi Leaders and Social Welfare: Two Examples from the Sudan," in *Social Welfare in Muslim Societies in Africa*, ed. Holger Weiss. Uppsala: Nordic Africa Institute.

——. 1999. "'Where East Meets West': The Development of Qur'anic Education in Darfur," *Islam et sociétés au sud du Sahara* 13.

Sells, Michael. 2006a. "The Young Woman at the Kaʿba—Love and Infinity," on the Ibn Arabi Society section of Itunes.com (released September 24).

——. 2006b. *Approaching the Qur'an: The Early Revelations*. Ashland: White Cloud Press.

——. 2000. *Stations of Desire: Love Elegies from Ibn 'Arabi and New Poems*. Jerusalem: Iblis Press.

——. 1994. *Mystical Languages of Unsaying*. Chicago: University of Chicago Press.

Sharma, Aradhana and Akhil Gupta. 2006. "Introduction: Rethinking Theories of the State in an Age of Globalization," in *The Anthropology of the State: A Reader*, eds. Aradhana Sharma and Akhil Gupta. Malden: Blackwell.

Sidahmed, Abdel Salam. 1996. *Politics and Islam in Contemporary Sudan*. New York: St. Martin's Press.

Siddiq, Muhammad Khalifa. 2015. "Abʿād iltiḥāq al-ṭalaba al-sūdāniyīn bi-Dāʿish" (Dimensions [of the Phenomenon] of the Sudanese Students Who Joined ISIS), *al-Rāṣid*, issue 148.

Silverstein, Brian. 2007. "Sufism and Modernity in Turkey: From the Authenticity of Experience to the Practice of Discipline," in *Sufism and the 'Modern' in Islam*, ed. Martin van Bruinessen and Julia Day Howell. London: IB Tauris.

Simone, T. Abdou Maliqalim. 1994. *In Whose Image? Political Islam and Urban Practices in Sudan*. Chicago: University of Chicago Press.

Sirriyeh, Elizabeth. 1999. *Sufis and Anti-Sufis: The Defence: Rethinking and Rejection of Sufism in the Modern World*. London: Curzon.

Skovgaard-Peterson, Jakob. 1997. *Defining Islam for the Egyptian State: Muftis and Fatwas of the Dār al-Iftā*. Leiden: Brill.

Soares, Benjamin and Filippo Osella. 2009. "Islam, Politics, Anthropology," in *Islam, Politics, Anthropology*, eds. Filippo Osella and Benjamin Soares. Malden: Blackwell.

Starrett, Gregory. 1998. *Putting Islam to Work: Education, Politics and Religious Transformation in Egypt*. Berkeley: University of California Press.

Steinmetz, George, ed. 1999. *State/Culture: State Formation after the Cultural Turn*. Ithaca: Cornell University Press.

Stenberg, Leif. 1996. *The Islamization of Science: Four Muslim Positions Developing an Islamic Modernity*. Lund: Almqvist and Wiksell International.

Stevens, Jacqueline. 1999. *Reproducing the State*. Princeton: Princeton University Press.

Stolow, Jeremy. 2010. *Orthodox by Design: Judaism, Print Politics and the Artscroll Revolution*. Berkeley: University of California Press.

Sullivan, Winnifred Fallers. 2005. *The Impossibility of Religious Freedom*. Princeton: Princeton University Press.

Sullivan, Winnifred Fallers, Robert Yelle, and Mateo Taussig-Rubbo, eds. 2011. *After Secular Law*. Stanford: Stanford University Press.

Taha, Mahjub 'Ibayd. 1994. "Ḥawl uṣūṣ al-ta'ṣīl fī majāl al-ʿulūm al-ṭabīʿiyya" (On the Foundations of Fundamentalization in the Field of the Natural Sciences), *al-Ta'ṣīl*, issue 1 (December).

al-Tahir, Ahmad Muhammad. 2004. *Jamāʿat Anṣār al-Sunna al-Muḥammadiyya: nashʾatuhā, manhajuhā, ahdāfuhā* (The Ansar al-Sunna Group: Its Development, Its Method, Its Goals). Riyadh: Dār al-Faḍīla li-l-Nashr wa-l-Tawzīʿ.

al-Tayyib, al-Tayyib Muhammad. 2005. *al-Masīd*. Khartoum: Dār ʿIzza li-l-Nashr wa-l-Tawzīʿ.

al-Tihami, ʿUmar. Ca. 2002. *Shiʿr al-Buraʿī fī mīzān al-kitāb wa-l-sunna* (The Poetry of al-Buraʿi on the Scales [of Judgment] of Qurʾan and Sunna). No publisher.

Tisdal, Simon. 2008. "Khartoum's Boom: Sudan Is Modernising Quickly and Oil Revenues Are Turning the Country's Capital into an Economic Powerhouse," *Guardian*, March 11.

Trimingham, J. S. 1965 (1949). *Islam in the Sudan*. London: Frank Cass.

Trouillot, Michel-Rolph. 2001. "The Anthropology of the State in the Age of Globalization: Close Encounters of the Deceptive Kind," *Current Anthropology* 42:1.

al-Turabi, Hasan. 2009a. *al-Ḥaraka al-islāmiyya fī-l-Sūdān: al-manhaj, al-kasb, al-taṭawwur* (The Islamic Movement in Sudan: Its Program, Its Accomplishments, Its Development). Beirut: Arab Scientific Publishers.

——. 2009b. "The Islamic State," in *Princeton Readings in Islamist Thought: Texts and Contexts from al-Banna to Bin Laden*, eds. Roxanne Euben and Muhammad Qasim Zaman. Princeton: Princeton University Press.

——. 1995. "al-ʿAmal al-islāmī al-muʿāṣir—naẓarāt wa-l-ʿibr" (Contemporary Islamic Work—Reflections and Lessons Learned), in *al-Mashrūʿ al-islāmī al-Sūdānī: Qiraʾāt fī-l-fikr wa-l-mumārasa* (The Sudanese Islamic Project: Readings in Its Philosophy and Practice), no editor listed. Khartoum: Markaz al-Dirāsāt wa-l-Buḥūth al-Ijtimāʿiyya.

ʿUmar, Amin Hasan. 1995. "Ruʾya jāmiʿa li-mashrūʿ al-nahḍa al-ḥaḍāriyya al-shāmila" (Comprehensive Vision of the Project for Complete Civilizational Renaissance), in *al-Mashrūʿ al-islāmī al-Sūdānī: qiraʾāt fī-l-fikr wa-l-mumārasa* (The Sudanese Islamic Project: Readings in its Philosophy and Practice), no editor listed. Khartoum: Markaz al-Dirāsāt wa-l-Buḥūth al-Ijtimāʿiyya.

ʿUmar, Ibrahim Ahmad. 1998. "Kalimat maʿālī Wazīr al-Taʿalīm al-ʿĀlī wa-l-Baḥth al-ʿIlmī" (The Speech of his Highness the Minister of Higher Education and Scientific Research), in *Kitāb buḥūth nadwat tansīq juhūd al-taʾṣīl wa islāmiyyat al-maʿrifa* (A Book of Research from a Symposium on the Coordination of the Efforts of Fundamentalization and the Islamization of Knowledge), ed. ʿIsam Muhammad ʿAbd al-Majid Ahmad. Khartoum: The Ministry of Higher Education and Scientific Research.

——. 1995. "al-ʿIlm al-islāmī ʿalā ṭarīq al-bināʾ" (Islamic Knowledge on the Path of Construction"), *al-Taʾṣīl*, issue 2 (May).

Van der Veer, Peter. 2001. *Imperial Encounters: Religion and Modernity in India and Britain*. Princeton: Princeton University Press.

Van Linschoten, Alex Strick, and Felix Kuehn, eds. 2012. *Poetry of the Taliban*. New York: Columbia University Press.

Varzi, Roxanne. 2006. *Warring Souls: Youth, Media and Martyrdom in Post-Revolutionary Iran*. Durham: Duke University Press.

Villalon, Leonardo. 1995. *Islamic Society and State Power in Senegal: Disciples and Citizens in Fatick*. Cambridge: Cambridge University Press.

Vogel, Frank. 1997. "Siyasa Shar`iyya [Governance in Accordance with Divine Law]," in *Encyclopaedia of Islam* [New Edition]. Leiden: E.J. Brill, 1997.

Voll, John. 1997. "Islam, Islamism and Urbanization in Sudan: Contradictions and Complementaries," in *Population, Poverty and Politics in Middle East Cities*, ed. Michael E. Bonine. Gainesville: University Press of Florida.

——. 1971. "The British, the *ʿulamāʾ*, and Popular Islam in the Early Anglo-Egyptian Sudan," *International Journal of Middle East Studies* 2:3.

Von Vacano, Diego. 2015. "The Scope of Comparative Political Theory," *Annual Review of Political Science* 18.

Wagemakers, Joas. 2009. "The Transformation of a Radical Concept: *al-wala' wa-l-bara'* in the Ideology of Abu Muhammad al-Maqdisi," in *Salafism: Islam's New Global Movement*, ed. Roel Meijer. New York: Columbia University Press.

Walton, Jeremy. 2015. "Labours of Inter-Religious Tolerance: Cultural and Spatial Intimacy in Croatia and Turkey," *The Cambridge Journal of Anthropology* 33:2.

Warburg, Gabriel. 2003. *Islam, Sectarianism and Politics in Sudan since the Mahdiyya*. Madison: University of Wisconsin Press.

——. 1978. *Islam, Nationalism, and Communism in a Traditional Society: The Case of Sudan*. London: Frank Cass.

——. 1971. *The Sudan under Wingate: Administration in the Anglo-Egyptian Sudan, 1899–1916*. London: Frank Cass.

Wedeen, Lisa. 2008. *Peripheral Visions: Publics, Power, and Performance in Yemen*. Chicago: University of Chicago Press.

Werbner, Pnina and Helene Basu. 1998. *Embodying Charisma: Modernity, Locality and the Performance of Emotion in Sufi Cults*. New York: Routledge.

White, Jenny. 2013. *Muslim Nationalism and the New Turks*. Princeton: Princeton University Press.

Wickham, Carrie Rosefsky. 2013. *The Muslim Brotherhood: Evolution of an Islamist Movement*. Princeton: Princeton University Press.

——. 2002. *Mobilizing Islam: Religion, Activism and Political Change in Egypt*. New York: Columbia University Press.

Willemse, Karin. 2012. "*Zawiya, Zikr* and the Authority of Shaykh 'al-Pepsi': The Social in Sacred Place-Making in Omdurman, Sudan," in *The City: The Making of Muslim Sacred Places and Urban Life*, eds. Patrick A. Desplat and Dorthea E. Schulz. Biefeld: Transcript Verlag.

——. 2007. *One Foot in Heaven: Narratives on Gender and Islam in Darfur, West Sudan*. Leiden: Brill.

Wineger, Jessica. 2006. *Creative Reckonings: The Politics of Art and Culture in Contemporary Egypt*. Stanford: Stanford University Press.

Wingate, F. R. 1968 [1891]. *Mahdism and the Egyptian Sudan*. London: Frank Cass and Co.

Wood, Graham. 2015. "What ISIS Really Wants," *Atlantic Monthly* (March).

Zaman, Muhammad Qasim. 2002. *The Ulama in Contemporary Islam: Custodians of Change*. Princeton: Princeton University Press.

Zayn al-'Abadin, Al-Tayyib and Mudaththir 'Abd al-Rahim. 2004. *al-Islām fī-l-Sūdān: buḥūth mukhtāra min al-mu'tamar al-awwal li-Jamā't al-Fikr wa-l-Thaqāfa al-Islāmiyya* (Islam in Sudan: Research Chosen from the First Conference for the Islamic Ideas and Culture Group). Khartoum: Dār al-Aṣāla.

Zeghal, Malika. 2013a. "Competing Ways of Life: Islamism, Secularism, and Public Order in the Tunisian Transition." *Constellations* 20:2.

——. 2013b. "The Implicit Sharia: Established Religion and Varieties of Secularism in Tunisia," in *Varieties of Religious Establishment*, eds. Winnifred Fallers Sullivan and Lori G. Beaman. Burlington: Ashgate.

Archival Materials

FO = Foreign Office Archives. British Government Archives, Public Records Office, London.

PRO = Public Records Office Archives. British Government Archives, Public Records Office, London.

SAD = Sudan Archive, Durham. University of Durham Library.

Index

Abaza, Mona, 98–99n1, 99n2
ʿAbdallab people, 49
ʿAbd al-Aziz, Mahmud, 154n21
ʿAbd al-Khaliq, ʿAbd al-Rahman,184–85
ʿAbd al-Rahman, Jaʿfar, 61, 62
ʿAbduh, Muhammad, 43, 47–48
Abrams, Philip, 10n10
Administration for the Fundamentalization of Knowledge (*Idārat Taʾṣīl al-Maʿrifa*), 101, 102
aesthetics, 149n13; the aesthetic dimension of contemporary reform movements, 132–33; the insertion of social power through aesthetics, 148–49
African International University (*Jāmiʿat Ifrīqiyā al-ʿĀlamiyya*), 73
Agrama, Hussein, 31n2; on Islamic law within the Egyptian state, 23–24
Ahmed, Einas, 63n9, 79n30; on state power challenges to Sudanese Islamists, 182–83n24
ʿAli, Haydar Ibrahim, 58–59n3
al-Amin, al-Amin ʿUmar (Shaykh al-Amin), followers of, 116–17
Anderson, Jon, 7, 9n9
Annales school of history, critique of, 179–80
Ansar al-Sunna (*Anṣār al-Sunna al-Muḥammadiyya*), 109, 151n16, 181–83, 182–83n24; approach of to religious minorities and the relationship between Muslims and non-Muslims, 189–94, 190n29, 193–94n34; on the promotion of correct doctrine, 185–86; relationship of to the government, 182n22, 182–83n24; on theological doctrine (*ʿaqīda*) as the object of political contestation, 183
anthropology, 4n6; of art and poetics, 157n25; of Islam, 6
Arab Spring, 1, 62
Arabness, as a new and hybrid identity in Sudanese history, 67n14
Aretxaga, Begoña, 10n10
Asad, Talal, on the secularization theory, 34, 34n9
al-ʿAtabani, Ghazi Salah al-Din, 60, 201
authority, formal structures of, 5, 9–10, 12, 22, 31, 37, 63, 78, 170–71, 177; shifts in religious, 37–38, 44, 54, 78, 105, 107, 114, 133–35, 142, 163, 169, 171, 173, 207, 212–15
al-Azhar University (*Jāmiʿat al-Azhar*), 5, 42, 43

Babikir, Hamid Ahmad, on revelation to non-prophets, 109
bakhra (a curative device used in "prophetic medicine"), and Sufi theories of knowledge, 111–12
Bakht al-Ridda, 3
al-Banna, Hasan, 181
al-Bashir, ʿIsam Ahmad, 103
al-Bashir, ʿUmar: speech of at the International Conference for Christian-Islamic Dialogue: For the Continuance of Peace and the Strengthening of National Unity, 188–89, 189n26; speech of at Qarri, 49–55
Baumgarten, Alexander, 149n13
Benjamin, Walter, 144–45
Bernal, Victoria, 20; on the Sudanese "Islamic revival," 26n24
bin Laden, Osama, 35–36; expulsion of from Sudan, 60–61n6
Brown, Wendy, 4, 189n26
Browne, C. P., 38–39; description of a Sufi *dhikr* ceremony, 39–40, 39n16, 40n20; view of Islam as a religion of surrender, 39
al-Buraʿi (Shaykh ʿAbd al-Rahim Muhammad Waqiʿ Allah), 16–17, 16n17, 139, 146, 158–59, 161–62, 163, 166, 167, 167n8, 169; hagiographies of, 162–63; on the ills of urban migration, 126–27; his mode of Islamic politics, 172; and the public sphere, 17–18
Bush, George W., 41n21
Butler, S. S., 40n18; description of a Sufi *dhikr* ceremony, 40

Canartel (Canar Telecommunication Co.), 56–57, 58, 91